Journal of the Early Book Society

for the Study of Manuscripts and Printing History

Edited by Martha W. Driver

Volume 21, 2018

Pace University Press
41 Park Row
New York, NY 10038

Printed in the United States of America

ISBN: 978-1-935625-29-2
ISSN: 1525-6790

Member

Council of Editors of Learned Journals

™ The paper used in this publication meets the minimum requirements of American National Standard for Information Sciences—Permanence of Paper for printed Library Materials ANSI Z39.48—1984.

The *Journal of the Early Book Society* is published annually. *JEBS* invites longer articles on manuscripts and/or printed books produced between 1350 and 1550. Special consideration will be given to essays exploring the period of transition from manuscript to print. Authors are asked to follow *The Chicago Manual of Style.* A Works Cited list at the end of the text should include city, publisher, and date. Manuscripts are to be sent, in triplicate, along with an abstract of up to 150 words, to Martha Driver, Early Book Society, Department of English, Pace University, 41 Park Row, New York, New York 10038. Only materials accompanied by a self-addressed, stamped envelope (or international reply coupon) will be returned. Members of the Early Book Society who are recent authors may send review books for consideration to Susan Powell, Reviews Editor, 7 Woodbine Terrace, Headingley, Leeds LS6 4AF, England. Brief notes on recent discoveries, highlighting little-known or recently uncovered texts and/or images, may be sent to Alexandra Gillespie, Centre for Medieval Studies, 125 Queen's Park, 3rd Floor, Toronto, ON MSS 2C7, Canada. Subscription information may be obtained from Martha Driver or from Pace University Press.

Those interested in joining the Early Book Society or with editorial inquiries may contact Martha Driver by post or e-mail (MDriver@Pace.edu). Information may also be found at <www.nyu.edu/projects/EBS>. For ordering information, call Pace University Press at 212-346-1405 or visit http://www.pace.edu/press. Institutions and libraries may purchase copies directly from Ingram Library Services (1-800-937-5300).

The editor wishes to thank Gill Kent, Julia Ruth Dillon, Derek A. Pearsall, the Pace University Press Graduate Assistant Jessica Estrella, and Stephanie Hsu, Associate Director, Pace University Press, for their help and advice on this issue.

Journal of the Early Book Society

For the Study of Manuscript and Printing History

Contents

Articles

Anthoine Vérard's Books for Henry VII 1
MARY BETH WINN

Compiling Practices in Printed English Paratexts 1500–1550 27
MARI-LIISA VARILA

"Erthe upon Erthe" Revisited 53
NANCY P. POPE

Rethinking Gender and Language in Stephen Scrope's *Epistle of Othea* 97
MISTY SCHIEBERLE

Anne of Cleves in Book and Manuscript 123
VALERIE SCHUTTE

Nota Bene: Brief Notes on Manuscripts and Early Printed Books Highlighting Little-Known or Recently Uncovered Items or Related Issues

Contrary Virtues and Apostles' Names in San Marino, Huntington Library MS HM 142 149
MARTHA RUST

Another Woman Reader of John Gower's *Confessio Amantis*: Jacquetta of Luxembourg and Cambridge, Pembroke College MS 307 159
SARAH WILMA WATSON

Punctuating Malory's *Morte Darthur* 171
HELEN COOPER

De Worde's Edition of Trevisa's Translation of *De proprietatibus rerum* (c. 1495) and its Relationship to MS Plimpton 263 185
A. S. G. EDWARDS

Caxton at Work: How the Temporale of the *Golden Legend* Was Made 197
JOHN SCAHILL

Notes on the Early Modern Additions to an Italian Fourteenth-Century Book of Hours 215
CAROLINE KONCZ

The Contents of Vulgate Bibles Produced in England 233
RALPH HANNA

A London Expatriate Scribe? John Vale in Portugal 243
JOE STADOLNIK

Two Manuscripts of the *Practica Phisicalia Magistri Johannis de Burgundia* and their Censorship 251
PATRICK OUTHWAITE

Dating by Ductus: Differentiating Pen Stroke from Pen Angle in the Construction of Anglicana "d" 259
AMY CONWELL

Descriptive Reviews

Michelle P. Brown, Ildar H. Garipzanov and Benjamin C. Tilghman, eds. 275
Graphic Devices and the Early Decorated Book
CYNTHIA JOHNSTON

Margaret Connolly and Raluca Radulescu, eds. 279
Editing and Interpretation of Middle English Texts: Essays in Honour of William Marx
PAMELA ROBINSON

Emily C. Francomano 283
The Prison of Love: Romance, Translation, and the Book in the Sixteenth Century
JANE H. M. TAYLOR

Ralph Hanna 285
Patient Reading / Reading Patience: Oxford Essays on Medieval English Literature
OLIVER PICKERING

Philippa Hardman and Marianne Ailes 289
The Legends of Charlemagne in Medieval England: The Matter of France in Middle English and Anglo-Norman Literature
KEITH BUSBY

Mary Kane and Jane Roberts, eds. 293
Kane from Canada
SUSAN POWELL

Omar Khalaf, ed. 297
Alexander and Dindimus, Edited from Oxford, Bodleian Library, MS Bodley 264
VERONICA O'MARA

S. J. Ogilvie-Thomson, ed. 301
The Index of Middle English Prose: Handlist XXIII: The Rawlinson Collection, Bodleian Library, Oxford
SUSAN POWELL

Susan Powell 305
The Birgittines of Syon Abbey: Preaching and Print
MARY ERLER

R. M. Thomson 309
The Fox and the Bees: The Early Library of Corpus Christi College Oxford: The Lowe Lectures 2017
RALPH HANNA

Daniel Wakelin 311
Designing English: Early Literature on the Page
SUSAN POWELL

Jocelyn Wogan-Browne, Thelma Fenster, and Delbert Russell, eds. and trans. 315
Vernacular Literary Theory from the French of Medieval England: Texts and Translations, c. 1120–c. 1450
JANE H. M. TAYLOR

About the Authors 319

Anthoine Vérard's Books for Henry VII

MARY BETH WINN

The editions produced by the enterprising Parisian publisher, Anthoine Vérard, have attracted much attention in recent years, requiring updates, therefore, to the bibliography contained in my study of 1997.[1] Likewise, my consideration of French books for English readers, presented at the Early Book Society meeting in Durham in 2004, could not include various copies that have since come to light. In collaboration with Louis-Gabriel Bonicoli, whose dissertation on the illustrations of Vérard has brought critical new insights to the publisher's production,[2] I am at work on a database that will include copy-specific information on all the known copies of all of Vérard's editions and manuscripts,[3] but I would like to focus here on Vérard's books for Henry VII.

Henry VII ascended the throne of England in 1485, the year that Vérard issued his first book in Paris. During the course of his reign, Henry acquired numerous manuscripts but focused particularly on printed books, especially the deluxe vellum examples produced by Anthoine Vérard. Janet Backhouse notes that:

> Henry's taste for them reflects not so much a parsimonious approach to the purchase of books, nor even a deliberate choice of the printed text in preference to that written out by hand, but rather a leaning towards current French fashion, in contrast to the taste for Flemish work shown by Edward IV.[4]

It should be remembered that Henry employed a secretary for the French language, Jean Meautis, who is named in his accounts on March 21, 1494.[5]

The French connections are also evident in the organization of the king's library. In the very first year of his reign, on December 5, 1485, Henry created the office of "Stationer to the King," a post initially held by Peters Actors of Savoy.[6] As Duff noted, the title itself indicated that most books were imported,[7] and it was changed to Royal *Printer* in 1501 for William Faques (d. 1508), himself a printer. Henry also established the royal library as a separate department within his household and added the office of Royal Librarian to care for it. Quentin Poulet, a native of Lille, was first appointed to the post and was paid from the royal accounts (1499–1503) not only for books delivered but for "claspes and garnyshing," binding, and copying.[8]

Henry's accounts record payment on September 20, 1499, "to a Frensheman for sertain bokes" amounting to an impressive £56 4s, indicative of a large number of books. Another payment, March 15, 1505, specifies payment "to a Frensheman for *printed* bokes." Although several entries record payment for writing (i.e., copying) a book,[9] others specifically mention *printed* books: on November 13, 1495, "to Hugh Denes for printed bokes, 13s. 4d." Hugh Denes is elsewhere paid for a lute and a musk ball, so his trade was not limited to books.[10] On June 18, 1502, the privy purse expenses record: "To Antony Verard for two bokes called the Gardyn of Helth." We return to this title below.

One might ask whether it was the king who sought Vérard's books or Vérard who sought the king's patronage. Lotte Hellinga notes that by 1489, "Henry VII had fully grasped the political potential of the press," engaging William Caxton to translate and print an edition of Christine de Pizan's *Faits d'armes et de chevalerie.*[11] The king's personal taste, however, "was largely for works in French, both manuscripts and printed versions obtained from Flanders and Paris."[12] Vérard was undoubtedly eager to satisfy the king's desires, and Henry's reign accounted for the first appreciable collection of printed books in the English royal library. With the exception of a Missal for the Use of Sarum, Vérard's books for Henry are all in French, and most of them seem to have been illuminated in Paris before being exported—or indeed delivered—to England.

Around 1490, Vérard launched his series of deluxe vellum copies for the French king Charles VIII, but as early as 1493 he seems to have sought or gained Henry's attention. A vellum illuminated copy of Boccaccio's *Des nobles femmes,* published by Vérard on April 28, 1493, is listed in Henry's Richmond inventory (no. 71)[13] and is now bound in red velvet, which presumably replaced a similar earlier binding.[14] I suspect that Vérard's attention to the English king became even more pronounced in 1494, when the French king Charles VIII left Paris for the Italian campaigns. Vérard produced at that time his most ornate book for Henry: the *Boèce de consolation* (London BL, IB 41165 [C.22.f.8]). Printed on vellum, this book shows Vérard himself kneeling before the king to offer his gift, in a full-page miniature painted by one of the best artists of the period, the Master of Jacques de Besançon. In the prologue, which originally dedicated the work to Charles VIII, the printed name of the French king was erased and that of Henry inserted by hand in its place.[15] Such details are the hallmark of Vérard's presentation copies. It is worth noting with Janet Backhouse that the vellum printed books "were never a poor man's substitute for illuminated manuscripts but major acquisitions in their own right."[16]

Vérard prepared deluxe copies of seven other editions for Henry VII, identified through dedications or armorial bearings, as I discuss elsewhere.[17] Only recently made known, however, is a vellum copy of Vérard's edition of the *Ortus sanitatis*, now housed in the library of Transylvania University in Lexington, Kentucky.[18] Published between October 25, 1499, and 1502,[19] Vérard's edition provides the earliest French translation of the *Hortus sanitatis*, the first natural history encyclopedia to include sections on mammals, birds, fish, and stones, as well as plants and the qualities of urines. The entries for each section were presented in alphabetical order, with both Latin and French names. In addition to describing the characteristics of each subject, the book explained its benefits and uses, so that it offered both knowledge of the entire natural world and a guide to health, hence its title, *Le jardin de santé*, or Henry's "Gardyn of Helth."[20] An index at the end listed chapters to address various maladies or concerns: "*Contre les ulceres des intestins ou boyaulx*," "*pour recouvrer jeunesse*." Its medicinal and scientific value did not exclude consideration of such fabulous creatures as the mermaid, the unicorn, and the mandrake, male and female. But the fame of the book was assured by its illustrations, for it contained images for every one of its thousand entries, providing an unparalleled iconographic program.

Figure 1. Woodcut presentation scene used by Anthoine Vérard (reproduced from John Macfarlane, *Antoine Vérard*, London: 1900), Pl. XXIV.

A Latin edition had been published in Mainz by Jacob Meydenbach in 1491,[21] but Vérard copied the woodcuts that had appeared in the

Figure 2. *Ortus sanitatis* (Paris: Vérard, [between X 1499 and 1502]). Lexington, Kentucky, Transylvania University Library, Special Collections, Clara Peck Collection QK41.H6 V4, vol. 1, fol. a1v.

Strasbourg edition of around 1497,[22] adding a few of his own. His two-volume edition contains five large and 1,088 small woodcuts, all of which have been illuminated in this copy.[23] Eleven pages have painted borders, incorporating the arms and badges of Henry VII. Each major section of the text begins with a full-page woodcut, Vérard's often-used dedication scene (Fig. 1) appearing at the beginning of volume I, folio a1v. The woodcut, measuring 157 millimeters by 132 millimeters, leaves ample space on the page (346 x 230 mm) for the royal arms of England (below) and the portcullis (above), each supported by a dragon and a greyhound (Fig. 2). The floral borders on each side incorporate the red rose of the Tudors. It should be noted, however, that the painter made no attempt to depict the king; he followed the outlines of the woodcut in which the principal figures are a seated cleric and a standing man, generic representations of author and donor or perhaps patron. Facing this page is the author's prologue, "*Le prohesme de l'acteur,*" which begins on folio a2r, again surrounded by painted borders, with red roses and the royal badge of the portcullis with supporters (Fig. 3).

Volume II (fol. A1v) begins with a striking woodcut of a skeleton to introduce the "*Traicté des bestes*" (Fig. 4). The captions are in Latin, with no attempt made to translate them into either French or English. The painted borders here and on the facing page again incorporate the royal arms, portcullis, and roses. For the "*Traicté des oyseaux*" that begins on folio K4v [59v], Vérard used another of his presentation woodcuts, this time representing the king on horseback receiving the book as he departs for a hawking party (Fig. 5). This woodcut (215 x 160 mm) originated with Guillaume Tardif's treatise, *L'art de faulconnerie*, dedicated to Charles VIII and printed by Vérard

Le iardin de sante translate de latin en francois.

Le prohesme de lacteur.

Figure 3. *Ortus sanitatis*, Transylvania University, vol. 1, fol. a2r, *"Le prohesme de l'acteur."*

on January 5, 1492/3.[24] The decorated borders surrounding the woodcut again contain the English royal arms, portcullis and roses.

For the "*Traicté des poissons*" (vol. II, fol. R1v [97v]), the prologue begins below the same presentation woodcut that was used in volume I (Fig. 1). This time, however, printed borders framed the page in all copies of the edition, so in the vellum copy, new borders were painted over the printed ones, again incorporating the royal arms. A smaller woodcut of the writer (vol. II, fol. AA1v) was used for the "*Traictié des pierres*," and on that page the royal arms in the lower border have been partially erased.

For the final "*Traicté des urines*," however, a new full-page woodcut (182 x 131 millimeters) is introduced (vol. II, fol. aaa1v), apparently made for this edition (Fig. 6). It represents an apothecary shop and was copied from an earlier example used in the Latin edition of around 1497.[25] In Henry

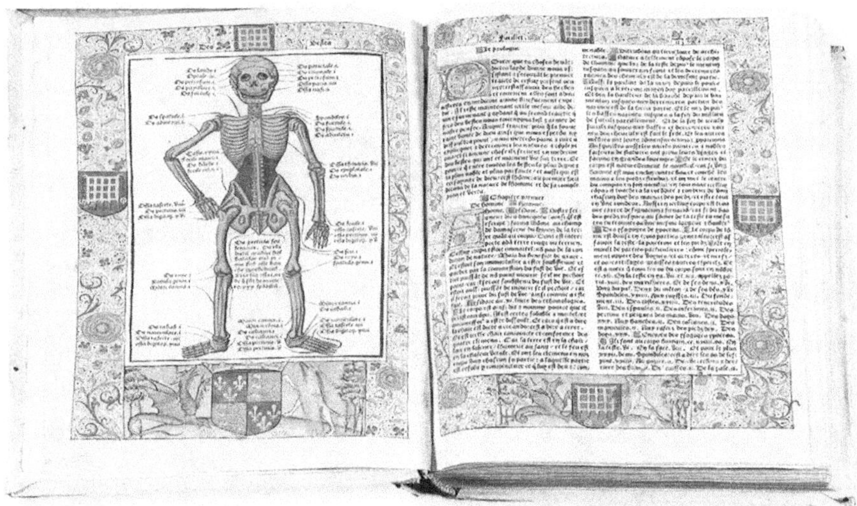

Figure 4. *Ortus sanitatis,* Transylvania University, vol. 2, fol. A1v-A2r, *"Le Traicté des bestes."*

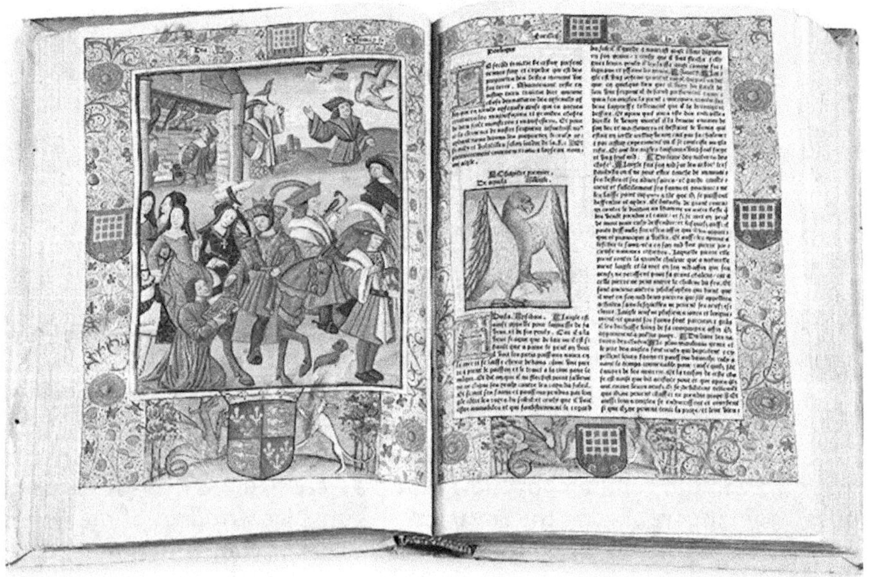

Figure 5. *Ortus sanitatis,* Transylvania University, vol. 2, fol. K4v-K5r, *"Le Traicté des oyseaux."*

Figure 6. *Ortus sanitatis*, Transylvania University, vol. 2, fol. aaa1v, *"Le Traicté des urines."*

Figure 7. *Ortus sanitatis*, Transylvania University, vol. 2, fol. K2v, *"De unicorno. Licorne."*

VII's copy it is surrounded by borders, although the greyhound supporter has been partly defaced.

These examples show that this vellum copy was personalized for Henry VII through the use of the borders, by adding royal arms, badges, and roses, rather than through any change in text or miniatures. The borders are added only to pages with large woodcuts or which begin a new treatise, not to pages with only small images. For example, the woodcut of the "*licorne*" represented in the lap of a virgin is painted but without added borders to the page (Fig. 7). While neatly painted, these pages show no special treatment for the king; neither do the large miniatures. The king is not represented in the first presentation scene of volume I, and although volume II begins with a woodcut of a king on horseback, only the arms and badges in the borders identify him as the king of England. Despite its royal decoration, the copy probably never entered Henry VII's collection. One prior critic, whose unsigned notes were transmitted with the book to Transylvania University, posited that Henry could perhaps not afford it, for in 1502, Ferdinand V was demanding a refund of Catherine of Aragon's dowry, since Prince Arthur had died in April of that year.

The provenance of the book is not attested until the seventeenth century, when it belonged to the Landgraves of Hesse.[26] The English bookseller Osborne sold it in the eighteenth century. Clara Peck (1896–1983), "a discriminating collector of sporting literature, particularly the history of the horse," and of natural history,[27] acquired the *Hortus sanitatis* at an unknown date. Although Peck is said to have purchased "her greatest books" beginning in the 1930s from the renowned antiquarian bookseller Dr. A. S. W. Rosenbach,[28] the biography of Rosenbach makes no mention of the *Hortus sanitatis,* although it calls Clara Peck "one of the country's foremost *femmes bibliophiles.*"[29] She also purchased titles, however, from H. P. Kraus.[30] At her death, she bequeathed some 885 items, of which 470 are considered rare, to Transylvania University in Lexington, Kentucky, where she had maintained a horse farm. The book received unwanted attention when it was stolen from the Transylvania University Library along with other treasures in 2004, but it was quickly recovered.[31]

What makes the book's history even more curious is the fact that, as noted above, Henry's accounts record a payment to Vérard of £6 for a copy of the "Gardyn of Helth" or *Ortus sanitatis,* a paper copy of the edition (BL C.22.f.9) that has been in the Royal Library since its publication. An old catalogue number "620," partially cut off, indicates its presence in the Westminster Inventory of 1542.[32] Why Henry would have purchased a paper copy of the *Ortus* when a vellum copy had apparently been decorated for him remains a mystery. Two other copies bearing the English royal arms seem likewise never to have entered the royal collection: the *Omelies Saint Gregoyre,* published in 1501 and now in Paris, BnF Rés. Vélins 305,[33] and the *Pelerinage de vie humaine,* housed in the Huntington Library in San Marino, California, RB 103394.[34]

An even more curious example is the substitution, by hand, of "*Henry septiesme*" over the erased name of Charles VIII in a vellum copy of the *Orloge de sapience* now in the New York Public Library.[35] Did Vérard prepare the books in anticipation of recompense that never materialized? Were the copies ordered, by the king or by a courtier wishing to offer them as gifts, and then not purchased, for financial or other reasons? Speculations are simpler to formulate than answers. One element, however, should not be overlooked: the artistic quality of the books is not the finest of Vérard's productions. The fact that he used in the *Ortus sanitatis* a woodcut for the presentation scene, rather than having a new miniature painted (as for the *Boèce*) indicates what we might call the "mass-produced presentation copy."

Although the majority of Vérard's three hundred editions were of French texts or translations, he also produced a significant number of liturgical books in Latin. These include over eighty Books of Hours, six Missals, and two Manuals. Of these, two editions of Hours, two Missals and one Manual were for the Use of Sarum and therefore destined for the English market. All of them were issued within a very few years, around 1503 to 1508, and they bring to light connections with two other cities known for their part in the English book trade: Rouen and Antwerp. The vellum copy of the *Horae ad usum Sarum* published around 1505 and housed at the Royal Library of Copenhagen has been digitized,[36] and I provide there a brief commentary on the edition. The late Erik Drigsdahl made a full description of the contents.[37]

The Missals have received little attention, and one of Vérard's editions bears specific reference to Henry VII. Missals contain the services said at the altar throughout the year and consist of four major sections: the Calendar of fixed feasts, the *Temporale* or Proper of Time (services for seasonal festivals, from the first Sunday in Advent through the last Saturday in Trinity term), the *Proprium sanctorum* or Proper of Saints (services for fixed festivals beginning with St. Andrew's Eve [November 29]), and the *Commune Sanctorum* or Common of Saints (services common to several occasions or frequently repeated, such as the marriage ceremony or services for several martyrs). The *Temporale* is followed by the core of the text: the Ordinary and the Canon of the Mass, the canon often printed on vellum and in larger type, prefaced by a full-page illustration, usually of the Crucifixion.

The earliest Missal for Sarum use was commissioned by Caxton from the Parisian printer Guillermus Maynyal in 1487 (ISTC im00719200). Twelve other incunable editions are known, and twelve more for the first decade of the sixteenth century.[38] Martin Morin of Rouen was the first French printer after Maynyal to produce Missals for Sarum use, and he helped to establish Rouen as a printing center for service books for England. Morin's edition of 1497 is a folio volume of 288 leaves, with a large woodcut to illustrate the beginning of each section of text.[39] For example, the Resurrection is depicted on folio P1 [107] for Easter; the border at the bottom of the page has an empty shield for the arms of a future owner, but also the fleur-de-lis and ermine of France and Brittany.[40] The canon is illustrated by two full-page woodcuts on facing pages: the Crucifixion and God the Father (fols. O3v–O4r [101v–102r]). By around 1500,[41] Morin had added a title page with two important innovations: the use of his name within the capital M of the title word, and the woodcut of St. George slaying the dragon (Fig. 8). This woodcut (or copies thereof) would reappear in numerous editions, not only of the Missal but of other texts for England.[42]

Vérard published two Missals for the Use of Sarum: one dated June 29, 1504 (STC 16180), the other, April 27, 1508 (STC 16182a).[43] His 1504 edition has the exact collation of Morin's 1497 edition and uses the same woodcuts (or copies) and borders containing fleurs-de-lis and ermine. This is, I believe, the first time that Vérard copied a Rouennais edition, but he took care in the colophon to identify himself as a Parisian merchant ("*Impensa honesti viri Anthonii verard mercatoris Parisien*").[44]

Vérard's Missal of April 27, 1508, is known from two copies, both of which bear the title page with his name within the capital M (Fig. 9), imitating Morin's earlier version.[45] This is the only indication of Vérard's involvement in the edition. Even more unusual is that the colophons in the two copies name different publishers, indicating two separate issues. The Oxford copy states that it was printed at the expense of Jean Huvyn and Guillaume Bernard, who are described as merchants: "*Impensa honestorum virorum Johannis Huuyn et Guillermi bernard mercatorum.*"[46] The copy in Saint Petersburg provides instead the name of Wynkyn de Worde: "*Impensa magistri wynandi de worde mercatoris.*"[47] Both copies are printed on paper, but the leaves of the Canon are printed on vellum.[48]

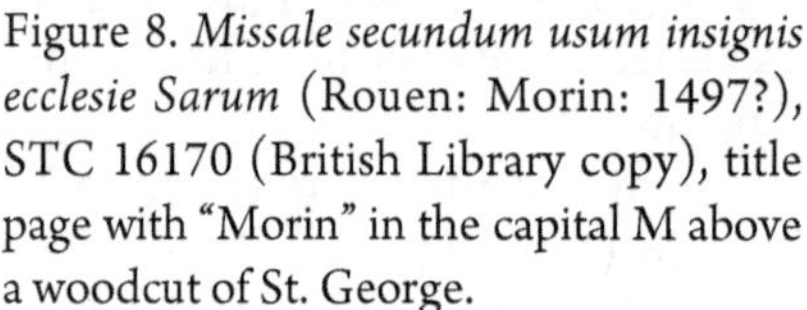
Figure 8. *Missale secundum usum insignis ecclesie Sarum* (Rouen: Morin: 1497?), STC 16170 (British Library copy), title page with "Morin" in the capital M above a woodcut of St. George.

Figure 9. *Missale secundum usum insignis ecclesie Sarum* (Rouen: J. Huvyn, G. Bernard, A. Vérard, April 27, 1508), The Bodleian Library, University of Oxford, Gough Missals 27, title page with "Anthoyne Verard" in the capital M above the woodcut of St. George.

Figure 10. *Missale secundum usum insignis ecclesie Sarum* (Rouen: J. Huvyn, G. Bernard, A. Vérard, April 27, 1508), The Bodleian Library, University of Oxford, Gough Missals 27, fol. O4r [102r], Henry VII at prayer beneath the Crucifixion.

The woodcut (170 x 167 mm) on the title page representing St. George slaying the dragon, with the royal arms to the left, also copies Morin's.[49] An even more striking woodcut in this edition, however, suggests that the Missal was a royal commission. A full-page image (305 x 193 mm) printed on folio O4r of the Canon depicts the Crucifixion within the initials IHS (Fig. 10). Christ on the cross occupies the central descender of the H, with the letters "INRI" (*Iesus Nazarenus Rex Iudaeorum* [Jesus of Nazareth, King of the Jews]) above his head, beneath the figure of a pelican showering blood from its wounded breast onto four smaller birds in the nest below. A banderole at the top of the image bears the text "*Maiorem caritatem nemo habet*" (Greater love has no one). Blood from Christ's wounded hands, feet, and side spurts into chalices held by angels. To the left, the Virgin Mary stands within the letter I in front of a man holding a spear, his left hand raised to his eye, facing the wound in Christ's side. To the right, within the smaller descender of the letter H, John the Evangelist stands in front of a soldier holding the sponge with vinegar at the end of a pole and pointing toward a banderole with the words "*Salva temet ipsum*" (Save yourself). The letter S incorporates an armored Roman soldier holding the staff with the letters SPQR (*Senatus Populusque Romanus*); another figure behind him points to a banderole with the phrase "*Vere filius dei erat*" (Truly he was the son of God).

Beneath this remarkable scene, a king identified as "*Henricus Septimus*" kneels in prayer, a book and staff on the altar before him. Behind him kneels another young man wearing a smaller crown and dressed in the same ermine-lined cloak as the king. He must be Henry's heir and by then his only surviving son, the future Henry VIII.[50] Henry's arms and portcullis badge are displayed to the right, within a garland of emblematic roses descending from the foot of the H. In all the editions produced by Vérard, nowhere else have I found this woodcut. Facing it on folio O3v [101v] is a smaller woodcut of Christ displaying the stigmata (Fig. 11), below which are printed three Latin prayers for Henry VII, described as "our king." These woodcuts are used in place of the full-page Crucifixion and God the Father usually found as illustrations for the Canon in Missals of the Morin model. Since the texts are printed on the reverse side of these images, they must have been specially prepared for this edition. The leaves are printed on vellum and are found in both extant copies of the edition, even though, as noted above, they were published by two different groups in London and Rouen.

The connection with Henry VII remains to be clarified, as does a source for the woodcut. A famous panel painting in the Royal Collection at Hampton Court Palace represents Henry, his wife, Elizabeth of York, and their seven children kneeling below a rendering of a battle between St. George and the dragon. Of the three sons depicted behind the king, only Henry was alive at the time the painting was made (ca. 1503–1509), as were only two of the four daughters kneeling behind their mother, who had also died. The "figures thereby symbolise the progeny of Henry VII and Elizabeth of York and symbolise the new Tudor dynasty."[51] The panel is dated to the last years of Henry's life, thus is exactly contemporaneous with the woodcut. Was this Missal, like the panel, destined for a particular chapel?

Richard Pynson, who was appointed the King's Printer in 1506/1507, often used a heraldic image to signal a royal connection,[52] and perhaps Pynson's Missal of 1504 served as Vérard's model.[53] The title page of that Missal declares that it was "*mandato et impensa*" by Henry VII,[54] and a full-page woodcut at the beginning of the volume displays the royal arms supported by a dragon and greyhound beneath a Tudor rose with angels bearing lines in praise of the king (Fig. 12):[55]

Hec Rosa virtutis de celo missa sereno
Eternu(m) florens regia sceptra feret.

[This Rose of virtue sent from mild heaven
Ever blooming will bear the scepter royal.]

Below the cut appears a six-line elegiac poem:

Septimus Henricus Regum nitidissima gemma
Ecclesie christi cultor (et) egregius
Talia mille premi tam sancta volumina fecit:
Ad decus etherei Regis (et) ecclesie.
Hoc igitur quicunq(ue) legis Missale sacerdos
Pro tanto ad christum principe funde preces.

[Henry VII, the most brilliant jewel of kings
and notable patron of the church of Christ,
has caused a thousand of such holy books to be printed
for the glory of the heavenly King and of the church.
So, O priest, whoever you are who reads this Missal
pour out your prayers to Christ for this great prince.][56]

The canon is introduced by a full-page woodcut of the Crucifixion, but on the page preceding the woodcut, at the bottom of the second column, are the same prayers for the king as in Vérard's edition.[57] The texts are almost identical, but Pynson adds, "*et fundator noster*" to the reference to the "excellent king," whereas Vérard deletes the reference to "founder." However, Vérard's layout gives greater prominence to the texts and further calls them to the reader's attention by their placement facing the woodcut of the king (fig. 11). The prayers printed in Vérard's edition are introduced by a heading in red type beneath an image of the haloed Christ showing his stigmata, with banderoles on either side proclaiming "*Jhesus est || Amor meus.*" Two roses, with the initials "IHS" on the left and "MA" on the right, frame the heading, printed in red type: "*Sequuntur orationes in missis dicen || de pro bono felici ac prospero statu cri || stianissimi atq(ue) excellentissimi regis no || stri Henrici septimi*"[58] [The following are the prayers to be said in masses for the good fortune and prosperity of our most Christian and most excellent king Henry the seventh].

Jhesus est | Amor meus

IHS | M

Sequuntur orationes in missis dicen de pro bono felici ac prospero statu cri stianissimi atq; excellentissimi regis no stri Henrici septimi.

Quesumus omps & misericors de9 vt rex noster henric9 septimus qui tua miseratione regni suscepit guberna cula virtutū oim percipiat incrementa quibus decēter orna tus viciorū voraginē deuitare: corporis incolumitate gaude re: hostes superare: & in tranquilla pace du3 in humanis aget tam feliciter possit sua tempora pertransire vt post huius vi te decursum ad te qui via veritas & vita es graciosus valeat peruenire.

Secretum.

Munera quesumus domine oblata sanctifica: vt nobis vnigeniti tui corpus et sanguis fiant et famulo tuo Henrico septimo regi nostro obtinēdū anime corporisq; salu tem: et ad peragendum in firma fide & solida pace iniunctu3 sibi officium te largiente vsquequaq; proficiat.

Post communio.

Hec quesumus domine salutaris sacramenti perceptio famulum tuum Henricum septimum regem nostrum ab omnibus tueatur aduersis quatenus diuturnam & ꝓsperam vitam in tranquillitate ecclesiastice pacis obtineat: et post huius vite decursum ad eternam beatitudinem tua gra cia cooperante perueniat.

Figure 11. *Missale secundum usum insignis ecclesie Sarum* (Rouen: J. Huvyn, G. Bernard, A. Vérard, April 27, 1508), The Bodleian Library, University of Oxford, Gough Missals 27, fol. O3v [101v], prayers for Henry VII.

In Vérard's edition, the prayers read[59]:

> Quesumus om(ni)p(otens) (et) misericors de(us) ut rex noster henric(us) || septimus qui tua miseratione regni suscepit guberna || cula virtutu(m) o(mn)i(u)m percipiat incrementa quibus dece(n)ter orna || tus vicioru(m) voragine(m) deuitare: corporis incolumitate gaude || re: hostes superare: (et) in tranquilla pace dum in humanis aget || tam feliciter possit sua tempora pertransire ut post huius vi || te decursum ad te qui via veritas (et) vita es graciosus valeat peruenire.[60]
>
> Secretum[61]
>
> Munera quesumus domine oblata sanctifica: ut nobis || unigeniti tui corpus et sanguis fiant et famulo tuo || Henrico septimo regi nostro obtine(n)du(m) anime corporisq(ue) salu || tem: et ad peragendum in firma fide (et) solida pace iniunctum || sibi officium te largiente usquequaq(ue) proficiat.[62]
>
> Post communio
>
> Hec quesumus domine salutaris sacramenti perceptio || famulum tuum Henricum septimum regem nostrum || ab omnibus tueatur aduersis quatenus diuturnam (et) p(ro)spe || ram vitam in tranquillitate ecclesiastice pacis obtineat: et || post huius vite decursum ad eternam beatitudinem tua gra || tia cooperante perueniat.[63]

The page is surrounded by printed borders of flowers and birds, with the footpiece displaying two angels holding an empty shield on a field of fleurs-de-lis and ermine, motifs of France and Brittany. In the Oxford copy, the printed area measures 247 by 177 millimeters on a page 322 by 220 millimeters; pages in the Saint Petersburg copy are slightly larger, 356 by 245 millimeters.

For his 1508 edition of the Missal, did Vérard copy Pynson but order a new woodcut in honor of Henry VII? Did he prepare this edition especially for the king as a commission or in hopes of obtaining one? His hopes may have been thwarted in any event, because of Henry's death only a year later, on April 21, 1509. By then, the position of "royal printer" had been established and printing in England had greatly expanded, reducing the number of books imported from France. Vérard himself ceased producing books in 1512 or 1513. Since then, scholars and bibliophiles alike have continued to discover, examine, and admire his editions, including the deluxe copies destined for Henry VII.

Septimus Henricus Regum nitidiſſima gemma
Eccleſie chꝛiſti cultoꝛ ⁊ egregius
Talia mille pꝛemi tam ſancta volumina fecit:
Ad decus etherei Regis ⁊ eccleſie.
Hoc igitur quicunqꝫ legis Miſſale ſacerdos
Pꝛo tanto ad chꝛiſtum pꝛincipe funde pꝛeces.

Figure 12. *Missale secundum usum insignis ecclesie Sarum* (London: Richard Pynson, 1504), STC 16179, fol. 9v, poem praising Henry VII beneath his coat of arms.

NOTES

1. Mary Beth Winn, *Anthoine Vérard, Parisian Publisher, 1485–1512: Prologues, Poems, and Presentations* (Geneva: Droz, 1997). A special issue of *Le Moyen Français* was devoted to Antoine Vérard in 2011 (vol. 69) and included a bibliography compiled by Mariagrazia Ricci for the years 1995–2011, but other studies have been published since then.
2. Louis-Gabriel Bonicoli, "La Production du libraire-éditeur parisien Antoine Vérard (1485–1512): Nature, fonctions et circulation des images dans les premiers imprimés illustrés," doctoral thesis, Université Paris Ouest Nanterre La Défense, 2015.
3. The database will be housed at the University at Albany, SUNY.
4. Janet Backhouse, "The Royal Library from Edward IV to Henry VII," in the *Cambridge History of the Book in Britain, Volume III: 1400–1557*, ed. Lotte Hellinga and J. B. Trapp (Cambridge, UK: Cambridge University Press, 1999), 272.
5. See Samuel Bentley, ed., "Extracts from the Privy Purse Expenses of King Henry the Seventh, from December A° 7, 1491, to March A° 20, 1505," in *Excerpta Historica or Illustrations of English History* (London: Samuel Bentley, 1831, 85–133), 97. Meautis continued to hold this office under Henry VIII in conjunction with his appointment in 1509 as clerk of the king's council. A.F. Pollard, "Council, Star Chamber, and Privy Council under the Tudors," *The English Historical Review* 37, no. 147 (July 1922, 337–360), 347.
6. The appointment reads:

   > Grant for life to Peter Actoris, born in Savoy, of the office of Stationer to the King; also license to import, so often as he likes, from parts beyond the sea, books printed and not printed into the port of the city of London, and other ports and places within the kingdom of England, and to dispose of the same by sale or otherwise without paying customs, etc. thereon and without rendering any accompt thereof.

   Edward Gordon Duff, *A Century of the English Book Trade* (London: Bibliographical Society, 1948), xiii. It is presumably this "Master Peter" who, on June 14, 1495, received payment from the king's privy purse for expenses "for sertain bokes opon a bille." See Bentley, ed., "Extracts," 103. He is named in a later entry, August 15, 1501: "To Peter Auctor for v. printed bokes, 14s." Henry R. Plomer, "Bibliographical Notes from the Privy Purse Expenses of King Henry the Seventh," *The Library* 3rd ser., 4 (1913): 296.

7. "At this time so little printing was done in England, almost all books being imported, that no Printer to the King was appointed, but only a Stationer to the King." Duff, *Century*, xiii.
8. He received 8s for "ii Saulter Bokes" on May 7, 1499, £1 for "iii bokes" on December 14, 1499, £10 for "claspes and garnyshing of the Kinges boke" on March 25, 1501, 7s 8d for "bynding of 7 bokes and carriage of the same" on March 19, 1502, £1 6s 8d for "writing of 2 rolls of the fundacon of the Kinges almose houses at Westminster" on January 31, 1503. These and subsequent references are cited from Bentley, "Extracts."
9. January 2 and May 21, 1492; December 8, 1494.
10. The printers at Westminster were paid in 1499, while Richard Pynson the printer was rewarded in 1503 and in 1504, specifically for "massebokes to be printed" (£10). Pynson held the title of "impressor regius" beginning in 1506/7, according to Pamela Neville-Sington, "Press, Politics and Religion," in *The Cambridge History of the Book in Britain, Volume III: 1400–1557*, ed. Lotte Hellinga and J. B. Trapp (Cambridge, UK: Cambridge University Press, 1999), 579.
11. Lotte Hellinga, *William Caxton and Early Printing in England* (London: British Library, 2010), 102. The French edition, entitled *L'art de chevalerie selon Vegece,* was published by Vérard on June 26, 1488 (ISTC ic00471000); the English *Fayt of armes and of Chyvalrye* in 1489 (ISTC ic00472000).
12. Hellinga, *William Caxton,* 104.
13. See James P. Carley, *The Libraries of King Henry VIII* (London: British Library, 2000), 19.
14. In this copy (London BL, IB41132b) the woodcuts have all been illuminated, and the first leaf (following two missing leaves) is covered with a new full-page miniature of Pyramus and Thisbee in place of the original preface to the French queen, Anne de Bretagne. While the deletion of the dedication to the French queen in a copy destined for the English king is understandable, the significance of the chosen image remains unclear.
15. See the reproduction in Winn, *Anthoine Vérard,* 323.
16. Backhouse, "Royal Library," 272.
17. Winn, *Anthoine Vérard,* 138–153.
18. Special Collections, Clara Peck Collection QK41.H6 V4. About this copy, see Simonetta Cochis, "Le jardin de santé," in *Transylvania Treasures* 1.1 (2008), 4–5, http://libguides.transy.edu/SpecialCollections/TransyTreasures. I thank Professor Cochis for most of the photos contained in this article. Vérard's title page employs the spelling *"Ortus,"* while the prologue introduces the work as *"Le jardin de santé,"* but most Latin editions are entitled *"Hortus sanitatis."*

19. ISTC ih00490000; GW 13551; John Macfarlane, *Antoine Vérard* (London: 1900; rpt. Geneva: Slatkine, 1971), 140. Thirty-two copies and fragments are known. Copies in Neuchatel (http://www.e-rara.ch/id/1933704) and Valenciennes (https://patrimoine-numerique.ville-valenciennes.fr/ark:/29755/B_596066101_INC_83) have been digitized.
20. Editions published before 1500 are cited in the ISTC and GW. Scientific works are relatively rare among early printed editions, and the online catalogue of the Valenciennes public library asserts that Vérard's edition is *"le premier ouvrage encyclopédique d'histoire naturelle à avoir été imprimé en langue vulgaire dès 1485."* For other works, see Arnold C. Klebs, *Incunabula scientifica et medica* (Bruges, Belgium: 1938; rpt. Hildesheim, Germany: G. Olms, 1963). The 2013 issue of the journal *Kentron* is devoted to the *Hortus sanitatis*, with articles on the text, illustrations, and incunable editions. See also Brigitte Gauvin, Catherine Jacquemard, and Marie-Agnès Lucas-Avenel, "L'Hortus sanitatis: transmission et réorganisation de la matière encyclopédique au xve siècle," in *Revue d'Histoire des Textes* 7 (2012): 353–369.
21. The vellum copy in Cambridge University Library has been digitized: https://cudl.lib.cam.ac.uk/view/PR-INC-00003-A-00001-00008-00037/12.
22. ISTC ih00488000; GW 13549. A digitized copy of Munich, BSB-Ink H-390 can be viewed at http://daten.digitale-sammlungen.de/~db/0002/bsb00027852/images/index.html?id=00027852&grosser=&fip=193.174.98.30&no=&seite=1.
23. Of the extant copies, Henry VII's is the only complete copy on vellum. One other illuminated vellum copy of each volume is known: vol. 1 in Paris, BnF Rés. Vélins 503, and vol. 2 at the Musée des Beaux Arts de la Ville de Paris, Petit Palais, Dutuit Collection, B.138. They may or may not have belonged together. Images from the Dutuit copy of vol. 2 are online at http://parismuseescollections.paris.fr/fr/petit-palais/oeuvres/traictie-des-bestes-oyseaux-poissons-pierres-precieuses-et-orines-par-jean-cuba.
24. ISTC it00015900; Macfarlane, *Antoine Vérard*, 22. For the painted woodcut in the vellum copy of this edition (Paris, BnF Rés. Vélins 1023), see http://gallica.bnf.fr/ark:/12148/btv1b8626776h/f13.item. Note that it lacks painted borders.
25. Reproduced in Hugh W. Davies, *A Catalogue of a Collection of Early French Books in the Library of C. Fairfax Murray* (London: Privately Printed, 1910), 1: 243.
26. The names of Hermann (of Rottenburg) and Ernest (of Hesse-Rheinfels, d. 1693) appear on the title page of vol. 1.

27. A. S. G. Edwards, "Peck, Clara S." in *Oxford Companion to the Book* (Oxford: Oxford University, 2010).
28. Robert Nikirk, "Miss Clara Peck, Book Collector," *Kentucky Review* 11.3 (1992): 44–57.
29. Edwin Wolf II with John F. Fleming, *Rosenbach: A Biography* (Cleveland and New York: World Publishing Co., 1960), 393.
30. For information about Clara Peck's bequest, photographs, and generous assistance with queries about the *Ortus sanitatis*, I am extremely grateful to B. J. Gooch, Special Collections Librarian at Transylvania University.
31. About the theft by four students, who attacked the Special Collections librarian with a stun gun, see articles cited at http://homepages.transy.edu/~subrown/booktheft/theft.htm. Posted there are twenty-four images from the *Hortus sanitatis*. In 2010, one of the thieves, writing under the name Chas Allen, penned a book about the theft: *Mr. Pink: The Inside Story of the Transylvania Book Heist.* The heist has just been made into a movie, *American Animals,* directed by Bart Layton and shown at the Sundance Film Festival in Park City, Utah, January 19–27, 2018. See Guy Lodge, "Film Review: 'American Animals,'" *Variety,* January 19, 2018, http://variety.com/2018/film/reviews/american-animals-review-1202669037/.
32. .See Carley, *Libraries,* 89.
33. Joseph B. B. Van Praet, *Catalogue des livres imprimés sur vélin de la Bibliothèque du Roi,* Paris: 1822–1828, 1: 283, no. 390, traces its provenance from Cardinal Dubois (1725) through La Haye (1764), Gaignat (sale catalogue I, 70:252), La Vallière (1783–88, catalogue I, 181:502), and MacCarthy (1815, catalogue I, 92:572), after which it entered the Bibliothèque nationale de France.
34. About these books, see Winn, *Anthoine Vérard,* 144, with reproduction on 145 of fol. a4 of the Pelerinage.
35. *Orloge de sapience,* New York Public Library *1493; see Winn, *Anthoine Vérard,* 143–144, 286–287.
36. "Anthoine Vérard, *Hore beate virginis Marie ad usum Sarum* (Paris, c. 1505)," Royal Danish Library, http://www.kb.dk/permalink/2006/manus/9/.
37. CHD Institute for Studies of Illuminated Manuscripts in Denmark, http://manuscripts.org.uk/chd.dk/inc/perg19.html.
38. I have used the online indices of the ISTC and the USTC for these figures, but caution is needed because of difficulties in distinguishing among closely related editions. A case in point is that Vérard's 1508 edition is not cited by the USTC.

39. STC 16171. The copy held by Boston Public Library has been digitized and can be viewed at https://archive.org/details/missalesecundumv00cath.
40. Three other woodcuts of this size illustrate the other sections of text: the first Sunday in Advent by "*Ad te levavi animam meam*" with an image of the Mass; St. Andrew's Eve at the beginning of the *Proprium sanctorum* (fol. a1 [157]), with an image of the martyrdom of St. Andrew; and the *Commune sanctorum* (fol. i1 [217]), with a four-part image of the saints and martyrs.
41. STC 16170, originally dated after 1500, but revised to ca. 1505; see ISTC im00721750. However, see n. 45 below.
42. According to Édouard Frère, *De l'imprimerie et de la librairie à Rouen, dans les XVe et XVIe siècles, et de Martin Morin, célèbre imprimeur rouennais* (Rouen, France: 1843), 52, Morin first used an image of St. George in a Missal of 1497. Morin's 1501 Missal was produced by Jean Huvin, the publisher of Vérard's Missal.
43. Both editions are reproduced in Early English Books Online (eebo.chadwyck.com), but the film used for the 1508 edition is so light that the pages are almost illegible.
44. As early as 1489, Vérard had hired printer from Rouen, Jean Le Bourgeois, to print the prose romance *Tristan*, but he usually employed printers in Paris. Other Rouennais stationers, identified in the colophon as Jean de Burges, Jacques Cousin, and Pierre Huvin, collaborated with Vérard on an edition of a book of Hours for the Use of Rouen, dating from after 1503. The almanac is for 1503–1520 (USTC 26043; Macfarlane, *Antoine Vérard*, 249). Jacques Cousin (1503–1517), issued several editions of Missals, Hours, and a Manual for Sarum Use. See Duff, *Century*, 34.
45. The same capital M with his name appears on the title page of his Missal for the Use of Rouen. I thank Dominique Coq for this information about the copy located in Rouen, Bm, Inc g-141. If the Rouen Missal appeared as early as 1496, then the use of the capital M predates the Sarum Missal by a decade. Since it seems likely that Vérard copied Morin, this suggests that Morin, too, began using an M with his name before 1500.
46. Gough Missals 27 in the Bodleian Library. This is the copy filmed for EEBO, but the reproduction is too light to read. The full colophon is recorded in Richard Gough, *Catalogue of Sarum and York Missals* (London: 1780), 13. I am very greateful to Jo Maddocks, Assistant Curator of Rare Books, Bodleian Libraries, for additional information about this Missal.
47. Saint Petersburg, National Library, 15.52.7.23. This copy was apparently unknown to George D. Painter, Dennis E. Rhodes, and Howard M. Nixon, who cite only a fragment of a 1508 edition bearing the name of

the London publisher in their article: "Two Missals Printed for Wynkyn de Worde," *British Library Journal* 2.2 (1976): 159–171, at 160. The fragment of four leaves now in Oxford [STC 16182a.5] includes the colophon. The fragment of two leaves in the Durham University Library could be from either issue. I am grateful to the late Dr. Ian Doyle for showing it to me in 2004 and to Richard Higgins for identifying it now under the shelfmark Add.MS. 1950/b/4.

48. It is not unusual for vellum leaves of the Canon to be inserted in paper copies. A similar example is found in copies of the Sarum Missal published by Pynson on January 10, 1500. As Katja Airaksinen states, "A number of copies may have been printed in such a manner, including this bifolium on vellum within a paper copy in order to provide protection and grandeur for the most used and important part of the Missal." See Katja Airaksinen, "The Morton Missal: The Finest Incunable Made in England," *Transactions of the Cambridge Bibliographical Society* 14.2 (2009): 147–179, at 159.
49. Vérard also uses this woodcut in his edition of the *Art of Good Lywyng*, published on May 30, 1503 (STC 791). See the digitized copy at https://gallica.bnf.fr/ark:/12148/bpt6k990545t/f1.item.
50. His son Arthur had died in 1502.
51. Commentary accompanying the reproduction of the painting online: https://www.royalcollection.org.uk/collection/401228/the-family-of-henry-vii-with-st-george-and-the-dragon.
52. See especially A. S. G. Edwards and Carol M. Meale, "The Marketing of Printed Books in Late Medieval England," *The Library* 6.14 (1993): 95–124. The cut they reproduce as fig. 5 is the one used in the Missal, which demonstrates that it appeared at least as early as 1504, rather than 1513 as they suppose.
53. Pynson's Missal of 1500 (STC 16173; ISTC im00721550) uses a different woodcut of the king's arms, and its colophon reveals its commissioning by Cardinal John Morton, Archbishop of Canterbury. See Airaksinen, "Morton Missal."
54. Missale ad vsum insignis [et] preclare eccclesie [sic] Sarum: pulcherrimis eleme[n]tis (vt res ipsa indicat) pressum: additis q[uam] plurimis commoditatibus que in ceteris huiusmodi codicibus non habentur. Nam que in illis annotata fuere. no[n] sine summo labore inuenta sunt: hic autem in suis locis ad plenum perscripta sunt: appositis ipsius ecclesie institutis, co[n]suetudinibus, singulisq[ue] festis. vna cum suis prosis. Et si que abera[n]t, suo loco adiectis. Titulis preterea numerorum ac me[n]sium notis pensiculate collatis: vt nusq[uam] numerus numero

non respondeat. Quo sacrificantibus omnia facillime occurrant. Adiunctis quoq[ue] [et] in fine appositis aliquibus nouis officiis non paru[m] necessariis. Quod quidem impressum est atq[ue] vigilantissimo studio castigatum examinatumq[ue] in opulenti ciuitate London. per Richardum Pynson huius artis ingeniosissimu[m]. Mandato [et] impensa serenissimi [christ]ianissimisq[ue] [et]omni virtutum genere prediti Regis Henrici septimi: ad indiuidue trinitatis et intemerate v[ir]ginis Marie totiusq[ue] militie celestis laudem decus [et] sempiternam gloriam. Anno vero a natali christiano Millesimo quingentesimo quarto, decimo kalendas Ianuarii. (London: Printed by Richard Pynson, 1504 [10 Kalendas Januarii]).

55. This woodcut is lacking in the copy now in the John Rylands Library, Manchester.
56. For the translation of Pynson's texts as well as invaluable information about Pynson's Missals, I am very grateful to Professor Daniel J. Sheerin.
57. These prayers are also handwritten on the rear flyleaf of the "Morton Missal" (Oxford, Bodl. M276-1), but with three additional prayers. See Airaksinen, "Morton Missal." Manuscript prayers to Henry VII have also been added at the end of the British Library copy (BL IB. 40686) of the Sarum Missal published in Paris in 1497 by Ulrich Gering and Berthold Rembolt for Wynkyn de Worde, Michel Morin, and Pierre Levet. See Painter, Rhodes, and Nixon, "Two Missals," 165; unfortunately the texts are not cited, so I have been unable to determine whether they are the same as those printed in Vérard's edition.
58. In the Saint Petersburg copy, the name "*Henrici septimi*" has been partially and poorly erased, leaving the letters "ti" and the red final period still visible. "*Jacobi quin*" is handwritten in black ink in its place, ending with the final red printed letters "ti."
59. The prayers are included in Francis Henry Dickinson, *Missale ad usum insignis et praeclarae ecclesiae Sarum* (Burntisland, Scotland: E Prelo de Pitsligo, 1883), 562–563. William Maskell, *The Ancient Liturgy of the Church of England,* According to the Uses of Sarum, 2nd ed. (London: William Pickering, 1846), 184, cites the texts from a 1516 edition of the Sarum Missal where the king's name has become "*Henricus octavus.*"
60. Omnipotent and merciful God, we pray that our king Henry the seventh, who through your compassion undertook the governing of the kingdom, may assume an increase of all virtues appropriately adorned to avoid the abyss of vices, to rejoice in soundness of the body, to conquer enemies, and may he govern in tranquil peace while among mortals. May he blessedly be able to pass through his time so that after the course of

his life he be able to come through as pleasing to you who are the way, the truth and the life.

I am very grateful to Richard Collier for translations of these prayers.

61. The headings "*Secretum*" and "*Post communio*" are printed in red type.
62. We pray, Lord, that the gifts offered be sanctified, so that they become the body and blood of your only-born son for us and for your servant Henry the seventh our king, and that salvation be obtained by the spirit and body and that by working through strong faith and firm peace together he may advance his office always bountifully for you.
63. We pray, Lord, that this healthful taking of the sacrament may protect your servant our king Henry the seventh from all adversaries so that he may obtain a long and prosperous life in the tranquility of the peace of the church and after the course of his life he may by your grace achieve eternal beatitude.

WORKS CITED

Websites for Primary Works

Hortus sanitatis. Mainz: Jacob Meydenbach, 1491. Cambridge University Library. https://cudl.lib.cam.ac.uk/view/PR-INC-00003-A-00001-00008-00037/12.

Missale secundum usum insignis ecclesie Sarum. Paris: Vérard, 1504. STC 16180 (Cambridge University Library copy). http://eebo.chadwyck.com.

Missale secundum usum insignis ecclesie Sarum. Rouen: J. Huvyn , G. Bernard, A. Vérard, 1508. STC 16182a (Bodleian Library copy). http://eebo.chadwyck.com

Ortus sanitatis. Vérard. Neuchâtel. http://www.e-rara.ch/id/1933704.

Ortus sanitatis. Vérard. Valenciennes. https://patrimoine-numerique.ville-valenciennes.fr/ark:/29755/B_596066101_INC_83.

Ortus sanitatis. Vérard. Paris, Petit Palais. http://parismuseescollections.paris.fr/fr/petit-palais/oeuvres/traictie-des-bestes-oyseaux-poissons-pierres-precieuses-et-orines-par-jean-cuba.

Tardif, Guillaume. *L'art de faulconnerie.* Paris: Vérard, 1492/3. http://gallica.bnf.fr/ark:/12148/btv1b8626776h/f13.item.

Secondary Works

Airaksinen, Katja. "The Morton Missal: The Finest Incunable Made in England." *Transactions of the Cambridge Bibliographical Society* 14.2 (2009):147–179.

Antoine Vérard. Le Moyen Français 69 (2010).

Backhouse, Janet. "The Royal Library from Edward IV to Henry VII." In *The Cambridge History of the Book in Britain, Volume III: 1400–1557*, ed. Lotte Hellinga and J. B. Trapp, 267–281. Cambridge, UK: Cambridge University Press, 1999.

Bentley, Samuel, ed. "Extracts from the Privy Purse Expenses of King Henry the Seventh, from December A° 7, 1491, to March A° 20, 1505. In *Excerpta historica: or, Illustrations of English History*, 85–133. London: Samuel Bentley, 1831.

Bonicoli, Louis-Gabriel. "La production du libraire-éditeur parisien Antoine Vérard (1485–1512): Nature, fonctions et circulation des images dans les premiers imprimés illustrés." Doctoral thesis, Université Paris Ouest Nanterre La Défense, 2015.

Carley, James P. *The Libraries of King Henry VIII*. London: British Library, 2000.

Cochis, Simonetta. "Le jardin de santé." *Transylvania Treasures* 1.1 (2008):4–5. http://libguides.transy.edu/SpecialCollections/TransyTreasures.

Davies, Hugh William. *A Catalogue of a Collection of Early French Books in the Library of C. Fairfax Murray*. London: Privately Printed, 1910.

Dickinson, Francis Henry. *Missale ad usum insignis et praeclarae ecclesiae Sarum*. Burntisland, Scotland: E Prelo de Pitsligo, 1883.

Duff, Edward Gordon. *A Century of the English Book Trade*. London: Bibliographical Society, 1948.

Edwards, A. S. G. "Peck, Clara S." In *Oxford Companion to the Book*. Oxford: Oxford University, 2010.

———, and Carol M. Meale. "The Marketing of Printed Books in Late Medieval England." *The Library* 6.14 (1993):95–124.

Frère, Édouard. *De l'imprimerie et de la librairie à Rouen, dans les XVe et XVIe siècles, et de Martin Morin, célèbre imprimeur rouennais*. Rouen, France: 1843.

Gallica Digital Library. http://gallica.bnf.fr/accueil/?mode=desktop.

Gauvin, Brigitte, Catherine Jacquemard, and Marie-Agnès Lucas-Avenel. "L'Hortus sanitatis: transmission et réorganisation de la matière encyclopédique au xve siècle." *Revue d'Histoire des Textes* 7 (2012):353–369.

Gesamtkatalog der Wiegendrucke (GW). http://www.gesamtkatalogder-wiegendrucke.de.

Hellinga, Lotte. *William Caxton and Early Printing in England*. London: British Library, 2010.

Incunabula Short-title Catalogue (ISTC). http://data.cerl.org/istc/_search.

Klebs, Arnold C. *Incunabula scientifica et medica*. Bruges, Belgium: 1938; rpt. Hildesheim, Germany: G. Olms, 1963.

L'Hortus sanitatis. Thematic issue. *Kentron: Revue pluridisciplinaire du monde antique* 29 (2013).

Macfarlane, John. *Antoine Vérard.* London: 1900; rpt. Geneva: Slatkine, 1971.

Maskell, William. *The Ancient Liturgy of the Church of England, According to the Uses of Sarum*, 2nd ed. London: William Pickering, 1846.

Neville-Sington, Pamela. "Press, Politics and Religion." In *The Cambridge History of the Book in Britain, Volume III: 1400–1557*, ed. Lotte Hellinga and J. B. Trapp, 576–607. Cambridge, UK: Cambridge University Press, 1999.

Nikirk, Robert. "Miss Clara Peck, Book Collector." *Kentucky Review* 11.3 (1992):44–57.

Painter, George D., Dennis E. Rhodes, and Howard M. Nixon. "Two Missals Printed for Wynkyn de Worde." *British Library Journal* 2.2 (1976): 159–171.

Plomer, Henry R. "Bibliographical Notes from the Privy Purse Expenses of King Henry the Seventh." *The Library* 3rd ser., 4 (1913): 291–305.

Pollard, A.F. "Council, Star Chamber, and Privy Council under the Tudors," *The English Historical Review* 37, no. 147 (July 1922): 337-360.

Van Praet, Joseph B. B. *Catalogue des livres imprimés sur vélin de la Bibliothèque du Roi.* Paris: 1822–1828.

Winn, Mary Beth. *Anthoine Vérard, Parisian Publisher, 1485–1512: Prologues, Poems, and Presentations.* Geneva: Droz, 1997.

Wolf, Edwin II, with John F. Fleming. *Rosenbach: A Biography*. Cleveland and New York: World Publishing, 1960.

Compiling Practices in Printed English Paratexts 1500–1550

MARI-LIISA VARILA

Many early English texts survive in manuscript compilations created by book producers, early owners, or book collectors. Manuscript compilations relatively rarely contain explicit commentary on the selection and organization of texts. With manuscripts produced in the bespoke mode or copied for private use, the reader would typically have already had an idea of what would be included in the product and why. Many early printed books are also compilations and adaptations of earlier material. The paratextual elements in these books occasionally shed light on the processes of text production and compilation. In speculative production of printed books, there may have been more reason to justify decisions related to the production of a given edition. In paratextual spaces—for example, title pages and prefaces—text producers could explain their rationale to the potential customers.

This study addresses the textual agency of late-medieval and early-modern compilers as presented on English title pages and other front matter from 1500 to 1550. I first examine verbs related to compiling practices found on title pages. I then focus on the various uses of the verb *compile* in context, drawing examples from prefaces and letters to the reader. Finally, I compare printed comments on compiling activities to late-medieval and early-modern manuscript practices, suggesting that evidence from printed paratexts may also advance our understanding of manuscript production.

Compilers and Compilations

The importance of compiling activities in the production of texts and books has been widely recognized in previous research into the history of the book, both manuscript and early print.[1] An often-repeated description by Bonaventure places medieval text workers into four categories: scribes, who copied the words of others; compilers, who put together the work of others without adding anything of their own; commentators, who combined their work with that of others but focused on the contributions of others, and finally, authors, who combined their work with that of others but focused on their own contribution.[2] Drawing on this and other medieval negotiations of authorship, A. J. Minnis observes that while late-medieval authors were held accountable for their work, compilers, working with the texts of others, could conveniently avoid such responsibilities.[3]

Malcolm B. Parkes notes that in the later medieval period:

> a compiler was perceived as one who imposed a new organization on material derived from the works of others. The compiler assembled, after a process of critical evaluation, concise and important extracts from sources regarded as authoritative and disposed them according to a scheme, or sometimes the framework of a general topic, characterized by its usefulness.[4]

For Parkes, the logical organization and reorganization of material are an essential aspect of a compiler's work. Minnis elucidates the ways in which such impulses show in the text-organizational work of medieval authors, for example, in Ranulf Higden's *Polychronicon* and Geoffrey Chaucer's *Canterbury Tales*.[5]

Much of the discussion on the compiler's role has focused on the medieval period. However, Ann M. Blair notes that compiling was "generally a valued literary and scholarly activity" throughout the medieval period and well into the early modern, with criticism on the basis of unoriginality generally not arising before the seventeenth century.[6] While some ancient and medieval practices of compiling remained in use in the early-modern period, the diversification of readers and writers also allowed for new ways of collecting and organizing text. Early-modern commonplace books (collections of quotations under thematic headings) were based on ancient models but were also related to medieval *florilegia* and mirrors for princes.[7] Guidelines were available for compiling texts and extracts, but not all compilers followed such models. Earle Havens characterizes the history of commonplace books as a "history of a 'tradition' that stubbornly refused to be traditional."[8] Parkes notes that compilation as a genre evolved over time, and to track these developments, it is necessary to study individual compilations in detail.[9] Compilations thus resist categorization to a degree.

Compiling is a thorny concept also because it can denote a physical or a textual process—or both. As Jeffrey Knight puts it, early-modern readers and writers "did not simply think of their books as aggregations of text; they physically aggregated, resituated, and customized them."[10] In the physical sense, gatherings and booklets were brought together in codex form in more or less planned constellations. In the textual sense, works, extracts, and brief texts were taken out of their previous context and resituated among other select materials. Compiling was also a linguistic process. Compilers selected, reworked, and rearranged texts and had the opportunity to edit the language of those texts when reproducing them in a new context. They could, for instance, translate or modernize their source texts or modify their paratextual framing. They could also lend cohesion to the collection by introducing a systematic visual program for texts taken from different sources.[11]

Despite considerable scholarly attention to compiling as a major phenomenon in the history of books and texts, compilers as textual agents remain somewhat elusive to book historical and linguistic research alike. Looking at compilers as language users is not an easy task, as the language of the compiler is often interwoven with the language of their source materials. Thomas Kohnen approaches the various roles of commonplace book compilers from a historical pragmatics perspective, noting that compilers may shift between the roles of text receiver (reader), text composer (author), text copyist (scribe), and text sender (recording the text for future readers, potentially including themselves).[12] Compilers often have double agency in text production. Authors, scribes, printers, translators, booksellers, and book owners could all act as compilers, producing material either for their own purposes or for others.

This paper seeks to understand early-sixteenth-century ideas of compiling through an investigation of paratextual elements in books printed in English from 1500 to 1550. Although my focus is on printed books, the motivation behind this study also arises from research into manuscript and hybrid compilations. The interaction between manuscript and print during the early stages of print culture has been brought to the fore of book historical research during the past few decades. Alexandra Walsham and Julia Crick argue that the interaction and hybridity of manuscript and print should be seen "as a keynote of the culture of communication in this period."[13] Many readers and text producers regularly operated with both media: texts were prepared in manuscript form for printing, and printed texts were copied by hand. Extracts copied from longer works—manuscript or print—often appear in manuscript compilations. However, it is not always easy to identify them in their manuscript context, as they may have been integrated into their new surroundings with no source references.[14] While prefaces to longer works may describe the text-production process of the author/translator –compiler in the context of the textual product, explicit comments by scribe–compilers regarding the physical product are rare.

Paratextual spaces for commenting on texts and text production are not identical in manuscript and print. Margaret M. Smith notes that the title page is primarily a feature of the printed book that developed as a response to the practicalities of speculative production of multiple copies of the same work. It worked as an identifying label and, later, as an advertisement for books in storage and on sale.[15] Title pages are relatively rare in manuscripts, especially those predating print. With manuscript trade, the agreement between the producer and purchaser would typically have ensured that purchasers already knew which text(s) they would receive, and manuscripts would not generally have been stored for a lengthy period awaiting potential buyers.[16] Those compiling manuscripts for their own use might not have found it necessary to record their reasons for the inclusion of a given text or extract. However, the openings and closings of both manuscript and print texts and books—such as rubrics, prologues, and colophons—are potential paratextual sites of commentary on compiling practices. Despite the differences between the media and modes of text production, this study proceeds from the premise that compilers at work in the early sixteenth century shared some of their rationale independent of the medium used: in other words, that some principles and practices of producing a compilation would have been common to both manuscript and print production.

The Present Study

The materials for this study were collected from the *Early English Books Online* (*EEBO*) database. *EEBO* contains digital images of copies of most editions printed in the British and Irish Isles in the period studied and full-text versions of many of the titles.[17] I have used *EEBO* in three different ways: by consulting images, by conducting full-text searches through the *EEBO* interface, and by searching a dataset of title-page metadata collected from *EEBO*.[18] The metadata dataset contains title-page information (title, printer, and year of publication) of all editions in *EEBO* from 1500 to 1550, including those editions for which full-text versions are not available.

Using *EEBO* enabled me to access a comprehensive corpus of early English editions, and a similar analysis would not have been feasible by consulting copies in situ. However, some inaccuracies are likely to remain. For example, the metadata for some items is necessarily conjectural, and the title field of the metadata occasionally includes other elements such as colophons. The overall survey presented in the next section therefore shows general tendencies in the data, but it cannot be treated as a statistical account. The close reading of examples in their context is intended to balance the picture arising from the overall survey.

The title-page dataset was consulted using the corpus software AntConc.[19] I created a word list of all the words in the dataset and identified verbs connected to compiling practices. Five verbs were selected for further scrutiny: *add, collect, compile, gather,* and *take+out.* I counted the relevant occurrences of these verbs on English title pages by searching the dataset and analyzing the results manually. Common polysemic verbs such as *make* were left out of the study, as the manual analysis of all instances of them would not have been feasible. For the same reason, instead of *take,* the less frequent and semantically more restricted phrasal verb *take out* (referring to extracting text) was selected for analysis.

Next, I examined the verb *compile* in context by searching the EEBO-TCP full-text corpus.[20] I limited the search to prefaces and letters to the reader by using the *EEBO* advanced search function "Limit full text keyword(s) within . . ." and selecting the fields *Prefaces* and "*To the reader.*" The texts of the works proper were left out of the present study, as I expected that explicit comments related to the book-production process would be more common in prefatory material and that such paratextual comments could fruitfully be compared to title-page usages.

Finally, I compared print practices to phenomena highlighted in previous research into manuscript compilations. For this part, searching a large corpus was not feasible for two reasons: editions of entire manuscript compilations are relatively rare, and paratextual material and details of manuscript context are often missing from text-focused linguistic corpora. In establishing parallels between compilers' activities in manuscript and print, I rely on the important work done in the field of manuscript studies. The following three sections focus respectively on the occurrence of compiling verbs on title pages, the word *compile* in context, and parallels between print and manuscript practices.

Compiling on Early English Title Pages

The main language used on the title pages of English editions from 1500 to 1550 found in *EEBO* is most commonly Latin or English. Of the 3,775 title pages surveyed, 2,449 mainly employ English, 1,292 Latin, and only 34 other languages (under 1 percent of the dataset). For the first three decades studied, Latin is the most common language on title pages. Of the 443 title pages in 1500 to 1510, 238 mainly employ Latin and 192 English; of the 461 title pages in 1511 to 1520, 296 primarily use Latin and 161 English. In 1521 to 1530, Latin (405 title pages) is still more common than English (282). In the 1530s and 1540s, English becomes the dominant language. In 1531 to

1540, English is the preferred language on 672 title pages and Latin on 206; the corresponding numbers for 1541 to 1550 are 1,142 (English) and 147 (Latin). The 2,449 English title pages from 1500 to 1550 form the basis for the following analysis. Although some problematic hits likely remain, this number is a useful estimate of the scope of the data. I have not sampled the data, which means that the 1,142 English title pages from the 1540s make up almost one half of the materials analyzed.

I examined instances of the five compiling verbs selected for further analysis: *add, collect, compile, gather,* and *take+out*. I searched the title-page dataset for past participle (*-ed*) forms of these verbs to find examples where the compiling processes are described as completed actions. An example of such a usage is the following: "Here begynneth a lytel treatyse called the contrauerse bytwene a louer and a Iaye lately compyled" (STC 10838.7, A1r).[21] Table 1 shows the raw numbers for this stage of the analysis.

The survey in Table 1 shows that compiling verbs found their way onto English title pages, especially toward 1550. The most prominent of the five verbs is *compiled* itself (127 occurrences). *Added* and *gathered* are also relatively common, especially in the last two decades of the survey. The first attestation of the verb *collect* in English in the *Oxford English Dictionary Online* (*OED Online*) is from 1573, but the past participle *collect* (without the *-ed* ending) is attested already in the fifteenth century. The use of this verb on early English title pages may reflect the influence of Latin models on English title-page formulae.[22] Table 1 shows a relative increase in the use of compiling verbs toward 1550 (the percentages for each decade were calculated by dividing the number of verb occurrences by the number of English titles). All relevant verb forms were counted, including multiple instances on the same title page. For example, the title page of STC 23899 contains two relevant items: "Floures for Latine spekynge selected and *gathered* oute of Terence. . . . *Compiled* by Nicolas Vdall" (π1r, my emphasis). In terms of the percentages in Table 1, this means that in the 1540s, compiling verbs do not necessarily occur in approximately 20 percent of *editions*, but the relative use of these verbs on title pages increases.

The results do not mean that compiling itself became more common during this period. The amount of information given on the title page generally increases towards 1550. Smith notes that "once the title-page advanced from the modest label-title to a more informative and decorative form, its function grew from mere identification to promotion" of the book and/or its printer.[23] It seems feasible that the increasing use of compiling verbs is related to the more general transformation of the title page into a promotional space. Indeed, the verb *compile* typically occurs on title pages in a context where the main focus is on identifying the book producers. In a majority of instances, *compile* occurs together with the preposition *by* in phrases identifying the

Table 1. Instances of compiling verbs on English title pages 1500 to 1550

	1500–1510	**1511–1520**	**1521–1530**	**1531–1540**	**1541–1550**	**Total**
Compiling verbs on title pages						
Total number of English title pages	192	161	282	672	1,142	**2,449**
Total number of compiling verbs	10	8	33	69	222	**342**
Verb forms per number of titles (%)	5.21%	4.97%	11.70%	10.27%	19.44%	**13.96%**
Occurrences by verb						
added	0	1	7	26	62	**96**
collected	0	0	2	2	20	**24**
compiled	9	7	20	21	70	**127**
gathered	0	0	4	17	58	**79**
taken+out	1	0	0	3	12	**16**

compiler: "compiled by Erasmus Roterodame" (STC 10505); "practysyd & compyled by the moost experte mayster Iherome of Bruynswyke" (STC 13434). The focus is on identifying and promoting the compiler rather than on describing the text-production process.

In the case of translated compilations, the translator may be identified after the compiler. Occasionally, the language of the original compilation is specified: "compyled in frenche by lady Margarete quene of Nauerre, and aptely translated into Englysh by the ryght vertuouse lady Elyzabeth doughter to our late souerayne Kynge Henri the. viij" (STC 17320). The commissioner, dedicatee, or intended audience of the edition may also be named: "compyled in latyn by Domynike Mancyn: and translate into englysshe: at the desyre of syr Gyles Alyngton knyght: by Alexander Bercley prest and monke of Ely" (STC 17242); "trewly compyled for the right high, excellent, and most vertuous lady, the lady Mary of Englande, doughter to our most gracious souerayn lorde kyng Henry the eight" (STC 7377). Occasionally, the title specifies a wider intended audience, as in "compyled for the commodite of al christen people. By D. Urbanum Regium" (STC 20843).

For comparison, the verb *gather* most commonly occurs on title pages together with the preposition *out*, as in "Floures for Latine speakyng selected and gathered oute of Terence" (STC 23899). *Gathered out* is more common than *gathered by*, and *collected out* is more common than *collected by*. As with instances of the phrasal verb *taken+out*, the focus is on identifying the source works and authors rather than the compiler (who may remain anonymous). In most instances of *gathered by*, the "gatherer" is identified only by name. An exception is STC 24781, where the gatherer is advertised as "the famous clerke Master Peter viret, Frenchman." The verb *add* is usually preceded by the name of the main text and followed by a noun phrase advertising additional contents: "The regiment of life, whereunto is added a treatise of the pestilence, with the boke of children" (STC 11970); "The psalter or boke of the Psalmes where vnto is added the letany and certayne other deuout prayers" (STC 2375).

Compiling verbs on title pages may thus be seen as part of the emerging strategy of using the title page to promote the book and advertise the quality of the physical and textual manufacturing process.[24] The five verbs typically occur in phrases identifying and advertising the author, compiler, and/or source work and in phrases highlighting additions to the main text. However, the brief formulae used on title pages do not typically elaborate on the nature of compiling as a text-production process. The semantic interpretation of verbs related to the production of books, works, and texts during the early sixteenth century is not a straightforward procedure. A single verb may reflect different kinds of compiling processes. I therefore continue by examining occurrences of the verb *compile* in context. Subjecting this verb to further scrutiny in a study of compilation practices may seem an obvious choice. However, of the five verbs surveyed above, *compile* was also the one most commonly found on title pages and the only one found in the dataset throughout the period studied.

Compiling in Context

In what follows, I explore lengthier examples from paratextual matter, primarily prefaces and letters to the reader. These could be written by authors, translators, printers, or other people participating in the production process or endorsing the finished product. Paratext offered the text and book producers a space for explaining their rationale of production and presentation. Prefatory matter occasionally contains very detailed accounts of how the work or the specific edition came to be. Although these accounts may have been produced with a degree of narrative freedom, they nevertheless offer a glimpse into compiling practices. Even conventional descriptions reflect contemporary expectations of how material could or should be compiled.

The first two definitions of *compile* in the *OED Online* (s.v. *compile,* v. 1; 2a) are both relevant for analyzing sixteenth-century usages of the verb. The earlier sense (v. 2a) is glossed as: "To make, compose, or construct (a written or printed work) by arrangement of materials collected from various sources."[25] The first attestation for this sense is from Trevisa's translation of Ranulf Higden's *Polychronicon* (1387). Chaucer fashions himself a compiler around the same time, noting in the *Treatise on the Astrolabe* that he is "but a lewd compilatour of the labour of olde Astrologiens."[26] The first attestation for the other relevant sense of the verb *compile* (v. 1) is slightly later, circa 1425. The definition reads: "To collect and put together (materials), so as to form a treatise; to collect into a volume."[27] Judging from the synonyms used in the definitions, the earlier sense (v. 2a) is perhaps more authorial; it is glossed using *make* and *compose,* and the focus is on the work. The definition for v. 1, in turn, contains the verbs *collect* and *put together*. According to the interpretation of the *OED Online,* the verb *compile* also has two additional senses that are attested only in the fifteenth and sixteenth centuries. The first one of these is "to compose an original work" (v. 3) and the second one is "to translate" (v. 4). There is obviously overlap between these different senses, and the boundaries between the text-production processes themselves are not clear-cut. The status of compiling as an authorial or nonauthorial activity seems to fluctuate during this period, reflecting different practices.

The verbs *compile* and *make* occasionally occur in a binomial structure, but it is not apparent whether they should be read synonymously or understood as different textual activities. *Make* is already used in the sense "To compose, write as the author" in Old English, while *compile* enters the English lexis in the medieval period.[28] Such synonymous or near-synonymous binomials have been discussed especially with regard to medieval English writers. Germanic and Romance vocabularies were sometimes combined into binomials of mixed origin, similarly to the pairing of *compile* and *make* in the above examples.[29] Building on earlier studies, Ronald Waldron argues that contrary to some earlier suggestions, such binomials do not appear to be motivated by a wish to familiarize the audience with new romance loan-words. Instead, his analysis lends some support to James Greenough and George Lyman Kittredge's suggestions that in some cases the binomials may have been a translator's solution to the problem of covering the "whole meaning intended by the writer" in the source language.[30] Analyzing the semantics of Latin compiling verbs might thus shed more light on the English usages as well.

Make and *compile* occur as a binomial in the letter to the reader in the *Pylgremage of Pure Deuotyon* (STC 10454): "for whiche intent and purpose the sayd most noble and famous clarke D[e]siderius Erasmus, compiled & made this dialoge in Laten, as it foloweth herafter nowe lately translated into our mother the Englishhe tonge" (†6v). The binomial "compiled & made" suggests an authorial contribution made by Erasmus. The title page of the edition also declares that the work was "deuysyd and set forthe" in Latin by Erasmus (†1r). Another example of the combination of *compile* and *make* is on the title page of the English translation of Hieronymus Brunschwig's *Liber de arte distillandi* (*The Vertuose Boke of Distyllacyon of the Waters*, STC 13435). The title page stresses the time and labor that went into producing the work, declaring that it was "fyrst made and compyled by the thyrte yeres study and labour of the moste connynge and famous master of phisyke, Maister Iherom brunswyke" (¶1r). A binomial structure is also used in the incipit of the original German work: "zesammen colligiert vnnd gesetzt von Hieronymo Brunschwygk" ("collected together and set forth" by Brunschwig).[31]

In the above examples, *compile* and *make* may be read as synonyms referring to original contribution or interpreted as indicating different textual activities. The two verbs might be considered chronologically as two different stages in the text-production process. However, in the two examples, the order of the verbs is reversed: Erasmus "compiled and made" his work, while Brunschwig "made and compyled" his book. The latter order is more commonly found on title pages in 1500 to 1550. Conversely, when *compiled* is the first verb in a binomial structure, it is typically followed by *set forth* or *put forth*. If the verbs are interpreted as reflecting production stages, then, *make* might stand for composing the work, *compile* for the text-organization and editing process, and *set/put forth* for the publication. However, there are too few instances of the binomial *compile/make* in the dataset to support any strong conclusions, and internal variation suggests that at least for some language users the two verbs might have been synonymous.

A lengthier passage where *compile* occurs with *make* is found in the 1500 edition of the *Life of St. Catherine of Siena* (STC 24766.3). Here, the verbs do not form a binomial but are used in close proximity to each other. In the introduction, the translator notes:

> This legende compyled a worshypfull clerke fryer Reymond of the ordre of saynt domynik doctor of deuynyte and confessour of this holy virgyn / But in this translacion I leue of the two prologues whiche in the begynnyng the same clerke made in latyn. The whiche passeth your vnderstondyng. (A1r)

The legend itself is "compiled" by Reymond of Capua, while the prologues are "made" by him. The verb *make* might here be a stronger indication of original composition than *compile*: the text of the legend was most likely based on an earlier tradition, while the prologues seem novel authorial contributions. Later in the introduction, there is another reference to the "worshypfull clerke" that "compyled this boke in latyn" (A1r). Here, the verb *compile* refers to the *book*. It is unclear whether *book* refers to the main text (the legend) only or whether it also covers paratextual elements (such as the prologues). As the prologues were left out of the translation, *this boke* is perhaps better understood as a reference to the main text. If this is the case, the use of *compile* in a less authorial sense appears consistent here: the verb refers to the reworking of preexisting material rather than original composition.

In addition to *make*, *compile* also occurs together with other verbs related to text production. In the dedicatory letter to *The Art or Crafte of Rhetoryke* (STC 5947), based on Philipp Melanchthon's *Institutiones rhetoricae*, Leonard Cox notes, "I haue partely translated out a werke of Rhetorique wryten in the Latin tongue: and partely compyled of myn owne: and so made a lytle treatyse in maner of an Introductyon into this aforesayd Science: and that in our Englysshe tongue" (A3r). In this case, *translating* and *compiling* are presented as separate textual activities. The verb *make* refers to the whole text-production process, the result of which is Cox's treatise.

The verb *compile* may also denote text-organizational work. In the introduction to the *Life of St. Catherine of Siena*, the reader is told:

> This boke shall be deuyded in thre partyes and eche parte of the boke shal be departed in to diuerse chapyters / whiche

> chapyters been compyled to gyder in the begynnyng in manere of a kalendre that ye mowe redely fynde: What matere in the boke ye desyre to here or rede. (STC 24766.3, A1r)

This statement is immediately followed by the list of contents.

Another usage encompassing the processes of extracting and combining materials is found in the *Dictionary of Sir Thomas Eliot* (STC 7659). After the end of the dictionary proper, and preceding lists of different systems of weights and measures, there is a brief note titled "To the honest and gentylle readers." It begins:

> To the more playne declaration of these tables folowynge, briefely compiled out of the bokes of Georgius Agricola, and Robertus Senalis, whiche wrate last and most exactly of poises & measures, It shal be expedient to the reder to haue in remembrance these thynges folowynge. (2L6r)

The material has been drawn from at least two different sources, evaluated, brought together, and finally equipped with a prefatory guide to the reader. These text-organizational uses of *compile* evoke Parkes's definition of the later medieval compiler's role as someone who critically evaluated, assembled, and organized material.

The text-organizational and material aspects of compiling are both prominent in the following example. In his letter to the reader found in the so-called *Hall's Chronicle* (STC 12721), the printer Richard Grafton describes the formation of the work. He notes that the author:

> was a man in the later tyme of his lyfe not so paynfull and studious as before he had ben: wherefore he perfited and writt this historie no farther then to the foure and twentie yere of kyng Henry the eight: the rest he left noted in diuers and many pamphletes and papers, whych so di[li]gently & truly as I coulde, I gathered thesame together, & haue in suchewise compiled them, as may after thesaied yeres, apere in this woorke: but vtterly without any addicion of myne. (❧3v)

This example presents compiling as a very concrete and physical process, done on the basis of "diverse and many pamphlets and papers."[32] Two different verbs are used: *gather* refers to the physical bringing together of source materials, while *compile* is used of the organization process. Compiling is here nonauthorial, done by the printer, but it results in an authorial text, without any addition by the printer—or so he claims. Such assertions can be read as a continuation of what Minnis terms the compiler's "typical disavowal of responsibility" in the context of medieval literature.[33] By claiming that the text is authorial, the compiler can avoid criticism based on its contents.

However, Grafton did develop the paratextual framing of the work. He notes in the same edition that "so sone as my leasure wil serve, for thine ease & ready fyndyng of any thyng herein conteyned I purpose to gather an exact table of the whole woorke" (❧3v). He fulfills this promise in the 1550 edition (STC 12723, Grafton [and Steven Mierdman]). The preface to this edition is different. Grafton notes that while the author's text could have been "augmented or amended" in some places:

> [y]et for asmuche as a dead man is the auchtor therof, I thought yt my duety to suffer hys worke to be hys awne, and therefore haue altered nothyng therein. But wher I promysed for the ready fynding of suche thinges as are herin conteygned to gather an exact table, I haue now performed my promes herin and haue (after my best maner, and so diligently as I can) deuysed for the history of euery seueral kyng, a seuerall table. ($^{\pi}$A3v)

As in the earlier edition, Grafton presents himself as unwilling to change authorial readings but adds a paratextual layer that helps the reader navigate the text: alphabetical indices after all major sections of the work. Grafton then continues by explaining how the tables are organized. The margins of the main text are equipped with roman numerals for every ten lines (x, xx, xxx, xl). References in each table are given by leaf, side of leaf, and line number (e.g., ii.ii.xii for second leaf, verso, line 12). Given that the book contains over one thousand pages, this device must have been both laborious to create and very useful to the reader. Grafton here adopts the role of a compiler (or editor) who avoids meddling with the authorial text but assumes text-organizational duties through preparing a new navigational tool to aid the reader.

Following Grafton's letter to the reader in both editions, there are two lists of sources, containing both authorities and works. The first list is titled: "The names of the auchtors aswell [*sic*] Latin as other out of the whiche this worke was first gathered, and after compiled and conioyned" (STC 12721, ❧4r). Here, as in Grafton's preface cited above, *gathering* is clearly presented as a textual—and perhaps physical—activity that precedes the process of *compiling*. The list of Latin, French, and English sources is followed by a note on the bottom of the page: "And out of other diuers Pamphlettes, the names of whom are to moste menne vnknowen" (STC 12721, ❧4r; STC 12723 $^{\pi}$A4r, reads "diuers other Pamphlettes"). These lists of sources and the mention of "diuers Pamphlettes" by lesser-known authors highlight the presence of multiple and often anonymous voices present in compilations.

Comparing Print and Manuscript Practices

Grafton's reference to "diverse pamphlets" provides a convenient starting point for examining parallels between print and manuscript practices. The adjective *diverse* is a marker of multiplicity and hence potentially of contents compiled from various sources. An initial search using the dataset of the present study finds sixty-two instances of *diverse* on English title pages from 1500 to 1550. Physically and textually diverse compilations are commonly encountered in the surviving corpus of late-medieval and early-modern manuscripts, and the adjective *diverse* also features in them. For example, the table of contents of Richard Hill's sixteenth-century commonplace book is titled: "The table of the contentes with in this bok whiche is a boke of dyueris tales & balettes & dyueris Reconynges & c."[34] The adjective also occurs in manuscript compilations in references to source texts and authors. In the partial Middle English translation of Latin gynecological texts in Glasgow University Library MS Hunter 403, for instance, it is noted that the "book was drawn out of divers books of medicines concerning the diseases of women" (347).[35] As the adjective *diverse* features in both manuscript and print to mark the multiplicity of contents or sources, it could be used as a keyword for locating more examples of compiling practices.

Another practice encountered in both print and manuscript compilations is the grouping of related texts for easier consultation. Printed books could combine related texts, resulting in a constellation of material that could be used together. For example, almanacs such as the *Kalender of Shepherds* brought together calendrical information, prognostications, and other useful advice.[36] Manuscript compilations, even when they seem to lack an overall theme or scheme, also often contain groups of texts related to the same topic. Units where a given theme or subject seems to have guided the production process may take the form of sections, gatherings, or booklets. For example, in bringing together a series of related texts, tables, and figures, the second quires of New Haven, Beinecke MS 558, and Medical Historical Library MS 26 might be characterized as astrological "calculus books."[37] Individual, thematic gatherings or booklets may also have been produced speculatively and later bound into larger volumes.[38]

Some prefatory texts explicitly comment on such text-organizational procedures. In his letter to the reader, Humphrey Lloyd, the translator of the *Treasury of Health* (STC 14651.5), explains how and why he has revised the source text:

> unto whiche worke conteyninge alonly the symple and bare practyse, I dyd adde before everye chapiter as brefely as I coulde, the causes and sygnes of the sicknesses and dyseases, trustyng therby both to gratifye and somwhat ease the paynes of the reader so that he nede not elles where to seke the causes and sygnes of suche diseases whose remedyes wer conteyned in this boke. (A2v–A3r)

The translator notes that as the source text contained only the "simple and bare practice," he *added* the causes and signs of each disease in the corresponding chapters to help the reader use and navigate the book. Such comments echo the text producers' claims to help the reader that are discussed in the previous section and Parkes's definition of a compiler as a critical assembler and organizer of material. Lloyd's reasoning also resembles practices described in medieval textual compilations, such as the prologue to Guy de Chauliac's *Cyrurgie*. The author notes (in English translation) that the:

> resoun of this exposicioun or gadryng togedre was noght defaute of bookes, but rather onhede and profit. Every man may not have alle bookes, and if he hadde, it were irkesome or noye to rede hem and goodly to holde all thing in mynde. And in construccionns always bettre thinges cometh.[39]

The value of collecting related information within one book is stressed by both Guy de Chauliac and Humphrey Lloyd.

Lloyd also lists other alterations and additions he has made to the source text. However, he still claims to have set everything forth "as truly & as nye the authores mynd" as he could (A3r). Much like the printer-compiler Grafton's claims to have presented the work without any addition of his own, the translator-compiler Lloyd's wording suggests that the process of augmenting the source text by including related material was not exactly authorial in the sense of original composition. In both manuscript and print, the grouping together of related texts can be seen to facilitate the reading and use of the resulting book. In relation to print, it could be argued that such commentary reflects early *editorial* concerns: preserving the authorial text while rendering it more reader-friendly, especially through text organization and the addition of paratextual devices such as tables and indices. However, the scribe-compilers of physical compilations—anthologies, "miscellanies," or other multitext manuscripts—often refrain from commenting on such practices even if the material context commonly suggests that similar forces are at play.

My final example concerns the utilization of extra space in manuscript and print. There is some evidence for the spatial strategies of printers, such as the use of half-sheets where the text did not require another full gathering. These practices are rarely reported to the readers. However, I have found one very explicit comment reflecting a printer's spatial concerns. The English translation of Juan Luis Vives's *An Introduction to Vvysedome* (STC 24848) was printed by Thomas Berthelet in 1544. The main text of the edition ends on the second recto page of the last gathering of the octavo edition (I2r). On the next recto page, the book producers prominently state: "For the fyllyng of void pages here folowing, we haue inserted certain floures of moste notable sentences of wise men, gathered together by Erasmus of Roterodam, and translated in to Englyshe." The text producers are here collectively referred to with the first-person plural pronoun *we*. However, as the motivation behind this insertion seems to arise from the physical form of the book, it probably reflects the agency of the printer. The main text, *An Introduction to Vvysedome*, is translated by Richard Morison, but according to the *English Short Title Catalogue*, the additions come from translations by Richard Taverner and the printer Berthelet himself. As the sayings are attributed to "wise men," they suit the theme of the main text. While providing the reader with more related information, these "flowers" also conveniently fill the last gathering of the edition.

The book producers' choice explicitly to justify their decision on spatial rather than thematic grounds is, perhaps, slightly curious. Neither are the additional contents advertised on the title page of the edition.[40] However, even if Berthelet's explicit comment is a rare instance, similar practices can be found in his other editions. In Berthelet's Latin edition of the psalm compilation attributed to John Fisher (STC 2994), the last psalm ends on L7r (L being the last signature of the edition). A prayer, "Precatio pro rege," is placed on L7v–L8r before Berthelet's colophon on the last page, L8v. In the English translation Berthelet published in the same year (STC 3002), the last psalm ends on L5v. Two prayers—"A prayer for the kyng" and "A prayer for men to saie entryng into battaile"—are inserted on L6r–L7v before Berthelet's colophon on L8r, the last recto page of the edition. Incidentally, both editions date from 1544, the same year as the Vives edition. The motivation for the inclusion of one or two prayers in these editions may well be the same stated in the Vives edition: to fill the last gathering.

The practice of utilizing blank space is also familiar from manuscript culture. In manuscript compilations, pages and leaves originally left blank were often made use of by scribes and readers who inserted texts and notes in these spaces. Such additions may be thematically related to the surrounding material, similarly to the "flowers" inserted by Berthelet. For example, recipes and charms were commonly added on the blank leaves of practically oriented manuscripts.[41] Unrelated texts or annotations, such as family birthdays and marriages, could also be inserted in these spaces (as, for instance, in

Beinecke MS 558, fol. 63v, and MS Ashmole 829, fol. 115r–v). The utilization of blank space is perhaps rarely commented on by text producers in general, but traces of similar practices exist in both manuscript and print. However, unlike a reader or owner, a printer could not have included private notes in blank space. When filling empty space with additional material, Berthelet had to cater to his prospective customers in terms of the chosen theme and contents. Personal annotations in manuscript compilations are thus better compared to handwritten insertions in copies of printed editions.

Conclusion

In this paper, I examine mentions of compiling processes in early printed paratexts in order to shed light on compilers as textual agents and compiling as a textual activity. I suggest that early-sixteenth-century compiling practices might be investigated through keyword-based searches followed by close reading of these words in context. Furthermore, I argue that manuscript and print compiling practices can be fruitfully compared and contrasted to shed more light on how compilations, as textual, linguistic, and physical objects, were created and perceived.

On early English title pages, the most common context for compiling verbs can be considered promotional. The verb *compile* typically occurs in phrases identifying the compiler and advertising their credentials. *Gather, collect* and *take+out* more often highlight the source work(s) than the compiler, and *add* foregrounds supplementary contents provided by the book producers. The close reading of examples of the verb *compile* in context suggests that while the verb is found in potentially synonymous binomials such as *compiled and made,* some early-sixteenth-century text producers may have thought more carefully about the relationship between *compile* and other text-production verbs. A more comprehensive comparative survey of text-production verbs might help tease out more nuances in the use of these verbs.

Some uses of the word *compile* indicate that text producers may have viewed compiling as something akin to modern editorial work. Compilers may state their unwillingness to meddle with the authorial language and yet perform editorial interventions such as adding paratextual devices of their own design or reorganizing the contents. This is the case, for example, in the printer–compiler Grafton's editions of *Hall's Chronicle* and the translator–compiler Lloyd's letter to the reader in the *Treasury of Health.* Looking at compilers as editors might provide a useful perspective to the study of compiling practices in the sixteenth century.

Comparing manuscript and print practices can also shed more light on late-medieval and early-modern compiling as a textual activity. Parallels include, for example, text-organizational procedures such as the grouping together of related texts. The utilization of space left blank in the initial production stage also seems to be a practice evident in both manuscript and print, but such spaces are used in different ways. Thematic insertions made by a scribe or printer during or soon after the initial production stage may be relatively invisible compared to the more personal annotations by readers and owners in manuscripts or individual printed copies.

Methodologically, the present study provides one possible model for collecting evidence of sixteenth-century text-production processes. Similar work could be conducted on a larger selection of verbs, on other word classes, and by extending the dataset diachronically or in terms of media. Comparisons across paratextual elements and different languages would be helpful in determining how conventions and innovations travel between different types of paratexts and different languages. Finally, it would be fruitful to compare text producers' statements with the actual contents of their products in order to see to what extent the claims they make in the paratextual spaces are accurate.

University of Turku

Acknowledgments

I am grateful to the anonymous reader for his or her helpful suggestions and to Professor Julia Boffey, Professor Wendy Scase, and the members of the Philological Colloquium at the Department of English in Turku for their insightful comments on an earlier draft.

NOTES

1. See, e.g., the chapters in Margaret Connolly and Raluca Radulescu, eds., *Insular Books: Vernacular Manuscript Miscellanies in Late Medieval Britain* (Oxford: Oxford University Press/British Academy, 2015); Karen Pratt, Bart Besamusca, Matthias Meyer, and Ad Putter, eds., *The Dynamics of the Medieval Manuscript: Text Collections from a European Perspective* (Göttingen, Germany: V&R Unipress, 2017); Margaret Connolly, "Compiling the Book," in *The Production of Books in England 1350–1500*, ed. Alexandra Gillespie and Daniel Wakelin (Cambridge, UK: Cambridge University Press, 2011), 129–149; Malcolm B. Parkes, "The Influence of the Concepts of *ordinatio* and *compilatio* on the Development of the Book," in *Scribes, Scripts and Readers: Studies in the Communication, Presentation and Dissemination of Medieval Texts*, ed. Mary A. Rouse and Richard H. Rouse (London: Hambledon Press, 1991), 35–69; Malcolm B. Parkes, "The Compilation of the Dominican Lectionary," in *Literarische Formen des Mittelalters: Florilegien, Kompi-*

lationen, Kollektionen, ed. K. Elm (Wiesbaden, Germany: Otto Harrassowitz, 2000), 91–106; Jeffrey Todd Knight, *Bound to Read: Compilations, Collections, and the Making of Renaissance Literature* (Philadelphia: University of Pennsylvania Press, 2013).

2. Bonaventure, "Procemium Sancti Bonaventuræ in Librum Primum Sententiarum," in *Doctoris Seraphici S. Bonaventurae Opera Omnia*, vol. I. (Ad Claras Aquas (Quaracchi): Typ. Coll. S. Bonaventurae, 1882), 14–15. See also A. J. Minnis, *Medieval Theory of Authorship*, 2nd ed. (Aldershot, UK: Wildwood House, 1988), 94–103.
3. Minnis, *Medieval Theory*, 100–103.
4. Parkes, "Dominican Lectionary," 91.
5. Minnis, *Medieval Theory*, 190–210.
6. Ann M. Blair, *Too Much to Know: Managing Scholarly Information before the Modern Age* (New Haven, CT, and London: Yale University Press, 2010), 176.
7. Ann Moss, *Printed Commonplace-Books and the Structuring of Renaissance Thought* (Oxford: Clarendon, 1996).
8. Earle Havens, *Commonplace Books: A History of Manuscripts and Printed Books from Antiquity to the Twentieth Century* (New Haven, CT: Beinecke Rare Book and Manuscript Library, 2001), 10.
9. Parkes, "Dominican Lectionary," 91; see also Havens, *Commonplace Books*, 65–66; Julia Boffey and A. S. G. Edwards, "Towards a Taxonomy of Middle English Manuscript Assemblages," in *Insular Books: Vernacular Manuscript Miscellanies in Late Medieval Britain*, ed. Margaret Connolly and Raluca Radulescu (Oxford: Oxford University Press/British Academy, 2015), 263–279.
10. Knight, *Bound to Read*, 8.
11. See, e.g., A. S. G. Edwards, "Bodleian Library MS Arch. Selden B.24: A "Transitional" Collection," in *The Whole Book: Cultural Perspectives on the Medieval Miscellany*, ed. Stephen G. Nichols and Siegfried Wenzel (Ann Arbor: University of Michigan Press, 1996), 63.
12. Thomas Kohnen, "Commonplace-Book Communication: Role Shifts and Text Functions in Robert Reynes's Notes Contained in MS Tanner 407," in *Communicating Early English Manuscripts*, ed. Päivi Pahta and Andreas H. Jucker (Cambridge, UK: Cambridge University Press, 2011).
13. Alexandra Walsham and Julia Crick, "Introduction: Script, Print, and History," in *The Uses of Script and Print, 1300–1700*, ed. Julia Crick and Alexandra Walsham (Cambridge, UK: Cambridge University Press, 2003), 12.
14. See, e.g., Connolly, "Compiling the Book," 138; Julia Boffey, "From Manuscript to Print: Continuity and Change," in *A Companion to the*

Early Printed Book in Britain 1476–1558, ed. Vincent Gillespie and Susan Powell (Cambridge, UK: D. S. Brewer, 2014), 22.

15. Margaret M. Smith, *The Title-Page: Its Early Development 1460–1510* (London and New Castle, DE: British Library and Oak Knoll Press, 2000), 22–23.
16. Ibid., 22–27; on speculative manuscript production, see, e.g., Linne R. Mooney and Lister M. Matheson, "The Beryn Scribe and His Texts: Evidence for Multiple-Copy Production of Manuscripts in Fifteenth-Century England," *The Library* 7th ser., 4 (2003): 327–370; Linda Ehrsam Voigts, "The 'Sloane Group': Related Scientific and Medical Manuscripts from the Fifteenth Century in the Sloane Collection," *British Library Journal* 16 (1990): 26–57.
17. The *EEBO* website states that for the Early English Books I dataset (1475–1640, based on STC I), bibliographic catalogue entries are available for Units 1–86 of the 87 units into which the material has been divided, while image sets are available for Units 1–80. For Early English Books II (1641–1700, based on Wing and STC II), catalogue information and image sets are available for 132 of the 135 units (as of June 2011). The coverage of *EEBO* is thus high but not exhaustive. See further, Early English Books Online, "About *EEBO*," https://eebo.chadwyck.com/marketing/about.htm, accessed January 29, 2018.
18. The dataset was originally compiled by Aki Aarnio, Aino Haataja, and Jenna Puolamäki in 2016–2017 for an analysis of promotional conventions on early English title pages (Mari-Liisa Varila and Matti Peikola, under review). I am grateful to our interns for all their help.
19. AntConc Homepage, http://www.laurenceanthony.net/software/antconc.
20. This stage of the analysis was conducted using the *EEBO* interface and EEBO-TCP Phase I data, containing approximately 25,000 texts. Phase II is expected to add full texts for a further 45,000 books. Phase I texts are thus not necessarily representative of the whole corpus.
21. Abbreviations in examples have been silently expanded.
22. *OED Online*, 2nd ed., s.v. *collect*, v.
23. Smith, *Title-Page*, 22–23.
24. Ibid., 91–108.
25. *OED Online*, 2nd ed., s.v. *compile*, v. 2a.
26. Walter W. Skeat, ed. *The Complete Works of Geoffrey Chaucer*, vol. 3 (Oxford: Clarendon Press, 1894), 176; see Minnis, *Medieval Theory*, 190–210.
27. *OED Online*, 2nd ed., s.v. *compile*, v. 1.
28. *OED Online*, 3rd ed., s.v. *make*, v. 4a.

29. For a summary of research into binomials in the history of English, see, e.g., Sandra Mollin, *The (Ir)reversibility of English Binomials: Corpus, Constraints, Developments* (Amsterdam: John Benjamins, 2014), 109–114.
30. Ronald Waldron, "Doublets in the Translation Technique of John Trevisa," in *Lexis and Texts in Early English: Studies Presented to Jane Roberts*, ed. Christian J. Kay and Louise M. Sylvester (Amsterdam: Rodopi, 2001), 272–277; James Bradstreet Greenough and George Lyman Kittredge, *Words and Their Ways in English Speech* (New York: Macmillan, 1902), 115.
31. *Liber de arte distillandi* (Strasbourg: Johann Grüninger, 1500), A2r.
32. For material practices of compiling, see, e.g., Blair, *Too Much to Know*, 210–229.
33. Minnis, *Medieval Theory*, 192–197.
34. Oxford, Balliol College, MS 354, p. 6.
35. Glasgow University Library MS Hunter 403, p. 347; Linda Ehrsam Voigts and Patricia Deery Kurtz, *Scientific and Medical Writings in Old and Middle English: An Electronic Reference* (Ann Arbor: University of Michigan Press, 2000), CD-ROM, eVK2 7366.00.
36. Martha W. Driver, "When Is a Miscellany Not Miscellaneous? Making Sense of the *Kalender of Shepherds*," *Yearbook of English Studies* 33 (2003): 199–214.
37. Mari-Liisa Varila, "In Search of Textual Boundaries: A Case Study on the Transmission of Scientific Writing in 16th-Century England" (PhD diss., University of Turku, 2016), 231–244.
38. Julia Boffey and John J. Thompson, "Anthologies and Miscellanies: Production and Choice of Texts," in *Book Production and Publishing in Britain 1375–1475*, ed. Jeremy Griffiths and Derek Pearsall (Cambridge, UK: Cambridge University Press, [1989] 2007), 290; Connolly, "Compiling the Book," 139–140.
39. Paris, Bibliothèque Nationale MS anglais 25, ff. 2r–2v, as edited in Jocelyn Wogan-Browne, Nicholas Watson, Andrew Taylor, and Ruth Evans, eds., *The Idea of the Vernacular. An Anthology of Middle English Literary Theory, 1280–1520* (University Park: Pennsylvania State University Press, 1999), 61–64.
40. Berthelet's later edition of the *Introduction to Wisedome* (STC 24848.5) combines Vives's work with two longer works, the *Banket of Sapience* and *Preceptes of Agapetus*, and lists all three on the title-page.
41. See, e.g., Connolly, "Compiling the Book," 140.

WORKS CITED

Primary Sources

Manuscripts

Glasgow, University of Glasgow MS Hunter 403
New Haven, Beinecke Rare Book and Manuscript Library MS 558
New Haven, Medical Historical Library MS 26
Oxford, Balliol College MS 354
Oxford, Bodleian Library MS Ashmole 829

Printed Editions

Copies of printed editions were consulted via *EEBO:*

Brunschwig, Hieronymus. *The Noble Experyence of the Vertuous Handy Warke of Surgeri.* [London: Peter Treveris, 1525]. STC 13434.

———. *The Vertuose Boke of Distyllacyon of the Waters.* [London: Laurence Andrew, 1527]. STC 13435.

Cox, Leonard. *The Art or Crafte of Rhetoryke.* [London: Robert Redman, 1532]. STC 5947.

Du Wés, Giles. *An Introductorie for to Lerne to Rede, to Pronounce, and to Speake Frenche Trewly.* [London: Thomas Godfray, 1533?]. STC 7377.

Elyot, Thomas. *The Dictionary of Syr Thomas Eliot Knyght.* London: Thomas Berthelet, [1538]. STC 7659.

Erasmus, Desiderius. *Pylgremage of Pure Deuotyon.* [London, 1540?]. STC 10454.

———. *Preparation to Deathe.* [London: Thomas Berthelet, 1538]. STC 10505.

Feylde, Thomas. *Contraverse bytwene a Louer and a Jaye.* London: Wynkyn de Worde, [1527?]. STC 10838.7.

[Fisher, John]. *Psalmi seu precationes ex variis scripturae locis collectae.* [London: Thomas Berthelet], 1544. STC 2994.

———. *Psalmes or Prayers Taken out of Holye Scripture.* [London: Thomas Berthelet, 1544]. STC 3002.

Goeurot, Jean. *The Regiment of Life.* [London: Edward Whitchurch, 1550]. STC 11970.

Hall, Edward. *The Vnion of the Two Noble and Illustrate Famelies of Lancastre [and] Yorke.* [London]: Richard Grafton, 1548. STC 12721.

———. *The Vnion of the Two Noble and Illustre Famelies of Lancastre [and] Yorke.* London: Richard Grafton [and Steven Mierdman], 1550. STC 12723.

John XXI, Pope. *The Treasury of Healthe.* [London: William Copland, 1550]. STC 14651.5.

Mancinus, Dominicus. *The Myrrour of Good Maners.* [London: Richard Pynson, 1518]. STC 17242.

Margaret of Navarre. *A Godly Medytacyon of the Christen Sowle.* [Wesel: Dirik van der Straten, 1548]. STC 17320.

The Psalter or Boke of the Psalmes. [London: Roger Carr for Anthony Smyth, 1548]. STC 2375.

Raymond of Capua. *The Lyf of Saint Katherin of Senis.* [Westminster: Wynkyn de Worde, 1500?]. STC 24766.3.

Rhegius, Urbanus. *A Declaration of the Twelue Articles of the Christen Faythe.* [London: Steven Mierdman for Walter Lynne, 1548]. STC 20843.

Terence. *Floures for Latine Spekynge Selected and Gathered out of Terence.* [London: Thomas Berthelet, 1534]. STC 23899.

[Viret, Pierre]. *A Notable Collection of Diuers and Sondry Places of the Sacred Scriptures.* London: Anthony Scoloker, [1548]. STC 24781.

Vives, Juan Luis. *An Introduction to Vvysedome.* [London: Thomas Berthelet, 1544]. STC 24848.

———. *Introduction to Wisedome.* With *Banket of Sapience* and *Preceptes of Agapetus.* [London]: Thomas Berthelet, [1546]. STC 24848.5.

Secondary Sources

Blair, Ann M. *Too Much to Know: Managing Scholarly Information before the Modern Age.* New Haven, CT, and London: Yale University Press, 2010.

Boffey, Julia. "From Manuscript to Print: Continuity and Change." In *A Companion to the Early Printed Book in Britain 1476–1558*, ed. Vincent Gillespie and Susan Powell, 13–26. Cambridge, UK: D. S. Brewer, 2014.

———, and A. S. G. Edwards. "Towards a Taxonomy of Middle English Manuscript Assemblages." In *Insular Books: Vernacular Manuscript Miscellanies in Late Medieval Britain*, ed. Margaret Connolly and Raluca Radulescu, 263–279. Oxford: Oxford University Press/British Academy, 2015.

———, and John J. Thompson. "Anthologies and Miscellanies: Production and Choice of Texts." In *Book Production and Publishing in Britain 1375–1475*, ed. Jeremy Griffiths and Derek Pearsall, 279–315. Cambridge, UK: Cambridge University Press, [1989] 2007.

Bonaventure. "Prœmium Sancti Bonaventuræ in Librum Primum Sententiarum." In *Doctoris Seraphici S. Bonaventurae Opera Omnia*, vol. 1, 1–15. Ad Claras Aquas (Quaracchi): Typ. Coll. S. Bonaventurae, 1882.

Connolly, Margaret. "Compiling the Book." In *The Production of Books in England 1350–1500*, ed. Alexandra Gillespie and Daniel Wakelin, 129–149. Cambridge, UK: Cambridge University Press, 2011.

———, and Raluca Radulescu, eds. *Insular Books: Vernacular Manuscript Miscellanies in Late Medieval Britain*. Oxford: Oxford University Press/ British Academy, 2015.

Driver, Martha W. "When Is a Miscellany Not Miscellaneous? Making Sense of the Kalender of Shepherds." *Yearbook of English Studies* 33 (2003): 199–214.

Edwards, A. S. G. "Bodleian Library MS Arch. Selden B.24: A "Transitional" Collection." In *The Whole Book: Cultural Perspectives on the Medieval Miscellany*, ed. Stephen G. Nichols and Siegfried Wenzel, 53–67. Ann Arbor: University of Michigan Press, 1996.

Greenough, James Bradstreet, and George Lyman Kittredge. *Words and Their Ways in English Speech*. New York: Macmillan, 1902.

Havens, Earle. *Commonplace Books: A History of Manuscripts and Printed Books from Antiquity to the Twentieth Century*. New Haven, CT: Beinecke Rare Book and Manuscript Library, 2001.

Knight, Jeffrey Todd. *Bound to Read: Compilations, Collections, and the Making of Renaissance Literature*. Philadelphia: University of Pennsylvania Press, 2013.

Kohnen, Thomas. "Commonplace-Book Communication: Role Shifts and Text Functions in Robert Reynes's Notes Contained in MS Tanner 407." In *Communicating Early English Manuscripts*, ed. Päivi Pahta and Andreas H. Jucker, 13–24. Cambridge, UK: Cambridge University Press, 2011.

Minnis, A. J. *Medieval Theory of Authorship*. 2nd ed. Aldershot, UK: Wildwood House, 1988.

Mollin, Sandra. *The (Ir)reversibility of English Binomials: Corpus, Constraints, Developments*. Amsterdam: John Benjamins, 2014.

Mooney, Linne R., and Lister M. Matheson. "The Beryn Scribe and His Texts: Evidence for Multiple-Copy Production of Manuscripts in Fifteenth-Century England." *The Library* 7th ser., 4 (2003): 327–370.

Moss, Ann. *Printed Commonplace-Books and the Structuring of Renaissance Thought*. Oxford: Clarendon, 1996.

Parkes, Malcolm B. "The Influence of the Concepts of *ordinatio* and *compilatio* on the Development of the Book." In *Scribes, Scripts and Readers: Studies in the Communication, Presentation and Dissemination of Medieval Texts*, ed. Mary A. Rouse and Richard H. Rouse, 35–69. London: Hambledon Press, 1991.

———. "The Compilation of the Dominican Lectionary." In *Literarische Formen des Mittelalters: Florilegien, Kompilationen, Kollektionen*, ed. K. Elm, 91–106. Wiesbaden, Germany: Otto Harrassowitz, 2000.

Pratt, Karen, Bart Besamusca, Matthias Meyer, and Ad Putter, eds. *The Dynamics of the Medieval Manuscript: Text Collections from a European Perspective*. Göttingen, Germany: V&R Unipress, 2017.

Skeat, Walter W. ed. *The Complete Works of Geoffrey Chaucer*. Vol. III. Oxford: Clarendon Press, 1894.

Smith, Margaret M. *The Title-Page: Its Early Development 1460–1510*. London and New Castle, DE: British Library and Oak Knoll Press, 2000.

Varila, Mari-Liisa. "In Search of Textual Boundaries: A Case Study on the Transmission of Scientific Writing in 16th-Century England." PhD diss., University of Turku, 2016.

———, and Matti Peikola (under review). "Promotional Conventions on English Title-Pages up to 1550: Modifiers of Time, Scope, and Quality." In *Norms and Conventions* (provisional title), ed. Claudia Claridge and Birte Bös. Amsterdam: John Benjamins.

Voigts, Linda Ehrsam. "The 'Sloane Group': Related Scientific and Medical Manuscripts from the Fifteenth Century in the Sloane Collection." *British Library Journal* 16 (1990): 26–57.

———, and Patricia Deery Kurtz. *Scientific and Medical Writings in Old and Middle English: An Electronic Reference*. Ann Arbor: University of Michigan Press, 2000. CD-ROM.

Waldron, Ronald. "Doublets in the Translation Technique of John Trevisa." In *Lexis and Texts in Early English: Studies Presented to Jane Roberts*, ed. Christian J. Kay and Louise M. Sylvester, 269–292. Amsterdam: Rodopi, 2001.

Walsham, Alexandra, and Julia Crick. "Introduction: Script, Print, and History." In *The Uses of Script and Print, 1300–1700*, ed. Julia Crick and Alexandra Walsham, 1–26. Cambridge, UK: Cambridge University Press, 2003.

Wogan-Browne, Jocelyn, Nicholas Watson, Andrew Taylor, and Ruth Evans, eds. *The Idea of the Vernacular. An Anthology of Middle English Literary Theory, 1280–1520*. University Park: Pennsylvania State University Press, 1999.

"Erthe upon Erthe" Revisited

NANCY P. POPE

Hilda M. R. Murray includes twenty-five texts in her 1911 volume, *The Middle English Poem, Erthe upon Erthe.*[1] They range from the first half of the fourteenth century to the first half of the seventeenth, and Murray traces some of their language to the "Dialogue of the Soul and Body" tradition, the earliest texts of which can be dated to the twelfth and thirteenth centuries.[2] Ten additional texts related to those Murray identifies have been discovered since her work. Four of them have been edited before now, without a thorough discussion of their relation to Murray's list of texts, and I have edited the other six in this article. The variety and number of witnesses found since 1911 suggest that Murray's conclusions should be revisited and the *Erthe* tradition as a whole should be reconsidered. Many of Murray's thoughts about her texts can be better supported now than when she wrote, but her thinking of diverse texts as variants of the same poem is no longer feasible. Instead, I view *Erthe* not as a single Middle English lyric in thirty-five copies but as a tradition within which a few poems have multiple witnesses but most texts are unique and to some extent original compositions.

What distinguishes members of this tradition from other medieval lyrics is their punning use of "earth" to name at least two referents: people and soil. The pun is clearly inspired by "*Memento homo quod cinis es et in cinerem reverteris*" [Remember, man, that you are dust, and unto dust you shall return], but Murray argues compellingly for an English-language origin for the *Erthe* tradition.[3] Her division of the poems into three groups is based on their sharing one or more stanzas, no matter how much the members of a group may differ otherwise. Thus, she identifies two texts as the A group on the basis of one similar stanza, twenty as the B group on account of five shared stanzas, and one as the C version, which she sees as a combination of material from A and B.[4] In an appendix, she adds a twenty-fourth text that she considers wholly unrelated.[5] Her twenty-fifth text, which appears only in her introduction, consists of one of the five shared stanzas in the B group. Various indices have put each *Erthe* poem discovered since 1911 into one of these groups.[6] Consequently, renaming all thirty-five texts would make identifying and comparing them difficult. I continue to use Murray's group letters and have added D and E to them: D for the poem she edited in her appendix and E for one of the *Erthe* texts she did not know, which combines material from B and D. References to texts use the group letter and item number in the following catalogue of all known copies.

CATALOGUE OF MANUSCRIPTS AND INSCRIPTIONS

Texts that Murray prints appear first in each of the group lists below; subsequently edited texts appear next; and texts I have edited appear last. Selected editors are named in parentheses,[7] *DIMEV* numbers are given in brackets,[8] and bibliographical information about editions other than Murray's and mine can be found in the notes.

MSS of the A Group

1. London, British Library, MS Harley 2253, fol. 59v (Murray) [6292-2].

2. London, British Library, MS Harley 913, fols. 62–63v (Murray, Harrington)[9] [6292-1].

3. Edinburgh, National Library of Scotland, Advocates MS 18.7.21, fol. 87v (Wilson)[10] [1167-1].

MSS of the B Group

1. W. Yates (Bateman,[11] Murray) [1170-13] (lost).

2. Lincoln, Cathedral Library, MS 91, fol. 279–279v (Murray) [1170-12].

3. Oxford, Bodleian Library, MS Selden Supra 53, fol. 159v (Murray) [1170-3].

4. London, British Library, MS Egerton 1995, fol. 55–55v (Murray) [6369-6].

5. London, British Library, MS Harley 1671, fol. 1* (Murray) [6369-7].

6. Philadelphia, University of Pennsylvania, MS Codex 721, fol. 91v (Fiedler,[12] Murray) [1170-14].[13]

7. Stratford-on-Avon, Guild Chapel, Chapel Lane, Mural Inscription (Wheler,[14] Murray) [1170, Inscriptions-1].

8. Oxford, Bodleian Library, MS Rawlinson C.307, fol. 2 (Murray) [1170-2].

9. London, British Library, MS Harley 4486, fol. 146 (Murray) [6369-8].

10. London, Lambeth Palace Library, MS 853, pp. 35–39 (Murray) [6369-11].

11. Oxford, Bodleian Library, MS Laud misc. 23, fols. 111v–112v (Murray) [6369-1].

12. London, British Library, MS Cotton Titus A.XXVI, fol. 153–153v (Murray) [1170-9].

13. Oxford, Bodleian Library, MS Rawlinson poet. 32, fols. 32v–35 (Murray) [6369-2].

14. Aberystwyth, National Library of Wales, MS Brogyntyn ii.1, *olim* Porkington 10, fols. 79v–81v (Murray) [1170-11].

15. Oxford, Balliol College, MS 354, pp. 434–435 (Murray) [1170-4].

16. London, British Library, MS Harley 984, fol. 72, fragment (Murray) [1170-10].

17. Cambridge, Magdalene College, MS Pepys 2553, p. 338 (Murray) [1170-7].

18. Cambridge, University Library, MS Ll.5.10, fol. 43v–44 (Murray) [1170-6].

19. Cambridge, Trinity College, MS R.3.21, fol. 33v (Murray) [1170-8].

20. Cambridge, Trinity College, MS B.15.39, fol. 170 (Murray) [6369-4].

21. London, Edmonton Church, Mural Inscription (Weever,[15] Murray) [1166-1].

22. Oxford, Corpus Christi College, MS 237, fol. 240v (Förster)[16] [1170-5].

23. London, Wellcome Library, MS 673, fol. 9 (Kane)[17] [6369-12].

24. London, British Library, MS Add. 37788, *olim* Tenison, fols. 83v–85v (Pope) [6369-5].[18]

25. San Marino, Huntington Library, MS HM 744, fols. 11v–12v (Pope) [6369-14].

26. Oxford, Bodleian Library, MS Bodley 220, fol. 106v–107 (Pope) [1170-1].

MSS of the C Group

1. Cambridge, University Library, MS Ii.4.9, fols. 67–68v (Murray) [1171-1].

2. London, British Library, MS Royal 17.A.XVI, fol. 30–30v (Pope) [1171-2].

MSS of the D Group

1. London, National Archives of the UK, Public Record Office E 175/11/16, *olim* PRO Exchequer Roll, K. R. Proc. Bundle 1 (Murray, Harrington)[19] [6293-3]; also London, British Library, MS Add. 25478, fol. 3–3v, a nineteenth-century transcription of it [6293-2].

2. New York, Pierpont Morgan Library, MS M957, fol. 126-126v, fragment (Pope) [6293-4].

3. Oxford, Bodleian Library, MS Holkham misc. 39, fol. 438 (Pope) [6293-1].

MS of the E Text

Cambridge, St. John's College, MS E.24, fols. 44–45 (Förster,[20] Pope) [6369-3].

In addition to the thirty-five texts of *Erthe* on the list above, there are five other MSS identified in the *DIMEV* as members of this tradition. Each one begins with part or all of the same couplet: "When life is most loved and death is most hated, / Then death draws his draft and makes man full naked." This couplet opens eleven of the thirty-five poems listed above, and it occurs elsewhere in two others. However, the following five MSS do not continue with any portion of *Erthe* after the introductory couplet, so they will not be discussed beyond the list below:[21]

1. Edinburgh, National Library of Scotland, Advocates MS 19.1.11, fol. 178v (Brown)[22] [6369-9].

   This folio contains two copies of the couplet with a unique third line lacking the word "earth"; in the same MS, folio 70r contains only the couplet.[23]

2. London, Lambeth Palace Library, MS 223, fol. 297 (Brown)[24] [6369-10].

   This contains only the couplet, plus an attribution: "*quod petrus Raynscroft.*"

3. Manchester, John Rylands Library, MS Lat. 201, fol. 227 (Fawtier & Fawtier)[25] [6369-13, 4490-7].

   This contains the couplet followed by a poem unrelated to the *Erthe* tradition.

4. Cambridge, St. John's College, MS D.5, fol. 121 [6369-15].

   This flyleaf contains an incomplete copy of the couplet followed by two incomplete copies of the first line of the couplet in different hands.

5. London, British Library, MS Add. 60577, fol. 92 [6369-16, 3353-4].

   This contains the couplet followed by another poem unrelated to the *Erthe* tradition. It has not been edited but can be read in the manuscript facsimile.[26]

DISCUSSION

All three of the A texts, the first two of the three D texts, and the E text appear in fourteenth-century manuscripts, whereas the third D text and all the B and C texts are found in fifteenth-century and later manuscripts. I discuss the groups in the order in which their earliest extant witnesses are written, beginning with A, going on to D and E, and ending with B and C.

The A Group

Murray puts two texts together to form the A group because the single stanza of A-1 resembles the first English stanza of A-2 more closely than either stanza resembles any other *Erthe* text:[27]

A-1	A-2
Erþe toc of erþe erþe wyþ woh,	Whan erþ haþ erþ iwonne wiþ wow,
Erþe oþer erþe to þe erþe droh,	Þan erþ mai of erþ nim hir inow.
Erþe leyde erþe in erþen þroh,	Erþ vp erþ falliþ fol frow;
Þo heuede erþe of erþe erþe ynoh.	Erþ toward erþ delful him drow.
	Of erþ þou were makid, *and* mon þou art ilich;
	In on erþ awaked þe pore *and* þe riche.

Clearly, the first four lines of A-2 are in the same meter and have the same rhyme scheme as A-1. The first, second, and fourth lines of each quatrain are also very similar, but the second and fourth lines have switched places and the third lines are not at all similar. Moreover, A-1 is a four-line poem, whereas A-2 consists of seven six-line stanzas in English alternating with Latin versions of them. The differences between the poems as a whole are greater than the resemblances between their first four lines. Nevertheless, these two poems may be considered members of a group because they are roughly contemporaneous; A-1 is dated 1331–1341, and A-2 1330–1342, at least thirty years earlier than any other extant witnesses in the *Erthe* tradition.[28]

A-1 is an outlier in this tradition in its brevity and its riddling quality. We have both intrinsic and extrinsic reasons to believe that the scribe may be the poet as well as the copyist of this poem. The extrinsic reason is the suitability of the text to its context, as has often been noted.[29] The intrinsic reason is its uniqueness among the thirty-five *Erthe* lyrics. In A-2, "earth" is used at most twice per line, except in parts of the third stanza; "earth" occurs three or four times in some lines of that stanza, with at most two meanings it in each line. Common to the other thirty-three is a punning use of the word "earth" twice in each line, at most. A-1 uses "earth" three times in every line, with two or three different meanings per line.[30] This poetical and punning achievement is likely to be original with its scribe, who has been credited with the authorship of other works in his hand.[31]

A-2 is also an outlier among the texts of *Erthe.* It is one of two such texts that use six-line stanzas rather than quatrains or couplets, but the other, B-14, has a two-syllable fifth line rather than A-2's full-length one, so the effect of its stanza is rather different. In addition, A-2 is one of three *Erthe* texts with Latin translations, but its Latin text is unique among them and has been judged a poetic achievement in its own right.[32] Finally, among its second through seventh stanzas, only one has close verbal similarities to any other poem in this tradition; five stanzas (thirty lines of verse) are either original, or occasionally, reminiscent of lines in the "Dialogue of the Soul and Body" tradition.[33] So at the very beginning of the extant written record of this tradition, A-1 and A-2 are two fundamentally different lyrics rather than two versions of the same poem.

The third text assigned to the A group was not known to Murray. It comes from National Library of Scotland Advocates MS 18.7.21, the preaching book of Franciscan friar John of Grimestone, written in 1372 in Norfolk.[34] This text was first noted by Brown in 1920 and first edited by Wilson in 1973.[36] It consists of four quatrains with lines that are half the length of those found in the other two A texts:

Herde maket halle,
And herde maket bour;
Herde reyset castel [Lines 3-4 resemble A-2, 6.5]
And herde reyset tour.

Wan herde is leyd in herde, [Lines 5-6 resemble A-2, 6.6]
Blac is his bour;
Þan sal herde for herde
Hauen many a bitter sour.

Wan herde hat herde [Lines 9-10 resemble A-2, 1.1]
Wonnen with wo,
And herde hat herde
Loken in his clo,

And herde hat of herde [Lines 13-14 resemble A-2, 1.2]
Ioyȝe rith inow,
Þan sal herde bewepen
Þat he [is] eer below.

Thus eight of its sixteen lines resemble A-2 in wording. However, lines 1 to 6 also resemble wording shared by the B, C, and E groups, and lines 9 to 10 resemble wording shared by the D group and E. There are also six lines (7–8, 11–12, and 15–16) that are unique to this poem. E would be as reasonable a text to group it with as A-2 is, if one were considering only similar wording. The manuscripts containing D-1 and E cannot be as precisely dated as John of Grimestone's book can be, but they are likely to have been written late in the century, much closer to A-3 than to A-1 and A-2. Given the metrical differences between this lyric and all the other fourteenth-century *Erthe* poems, it would ideally occupy its own single-member group. Still, it has one thing in common with A-1: it was probably composed by its scribe.

John of Grimestone's manuscript presents ample evidence that he was an original translator and adapter as well as a compiler.[37] He included 246 Middle English poems in his book,[38] of which only twenty-seven appear in other manuscripts.[39] Of these twenty-seven, six appear in John's book earlier than in other manuscripts and may be his own work.[40] Another seventeen, including *Erthe*, exist in manuscripts earlier than John's; ten of the seventeen appear in John's book in expanded or compressed forms or with significant revision of the wording.[41] John's text of *Erthe*, whatever its sources, resembles his other borrowed poems in its mix of unique, accurately quoted, and rewritten lines. It is as likely as most of the poems in his book to be John's own work.

The D Group and the E Text

The D group and the E text resemble each other so closely in some ways that they might be considered a single group, but in other ways their members are different enough to be classified as four separate works in the *Erthe* tradition. D-1 consists of a nine-stanza poem in Middle English plus translations of it in Latin and French.[42] E begins with five stanzas common to twenty-one of the twenty-six B texts and to both C texts (I postpone discussing them until the section on the B and C groups) and continues with nine stanzas not found in either B or C. Eight of these nine resemble eight of the nine stanzas in D-1. The two *Erthe* texts grouped with D-1 by the indices[43] are much shorter. D-2 is on the remaining fragment of a torn page; what remains are the beginnings of eleven lines, representing three stanzas from among those shared by D-1 and E. D-3 consists of one stanza common to D-1 and E, plus a Latin translation of it and a macaronic couplet. In addition to the general differences among these texts, there are unique lines in each of them. On the whole, therefore, it is more reasonable to call them different poems than to call them versions of the same poem.

Of these, Murray knew only the trilingual D-1, which she printed in an appendix. It appears on the back of a roll (E 175/11/16 in the National Archives) from the first half of the fourteenth century.[44] Judging solely by handwriting, this material was added to the roll late in the second half of the fourteenth century or possibly in the early fifteenth.[45] The English poem is in the West Midlands dialect, but some of its spellings are old-fashioned for the late fourteenth century, even in the West Midlands: *eorthe* rather than *erthe*, *-liche* for *-ly* in four different words (the adjective *dedliche* and the adverbs *mychfulliche*, *netfulliche*, and *grimliche*), and present-tense third-person singular verbs prefixed by i- (*isoeth*, *iworthe*, *iseoth*, and *ihere*). That the English poem is older in language than in handwriting suggests it had a lost source, whether written or oral. The Latin and French texts have corrections that, according to Harrington, suggest they also had a source.[46] Despite having later witnesses than the A group does, the D group and E may have been inspired by material as old as the inspiration for A-1 and A-2.

Neither D-2 nor D-3 has been fully edited before now.[47] D-2 occurs in Pierpont Morgan Library MS M. 957, a vellum manuscript dated about 1375, a miscellany whose last three folios have been largely torn out, leaving only a triangular fragment of each.[48] On the recto of the last fragment is this text, in an Anglicana hand:

What haþ erþe vpon erþe b–	[like D-1, 4.1 and E, 9.1]
Whan erþe seþ on erþe his–	[like D-1, 4.2 and E, 9.2]
And erþe in to erþe –	[like D-1, 4.3]
And erþe wexeþ –	[not like D-1 or E]
Whan erþe seþ –	[like D-1, 6.1 and E, 11.1]
And erþe lyþ –	[like E, 11.3]
And erþe –	
Þan erþe –	
Whan –	
And –	
A –	

The first six lines clearly identify this fragment as resembling D-1 and E equally. In addition, the last five lines, despite having only one or two words apiece, confirm that resemblance; three of the eight stanzas shared by D-1 and E have lines beginning When/And/And/Then, unlike any stanza in the A, B, and C groups. Yet this fragment indicates difference as well as similarity; it is clear that the manuscript once contained a somewhat different text from either D-1 or E, with its stanzas in a different order and with at least one unique line.

D-3 appears in Bodleian Library MS Holkham misc. 39, an early sixteenth-century manuscript in Anglicana script from Norfolk.[49] The *Erthe* poem appears amidst other fillers in the second half of the "amen" quire. It consists of four lines of English, three of Latin, and two macaronic lines. The scribe capitalized the first word in each line; I have expanded abbreviations and supplied periods.

Qwa*n* erde hath erde wyth wo i gete	[like D-1, 1.1 and E, 6.1]
And erde ys in erde wyth erde i reke	[not like D-1 or E]
And erde ys vnd*er* erde w^{t} vyrmys i frete	[like D-1, 1.3 and E, 6.3]
Þan chal erde on erde sone ben for ȝete.	[like D-1, 1.4 and E, 6.4]

Terra tenet t*erram* qu*ando* cu*m* ve sibi nacta
Et tellus t*er*ra sistat cu*m* pulu*ere* pacta
V*er*mib*us* est rosa tellus cu*m* sub *quoȝue* t*er*ra.

O vir bowt der*e* du*m* viuis they*ng* on þi*n* ber*e*.
Dico t*ibi* ver*e* sine fine þ*ou* chalt nowt ben here.

In its first quatrain, this short poem reproduces some familiar lines almost exactly and also produces one unique line; the quatrain resembles E and D-1 equally. Its next three lines then support Murray's contention that the Latin texts of *Erthe* are independent translations of the English.[50] She bases her argument on only two examples, in which the English as well as the Latin are different: A-2 and D-1. But lines 5 through 7 of D-3 purportedly translate the same English as that in D-1 and E while using only two of the same Latin words, *terra(m)* and *vermibus*. One possible explanation is that the scribe produced his own Latin translation. Since the bulk of the manuscript containing D-3 is a Latin-English dictionary in the same hand as the poem, its scribe was certainly fluent in both languages.

The macaronic couplet that closes his text is as unique as one of his English lines and all of his Latin ones. A draft of it appears on folio 446v, the last folio of the "amen" quire:

O vir dere bowt a [erasure of one letter] bere thynk on y
Dico tibi vere sine fine ye schalt not be here

I consider this a draft because it is rougher than the version that appears on folio 438r as the last two lines of the *Erthe* text. The couplet that closes D-3 has better meter and rhyme than this one and contains neither any erasures nor any unfinished words. The existence of a rough draft as well as a polished version suggests that at least this couplet is the work of the scribe. Whereas the damage done to the manuscript containing D-2 makes pronouncements about its originality speculative, D-3 is clearly an original text in more than half its lines, and its scribe is probably responsible for them.

E is one of the most important and least discussed texts of this widely varying poem.[51] Because it contains material from two otherwise separable traditions (the B and D groups), Max Förster considered it the oldest copy of the poem, but he presented no other evidence for dating this text earlier than A-1 and A-2.[52] The manuscript containing E, St. John's College (Cambridge) E.24, has been dated to the fourteenth century by its cataloguer.[53] A terminus a quo is established by the manuscript's containing a copy of *De spiritu Guidonis,* which was written between the January 1324 events it recounts and a 1327 letter referring to it.[54] Copies of this Latin text were made beyond the fourteenth century,[55] so its presence here does not give us a terminus ad quem. Likewise, neither the handwriting nor the East Midlands dialect of the poem (the only English-language item in the manuscript) establishes the end of its possible date range, although both look more like the fourteenth century than the fifteenth. Fortunately, Forshaw's work on the manuscripts of *Speculum ecclesie* suggests that this manuscript's copy of that text was written late in the fourteenth century.[56] If Forshaw is correct, then A-3, D-1, D-2, and E would all be roughly contemporaneous. So what evidence we have for dating these four texts makes it more logical to group A-3 with E than with A-1 and A-2.

However, grouping chronologically and verbally related poems in this way does not mean thinking of independent compositions, such as D-1 and E, as versions of the same work. The resemblance between D-1 and E is imperfect in the eight stanzas they share; not only does the wording differ to some extent in more than half the lines, but also the stanzas do not appear in the same order. E looks like a copy from a written exemplar because the words omitted by its scribe and inserted by him in superscript letters are all subjects or verbs in their sentences, not the words one would tend to omit if composing or writing from memory. (See "Editions," after conclusion of discussion, for my edition of E.) As Murray notes, the first line in D-1, "Whanne eorthe hath eorthe wiþ wrong igete," resembles the first line of A-2, "Whan erþ haþ erþ iwonne wiþ wow."[57] The resemblance is even stronger between this line in A-2 and the first line of E's sixth stanza, "Whan erþe hauet erþe with woo by zute," but there are no other significant parallels between A-2 and either D-1 or E. Rather, the D group and nine stanzas of E represent, as Murray says of D-1, a parallel tradition on the same themes as in the A, B, and C groups. Within the D group and E, as in the A group, no witness contains a faithful copy of one entire stanza of any other witness; accurate copying does not occur in any of the fourteenth-century texts of *Erthe*.

The B and C Groups

Murray puts twenty texts together to form the B group because sixteen of them share five stanzas, which I am calling stanzas a–e. Twelve of those sixteen also share two additional stanzas, which I am calling f–g. (The remaining four texts that Murray puts in the B group have some of these seven common stanzas.) Murray considers the B group to have two subgroups: the five-stanza version and the seven-stanza version.[58] However, among her B texts are six (B-9, 10, 11, 12, 13, and 20) that add to a–e or to a–g at least one of the same five other stanzas (h–l). On account of these further shared stanzas, Förster considers those six texts a third subgroup within the B group.[59] I agree with Förster in seeing three subgroups with more than one witness each: the five-stanza version (a–e), the seven-stanza version (a–g), and a twelve-stanza version that adds all of h–l to a–g. The only examples of fairly accurate copying among the thirty-five members of the *Erthe* tradition occur within these three subgroups. However, there are a number of B texts that Murray or Förster put in these subgroups that I consider separately because they contain unique material.

The Five-Stanza and Seven-Stanza Versions

Murray knew two examples, B-1 and B-2, of the five-stanza version without added material. They are essentially the same poem; they differ in one or two words per stanza, but the variants are roughly synonymous. Another seven versions that Murray edited, B-4 through B-7 and B-17 through B-19, are examples of the seven-stanza version without additions. Poems containing a–g agree with each other as closely as or more closely than the two a–e texts do. Because she knew many more examples of the seven-stanza version than of the five-stanza version, Murray had cause to wonder whether the longer text came into existence by expansion or the shorter text began as an excerpt.[60] However, the manuscript of E, the earliest surviving witness to any of the B stanzas, opens with stanzas a–e before proceeding through nine more stanzas that were discussed above with the D group. E therefore supports the argument Murray preferred, that the five-stanza version came first and then the seven-stanza version developed from it. The greater popularity of the seven-stanza version is possibly due to its concluding stanza, g, which ends with the hope of heavenly bliss, whereas stanza e ends with the certainty of physical decay.

E also supports all of Murray's preferred wordings in stanzas a–e. Murray discusses four variant readings that occur in these five stanzas, across those sixteen of her texts that include all five. She expresses a preference for the alliterating phrases in b-4 ("piteous parting") and c-4 ("sharp showers") rather than their nonalliterating alternatives (in b-4, "hard," "full hard," "heavy," or "doleful"; in c-4, "hard" or "grit"). She also prefers a version of d-1 that makes more sense to her than the variants, and she expresses no preference among the a-2 variants.[61] E has all three of her preferred readings, and its wording in a-2 likewise creates an alliterative phrase, "nobility of nought." There are five other variant readings in these five stanzas that Murray does not discuss, presumably because the variations look more like copying errors than like deliberate alterations. In all ten cases, E has the best readings in terms of alliteration, logic, or meter. Although E almost undoubtedly had a source, as discussed above, it preserves stanzas a–e in excellent, perhaps even original, condition.

Murray publishes two texts that may be grouped with the five- and seven-stanza subgroups. One of them, B-3, contains six of the seven stanzas in an unusual order, but with the most frequently occurring final stanza: a, b, c, f, d, g. Another, B-16, has only f and g at the top of a page following a lost leaf; I agree with Murray that it is likely to have been an example of the seven-stanza version.[62] Finally, two of the texts edited by others, B-22 and B-23, are also examples of the seven-stanza poem, bringing its witnesses to a total of nine. Overall, the two five-stanza poems Murray knew and the nine seven-stanza poems we have now are examples of fairly faithful copying. Stanza a loses its second line twice and gets a replacement once; stanza d's first line has two rather different forms, and its lines come in two different sequences. The other stanzas keep their lines in the same order with almost entirely the same wording throughout.

The Twelve-Stanza Version

Murray knew just two twelve-stanza poems, B-10 and B-11, with stanzas a–g plus the same five additional stanzas, which I call h–l, in the same order: a, b, c, d, h, i, j, e, f, k, g, l. Four of these five additional stanzas, h, j, k, and l, occur only in the *Erthe* tradition, to the best of my knowledge. Stanza i occurs also in the earlier *Fasciculus morum*.[63] All five stanzas have longer lines than a–g do, so the scribe or exemplar of B-10 inserts extra syllables in every line of e, f, and g, the stanzas that occur after longer-lined stanzas begin. The additions are superfluous to the poem's meaning, but they mean that Murray was looking at two different versions of the twelve-stanza type. Now that we have a total of four twelve-stanza poems (B-10, 11, 24, and 25), we can see more easily than Murray could that they form a subgroup. Indeed, three of the four are nearly identical, bringing the number of faithfully copied texts in the *Erthe* tradition to fourteen out of thirty-five. As mentioned above, Murray also knew four texts (B-9, 12, 13, and 20) that add one or more of stanzas h–l, but not all five of them, to different numbers of stanzas a–g. Where Förster considers such shared stanzas adequate reason to group these four texts with B-10 and 11, I see these four shorter poems as distinct from the twelve-stanza subgroup, and I discuss them separately.

Each of the four twelve-stanza poems has a small number of readings that disqualify it from being the exemplar of the subgroup. In addition to B-10's attempt to regularize the meter, the fourth line of its sixth stanza (i) contrasts "undevout" with "behated"; all other *Erthe* texts containing this stanza, as well as its earliest appearance in *Fasciculus morum*, contrast "loved" or "beloved" with "hated" or "behated." Also, the first line of B-10's seventh stanza (j) has "wretched" where the other texts have "wanting." Similarly, the third line of B-11's third stanza (c) has "all" instead of "up," which appears everywhere else, and the second line of its seventh stanza (j) has "wrappe" rather than the usual "happe." B-24's unique readings are its cancellation of "on þis" in its tenth stanza (k), where the others retain it, and two omissions, "ever" and "may," from the third and fourth lines of its twelfth stanza (l). B-25 has only one variant, "wretchedly" in the first line of its eleventh stanza (g), where the others have "wickedly." (See my editions of B-24 and B-25 in the "Editions" section below.)

Nevertheless, these four members of the twelve-stanza subgroup are copied with enough fidelity that one could reconstruct a hypothetical lost exemplar for them. Additional evidence that they might have a common exemplar comes from texts appearing alongside them in their manuscripts. Three of the four versions that contain all twelve stanzas (B-11, B-24, and B-25) are preceded by two prose works and a poem: Isidore's "O Man Know Thyself," Augustine's *De contemptu mundi*, and "Why Is This World Beloved." They occur in that order in B-24 and B-25; in B-11, after the two prose works, *Erthe* precedes "Why Is This World Beloved." The fourth twelve-stanza text, B-10, has "Why Is This World Beloved" before *Erthe* but omits both prose works. A lost booklet[64] consisting solely of four texts (in order, Isidore, Augustine, "Why," *Erthe*) is the simplest explanation of the close resemblances among the four manuscripts of the twelve-stanza version.

Other Members of the B Group

Starting with some portion of the *Erthe* tradition, several poems assigned to the B group go in diverse directions. B-8 and B-13 reproduce stanzas a–e but do not add f–g, so Murray puts them both in her five-stanza subgroup. (Förster agrees with Murray about B-8 but puts B-13 in the twelve-stanza subgroup because it includes four of h–l.) Yet B-8 is not a five-stanza poem; indeed, it has eight stanzas, the last three of which are unique. Interestingly, they serve the same functions as f–g do, moving from general statements to an exhortation addressed to the reader and ending with a prayer to God. So this eight-stanza poem has much the same structure and effect as the common seven-stanza version does, but it earns a separate place in the tradition for the uniqueness of its expression. B-13 is more unusual in altering the stanza form of the poem; every line is half its usual length, so a–e occupy ten stanzas. Stanzas added to a–e in B-13 consist of four of h–l and fourteen unique short-lined quatrains, the equivalent of seven stanzas in most *Erthe* poems. As a result, B-13 feels different even when its wording is familiar from the five- and twelve-stanza versions. The fact that almost half the text is unique enlarges that difference. Yet B-13's themes and wordplay, like B-8's, are consistent across borrowed and original stanzas.

Murray and Förster put two more poems, B-14 and 15, in the seven-stanza subgroup because they include all of a–g. Again, differences in form and content are sufficient to set them apart from other witnesses to those seven stanzas. B-14 uniquely supplies every quatrain a bob and wheel, as well as increasing the poem by five similar six-line stanzas. The material in the fifth and sixth lines of each stanza is unique to this text, so the effect of a familiar quatrain is sometimes reinforced but sometimes altered by its bob and wheel. Still, as in B-8 and B-13, B-14's themes and wordplay are consistent across its entire length. In seeming contrast, four of the nine quatrains that B-15 adds to the common seven cover the Nine Worthies, whereas the other five offer more explicit moralizing on mortality than is found in shorter poems in the *Erthe* tradition. Yet this unique material is shaped to convey the same general message as the seven common stanzas do: the Nine Worthies do not change the subject but exemplify it, and wordplay on "earth" continues in all nine stanzas to which this poem is the only extant witness.

The four remaining members of the B group are all related to the twelve-stanza version, but in significantly different ways. B-9 is an eight-stanza poem that adds one stanza from h–l (l) to the end of the seven-stanza version; the overall effect is much the same as in the seven-stanza poems, but achieved somewhat differently. B-12 is a six-stanza poem that begins as a very accurate copy of the twelve-stanza version. Halfway through the sixth stanza, the scribe abruptly ends the poem with a unique couplet of exhortation. These last two lines do not match each other or the first two lines of their stanza in meter, nor do they rhyme with the first two lines. The closing couplet's language is plainer and simpler than the rest of the poem, also; overall, the effect is nearly comical. B-20 reproduces nine stanzas from the twelve-stanza version (a, b, c, d, h, i, j, g, l) with considerable accuracy except for the omission of e, f, and k, the eighth, ninth, and tenth of the twelve stanzas. There is sufficient repetition of thought and wording in the twelve-stanza poems that B-20 achieves almost the same effect as they do, with three-quarters of their material. Finally, B-26 is unique in combining all of a–e with all of h–l while omitting f–g. It also presents its ten stanzas in a unique order and omits several words usually found in them. Most surprisingly, B-26 closes with stanza i rather than stanza l, which is the last stanza in every other poem that includes it. Making l the ninth stanza and i the tenth moves the reader from hope that the soul will go to heaven to despair that the body will be detestable after death. This is effective, but its effect is not the same as that of the twelve-stanza version's prayerful conclusion. (See my edition of B-26 in the "Editions" section below.)

Five of the B texts that I do not put in a subgroup include some or all of stanzas h–l, which are part of the twelve-stanza version. These poems, B-9, 12, 13, 20, and 26, turn out to differ with regard to the three texts that tend to occur in manuscripts of the twelve-stanza subgroup: Isidore's "O Man Know Thyself," Augustine's *De contemptu mundi,* and "Why Is This World Beloved." The manuscripts containing B-9, 12, and 13 have none of the fellow travelers, whereas the manuscripts of B-20 and 26 each have two: B-20 occurs with both prose works but not "Why," and B-26 follows Isidore and "Why" but not Augustine. I suggest that the makers of B-20's and 26's manuscripts had access to some copy of the booklet that I posit lies behind the twelve-stanza version. B-20's scribe omitted one of the three accompanying texts and three of the twelve stanzas; B-26's scribe omitted a different one of the three fellow travelers and two of the twelve stanzas, as well as reorganizing the other ten stanzas. These changes look more like scribal decisions than like accidents of transmission if B-20 and 26 share a source with the twelve-stanza version.

The C Group

Murray sees C-1 as a hybrid of the A and B groups, uniting the five-stanza version of B with material found in A-2. She is correct in identifying nineteen lines of C-1 as corresponding to stanzas a–e (minus one line), and the fact that these nineteen lines occur in only two passages of C-1 (ll. 1–10 and 27–35) may indicate that they were found together in the scribe's source. However, Murray's identification of five other passages of C-1 as corresponding to passages in A-2 is problematic. One problem is that three of the five passages in C-1 do not resemble their supposed parallels in A-2 closely enough; nine lines in C-1 (ll. 19–22, 41–44, and 38) echo lines in A-2's fifth, second, and sixth stanzas in only nine substantive words other than "erthe," and most of these shared words occur in different contexts in the two poems.[65] Still, Murray's other two sets of parallel passages (C-1's ll. 25–26 and 63–64 vis-à-vis lines in A-2's second and sixth stanzas) are strikingly similar. Their problem is that they are equally close to lines in various versions of an earlier poem, "Dialogue of the Soul and Body."[66] So Murray does not prove that C-1 is related directly to A-2; C-1 could as easily belong with the separate B poems. It cannot be put into any of B's subgroups both because it contains fifty-nine unique lines (and four shared only with C-2) and because it is not written uniformly in quatrains; Murray publishes it in stanzas based on the continuation of a rhyme sound, with the result that her edition's stanzas range from two to six lines.

C-2, which Murray did not know, looks even more like a member of the B group than C-1 does. (See my edition of C-2 in the "Editions" section below.) Like C-1, C-2 contains lines equivalent to stanzas a–e in two passages, eighteen at the beginning of its text and the other two at its end. Also like C-1, C-2 includes unique lines (but only twelve of them) as well as four lines found otherwise only in C-1, and it is not written uniformly in quatrains. Furthermore, C-2 does not contain either of the two passages in C-1 that resemble both A-2 and some versions of the "Dialogue of the Soul and Body," so it does not look at all like a mix of the A and B traditions. Finally, C-2 looks very much like a B version in one respect: its tenth stanza consists of a couplet found in twelve of the B texts (usually as an epigraph) but not in any of the A, D, or E texts. Therefore, I consider each of C-1 and C-2 to be a different poem in a single B-C group. They can be considered as a pair of related poems because of the lines they share that do not occur elsewhere and because of their presenting the poem in separable couplets rather than quatrains, but they are not the same poem.

Audiences

The audiences who were likely to have read this poem are as varied as the texts themselves. Two of the texts were inscribed on masonry (B-7 and B-21); nine of them were added to more or less unrelated texts, all but one of which had been written down by other scribes at some earlier time; and twenty-four of them were included in a scribe's own compilation. I consider the nine cases of later addition before turning to the twenty-four cases of planned inclusion.

The nine manuscripts in which *Erthe* appears as an unplanned addition to earlier contents tend to contain learned works. This group includes all three in the D tradition: the trilingual text (D-1) in Public Record Office E 175/11/16, a roll in the collection of the King's Remembrancer of the Exchequer; the fragmentary text (D-2) in Morgan M. 957, a trilingual manuscript; and the bilingual text (D-3) in Holkham misc. 39, a Latin-Middle English dictionary.

In the case of D-1, we can confidently say that the scribe himself was a professional civil servant. Only such a man would have had access to an Exchequer document, and he was evidently able to write three languages. In the case of D-3, the only text of these nine in the same hand as the rest of its manuscript, the scribe was likewise a professional, a lexicographer and translator, capable of producing macaronic verse. His manuscript is in this group because his version of *Erthe,* like the other fillers he put in his amen quire, is an addition to his completed dictionary. Three more of these nine texts likewise occur alongside writing in other languages: B-6 was added to University of Pennsylvania Ms. Codex 721, William of Pagula's Latin work, *Oculis sacerdotis,* a textbook for parish priests; B-9 was added to Harley 4486, after *Le livre de Sydrac,* a French compilation of philosophy and science; and C-2 occurs at the end of Royal 17.A.xvi, a bilingual collection of astronomical, ecclesiastical, geographical, and historical facts and figures.

The remaining three manuscripts are entirely in Middle English: B-3 is in Selden supra 53, a small anthology of poems by Hoccleve and Lydgate; B-5 is on the first flyleaf of Harley 1671, an imperfect copy of *The Way to Paradise,* a theological treatise; and B-16 is in Harley 984, Matthew's Gospel in a Wycliffite translation. By modern standards, most poems in the *Erthe* tradition seem fairly simple, so we might expect it to appeal to an audience we would likewise consider simple. But the scribes and the other likely readers of these nine manuscripts were well educated in one, two, or three languages, and they were interested in many kinds of learning.

Among the remaining twenty-four manuscripts are also a few learned compilations. Harley 2253 (A-1) and Harley 913 (A-2) are trilingual, in English, French, and Latin. Cotton Titus A.xxvi (B-12) contains Italian texts as well as texts in the same three languages as the Harley 2253 and 913; its subjects include botany, medicine, and naval architecture. Wellcome 673 (B-23) is largely a professional medical manuscript in Latin to which a few morally improving poems have been added in English. Even one of the monolingual manuscripts, Rawlinson poet. 32 (B-13), devotes ten folios to a history of philosophers. Adding these five copies to the nine discussed above, I conclude that more than a third of the poems in the *Erthe* tradition were written down for learned audiences.

Where we know or can guess the original audiences for the remaining nineteen manuscripts in this group of twenty-four, they cross the divide between clergy and laity. For instance, A-3 appears in what we know is a preaching handbook, Advocates 18.7.21; *Erthe* and the other Middle English lyrics in this work were meant to be used in sermons preached by the scribe, a Franciscan friar named John from Grimestone in Norfolk. We can surmise that manuscripts written entirely in Latin except for *Erthe,* such as Rawlinson C.307 and St. John's College, Cambridge, E.24 (containing B-8 and E, respectively), were intended for a clerical audience. There is no indication in these last two books that their sole item in English was supposed to be shared with the laity, as John of Grimestone's lyrics were; *Erthe* seems to have been included for the edification of the professional clergy themselves, as the other texts in each manuscript were.

We know a good bit about the laity for whom some of the other manuscripts were intended. For example, Robert Thornton was scribe and owner of Lincoln Cathedral 91, which includes B-2 and was created to provide both edifying and entertaining reading for his family in Yorkshire.[67] Similarly, in London, Richard Hill copied B-15 into Balliol 354, whose widely varying texts were intended for his own or his household's use.[68] Meanwhile, in Scotland, the Maitland family had Pepys 2553 made to preserve poems written by family members and other poems, including B-17; relatives arranged for a partial transcript of it (CUL Ll.5.10) at a much later date, suggesting that some of the poems, including B-18, continued to be valued.[69] The contents of other manuscripts suggest that at least those containing six more of our copies (B-4, 10, 13, 14, and 22, plus C-1) were likewise intended for lay audiences. The contents of these manuscripts include practical instruction on such topics as courtesy and venery, works designed for the early education of children, and worldly kinds of entertainment as well as entertaining kinds of religious edification.

In addition to crossing the clerical/lay division, *Erthe* apparently appealed to a variety of social circumstances. The specific patrons of two manuscripts with French texts, Harley 2253 (A-1) and Cotton Titus A.xxvi (B-12), are unknown, but they presumably belonged to the upper classes, as the Maitland family certainly did. Among the middle-class miscellanies, Lincoln Cathedral 91 (B-2) and Brogyntyn ii.1 (B-14) met the needs of country gentry, whereas Richard Hill and the owners of the "devotional anthologies" containing B-11 and 19 belonged to London's mercantile class.[70] In addition, manuscripts whose contents do not indicate their socioeconomic class give us physical clues; they vary in their use of paper and parchment, the presence or absence of illumination, and the professionalism of their scribes and rubricators to such an extent that we can deduce how much—or how little—money was invested in them. (However, it should be noted that while richly produced books can be associated with the possession of money, cheaply produced books may represent a low priority for the project rather than a low income on the part of the intended owner.) Murray's accurate observations about the chronological range of this poem (fourteenth to seventeenth centuries) and its geographical range (Scotland, Ireland, and all over England) can be expanded to include its appeal to diverse social classes and to both clergy and laity.

Conclusion

There are, then, three essentially independent traditions with multiple witnesses—A, B-C, and D—plus the singular E text that combines some B stanzas with some D ones. The two texts Murray put together to form the A group come from the 1330s and 1340s; A-3, D-1, D-2, and E come from later in the fourteenth century, after 1370; and the B-C texts plus D-3 come from the fifteenth century or later. The scribal activities that created multiple witnesses in each tradition include accurate copying, excerpting, adding new material, reformatting quatrains into couplets or six-line stanzas, changing the line length, and rewording. Of these activities, copying more or less accurately has produced only fourteen of the thirty-five versions: the B texts that contain only stanzas a–e or a–g or a–l (the five-, seven-, and twelve-stanza subgroups). Scribes who altered the poem on their own account or to please their audience produced all three texts assigned to the A group, twelve B texts, both C texts, all three texts assigned to the D group, and the E text. This poetic tradition, in its extant witnesses, does not indicate that the primary concern of its scribes was accurate transmission of a stable text.[71] Rather, twenty-one versions indicate scribal authorship to some extent,[72] with differing results. Most are fairly successful in conveying the same themes and having the same effects on their readers, but the unique and original ways in which their poems proceed should be respected.

EDITIONS

Generally, I stay close to the manuscript, italicizing expanded abbreviations, retaining superscript letters, and not correcting the text. One reason to have access to editions of all thirty-five poems in the *Erthe* tradition is that they vary in wording, spelling, and abbreviations. Each edition is accompanied by information about the manuscript presentation of the text and my specific editorial practices in its case. My editions of D-2 and D-3 appear in the discussion section of this article, but the following five poems are too long to incorporate in that manner.

B-24

B-24 is in British Library Additional 37788, a mid-fifteenth-century vellum manuscript written in the same professional Gothic Textualis book hand throughout; the dialect of this poem is East Midlands, probably near the border with Southern.[73] The poem is the fourth of five items in the body of this manuscript and is written in prose. Every stanza ends with a pilcrow (in lieu of any other punctuation), and most of the stanzas begin with a capital letter. The ends of each of the first three lines in every stanza are marked by a punctus, a punctus elevatus, or a virgula, depending on grammar. I reflect the careful punctuation of this scribe by using a period at the end of each stanza;

a capital letter at the beginning of each line; either a period or a comma for each punctus, including ones occurring within a line; and a semicolon for both instances of the punctus elevatus.

Whanne lyf is moost loued, & deeth is moost hatid;
þanne deeþ draw^t his drauȝt, & makiþ man ful nakid.

De terra plasmasti me &ce*tera*.

1. Erþe out of erþe is wondirli wrouȝt. [stanza a]
Erþe of erþe haþ gete a dignite of nouȝt.
Erþe upon erþe haþ sett al his þouȝt
How þ^t erþe upon erþe mai be hiȝ brouȝt.

2. Erþe upon erþe wolde be a king, [b]
But how erþe schal to erþe þenkiþ he no þing.
Wha*n*ne þat erþe biddiþ erþe hise rentis hoom bringe,
Þanne schal erþe out of erþe haue a piteuous p*er*tyng.

3. Erþe upon erþe wy*n*neþ castels & touris. [c]
Þa*n*ne seiþ erþe to erþe þis is al ouris.
Wha*n*ne erþe upon erþe haþ biggid up hise bouris,
Þa*n*ne schal erþe upon erþe suffre scharp schouris.

4. Erþe gooþ upon erþe as molde upon molde. [d]
So gooþ erþe upon erþe al glitering in gold
Lyk as erþe unto erþe neu*er*e go schuld,
& ȝit schal erþe unto erþe raþ*er* þan he wolde.

5. O þou wrecchid erþe þat on þe erþe traueilist nyȝt & day, [h]
To florische þe erþe, to peinte þe erþe wiþ wantowne aray,
Ȝit schalt þou erþe, for al þi erþe, make þou it neu*er* so qweynte or gay,
Out of þis erþe into þe erþe, þ*er*e to cly*n*ge as a clot of clay.

6. O wrecchid man whi art þou proud þ^t art of erþe makid. [i]
Hidir brouȝtist þou no schroud, but pore come þou & nakid.
Wha*n*ne þi soule is went out & þi bodi i*n* erþe rakid,
Þan þi bodi þat was rank & biloued of alle men is bihatid.

7. Out of þis erþe came to þis erþe, þis wanting garnement. [j]
To hide þis erþe to happe þis erþe to hi*m* was cloþing lent.
Now gooþ erþe upon erþe ruly raggid & rent;
Þ*er*fore schalt erþe undir þe erþe haue hidous turment.

8. Whi þat erþe loueþ erþe wondir me þink, [e]
Or whi þ^t erþe for erþe swete wole or swink.
For whanne þat erþe upon þe erþe is brouȝt wiþ i*n*ne þe bri*n*k,
Þan schal erþe of þe erþe haue a ruful stink.

9. Lo erþe upon erþe consider þou mai [f]
How erþe comeþ i*n* to erþe nakid al wey.
Whi schulde erþe upon erþe go stout or gay,
Wha*n*ne erþe schal passe out of erþe in a pore aray.

10. Wolde þ*er*fore þis erþe on þis erþe ~~on þis~~ hertili þink [k]
How þat erþe out of erþe schal haue a rising,
A*n*d þus erþe for erþe ȝelde streiȝt rekenyng,
Schulde neu*er*e erþe for erþe mysplese heuene ki*n*g.

11. Þou erþe upon erþe þ^t wickidli hast wrouȝt, [g]
While þat erþe is upon erþe turne aȝe*n* þi þouȝt,
& p*re*ie to god upon erþe þat al erþe haþ wrouȝt,
Þat erþe upon erþe to blis may be brouȝt.

12. Lord þ^t erþe madist for erþe & suffirdist peynes ille, [l]
Lete neu*er* þis erþe for þis erþe myscheue ne spille,
But þat þis erþe in þis erþe be worching þi wille,
So þat erþe fro þis erþe stiȝ up to þin hiȝ hille. Am*en*.

B-25

B-25 is in Huntington Library HM 744, a composite manuscript, of which the two-quire vellum section containing *Erthe* is mid-fifteenth century, written in four hands by three or four scribes;[74] this poem is consistently in an Anglicana hand and intermittently in the dialect of Norfolk.[75] It is the fifth item in the first quire, but the two quires may be considered a unit, because the sixth item begins in the first quire and concludes in the second quire. Given the evidence that both sections of the manuscript were written in London,[76] one must assume that the scribe of our poem was originally from Norfolk but residing in London; he changed *erþe* to the Norfolk spelling *erde* nearly one-third of the time. The poem is written as prose, but every stanza begins with a capital letter. Nothing marks the ends of most lines, but most of the stanzas end with punctuation; two of the four virgulas occur at the ends of stanzas and five of the other ten stanzas end with a punctus. I model my punctuation of the following edition on the punctuation of my edition of B-24, which was based on its scribe's usage.

Whan liif is most loued and deeþ most hatid,
[Þ]anne deeþ drawid his drauȝt and makiþ man ful nakid.

1. Erde out of erþe is wondirly wrouȝt. [stanza a]
Erþe of erde haue gete a dignite of nouȝt.
Erde upon erþe hat set al his þouȝt
How þat erþe upon erþe my be heȝe browȝt.

2. Erde upon erþe wold ben a king, [b]
But how erþe schal to erþe denkiþ he no þing.
Wanne þat erþe biddiþ erde his rentis hoom brenge,
Thanne schal erþe out of erde haue a piteuous per*tinge*.

3. Erde upon erde wynneþ castells and touris. [c]
Þan seiþ erde to erde þis is al ouris.
Wanne erde upon erþe haþ biggid up hise bouris,
Þanne schall erþe upon erþ[e] suffre scharp schouris.

4. Erde gooþ upon erde as moolde vpon moolde. [d]
So gooþ erde upon erþe alle gliteringe in golde
Like as erþe vnto erþe neuere goo schulde,
And ȝit schal erþe vnto erþe raþ*er* þan he wolde.

5. O þou wrechid erþe þt on þe erþe trauaeilist neȝt and day, [h]
To florische þe erde, to paynte þe erþe w[t] wantwne aray,
ȝit schalt þou erþe, fro al þin erþe, make dou it neuer so qweyn-te or gay,
Out of þis erþe in to þe erþe, þe*er* to clynge as a clot of clay.

6. O wrecchid man whi art þou so proud þ[t] art of erþe makid. [i]
Hider brouȝtist þou no schrowd, but pore come þou and nakid.
Whan*ne* þi soule is went out and þi boþi in erþe rakid,
Þan þi body þat was ra*n*ke and biloued of al men is bihatid.

7. Out of þis erde cam to þis erde þis wantinge granament. [j]
To hide þis erþe, to happe þis erþe to hym was cloþing lent.
Now gooþ erþe upon erde ruly raggid & to rent.
Þ*er*fore schal erþe vndir þe erþe haue hidous torment.

8. Whi þat erþe loueþ erde wonder me þink, [e]
Or whi þat erde for erþe swete wold or swinke.
For whan*ne* þat erþe upon erþe is browȝt w^t^ynne þe brynke,
Þanne schal erþe of þe erþe haue a ruful stink.

9. Lo erþe upon erde considere þou may [f]
How erþe comeþ in to erþe nakid al wey.
Whi schuld erþe upon erþe go stoute or gay,
Whanne erþe schal passe out of erþe in a poure aray.

10. Wold þerfore þis erþe on þis erþe on þis hertily þink [k]
How þat erþe out of erþe schal haue a rising,
And þus erþe for erþe ȝeelde streiȝt rikenynge,
Schuld neu*ere* erþe for erþe mysplese heuene kinge.

11. Þou erþe upon erþe þat wrecchidly hast wrouȝt, [g]
Whyle þat erþe is opon erþe turne aȝen þi þouȝt,
And pray to god upon erþe þ^t^ al erþe haþ wrouȝt,
Þat erþe upon erþe to blis may be brouȝt.

12. Lord þat erþe madist for erþe and sufferist peynes ille, [l]
Lete neu*ere* þis erþe for þis erþe myschefe ne spille,
But þ^t^ þis erþe in þis erþe be eu*ere* worchinge þi wille,
So þat erþe fro þis erþe may stiȝe up to þin hiȝ hille. Amen.

B-26

B-26 is in Bodley 220, a mixed paper and vellum manuscript from the first half of the fifteenth century. The first two of its five items are in one hand, and the scribe signs himself "Wellys I." at the end of the second item.[77] The third, fourth, and fifth items (B-26 is the fifth item) are written in another hand and are not signed. The handwriting of this second scribe has the general look of Anglicana and uses the Anglicana forms of *e*, *g*, *r*, and *s* exclusively, although the Secretary forms of *a* and *w* alternate with their Anglicana counterparts, sometimes in the same line. The scribe's dialect is southeast Midlands.[78] The poem is written in lines of verse, each beginning with a capital letter, and every pair of lines has been bracketed, as if the poem were written in couplets rather than quatrains. Half of the lines end with a punctus, and a punctus occurs inside some lines, but these internal punctuation marks do not correspond with either the grammar of the sentences or the meter of the verse; therefore, I supply punctuation only at the ends of lines.

1. Erthe oute of erthe ys wonderly wrought. [stanza a]
Erthe of erthe hath gote a dignyte of nought.
Erthe vp on erthe hath sette all hys þought
Howe erthe vp on erthe may be hye brought.

2. Erthe vp on erth wold be a kyng, [b]
But howe erthe shall to erth thenketh he no thyng.
Whanne that erthe bydds erthe hys rents home brynge,
Thanne shall erth oute of erthe haue a pytouse p*ar*tynge.

3. Erthe vp on erthe wynnyth castellys and tourys. [c]
Thanne seys erthe to erthe þis all ourys.
Whanne erth vp on erthe hath byggyd hys bourys,
Thanne shall erthe vp on erthe suffr^{e} harde shourys.

4. Erthe goeth vp on erth as molde vp on molde. [d]
Erthe goeth vp on erth glyteryng as golde
Lyke as erthe from erthe neuer go shulde,
But ȝit shall erth to erthe rather þanne he wold.

5. Wrecche erthe þat on erth travaylist nyȝt and day, [h]
To floressh and paynte þe erthe with wanton a ray,
Yit shall þou erth fro all þy erth make þou it never so qweynt or gay
Fro thys erthe in to erth clyng as a clott of clay.

6. Oute of þis erth cam thys erth wantyng garnement. [j]
To hyde þis erth to happe þis erth to hym was clothyng lent.
Nowe goth erthe vp on erth rewly raggyd and rente.
Therefor shall erth vnder ^{þe} erth haue hydouse turment.

7. Why þat þe erth loves þe erth wonder me thenke, [e]
Or why þat erth ~~for love of erth loves þe erth~~ for love of erth swete wole or swynk.
For whanne þat erth vp on erth ys brought with inne þe brynke,
Thanne shall erth of the erth haue a rewfull stynke.

8. Wolde erthe on the erth on þis hertely thynk [k]
Howe þat erth oute of erth shall haue a rysyng
And þus erthe f[or] þe erthe ȝilde streyte rekenyng,[79]
Shuld neuer erthe for þe erthe mysplease heuen kyng.

9. Lord, þat erthe madest for erthe and suffyrdist peynys ylle, [l]
Let neuer erthe for erth myscheve ne spylle,
But þat þis erthe in thys erthe be euer worchyng þy wylle.
So þat þe erth fro thys erthe stye vp to thyn hye hyll.

10. Wrecched man why art þou proude þat art of erth maked. [i]
Hydyr broughtyst þou no shroud bot pore come and naked.
Whanne þy soule is went out and þy body on þe erth raked,
Thanne þy body þat was so rank and loved of all men ys behated.

C-2

C-2 is in Cambridge University Library Ii.4.9, a fifteenth-century vellum manuscript that has been dated to 1420 and contains primarily calendrical texts.[80] The manuscript continued in use for some time, acquiring six texts on its first three folios and seven on its last four; C-2 is the seventh item added at the end of the manuscript. The hand in which C-2 is written occurs only in this text; the scribe writes in an Anglicana script and a Northern dialect.[81] He does not use the yogh, and his thorn and *y* are indistinguishable.[82] The poem consists of nineteen couplets, seven of which are written in lines of verse (1–3 and 9–12) while the remainder of the text is written as if it were prose, although a capital letter marks the beginning of each couplet. The ink has faded almost to illegibility in many places, and water damage has completely obliterated a few words at the lower left corner of the verso; these are indicated by underlined blanks in the edition. There is very little punctuation, so what appears here is almost entirely editorial. To facilitate comparison with Murray's edition of C-1, I group the couplets into monorhymed stanzas of two to six lines as she does.

1. Erth opon erth is varpyd & wroght. [B's stanza a, 1st in C-1]
Erth has takyn of erth anobylte o noght.
Erth on þ^e^ erth setts al is thought,
how erth opon erth may be hee broght. (*highe* in margin in later hand)

2. Erth opon erth getts tovns & towrs. [B's stanza c, 2nd in C-1]

þe*n* says erth to erth þis is al owris.
Bot qwen erth on þis erth has bygwd al is bowrys,
þen sal erth for erth swffwr scharpe schowrys.

3. Erth bydis erth is bowrys hom bring, [Half of B's stanza b, 8th in C-1]

þen sal erth for þis erth make make apete partyng.

4. Erth says tyl erth wond^er^ me thynke [B's stanza e, 9th in C-1]

þat erth for erth wold swet or swynke,
ffor qwen erth in erth is broght w^t^ in þ^e^ brynk^e^,
þen has erth noght of erth bot affowll stynk^e^.

5. Erth opon erthe wold fayn be a kyng, [Half of B's stanza b, 3rd in C-1]

bot þ^t^ he sal dy he thynkis no thyng.

6. Erth opon erth gos gleterand in gold [Half B's stanza d, 10th in C-1]

os erth on þis erth new^er^ dee solde.

7. yit may erth opon erth hew^er^ mynd make [Like 11th stanza in C-1]

how erth agwn in erth be layd in alayke.

[verso]

8. Erth veyns of erth new^er^ to haf i no^w^gh [Like half of 5th stanza in C-1]

or he be layd in erth os slo is in his slogh,

9. þe*n* sal erth vepe os he be soyn lowte [unique]
þ^t^ for erth be wayr w^t^ þi weght.

10. ffor qwen lyff is best lowyde & ded most hatyd, [Couplet found only in B texts and C-2]
þe*n* cowms ded & drayis is draght & makys man fwll naykyd.

11. y^{e} þ^{t} wayr in erth rich & stovt of astayt [unique]
& rod w^{t} rowt^{e} agayn reght boyd erte & late,
had he haldyn opon heght w^{t} none arang qatte
qwyll he lewyd in erth hayd he no make.
qwat is don for yar sawlys yar paynys for to slake,
ilk^{e} day may we se gwd hede & we take.

12. Siqw^{e} is erth closyd *in* erth os a_l_at is uf clay [unique]
and þ^{e} sawl is wendand a wyll win full way,
þen has erth non erth __ new is in faye
ffor þen as erth fell a kyng _____ for erth þ^{t} aye.

13. Erth wrots in erth _____ moldwarp in mold, [Half of B's stanza d, 10th in C-1]
And yit sal erth _____ erth langer þen he wold.

E

E is in Cambridge, St. John's College MS E.24. It is the only *Erthe* text I edit in this article that has been edited before. The very small number of letters I read differently from Förster do not create significant differences in the poem's meaning, and a twenty-first-century reader can simply ignore Förster's provision of excessive punctuation and "missing" words (all properly put in angle brackets). However, the layout of this text in Förster's article is likely to mislead many readers and ought to be corrected. After Förster edits the first five stanzas of E (a–e), which he numbers 1 to 5, he adds the two stanzas that are found in the seven-stanza version (f–g), numbering them 6 to 7, and then the five stanzas that are found in the twelve-stanza version (h–l), numbered 8 to 12, although there is no extant witness to all of h–l that puts them together in that order or as the poem's last five stanzas. Then he edits B-22. Finally, he returns to the St. John's College text, five pages after he left it, in order to edit its sixth through fourteenth stanzas, which he numbers 1 to 9, despite no manuscript evidence of any break between the poem's first five stanzas and its last nine.

The manuscript comes from late in the fourteenth century, and its *Erthe* poem is written in the East Midlands dialect. The poem is the fifth of twenty items in the manuscript, and the only one written in English rather than Latin. The scribe wrote the poem in lines of verse, each of which begins with a rubricated capital letter and most of which (51 of 58) end with a punctus. Couplets are bracketed in red. On the second of the three folios occupied by this poem, the scribe omitted and then inserted four words, as well as occasionally using *th* in place of thorn; there are no such errors or inconsistencies on the first and third folios. In the opening stanzas, he uses more abbreviations than many scribes do when writing in English. I use either a period or a comma at the end of each line and follow the scribe's example in not using medial punctuation. However, I divide the poem into quatrains instead of couplets to facilitate comparison with shared stanzas in other *Erthe* texts.

Wha*n* lyf is louyd & deþ ys most hatid,
Deþ drawiþ h^s drawȝtis & m*a*k^t ma*n* ful n*a*kid.

1. Erþ*e* owt of erþe ys wo*n*dirli wrowȝt. [stanza a]
Erþ*e* hath getyn of erþ*e* a nobli of nowȝt.
Erþ*e* apo*n* erþ*e* haþ sette al his þowȝt,
How erþ*e* upo*n* erþ*e* m*ay* be hye browȝt.

2. Erþ*e* upo*n* erþ*e* wolde be made a kynge. [b]
How erþ*e* schal to erþ*e* þynk^t he no þyng.
We*n* erth*e* biddiþ erþ*e* his rentis ho*m* to bringe,
þe*n* schal erþ*e* have of erþ*e* a petuos p*ar*tynge.

3. Erþe opo*n* erþe wynn^t castell*is* & towris. [c]
þe*n* seiþ erþe o*n* to erþe þis is al owris.
Whe*n* erþe upo*n* erþe haþ byggid his bowris,
þe*n* schal erþe for erþe suffur scharp schour*is*.

4. Erþe goþ upo*n* erþe as molde upo*n* molde. [d]
Erþ goþ upo*n* erþe as glisterynge as golde,
Lyk as erþe o*n* to erþe neu*er* go schulde,
& ȝut schal erþe on to erþe raþir the*n* wolde.

5. Why þat erþe louiþ erþe wondir me þi*n*ke, [e]
Or whi þat erþe for erþe wolde swete or swi*n*k.
Wha*n* erþe upo*n* erþe is browȝt w^t in þ*e* brinke,
þan schal erþe haue of erþe riȝt a foule stink.

6. Wha*n* erþe hauet erþe w^t woo by ȝute, [Like D-1, stanza 1]

And erþe in erþe by gynnyt to lete,
And erþe liþ in erþe w^t wormys y frete,
þan erþe ys yn erþe sone for ȝute.

7. Whan erþe wynt erþe so luþur to a wylde, [Like D-1, stanza 3]
And erþe on þis erþe eche day schal elde,
And erþe in erþe sone so a colde,
How may erþe in erþe be bolde.

8. Whan erthe on erthe þorow pryde styyth, [Like D-1, stanza 2]
And erthe on thys erþe to covytise wryyth,
And erthe in to erthe sone a ȝen heyyth,
þan erthe toward erþe to hevyn c*r*yeth.

9. What hauyþ erþe in erþe but woo. [Like D-1, stanza 4]
Whan [erþe] sieþ on erþe greueliche foo,
And erþe ne may on erþe ryde ne goo,
þan erthe a curseþ erþe þis worlde fareþ soo.

10. Whan [erþe] axyþ erthe whare be hur beste, [Like D-1, stanza 8]
þat erþe by hete erþe that he schulde y leste,
Whan erþe for erþe drawet to helle cheste,
þer erþe for erþe lesyt ioy wele an feste.

11. Whan [erþe] syeþ erþe to endynge drawe, [Like D-1, stanza 6]
And erþe is on þys erþe wiþ deþ aslawe,
And erþe lyth on erþe wyþ wormes y gnawe,
þan may erthe erthe y knawe.

12. Whan erþe schalle of o erþe nedeliche a ryse, [Like D-1, stanza 7]
And erþe y hure in erþe þe greueliche a syse,
And erþe ne may erþe lere no wyse,
þer schal erþe for erþe sorelyche a grise.

13. Man that [art] erþe & of erþe y makid, [unique]
And erþe in to erþe a ȝen thou schelt nakyd,
Ne let noȝt þin erþe for erþe ben a slaked,
And þin erþe for erþe in sawle ben a blaked.

14. Owre lorde þat on erþe for erþe was y bore [Like D-1, stanza 9]
And on erþe for erþe wiþ wondys to tore,
Wyte erþe uppon erþe þat owre ne be for lore,
And brynge owre erþe þer boote is y fore.
Amen.

Acknowledgments

I am grateful to many librarians for access to manuscripts and/or provision of photographic reproductions: Aberystwyth, National Library of Wales; Cambridge, St. John's College Library; Edinburgh, National Library of Scotland; London, British Library; London, National Archives; New York, Morgan Library; Oxford, Bodleian Library; and San Merino, Huntington Library. I am also grateful to the many scholars who are named in the notes, where their specific contributions are detailed. Pervading this article is the more general influence of three individuals: Ruth Evans, the Dorothy McBride Orthwein Professor of English, St. Louis University, whose reading of an earlier complete draft inspired this revision; Amy Reynolds, Postdoctoral Fellow in English, Washington University in St. Louis, who has been of assistance in many ways and who has given much support for the past five years; and my husband, Michael A. Thomas, who has enabled this project to grow from my first handling an *Erthe* manuscript in 2002 until now.

NOTES

1. Hilda M. R. Murray, *The Middle English Poem, Erthe upon Erthe, Printed from Twenty-Four Manuscripts* (London: Oxford University Press, 1911). In addition to the twenty-four counted in her subtitle, Murray reprints five related inscriptions found on burial markers; ibid., xxxvi–xxxviii. Only one of these is early enough to appear in Middle English verse indices and thereby raise the number of "Erthe" texts printed by Murray to twenty-five.
2. Ibid., xxx–xxxii.
3. Ibid., xxix–xxxiii.
4. Ibid., x–xxix.
5. Ibid., 41–46.
6. Carleton Brown, *A Register of Middle English Religious & Didactic Verse* (London: Oxford University Press for the Bibliographical Society, 1916–1920), assigns eight of the ten poems Murray had not edited to her groups, following her criteria; for example, he lists D-2 as a version of D-1 and E as a B text. George Kane, "The Middle English Verse in

MS Wellcome 1493," *London Medieval Studies* 2 (1951): 50–65, 58, assigns B-23 to the B group. Rossell Hope Robbins and John L. Cutler, *Supplement to the Index of Middle English Verse* (Lexington: University of Kentucky Press, 1966), group D-3 with D-1 and D-2.

7. Murray edited most of her texts from their manuscripts herself; I list earlier editors only in the four cases where she reprinted their editions because she could not access the originals.
8. Linne R. Mooney, Daniel Wayne Mosser, and Elizabeth Solopova, eds., *The DIMEV: an Open-Access, Digital Edition of the Index of Middle English Verse*, http://www.dimev.net/index.html.
9. Marjorie Harrington, "Of Earth You Were Made: Constructing the Bilingual Poem 'Erþ' in British Library, MS Harley 913," *Florilegium* 31 (2014): 128–133.
10. Edward Wilson, *A Descriptive Index of the English Lyrics in John of Grimestone's Preaching Book*, Medium Ævum Monographs n.s. 2 (Oxford: Blackwell, 1973), 27.
11. William Bateman, *Billyng's Five Wounds of Christ* (Manchester: Dean, 1814). Murray reprints Bateman's previously published edition of this text, the manuscript of which had been lost. Bateman's edition of the manuscript, a scroll belonging to William Yates of Manchester, was a "small impression of no more than forty copies, printed entirely for private distribution" (ibid., first unnumbered page after title page); I am grateful to Widener Library at Harvard University for a reproduction of Bateman's work.
12. H. G. Fiedler, "Earth upon Earth," *Modern Language Review* 3 (1908): 218–227, 219. Murray reprints Fiedler's previously published edition of this text, the manuscript of which was in private hands. Fiedler's edition contains one error—*brente* for *broute* in line 19—as can be seen in the University of Pennsylvania's digital facsimile of the manuscript: http://hdl.library.upenn.edu/1017/d/medren/2487538.
13. University of Pennsylvania Ms. Codex 721 is identical with a manuscript listed as No. 2A in Davis and Orioli Sale Catalogue 135 (1949), which appears in the printed indices of Middle English verse as an unlocated manuscript. To the best of my knowledge, I am the first to identify these entries as referring to the same text. I am grateful to the staff of Princeton University Library for a partial reproduction of the sale catalogue.
14. R. B. Wheler, *History and Antiquities of Stratford-upon-Avon* (Stratford-upon-Avon, UK: J. Ward, 1806), 98. Murray reprints Wheler's edition because the inscription had been covered with whitewash.
15. John Weever, *Ancient Funerall Monuments within the United Monarchie of Great Britaine* (London: T. Harper, 1631), 534. Murray reprints Weever's edition because the inscription had become illegible.

16. Max Förster, "Die älteste Fassung des mittelenglische Gedichtes Earth upon Earth," *Archiv für das Studium der neueren Sprachen und Literaturen* 138 (1919):55–56.
17. Kane, "Middle English Verse," 66–67.
18. This manuscript is first listed as "*olim* Tenison" in Robbins and Cutler, *Supplement*, 80, who cite Churchill Babington's edition of Pecock's *The Repressor of over much Blaming of the Clergy* (I. lxxii, n.) as their source. A comparison of the contents of BL Add. 37788 with the contents listed for Tenison's manuscript by Babington (I. lxxii, n.) shows that they are identical. Moreover, BL Add. 37788's online description says, "This MS. is the only one noticed by Churchill Babington in his preface to Pecock's *Repressor* (Rolls Series, 1860), p. lxx," and lists Tenison as a previous owner. The reason Robbins and Cutler did not recognize the version of "Erthe" mentioned by Babington as the version in BL Add. 37788 is that Babington listed the introductory couplet of the poem as the explicit of the previous item in the manuscript instead of as the incipit of "Erthe." So this version was assigned a new number, 704/17, when it had already been indexed as 3985/7 in Carleton Brown and Rossell Hope Robbins, *The Index of Middle English Verse* (New York: Columbia University Press for the Index Society, 1943), 638. To the best of my knowledge, I am the first to identify these two entries as referring to the same text.
19. Marjorie Harrington, "A Trilingual Version of 'Erthe upon Erthe' in the National Archives of the United Kingdom, E 175/11/16," *Journal of the Early Book Society* 19 (2016): 203–210.
20. Förster, "älteste Fassung," 57–61.
21. The benefits of the DIMEV and its print predecessors are immense, but the drawback to organizing by incipits is shown by these examples. On the one hand, the introductory couplet's absence separates many texts in the "Erthe" tradition from ones with which they otherwise belong; on the other hand, the introductory couplet's presence joins together ten versions identified as members of group B with the unique text I call E and with five witnesses that do not belong to the "Erthe" tradition at all.
22. Brown, *Register*, 1.505.
23. Librarians at the National Library of Scotland alerted me to this previously unlisted occurrence.
24. Brown, *Register*, 1.432.
25. E. C. Fawtier & R. Fawtier, "From Merlin to Shakespeare: Adventures of an English Prophecy," *Bulletin of the John Rylands Library* 5 (1918–1920): 388–392, 389.

26. Edward Wilson & Iain Fenlon, eds., *The Winchester Anthology: Facsimile Edition of B.L. Additional MS. 60577* (Woodbridge, UK: Brewer, 1981), 153.
27. Editions printed here are taken from Murray, *Middle English Poem*, 1.
28. For A-1, Carter Revard, "Scribe and Provenance," in *Studies in the Harley Manuscript: The Scribes, Contents, and Social Contexts of British Library MS Harley 2253*, ed. Susanna Fein (Kalamazoo, MI: Medieval Institute Publications, 2000), 21–109, argues that paleographically "much of [the manuscript] most closely resembles the holographs of 1340" (62). Susanna Fein, *The Complete Harley 2253 Manuscript*, 3 vols. (Kalamazoo, MI: Medieval Institute Publications, 2014), 1:2, attributes the work of the Ludlow scribe to the decade 1331–1341. For A-2, Michael Benskin, "The Hands of the Kildare Poems Manuscript," *Irish University Review* 20 (1990):163–193, 164, attributes Harley 913 to the 1330s; Peter Lucas and Angela Lucas, "Reconstructing a Disarranged Manuscript: The Case of Harley 913, a Medieval Hiberno-English Miscellany," *Scriptorium* 14 (1990): 286–299, 287, date it "c. 1330, or perhaps a little later." Alan J. Fletcher, "The Date of London, British Library, Harley MS 913 (the 'Kildare Poems')," *Medium Ævum* 79 (2010): 306–310, points out that the list of Franciscan houses must have been copied during or after 1338–1342, along with items adjacent to it, but as these are in a different booklet from "Erthe" (Lucas and Lucas, "Reconstructing," 291–297) the dating of "Erthe" may or may not be affected by Fletcher's observation.
29. Theo Stemmler, "Miscellany or Anthology? The Structure of Medieval Manuscripts: MS Harley 2253, for Example," in *Studies in the Harley Manuscript: The Scribes, Contents, and Social Contexts of British Library MS Harley 2253*, ed. Susanna Fein (Kalamazoo, MI: Medieval Institute Publications, 2000), 111–121, 115; Michael P. Kuczynski, "An 'Electric Stream': The Religious Contents," in *Studies in the Harley Manuscript*, 123–161, 143–144; and Susanna Fein, "A Saint 'Geynest under Gore': Marina and the Love Lyrics of the Seventh Quire," in *Studies in the Harley Manuscript*, 351–376, 353. Also, Susanna Fein, "Compilation and Purpose in MS Harley 2253," in *Essays in Manuscript Geography: Vernacular Manuscripts of the English West Midlands from the Conquest to the Sixteenth Century*, ed. Wendy Scase (Turnhout, Belgium: Brepols, 2007), 67–94, 78; and Carter Revard, "Oppositional Thematics and Metanarrative in MS Harley 2253, Quires 1–6," in *Essays in Manuscript Geography*, 95–112, 109–110. Most recently, Harrington, "Of Earth You Were Made," 108–113.
30. This count is my own. It is based on my reading of the quatrain, with birth indicated in the first line, the getting of love or of possessions

in the second, death in the third, and the end of desire for love or for possessions in the fourth. Russell A. Peck, "Public Dreams and Private Myths: Perspectives in Middle English Literature," *PMLA* 90 (1975): 465–466, reads the quatrain four other ways, further distancing it from the thirty-four longer, simpler texts.

31. For example, Matthew Fisher, *Scribal Authorship and the Writing of History in Medieval England* (Columbus: Ohio University Press, 2012), reviews previous attributions of *Fouke le Fitz Waryn* and the Anglo-Norman Bible stories to the scribe (ibid., 102) before arguing for the scribe's authorship of the Office of Thomas of Lancaster (ibid., 105–116) and the *Short Chronicle* (ibid., 116–140). Susanna Fein, "Literary Scribes: The Harley Scribe and Robert Thornton as Case Studies," in *Insular Books: Vernacular Manuscript Miscellanies in Late Medieval Britain,* ed. Margaret Connolly and Raluca Radulescu, Proceedings of the British Academy 201 (Oxford: Oxford University Press, 2015), 61–79, 66–67, suggests that the scribe also wrote *A Book of Dreaming* in English and three saints' lives in Latin.
32. Harrington, "Of Earth You Were Made," 105–137.
33. Murray, *Middle English Poem*, xxx–xxxii.
34. John of Grimestone names himself and gives the date of his book on fol. 9v; Wilson, *Descriptive Index,* xiii–xvi, discusses supporting evidence for the manuscript's original provenance.
35. Brown, *Register,* 2.79.
36. Wilson, *Descriptive Index,* 27, item 130. I reprint Wilson's edition.
37. Siegfried Wenzel, *Preachers, Poets, and the Early English Lyric* (Princeton, NJ: Princeton University Press, 1986), 113–115, argues from how small the percentage of verses is with any source or analogue that John of Grimestone was likely to be the author of the much larger percentage of verses found only in his book. My complementary argument is that the nature and extent of variation between John's verses and analogous versions make it likely he rewrote what he borrowed as well as writing what he did not find elsewhere.
38. Wilson, *Descriptive Index,* xi.
39. Ibid., xi–xii, lists twenty-five; Wenzel, *Preachers, Poets,* 114, counts twenty-seven.
40. John's text is the earliest extant one for the items that Wilson numbers 5, 7, 8, 198, 205, and 211.
41. Items 107, 186, and 213 are longer in John's book than in earlier versions; the expansions may be his own. There is no difference in length but considerable difference in wording in items 133, 154, and 182. Items 120, 127, 130 ("Erthe"), and 200 are shorter than earlier versions, and three of these four also differ significantly in wording.

42. Harrington, "Trilingual Version," 197–203, discusses the Anglo-Norman and Latin poems and their relation to the Middle English poem.
43. See note 6 for details.
44. The legal text on the roll has been identified as the Ordinances of 1311. It is unlikely to have been copied later than the repeal of the Ordinances in 1322. I am grateful to Dr. Jessica Nelson, medieval records specialist at the National Archives, for identifying this roll for me in 2013.
45. Harrington, "Trilingual Version," 198 and 211, thanks Teresa Webber for dating both hands.
46. Ibid., 199.
47. Harrington prints the first seven lines of D-3's nine lines in a footnote; ibid., 212.
48. The Morgan Library's CORSAIR Online Collection Catalog, http://corsair.themorgan.org/cgi-bin/Pwebrecon.cgi?BBID=145495, accessed October 11, 2014, gives the date. My transcription is diplomatic; the capital letters at the beginning of each line appear in the manuscript. I supply only a dash at the end of each incomplete line.
49. Richard Beadle, "Prolegomena to a Literary Geography of Late Medieval Norfolk," in *Regionalism in Late Medieval Manuscripts and Texts: Essays Celebrating the Publication of "A Linguistic Atlas of Late Medieval English,"* ed. Felicity Riddy (Cambridge, UK: D.S. Brewer, 1991), 89–108, 107, identifies the date and origin of the manuscript. I am grateful to Dr. Frank Coulson of the Ohio State University for helping me complete my first transcription of this text from a reproduction. All his speculations about illegibly reproduced letters proved accurate when I was able later to transcribe the manuscript itself. I am also very grateful to Dr. Bruce Barker-Benfield of Oxford's Bodleian Library for looking at the manuscript with me; among other useful observations, he brought the rough draft of the concluding couplet to my attention.
50. Murray, *Middle English Poem*, xxix–xxxiii. Harrington, "Trilingual Version," 200, agrees with Murray's claim that the English versions of A-2 and D-1 are the originals on which the Latin versions are based but refutes Murray's suggestion that A-2 might have inspired D-1. I agree with Harrington on both points.
51. Harrington, "Trilingual Version," is the only scholar I have seen discuss Förster's claims about the two poems he edited; other references I have found to his article only cite the Middle English editions. I am grateful to Dr. Patrick Brugh for helping me with Förster's scholarly German of 1919.
52. Förster, "älteste Fassung," passim. I disagree with Förster's unsupported assumption that E must be the earliest version of the poem and the

source of all the other versions, just because it combines material usually found separately. On the other hand, the language in Harrington, "Trilingual Version," 200 ("this text conflates material from two different strands, splicing together five stanzas from the first strand with eight stanzas from the second strand") implies that E is later than the B and D groups, whereas E is certainly the earliest witness to the five stanzas that occur in almost all B texts.

53. M. R. James, *A Descriptive Catalogue of the Manuscripts in the Library of St. John's College Cambridge* (Cambridge, UK: Cambridge University Press, 1913), 159.
54. Edward E. Foster, ed., *Three Purgatory Poems* (Kalamazoo, MI: Medieval Institute Publications, 2004), 15.
55. Ibid., 16.
56. H. Forshaw, "New Light on the *Speculum Ecclesie* of St. Edmund of Abingdon," *Archives d'Histoire Doctrinale et Litteraire de Moyen Age* 38 (1971): 7–33, 15.
57. Murray, *Middle English Poem*, 46.
58. Ibid., xviii.
59. Förster, "älteste Fassung," 40–44.
60. Murray, *Middle English Poem*, xviii.
61. Ibid., xxii–xxiii. Note that Murray was looking at stanzas a–e not only in the two five-stanza poems and the seven seven-stanza poems without additional material but also in all the longer poems she knew that include a–e.
62. Ibid., xviii.
63. Siegfried Wenzel, *Verses in Sermons: Fasciculus Morum and Its Middle English Poems* (Cambridge, MA: Mediaeval Academy of America, 1978), 147.
64. For comprehensive coverage of discussions regarding booklets, see Alexandra Gillespie, "Medieval Books, Their Booklets, and Booklet Theory," *English Manuscript Studies, 1100–1700* 16 (2012): 1–29.
65. Murray, *Middle English Poem*, xxvii, gives these passages in full in parallel columns.
66. Ibid., xxx–xxxi, gives the passages from *Body and Soul* and "Erthe" in full in parallel columns.
67. Susanna Fein, "Literary Scribes," 70–77.
68. Carol M. Meale, "Amateur Book Production and the Miscellany in Late Medieval East Anglia: Tanner 407 and Beinicke 365," in *Insular Books: Vernacular Manuscript Miscellanies in Late Medieval Britain*, ed. Margaret Connolly and Raluca Radulescu, Proceedings of the British Academy 201 (Oxford: Oxford University Press, 2015), 157–173, esp. 157–159.

69. Priscilla Bawcutt, "Scottish Manuscript Miscellanies from the Fifteenth to the Seventeenth Century," *English Manuscript Studies 1100–1700* 12 (2005):46–73, esp. 52–53; Priscilla Bawcutt, "The Earliest Texts of Dunbar," in *Regionalism in Late Medieval Manuscripts and Texts,* ed. F. Riddy (Cambridge, UK: D.S. Brewer, 1991), 183–198, esp. 190–194.
70. Margaret Connolly, "Books for the 'helpe of euery persoone þat þinkeþ to be saued': Six Devotional Anthologies from Fifteenth-Century London," *Yearbook of English Studies* 33 (2003):170–181, discusses Laud misc. 23 and Trinity College (Cambridge) R.3.21, which contain B-11 and B-19, respectively.
71. Richard Beadle, "Some Measures of Scribal Accuracy in Late Medieval English Manuscripts," in *Probable Truth: Editing Medieval Texts from Britain in the Twenty-First Century,* ed. V. Gillespie and A. Hudson (Turnhout, Belgium: Brepols, 2013), 223–239, 239, reaches a different conclusion for Middle English literature in general: "The average late medieval English scribe seems to have been, both by training and inclination, and within the limits of human frailty, as concerned as conscientious editors are with the stability and accuracy of their texts." *Erthe* is evidently an outlier.
72. The first chapter in Fisher, *Scribal Authorship,* 14–58, "The Medieval Scribe," has shaped my thoughts on this topic. More recently, Kathryn Kerby-Fulton, "Confronting the Scribe-Poet Binary: The Z Text, Writing Office Redaction and Oxford Reading Circles," in *New Directions in Medieval Manuscript Studies and Reading Practices: Essays in Honor of Derek Pearsall,* ed. S. Baechle, K. Kerby-Fulton, and J. Thompson (Notre Dame, IN: University of Notre Dame Press, 2014), 489–515, 491, observes that "three groups we used to think of as distinct—scribes, poetic imitators, and authors—can no longer always be seen quite so separately." Daniel Wakelin, *Scribal Correction and Literary Craft: English Manuscripts 1375–1510* (Cambridge, UK: Cambridge University Press, 2014), 305, prefers to keep these terms distinct while changing our application of them: "We might ask whether the term *scribe* is adequate for somebody who rewrites heavily; we might want to credit more of the people who rewrite texts with the title, instead, of *author,* as Matthew Fisher urges us to do."
73. Angus McIntosh, M. L. Samuels, Michael Benskin, Margaret Laing, Keith Williamson, and Vasilis Karaiskos, eds., *An Electronic Version of A Linguistic Atlas of Late Mediaeval English.* http://www.lel.ed.ac.uk/ihd/elalme/elalme.html, (hereafter ELALME) identifies *worch* for *work* as southeast Midlands to Southern; *-ith* for third-person singular present-tense verbs as Midlands, mostly east; *deeth* for *death* as Midlands, mostly east; and *sei-* for *say* as Midlands to Southern.

74. C.W. Dutschke, *Guide to Medieval and Renaissance Manuscripts in the Huntington Library* (San Marino, CA: Henry E. Huntingdon Library and Art Gallery, 1989), 250, describes the first two quires of HM 744 as containing ten items written in four hands; she identifies the first two hands as the same person's and suggests the possibility that the third hand also belongs to this scribe. In a meeting with Dr. Vanessa Wilkie, Curator of Medieval & British Historical Manuscripts at the Huntington Library, Dr. Wilkie advised me that the third hand is likely to belong to a different scribe.
75. ELALME situates fourteen of its twenty-three occurrences of *hat* for *hath* and fourteen of its twenty-four occurrences of *erde* for *erþe* in or adjacent to Norfolk. This scribe's tendency to equate a thorn with a *d* can also be seen in the substitution of *dou* for *þou* in line 21 and *boþi* for *bodi* in line 25.
76. The first two quires and an item added on the back flyleaf have connections to the family of Thomas Filer of London; Dutschke, *Guide*, 251. The other quires contain holograph poems by Thomas Hoccleve, likewise of London.
77. Theresa A. Halligan, ed., *The Booke of Gostlye Grace of Mechtild of Hackeborn* (Toronto: Pontifical Institute of Mediaeval Studies, 1979), 2, notes that a Carthusian monk named John Wells or Wellis is recorded as moving from one English Charterhouse to another in 1425, 1427, and 1439 and as dying at a fourth Charterhouse in 1445.
78. The poem's most distinctive spellings, *ʒilde* and *worchyng*, are used in both the southwest and southeast Midlands; the southeast is to be preferred, because ELALME's LP 6170 (London, British Library, Add. 37677, fols. 84–105) uses the same spellings as the poem does for other words they have in common, to a greater extent than other ELALME LPs.
79. The scribe left space for two letters after the f but wrote nothing in that space. There is no sign of an erasure.
80. British Library entry for Royal 17.A.xvi, permalink http://searcharchives.bl.uk/IAMS_VU2:IAMS040-002107247, most recently accessed July 22, 2017.
81. ELALME discusses a different item in this manuscript as LP 614 but does not identify its geographical origin. Five usages in our text (*-and* for the present participle ending, *bot* for *but*, *qw-* for *wh-*, *-s* for the third-person singular verb ending, and *sal* for *shall*) are either more prevalent in the North or occur only there. LPs 249, 1130, 1198, and 1285 are the only LPs with three, four, or all five of these usages; they are from Lancashire or Yorkshire.

82. Michael Benskin, "The letters <Þ> and <Y> in later Middle English, and some related matters," *Journal of the Society of Archivists* 7 (1982), 13–30, shows that using the same letter-form to write <Þ> and <Y> indicates a Northern or East Anglian scribe.

WORKS CITED

Babington, Churchill, ed. *The Repressor of Over Much Blaming of the Clergy*. 2 vols. Rolls Series 19. London: Longman, Green, Longman, and Roberts, 1860.

Bateman, William. *Billyng's Five Wounds of Christ*. Manchester: Dean, 1814.

Bawcutt, Priscilla. "The Earliest Texts of Dunbar." In *Regionalism in Late Medieval Manuscripts and Texts: Essays Celebrating the Publication of "A Linguistic Atlas of Late Medieval English,"* ed. Felicity Riddy, 183–198. Cambridge, UK: D.S. Brewer, 1991.

———. "Scottish Manuscript Miscellanies from the Fifteenth to the Seventeenth Century." *English Manuscript Studies 1100–1700* 12 (2005): 46–73.

Beadle, Richard. "Prolegomena to a Literary Geography of Late Medieval Norfolk." In *Regionalism in Late Medieval Manuscripts and Texts: Essays Celebrating the Publication of "A Linguistic Atlas of Late Medieval English,"* ed. Felicity Riddy, 89–108. Cambridge, UK: D.S. Brewer, 1991.

———. "Some Measures of Scribal Accuracy in Late Medieval English Manuscripts." In *Probable Truth: Editing Medieval Texts from Britain in the Twenty-First Century*, ed. V. Gillespie and A. Hudson, 223–239. Turnhout, Belgium: Brepols, 2013.

Benskin, Michael. "The Hands of the Kildare Poems Manuscript." *Irish University Review* 20 (1990): 163–193.

———. "The Letters <Þ> and <Y> in Later Middle English, and Some Related Matters." *Journal of the Society of Archivists* 7 (1982): 13–30.

Brown, Carleton. *A Register of Middle English Religious & Didactic Verse*. 2 vols. London: Oxford University Press for the Bibliographical Society, 1916–1920.

———, and Rossell Hope Robbins. *The Index of Middle English Verse*. New York: Columbia University Press for the Index Society, 1943.

Connolly, Margaret. "Books for the 'helpe of euery persoone þat þinkeþ to be saued': Six Devotional Anthologies from Fifteenth-Century London." *Yearbook of English Studies* 33 (2003): 170–181.

———, and Raluca Radulescu, eds. *Insular Books: Vernacular Manuscript Miscellanies in Late Medieval Britain*. Proceedings of the British Academy 201. Oxford: Oxford University Press, 2015.

Dutschke, C. W. *Guide to Medieval and Renaissance Manuscripts in the Huntington Library*. San Marino, CA: Henry E. Huntingdon Library and Art Gallery, 1989.

Fawtier, E. C., and R. Fawtier. "From Merlin to Shakespeare: Adventures of an English Prophecy." *Bulletin of the John Rylands Library* 5.3–4 (1919): 388–392.

Fein, Susanna. "Compilation and Purpose in MS Harley 2253." In *Essays in Manuscript Geography: Vernacular Manuscripts of the English West Midlands from the Conquest to the Sixteenth Century*, ed. Wendy Scase, 67–94. Turnhout, Belgium: Brepols, 2007.

———, ed. *The Complete Harley 2253 Manuscript*. 3 vols. Kalamazoo, MI: Medieval Institute Publications, 2014.

———. "A Saint 'Geynest under Gore': Marina and the Love Lyrics of the Seventh Quire." In *Studies in the Harley Manuscript: The Scribes, Contents, and Social Contexts of British Library MS Harley 2253*, ed. Susanna Fein, 351–376. Kalamazoo, MI: Medieval Institute Publications, 2000.

———. "Literary Scribes: The Harley Scribe and Robert Thornton as Case Studies." In *Insular Books: Vernacular Manuscript Miscellanies in Late Medieval Britain*, ed. Margaret Connolly and Raluca Radulescu, 61–79. Proceedings of the British Academy 201. Oxford: Oxford University Press, 2015.

———, ed. *Studies in the Harley Manuscript: The Scribes, Contents, and Social Contexts of British Library MS Harley 2253*. Kalamazoo, MI: Medieval Institute Publications, 2000.

Fiedler, H. G. "Earth upon Earth." *Modern Language Review* 3 (1908): 218–227.

Fisher, Matthew. *Scribal Authorship and the Writing of History in Medieval England*. Columbus: Ohio University Press, 2012.

Fletcher, Alan J. "The Date of London, British Library, Harley MS 913 (the 'Kildare Poems')." *Medium Ævum* 79 (2010): 306–310.

Forshaw, H. "New Light on the *Speculum Ecclesie* of St. Edmund of Abingdon." *Archives d'Histoire Doctrinale et Litteraire de Moyen Age* 38 (1971): 7–33.

Förster, Max. "Die älteste Fassung des mittelenglische Gedichtes Earth upon Earth." *Archiv für das Studium der neueren Sprachen und Literaturen* 138 (1919): 39–61.

Foster, Edward E., ed. *Three Purgatory Poems*. Kalamazoo, MI: Medieval Institute Publications, 2004.

Gillespie, Alexandra. "Medieval Books, Their Booklets, and Booklet Theory." *English Manuscript Studies, 1100–1700* 16 (2012): 1–29.

Halligan, Theresa A., ed. *The Booke of Gostlye Grace of Mechtild of Hackeborn*. Toronto: Pontifical Institute of Mediaeval Studies, 1979.

Harrington, Marjorie. "Of Earth You Were Made: Constructing the Bilingual Poem 'Erþ' in British Library, MS Harley 913." *Florilegium* 31 (2014): 105–137.

———. "A Trilingual Version of 'Erthe upon Erthe' in the National Archives of the United Kingdom, E 175/11/16." *Journal of the Early Book Society* 19 (2016): 197–215.

James, M. R. *A Descriptive Catalogue of the Manuscripts in the Library of St. John's College Cambridge*. Cambridge, UK: Cambridge University Press, 1913.

Kane, George. "The Middle English Verse in MS Wellcome 1493." *London Medieval Studies* 2 (1951): 50–67.

Kerby-Fulton, Kathryn. "Confronting the Scribe-Poet Binary: The Z Text, Writing Office Redaction and Oxford Reading Circles." In *New Directions in Medieval Manuscript Studies and Reading Practices: Essays in Honor of Derek Pearsall*, ed. S. Baechle, K. Kerby-Fulton, and J. Thompson, 489–515. Notre Dame, IN: University of Notre Dame Press, 2014.

Kuczynski, Michael P. "An 'Electric Stream': The Religious Contents." In *Studies in the Harley Manuscript: The Scribes, Contents, and Social Contexts of British Library MS Harley 2253*, ed. Susanna Fein, 123–161. Kalamazoo, MI: Medieval Institute Publications, 2000.

Lucas, Peter, and Angela Lucas. "Reconstructing a Disarranged Manuscript: The Case of Harley 913, a Medieval Hiberno-English Miscellany." *Scriptorium* 14 (1990): 286–299.

McIntosh, Angus, M. L. Samuels, Michael Benskin, Margaret Laing, Keith Williamson, and Vasilis Karaiskos, eds. *An Electronic Version of A Linguistic Atlas of Late Mediaeval English*. 2013. http://www.lel.ed.ac.uk/ihd/elalme/elalme.html.

Meale, Carol M. "Amateur Book Production and the Miscellany in Late Medieval East Anglia: Tanner 407 and Beinicke 365." In *Insular Books: Vernacular Manuscript Miscellanies in Late Medieval Britain*, ed. Margaret Connolly and Raluca Radulescu, 157–173. Proceedings of the British Academy 201. Oxford: Oxford University Press, 2015.

Mooney, Linne R., Daniel Wayne Mosser, and Elizabeth Solopova, eds. *The* DIMEV: *An Open-Access, Digital Edition of the Index of Middle English Verse*. http://www.dimev.net/index.html.

Morgan Library and Museum. CORSAIR Online Collection Catalog, Detailed Record for MS M.0957. http://corsair.themorgan.org/cgi-bin/Pwebrecon.cgi?BBID=145495.

Murray, Hilda M. R. *The Middle English Poem, Erthe upon Erthe, Printed from Twenty-Four Manuscripts*. London: Oxford University Press for the Early English Text Society, 1911.

Peck, Russell A. "Public Dreams and Private Myths: Perspectives in Middle English Literature." *PMLA* 90 (1975): 461–468.

Penn Libraries. Medieval & Renaissance Manuscripts Collection, MS Codex 721—William, of Pagula, ca. 1290–1332 [Oculus sacerdotis] (digitized). http://hdl.library.upenn.edu/1017/d/medren/2487538.

Revard, Carter. "Oppositional Thematics and Metanarrative in MS Harley 2253, Quires 1–6." In *Essays in Manuscript Geography: Vernacular Manuscripts of the English West Midlands from the Conquest to the Sixteenth Century*, ed. Wendy Scase, 95–112. Turnhout, Belgium: Brepols, 2007.

———. "Scribe and Provenance." In *Studies in the Harley Manuscript: The Scribes, Contents, and Social Contexts of British Library MS Harley 2253*, ed. Susanna Fein, 21–109. Kalamazoo, MI: Medieval Institute Publications, 2000.

Riddy, Felicity, ed. *Regionalism in Late Medieval Manuscripts and Texts: Essays Celebrating the Publication of "A Linguistic Atlas of Late Medieval English."* Cambridge, UK: D.S. Brewer, 1991.

Robbins, Rossell Hope, and John L. Cutler. *Supplement to the Index of Middle English Verse.* Lexington: University of Kentucky Press, 1966.

Scase, Wendy, ed. *Essays in Manuscript Geography: Vernacular Manuscripts of the English West Midlands from the Conquest to the Sixteenth Century.* Turnhout, Belgium: Brepols, 2007.

Stemmler, Theo. "Miscellany or Anthology? The Structure of Medieval Manuscripts: MS Harley 2253, for Example." In *Studies in the Harley Manuscript: The Scribes, Contents, and Social Contexts of British Library MS Harley 2253*, ed. Susanna Fein, 111–121. Kalamazoo, MI: Medieval Institute Publications, 2000..

Wakelin, Daniel. *Scribal Correction and Literary Craft: English Manuscripts 1375–1510.* Cambridge, UK: Cambridge University Press, 2014.

Weever, *Ancient Funerall Monuments within the United Monarchie of Great Britaine.* London: T. Harper, 1631.

Wenzel, Siegfried. *Preachers, Poets, and the Early English Lyric.* Princeton, NJ: Princeton University Press, 1986.

———.*Verses in Sermons: Fasciculus Morum and Its Middle English Poems.* Cambridge, MA: Mediaeval Academy of America, 1978.

Wheler, R. B. *History and Antiquities of Stratford-upon Avon.* Stratford-upon-Avon, UK: J. Ward, 1806.

Wilson, Edward. *A Descriptive Index of the English Lyrics in John of Grimestone's Preaching Book.* Medium Ævum Monographs, n. ser. 2. Oxford: Blackwell, 1973.

——— and Iain Fenlon, eds. *The Winchester Anthology: Facsimile edition of B.L. Additional MS. 60577.* Woodbridge, UK: Brewer, 1981.

Rethinking Gender and Language in Stephen Scrope's *Epistle of Othea*[1]

MISTY SCHIEBERLE

Christine de Pizan's *Epistre Othea* was by far her most widespread and popular work, instructing readers in moral and political virtues, teaching them how to read and apply exempla, and challenging them to dismiss antifeminist stereotypes rampant in literature and to embrace women's wisdom and counsel. Christine invents Othea, the goddess of wisdom and prudence, who advises Hector of Troy by recounting a hundred classical exemplars who embody vices and virtues (in poetic *textes*). In her own authorial voice, Christine then adds interpretations on moral and spiritual levels for her Christian readers (in prose *gloses* and *allegories*). Originally presented as a mirror for princes to Louis d'Orleans, and later to Jean of Berry, Queen Isabeau of France, Philip of Burgundy, and Henry IV of England, the *Othea* also enjoyed popularity as a chivalric instructional manual throughout the fifteenth and sixteenth centuries. There are forty-seven extant manuscripts, and there were early printed editions by Philippe Pigouchet (1499–1500), Philippe Le Noir (1522), the Widow Trepperel (1521?), and Raulin de Gautier (before 1534).[2] There are also three independent early English translations: Stephen Scrope's *Boke of Knyghthode* (ca. 1440); the anonymous *Lytle Bibell of Knyghthod* (ca. 1450), often attributed to Anthony Babyngton; and Robert Wyer's *.C. Hystoryes of Troye* (printed ca. 1540–1550).[3] Scrope, the focus of this study, clearly views knighthood as the *Othea*'s main topic: he refers to his production as a "Book off Knyghthode" or "Boke of Chevallry."[4] The natural question arises of whether, in his translation, this focus on the masculinized world of chivalric virtue eclipses Christine's interest in women and defending her gender. The scholarly consensus suggests that Scrope indeed represents an antifeminist perspective, but that consensus must be reconsidered, and I argue, modified once we examine his general practice of translation.

When Scrope first renders the *Othea* into Middle English, in the place of Christine's prologue, which addresses her dedicatee's greatness, her humble reference to "*la foiblesse / De feminin sens*" [the feebleness of feminine wisdom], and her assertion of the importance of her advice, he substitutes an original prose preface to his stepfather Sir John Fastolf.[5] Among other things, this preface attributes the work to male clerks and focuses almost exclusively on masculine authorities and on the Duke of Berry as an exemplar for Fastolf.

Because Scrope displaces Christine as author and misrepresents the origin of the *Othea*, it is no wonder that scholars have criticized his attitudes toward women and gender. Until recently, however, few scholars have looked beyond his preface—extant in only one manuscript—for evidence of Scrope's perspectives. A major aspect of the translation remains underexplored: the manuscript tradition of the *Epistle*, especially evidence of the accuracy of Scrope's translations of gendered words and characters. Analyzing these manuscript variants brings us closer to apprehending what Scrope thought of gender, beyond simply acknowledging that he must have considered the *Othea* appropriate reading for the "hye princesse" to whom one copy is dedicated.[6] A thorough exploration of the manuscript readings in fact complicates prior studies concerning whether Scrope was actively antifeminist, an average misogynist of his era, no more misogynist than the average man of his era, or was even aware of the significance of gender in Christine's *Othea*. Such an analysis indicates that, even if his preface displays a remarkable and plausibly willful ignorance about Christine and her role in the creation of the *Othea*, Scrope's actual translation, rather than exercising a purposeful antifeminist program largely registers an indifference to grammatical gender that results in the confusion of characters' genders, among other errors.

The manuscript circumstances of Scrope's translation are fairly complicated, even though there are only three copies: Cambridge, St. John's College MS H.5 (S); New York, Pierpont Morgan Library MS M 775 (M); and Warminster, Longleat Library and Archives, MS Longleat 253 (L).[7] S is the most complete manuscript, suffering only one major lacuna; M and L have more substantial gaps. Curt F. Bühler posits that Scrope generated a personal working copy from which three varying versions were made and dedicated to Fastolf, to Humphrey, Duke of Buckingham, and to the unnamed "hye princesse," and that from each of those versions today's three extant copies,

L, S, and M, respectively, preserving those dedications, eventually were made. None is in autograph, and no surviving manuscript was copied from either of the others.[8] However, Bühler acknowledges that S may in fact be the actual presentation manuscript for Buckingham, presumably because of its quality, relative completeness, and illuminations, including a presentation portrait of Scrope and Buckingham.[9] He dismisses the possibility of M as being the original copy for the "hye princesse," because it contains the arms of its owner, Sir John Astley (d. 1486), and "other tracts [*Sailing Directions* and an English *Secreta Secretorum*] . . . quite inappropriate for a lady," which he thought to be in the same hand.[10] However, Sonja Drimmer shows that the *Epistle* is independent from the other manuscript contents in terms of quire, scribe, and artist, and she argues that it is likely that Astley acquired the lady's manuscript and imposed his arms onto it.[11]

The most mysterious and inaccessible manuscript is L, the only witness that contains Scrope's preface to Fastolf in lieu of the prologue modeled on Christine's dedication to the Duke of Berry that appears in S and M.[12] The significant number of copying errors indicates that L is not Scrope's original; additionally, L lacks almost all of the scriptural quotations, occasionally containing the initial word of the Latin and once offering an English translation.[13] Thus, it is possible that in S and M, we may have the original presentation copies, but that is not the case for L. From a collation of manuscripts, it is clear that although the copies are generally quite closely related, L gives us access to some of Scrope's earliest readings (many of L's readings are closer to the French). While S and M retain some of Scrope's early readings, even some not copied by the L scribe, they also offer numerous variants introduced by their particular scribes.[14]

Scrope's exemplar is no longer extant, so we cannot confirm the exact quality of his translation. However, another volume from Fastolf's library aids us in reconstructing readings from Scrope's source: Oxford, Bodleian MS Laud misc. 570, which contains a French *Othea* copied from the same French exemplar after Scrope's translation.[15] This information is critical because, although modern scholarship relies on London, British Library, Harley MS 4431 to access Christine's final authorial version of the *Othea*, the Queen's Manuscript contains unique substitutions and errors not replicated in Laud misc. 570 (or any other French manuscript) and thus is not helpful in establishing the quality or tenor of Scrope's translation.[16] Nevertheless, Scrope's rendering has earned a reputation as a "good" translation largely on the basis of scholars' favorable comparison of it (and Laud misc. 570) to Harley 4431, coupled with their assertions of ways the other English translations—the *Lytle Bibell of Knyghthod* and Robert Wyer's early printed edition—go far astray from the readings in Harley 4431.[17]

Scholarship on Scrope's *Epistle* has focused primarily on the preface—understandably, since it is Scrope's main original composition. The preface introduces the work as a "Book off Knyghthode" designed to emphasize the Cardinal Virtues, which Scrope has translated for Fastolf to give his step-father guidance in enhancing his chivalric virtues (and perhaps persuade him to restore Scrope's withheld inheritance).[18] His version of the *Othea*'s origin has received significant scrutiny: he claims that the work was completed "at the instaunce and praer of a fulle wyse gentyl-woman of Frawnce called Dame Cristine" but was "compiled and grounded" by famous wise *men* of the University of Paris for the edification of John, Duke of Berry, a prominent and influential French royal family member, brother to Charles V and uncle of Charles VI (*Epistle* 122–123). Christine receives very little attention, as Scrope focuses more intently on the Duke as a model of military might and wisdom, an exemplar for Fastolf. The displacement of Christine's authorship is exacerbated by the fact that Laud misc. 570, copied from the same source as Scrope's translation, contains a presentation portrait of Christine personally offering her book to the Duke, which modern scholars know is an author portrait, though Scrope has interpreted Christine's role as that of patron. As a result of his misrepresentation of the work's origin and authorship, Scrope has been criticized as misogynist who denies Christine authorship and assumes that the intellectual elements of her text must have had a male-authored, university source.[19]

But there are more nuanced explanations. Jennifer Summit argues that Scrope recognizes in Christine's writing the opportunity for someone outside of traditional clerical and university authority to develop literary authority, and he essentially establishes himself further as the authoritative textual voice by defining himself against her femininity.[20] I have elsewhere suggested a modification of that last detail, arguing instead that Scrope in fact identifies with Christine, with Othea, and with their shared plight of needing to develop authority from traditionally powerless authorial positions. In my view, it is worth considering that Scrope misunderstands Christine to be a reasonably important patron who instigated the production of the *Othea* (which equally would warrant the Laud misc. 570 presentation portrait) and that when Scrope creates parallels between the Duke and Fastolf, he necessarily also creates a parallel between Christine and himself, one that carries over into his own identification with the female voices of the work itself.[21] In other words, Scrope's antifeminism is the passive sort that could not conceive of a female authority rather than the product of an active program or conscious desire to deny Christine all forms of authority, since he does believe that she is an influential patron.

Yet few scholars have examined the translated text itself in much detail. Marilynn Desmond explores the visual programs of Scrope's manuscripts while asserting that Scrope textually strives for the closest possible English equivalent to Christine's French.[22] I earlier suggested, largely on the basis of Curt F. Bühler's edited text, that Scrope accurately translates Christine's proto-feminist ideas, which is still generally true: he rarely meddles with her pro-women positions and does carefully render her lessons.[23] By taking such analysis a step further into all three manuscripts, however, my revised position is that we also must acknowledge that Scrope regularly evidences a hasty method of translation that simply cannot be bothered to represent accurately the gender in Christine's original. Ardis Butterfield has recently suggested that "roughness" is a useful term to encompass both the "elements in a translated text that signal its otherness, and the feeling that a language is being used without sufficient knowledge of, or facility in, its formal properties and idioms," which can help us understand the different kinds of linguistic fluency and competence evidenced in medieval English translations.[24] Scrope offers us perhaps the more traditional sense of a "rough" translation, and arguably one much less strategic than those texts that interest Butterfield: a translation produced quickly, and as a result, with varying degrees of accuracy.

Gender in Scrope's Manuscripts

I begin with the most obvious of Scrope's gendered misidentifications of characters before pursuing less-noticed errors and errors that are grammatical in nature. Scrope demonstrates a remarkable ignorance of mythology when he inexplicably deviates from the genders attributed to figures by classical traditions.[25] For instance, his Phoebe, in all three manuscripts, is masculinized:

> Unto Phebe resemble not; for why?
> *He* is to chaungeable and enemy
> To stedfastnes and to corage stronge,
> Malencolyous is and full of wronge.
>
> Phoebe is callid the mone, of whome the Monday hath *his* name; and to *him* is yoven the metall that we call silvere. (*Epistle* 20, ll. 19–25)[26]

Scrope's "his" in the prose might refer to "Monday," but no other day of the week receives a gendered pronoun, and "he" and "him" both refer to Phoebe. A similar problem plagues the representation of Echo in the *texte* of two manuscripts, yet it is contradicted in the *glose*:

Beware thou voide not fro thee Eccho,
Ne *his* pitous compleintes also;
Susteyne al *his* will, yif it may be,
For thou woste not what may come to thee.

The fabill seith that Eccho was a *womman* of fayrie.
(*Epistle* 104, ll. 15–20)[27]

S and L—the likeliest representations of Scrope's earliest efforts—record "his," and only manuscript M correctly reads "hire"; perhaps surprisingly, all three manuscripts immediately identify Echo as female in the first line of the glose and then go on to refer to her with "she" and "hire," as appropriate. Medusa suffers a similar fate, masculinized in all three manuscripts' *texte* warning that establishes Perseus, whom Scrope inexplicably calls "Persyval," as an exemplar:

Kepe thee wel fro the serpent Gorgon;
Bewar that thou loke not *him* uppon;
Have good sad mynde uppon Persyval
And he schal thee telle the story al.
(*Epistle* 67, ll. 23–26)

Scrope's gendering of the serpent as male comes from his perspective or assumptions, not the French grammar, in which "*serpent*" is feminine: "*De la serpent Gorgon te gardes, / Gard bien que tu ne la regardes*" [Protect yourself from the serpent Gorgon; / Guard well that you do not look upon her] (Laud misc. 570, fol. 63v; cf. Christine, *Epistre,* 277, ll. 2–5).[28] But when not dependent on articles and pronouns, when the French instead gives him "*damoiselle,*" Scrope correctly informs us at the outset of the *glose*: "Gorgon, as the fable seith, was a *gentilwomman* of sovereyne beaute," followed by "Phebus lay bi *hir* in the temple" (*Epistle* 67, ll. 28–29). Once changed into a serpent, Medusa remains female, until "Percivale" goes to battle the serpent and, in the S and L copies, "dide so myche that he smote of *his* hede" [*tant fist que le chef lui trancha*] (*Epistle* 68, l. 7). Scrope apparently misunderstands that "*le*" is masculine because of the masculine noun "*chef,*" not because of the owner's gender. This leads to incongruence between his grammar and his narrative, except in copy M, which correctly refers to "hire hed."

Could these instances of "his" and "him" simply be scribal errors, and only the M scribe is paying attention to gender, sometimes?[29] If these were the only mistakenly gendered figures, perhaps they could be scribal errors (even though the M scribe does not correct all such errors), but there are many more. Moreover, rather than being isolated to one witness, gendering errors more often appear in all three manuscripts, suggesting the strong likelihood that they originated with Scrope and his failure to think about grammar and narrative content simultaneously.

Scrope's masculine Atropos presents an unusual case of misgendering. The three female Fates spun, measured, and clipped the threads representing the lives of all humans, and Atropos, to whom fell the latter task, was identified logically with Death. Atropos-Death is marked as feminine by her role in classical mythology, the image in deluxe French *Othea* manuscripts (to which Scrope did not have access) of a disheveled yet threatening woman with unmistakable bared and sagging breast, and one single textual clue from Christine: a feminine past participle in the *allegorie* (Christine, *Epistre*, 249, l. 19).[30] Thus Scrope's depiction of Atropos as male could be primarily accidental—if he were ignorant of the Fates' gender or simply indifferent, or if he were aware of the more widespread iconographical and English literary representation of Death as male.[31] But a rushed translation may also be to blame.

According to all three manuscripts, Scrope translates Christine's opening lines "*Ayes a toute heur regart / Et a Atropos et a son dart*" [At all times pay attention / To Atropos and to her spear] as "Loke that at al tymes thou take good hede / Bothe to Acropos crafte and to his spede" (Laud 570, fol. 50v; cf. Christine, *Epistre*, 248, ll. 2–3; Scrope, *Epistle*, 45, ll. 10–11).[32] There is much confusion here: Scrope apparently misreads "*dart*" as "art," leading to his mention of the analogous term "crafte"; and, as in the case of Medusa, he seems to have assumed that a masculine pronoun "*son*" referred to the gender of the owner rather than a grammatically masculine object. At any rate, it seems that Atropos' true gender does not matter to Scrope, and he easily assumes that Christine's Death must be male. This gendering error may not persuade us of Scrope's authority as translator of classical myth, but it does not impede either the narrative or the moral lesson transmitted.

However, in another case indicative of Scrope's broader *modus operandi*, ignorance and imprecision make narrative events difficult to follow in chapters based on Phoebus's Raven and Minerva's Crow. In Christine's French grammar, "*le corbel*" [the raven], masculine, is distinct from "*la corneille*" [the crow], feminine. Both terms could technically refer to a crow, but classical mythology specifies that the Raven was Phoebus' servant and the Crow was Minerva's.[33] Christine's differently gendered choices help clarify, through masculine or feminine nouns and pronouns, which bird actor is which in the narrative. By contrast, Scrope's translation suffers greatly from his carelessness with regard to grammatical gender:

> *N'occis* pas Corinis la belle
> Pour le raport et la nouvelle
> Du corbel, car se *l'occioies,*
> Aprés tu t'en repentiroies. (Laud misc. 570, fol. 59r; cf. Christine, *Epistre,* 267, ll. 2–5)
> Corinis, the feire, *note* may thou noughte,
> For the reporte of the message broughte
> Be the ravin, for if thou *it slee,*
> Thou schalte aftir gretly repente thee.
> (*Epistle,* 60, ll. 2–5)

Although the *glose* (and any knowledge of mythology) makes clear that Corinis is Phoebus' victim, Scrope's *texte,* as if blissfully unaware of the narrative, presents the Raven as the god's target and misunderstands the French verb "to kill."[34] Later, the narrative descends into utter confusion in the companion chapter that records the interaction in which the Crow, based on her own experience, warns the Raven against reporting Corinis to Phoebus. The different genders of the French birds are essential to the transmission of the narrative, whereas Scrope's translation becomes a jumbled mess across all three manuscripts:

> Croy *la corneille* et son conseil,
> Jamais ne soies en esveil
> De male nouvelle apporter,
> Le plus seur est s'en deporter.
>
> *La corneille,* ce dit la fable, encontra *le corbel* quant *il* portoit la nouvelle a Phebus de s'amie Corinis qui se estoit meffaitte, et tant lui enquist que *il* lui dist l'achoison de son erre; mais *elle* lui desloua qu'*il* n'y alast par lui donner exemple d'*elle* meismes, qui pour semblable [case] avoit esté chacie de l'ostel Pallas ou jadis souloit estre moult avancie[e]. Mais *il* ne l'en volt croire, dont mal lui en ensuy. (Laud misc. 570, fols. 61v–62; cf. Christine, *Epistre,* 273, ll. 2–14)
>
> Beleve the crowe and *his* trewe counceille,
> And be nevir besy ne travaill
> In yvill tydingis to be the berere;
> Of thi demene thou maiste be the surere.

> The fable seith that the crowe mette the ravin whan *he* broughte the tidingis to Phebus of his love Corinis, the which had doon amys, and *he* requyred *him* so sore that *he* toolde *him* the cause of *his* journay. But *sche* disealowid *him* because *he* went not to yeve *him* example of the same, the which for a liche case had ben chaced out of Palles hous, where somtyme *he* was wonte to be gretly avaunced. But *he* wold not beleve *here*, for the which harme folowed to *him*. (*Epistle*, 64, l. 19-65, l. 1)[35]

In Scrope, once again, the feminine Crow becomes partially masculinized. The *texte*'s error plausibly could derive from taking "*son*" to refer to masculine owner rather than object, but a deeper indifference is at work in the *glose*. In the French, the nouns and the third-person pronoun forms are distinguished as masculine and feminine, except for the indirect pronoun "*lui*," used for either gender.

Scrope's refusal to adhere to the gendered forms and his reluctance to parse out which bird performs which actions results in an inconsistent use of "he" and "him" forms when, at least part of the time, the feminine forms are *required* to translate the narrative accurately:

> The [female] Crow met the [male] Raven when he [the Raven] was taking news to Phebus of his lover Corinis, who had done wrong, and she [the Crow] entreated him so much that he [the Raven] told her [the Crow] the reason for his errand. But she advised him against going by giving him example of herself, who for a similar reason had been chased from Pallas's household, where in the past she [the Crow] had been greatly promoted.

Scrope does not even try to keep the Raven and Crow separate: when any verb lacks an immediate noun subject, the actor becomes masculine, and he misses the fact that "*elle meismes*" refers to the Crow herself, not a similar example. Distinguishing the characters is possible in the French but not in Scrope's muddled translation. When in doubt, Scrope evidently assumes that a figure is masculine, that a masculine noun belongs to a masculine owner, and that a verb without an immediate subject refers to a male unless the narrative context is obvious.[36]

At best, Scrope is inconsistent, and his regular mistranslations betray a carelessness or haste in his approach to French grammar that also occurs in cases where gender itself is less relevant than the above. When the giant Polyphemus becomes enraged with jealousy over the relationship between Acis and Galatea, Christine's text notes that he saw them together and then "*fu surprins de soudaine rage,*" [he was taken with a sudden rage] (Laud misc. 570, fol. 66v; cf. Christine, *Epistre,* 283, ll. 11–12). Scrope carelessly translates, "Thanne were *thei* overleid with a sodeyne rage," despite the French verb's singular, not plural, form (*Epistle* 73, l. 11). In Chapter 19's treatment of Athamas and Ino, when the goddess of wrath makes them go mad, it is because "*la deesse virent tant espouentable*" [they saw the goddess so frightening] (Laud misc. 570, fol. 41v; cf. Christine, *Epistre,* 228, ll. 28–29). All manuscripts show evidence of fumbling with this phrase: the earliest version recorded in L notes "that the goodes saw theyme so ferefull," and S and M (or their exemplars) may omit "goodes" in an attempt to make more sense of the content, but "that thei sawe them so feerfull" is still inaccurate (*Epistle* 28, ll. 21–22). Even though some variants could be attributed to scribal error or correction, it seems unlikely that multiple scribes would commit consistently the same kinds of mistakes, much less the identical mistakes, that we find in most of the above examples.

Given Scrope's ignorance or indifference, a new problem arises: how do we separate Scrope the hasty translator from Scrope the potentially antifeminist translator, if that is even possible? The two would seem to collide in the translation of Christine's defense of Pasiphaë, which can serve as a useful example:

> Pour tant se Pasiphé fu fole,
> Ne vueilles lire a ton escole
> Que telles soient toutes femmes,
> Car il est maintes vaillans dames. (Laud misc. 570, fol. 57r; cf. Christine, *Epistre,* 263, ll. 2–5)
>
> Knowing that this Pasiphe was a fool,
> In no wise lerne thou not of *here* scool.
> Though that som wommen do soo amys,
> Yit right many goode there be, ywis. (*Epistle,* 56, ll. 24–27)

Christine refers to "*ton escole*" [your school], addressing masculine readers and admonishing them not to accept traditional male bodies of knowledge that claim all women are like Pasiphaë. Scrope turns "*ton escole*" into "here scool," a warning that the reader not learn from Pasiphaë herself, and he fails to dismiss the antifeminist staple that all women are like Pasiphaë, instead suggesting that *some* women are like her. He retains the defense that there are good women. He maintains Christine's *glose* interpretation of Pasiphaë's bestiality as instead the love of a bullish man and her warning that not all women are like Pasiphaë, and to be fair, he does not excoriate Pasiphaë further, as does the translator of the anonymous, independent translation, *The Lytle Bibell of Knyghthod,* who introduces a greater emphasis on her lewdness.[37] But Scrope either misses or resists Christine's opening critique of antifeminist thought and her insistence that men must contemplate and reject their stereotypes of women's sexuality. Still, Scrope paradoxically translates Christine's *glose* defenses while exhibiting the more expected antifeminism of his era in the *texte.*

This kind of disconnection is common throughout the *Epistle,* almost as if Scrope translated the *textes* independently from the *gloses* without stopping to consider the cohesion of the two parts, thus allowing inconsistencies to exist literally two lines apart. Grammatically, as in the cases of Echo and Medusa above, Scrope's Pasiphaë *texte* is flawed, but the *glose* is more correct. While I primarily am focused on gender inconsistencies, there are larger mistranslations that affect meaning in, for example, Chapter 17, where the *texte* claims that the goddess of madness strangled her children, instead of Athamas strangling his children (as the *glose* correctly reports), and Chapter 33, where Scrope's *texte* invites the reader to "remembre thee" of Neptune, as if the god were the exemplar, rather than to invoke Neptune in hours of maritime need, as the *glose* advises.[38] The number of similar errors suggests that Christine's compact and complex verse *textes* may have presented a particular challenge for Scrope. Indeed, he may have preferred to work in prose: his other major translation project, *The Dicts and Sayings of the Philosophers,* exclusively consists of prose, and the Longleat manuscript's preface to Fastolf indicates that when Scrope produced original material, he chose prose. In fact, one must wonder whether he delayed translating Christine's verse prologue until he prepared copies for other dedicatees, with whom he sought the more formal poet-patron relationship that her prologue describes.

Major (Scribal?) Manuscript Variants and Gender

Nevertheless, those searching for a more progressive view should not give up all hope. The typical indifference to or ignorance of gender in Scrope's manuscripts makes more meaningful the moments where a departure occurs. Regardless of what Scrope may have intended, amid all the scribal errors and corrections there are instances that seem to represent interpretation or deliberate tailoring that deviates from other copies. Because we cannot be certain if individual witnesses are more true to Scrope's original, isolated instances may indicate scribal rather than authorial alterations, but they still offer a potentially more complex consideration of gender than we previously thought possible in the Scrope manuscripts.

When Christine first introduces Othea, the *glose* identifies her as representing the "*sagece de femme*" [wisdom of woman] (Laud misc. 570, fol. 26v; cf. Christine, *Epistre*, 199, ll. 73–74). Scrope makes one of his few additions to Christine's text by inserting "man" into the statement, but the effect of his addition is different in L versus S and M. S and M record Othea as "wisedome of man or woman," as if genders possess separate types of wisdom, but L offers "wysedom of man *and* woman," as if they can both access all types (*Epistle* 6, ll. 18–19; *Epistle*, ed. Warner, 7).[39] Manuscripts S and M also replicate Christine's advice to the good knight to heed his wife's counsel "yif she be wise and wel condicioned," which manuscript L reinterprets: the knight should heed her counsel "if *he* be wyse and well condiciond" (*Epistle* 107, l. 20; *Epistle*, ed. Warner, 101; Laud misc. 570, fol 85r: "*elle*"). L makes the success of counsel dependent upon whether the knight himself possesses the proper qualities, putting the pressure for virtue on the recipient, not the giver, of counsel. Traditionally, concerns about the efficacy of counsel evoked anxiety in the counselor, who could never be certain his or her advice would be well received or heeded.[40] In L's suggestion that the recipient carries responsibility, this copy of Scrope comes closest to the perspective articulated in *The Lytle Bibell of Knyghthod*, which consistently lays at Hector's feet (or the reader's feet) the responsibility for taking and making good use of advice.[41]

Although there is not much, the most significant evidence for a progressive reading of Scrope appears in the M manuscript, the copy dedicated to the unnamed "hye princesse." While it is true that Scrope replicates almost all of Christine's positive views of women and makes few changes for his woman reader, there are small, unexplored differences that may indicate the tailoring of this copy for his dedicatee. The opening prologue now praises the "hye princesse" and her "good ladishipe" rather than the "ryght high prince" and his "mankyndlynes" (*Epistle* 4, ll. 14–24). Recall, too, that M alone refers to Medusa and Echo correctly as female (except in the Medusa *texte*, which still records "him"). M also omits the detail that Alcyone was removed from her husband's ship "with forse" (*Epistle* 96, l. 21), eliminating the potential violence of a forceful removal, and it no longer characterizes the nymph who loved Hermaphroditus as "ful of woo," leaving the reader to interpret her motivation for praying to the gods to join them forever (*Epistle* 100, ll. 13–14).[42] Additionally, M refers to Eolus, the god of wind who causes Ceyx's death as the "goddes" of winds, perhaps demonstrating an ignorance of mythology or perhaps constructing a female antagonist for Alcyone (*Epistle* 96, l. 22).[43]

But the clearest example that M may have been tailored for a woman reader occurs in the final chapter, when Christine enjoins her reader never to be ashamed to hear good advice from any person. Uniquely among the Scrope manuscripts, M reads "Be not ashamid to here trouthe and good techinge *of a woman* or of whom that ever seyeth it, for trouthe nobleth him that pronounceth it" (M fol. 274v; cf. *Epistle* 120, ll. 10–12; emphasis added).[44] As the work concludes, M emphasizes women's wisdom, a reminder to the copy's aristocratic female reader that her words can be important and powerful. These M alterations could be authorial, but we cannot be sure, because M offers a number of unique readings not attested in the other Scrope manuscripts and not linked to Laud misc. 570's French, which suggests that someone—Scrope or a scribe—made alterations to the English sense of the text.[45]

There is one instance in all three manuscripts that introduces women into the text, and because it lacks precedent in Laud misc. 570 or other French manuscripts, it likely originates with Scrope himself. When Scrope renders Christine's advice to embrace a patron saint ("*aucun saint*")—just as sailors should pray to Neptune—he advises "thei scholde take a singulere devocion to some seinte be devoute prayeres, be the which thei may calle to *him or hire* in there besynessis" (*Epistle* 44, ll. 24–26; Christine, *Epistre,* 247, l. 14–15, "*a lui*"). Despite his typical willingness to assume that nouns as well as pronouns with unclear antecedents are masculine, here Scrope acknowledges the power of patron saints—and perhaps his expectation for readers—of both genders. Admittedly, this example is not markedly pro-women, but it is a striking moment where pronouns and gender matter enough for our translator that he introduces the feminine even where Christine had not.

Conclusion

Whatever Scrope's perspectives may have been in real life about women and gender—and even if his preface to Fastolf evidences willful or intentional misogyny—his translation itself registers indifference to grammatical gender and to representations of women, a more passive form of misogyny rather than a deliberate antifeminist program. And this indifference matters, because it gives us a more accurate view of Scrope's process rather than reproducing our own notions about the nature of antifeminism in late-medieval England. His translation, as much as it follows Christine's didactic content with relative faithfulness, nevertheless mistranslates many French grammatical structures, much as we might find in first-year language students, especially when it comes to precision with pronouns.[46] I do not mean to suggest that Scrope did not know French grammar—he certainly is capable of translating correctly and often does—but rather that he did not care enough to parse out the grammatical gender of pronouns separately from the gender of subjects and objects every time. Of course, most translators try to balance expediency with conscientiousness and rarely succeed at both simultaneously. His imprecision and lack of revision may also share roots with the bureaucratic medieval copyists of legal proceedings, who were trained to translate oral proceedings in one language instantaneously into written records in another, with little time to process and no reason to return to edit their texts.[47]

It may be tempting for modern scholars to see antifeminism in Scrope's gendered errors, but extended collation of the three extant manuscripts makes it seem far more likely that they are not part of an underlying program but occur due to Scrope's haste and negligence. Therefore, it is difficult to assert that Scrope masculinizes women or has, specific intention behind his misgenderings; rather, he seems to have been more concerned with getting out Christine's messages about vices and virtues than with gender in any serious way. This evidence not only challenges the general conception of Scrope as antifeminist but also calls into question the quality of his translation.

Let me be clear: I do not mean to make excuses for the antifeminism apparent in Scrope's *Epistle*. After all, antifeminism need not be programmatic to be problematic. My point is that Scrope's antifeminism manifests itself as a part of a larger issue with his process of translation.

We have been reading Scrope on our terms—we know Christine was the author, even if he did not; we know the correct names and genders of the classical figures, even if he did not—and we have used that information to generate a portrait of Scrope as a well-intentioned but antifeminist translator. But when we read Scrope on his own terms, with a close attention to his apparent process of translation, what emerges instead is a sense of a writer rushing through his work, often paying little attention to the finer points of French grammar, which leads to many gendering errors that have little to do with actual human gender and would have been easily remedied had he known mythology better or reviewed his work to amend narrative incongruity. Perhaps Scrope was primarily interested in the morals—which he tends to get correct—and cared little for the accuracy of his narrative exempla. His subsequent translation of *The Dicts and Sayings of the Philosophers,* one of Christine's major sources, may suggest that indeed morality was his top priority.

Alternately, perhaps Scrope's haste could be explained by the fact that his initial dedicatee, his stepfather Fastolf, already owned and presumably could read the *Othea* in French. Moreover, Fastolf commissioned a second French copy, now Laud misc. 570, *after* Scrope's translation, and Laud misc. 570 seems to have had much more invested in it than even the best of Scrope's manuscripts, if the quality of script and illuminations are any indicators. In other words, Fastolf may not have needed or wanted Scrope's translation. We have tended to accept at face value Scrope's claim that he dedicates the translation to Fastolf in the hope that it would be efficacious at reforming his stepfather, but perhaps he was more of a realist and doubted that his stepfather would read the English version beyond the preface anyway.[48] After all, the next text Scrope wrote for Fastolf was the "Schedule of Grievances" outlining his mistreatment by his stepfather (c. 1452).[49] If the preface and *Epistle* were efforts to urge Fastolf more gently to reform, they evidently failed. Regardless of Scrope's purpose or doubts, we must view any misogynist elements within the broader context of a translator who seems indifferent to or ignorant of classical myth, French gendered pronouns, narrative cohesion, and it would seem, precision in translation.

University of Kansas

NOTES

1. Early versions of this article were presented at the Mid-America Medieval Association and at the Ohio State University Center for Medieval and Renaissance Studies Lecture Series; I am grateful to the audience for their generous and insightful feedback, especially Cynthia Brown, Kathy Krause, Linda Mitchell, Linda Voigts, Ethan Knapp, Sarah-Grace Heller, and Leslie Lockett. I also wish to thank the University of Kansas for sabbatical leave and the Hall Center for the Humanities Research Fellowship for supporting my work on this article and on my upcoming editions of Stephen Scrope's *Epistle of Othea* and the anonymous *Lytel Bibell of Knyghthod* for the TEAMS Middle English Texts series.
2. Gianni Mombello, *La tradizione manoscritta dell' "Epistre Othea" di Christine de Pizan: Prolegomeni all'edizione del testo* (Torino: Accademia delle scienze, 1967), provides description and analysis of all manuscripts to which he had access and, at 359–370, all early printed editions for which he could find evidence. Parussa, ed., *Epistre Othea*, 87–88, adds three manuscripts unexamined by or unknown to Mombello to bring the manuscript total to forty-seven. On the early printed editions, see also Cynthia J. Brown, "The Reconstruction of an Author in Print: Christine de Pizan and the Fifteenth and Sixteenth Centuries," in *Christine de Pizan and the Categories of Difference*, ed. by Marilynn Desmond, Medieval Cultures 14 (Minneapolis: University of Minnesota Press, 1998), 215–235.
3. For editions of the two fifteenth-century translations, see Stephen Scrope, *Stephen Scrope: The Epistle of Othea*, ed. Curt F. Bühler, Early English Text Society, o.s. 264 (Oxford: Oxford University Press, 1970); James D. Gordon, ed., *The Epistle of Othea to Hector. A 'Lytil Bibell of*

Knyghthod.' Edited from the Harleian Manuscript 838 (Philadelphia: University of Pennsylvania, 1942); and my own edition of both Scrope's *Epistle* and the *Bibell* (in process). Note that although the *Bibell* manuscript is dated closer to the turn of the sixteenth century, Gordon's linguistic analysis, xlvii-lxiii, dates the translation to ca. 1450. For recent studies of the translations, see Martha W. Driver, "Christine de Pisan and Robert Wyer: *The .C. Histoires de Troye,* or *L'Epistre d'Othea* Englished," *Gutenberg-Jahrbuch* 72 (1997): 125–139; and my *Feminized Counsel and the Literature of Advice in England, 1380-1500* (Turnhout: Brepols, 2014), 139–191, and "*The Lytle Bibell of Knyghthod,* Christine de Pizan's *Epistre Othea,* and the Problem with Authorial Manuscripts," *Journal of English and Germanic Philology* (forthcoming).

4. Scrope, *Epistle,* 122, ll. 9–10 and l. 24.
5. Scrope's Preface is preserved only in Warminster, Longleat Library and Archives, MS Longleat 253 (L); he later replaced it with a translation of Christine's Prologue to the Duke of Berry, which appears in Cambridge, St. John's College MS H.5 (S) and, partially, with some substitutions, in New York, Pierpont Morgan Library MS M 775 (M). See Scrope, *Epistle,* xiv–xviii, 3–4, and 121–124. For the Duke's Prologue, which is different from the Prologue in London, British Library MS Harley 4431 that appears in modern editions, see Gianni Mombello, "Per un'edizione critica dell'*Epistre Othea* di Christine de Pizan," *Studi Francesi* 25 (1965): 1–12, at 7–8.
6. Or perhaps he merely hoped the work might be pleasing enough to win him some favor with her, an effort that Sonja Drimmer, "Failure before Print: The Case of Stephen Scrope," *Viator* 46 (2015): 343–372, notes went unappreciated.
7. For more detailed descriptions of these items, see Curt F. Bühler's introduction to Scrope, *Epistle,* xiv–xviii; Kathleen L. Scott, *Later Gothic Manuscripts, 1390–1490, A Survey of Manuscripts Illuminated in the British Isles* (London: Harvey Miller, 1996), vol. 1, 264–266; Stephanie V. Gibbs, "Christine de Pizan's *Epistre Othea* in England: The Manuscript Tradition of Stephen Scrope's Translation," in *Contexts and Continuities: Proceedings of the IVth International Colloquium on Christine de Pizan (Glasgow 21–27 July 2000), Published in Honour of Liliane Dulac,* ed. Angus J. Kennedy et al. (Glasgow: University of Glasgow Press, 2002), vol. 2, 397–408; and Drimmer, "Failure before Print."
8. Scrope, *Epistle,* xxi–xxv. All citations of Scrope are to Bühler, unless otherwise noted. There are occasions when S and M agree against L, when S and L agree against M, and when M and L agree against S, leading to Bühler's proposition that each was made from an exemplar modified from Scrope's working copy.

9. Bühler in Scrope, *Epistle*, xiii.
10. Scrope, *Epistle*, xxiv.
11. Drimmer, "Failure before Print," 355–358. The princess is unidentified, though Bühler in Scrope, *Epistle*, xx–xxi, lists possibilities, all of whom he dismisses for various reasons: Eleanor Cobham (extremely unlikely), Anne Beauchamp, Anne Neville Stafford, and Anne de Vere. Jenni Nuttall, "Margaret of Anjou as Patron of English Verse?: The *Liber Proverbiorum* and the *Romans of Partenay*," *Review of English Studies* 67 (2016): 636–659, at 650, adds Margaret of Anjou to the list. Marilynn Desmond, "Reading and Visuality in Stephen Scrope's *Translatio* of Christine de Pizan's *Epistre Othea*," in *Thresholds of Medieval Visual Culture: Liminal Spaces*, ed. Elina Gertsman and Jill Stevenson (Woodbridge, UK: Boydell Press, 2012), 95–122, at 106, argues that the lady was Anne Neville Stafford, the Duke of Buckingham's wife, but evidence remains circumstantial. Although a "Pistill Othea" appears in the will of her daughter Anne de Vere, it is unclear whether that indicates an English copy or one of the many French copies in circulation. If the version preserved in M were produced for Neville Stafford, it would only amplify Drimmer's argument about Scrope's failure, since he would have produced two copies for the same household, decreasing further the circulation of his work; if M is indeed the original itself and a second Stafford family copy, these circumstances also may explain how Astley easily acquired the original.
12. The Longleat Library and Archives do not offer reproductions. Stephen Scrope, *The Epistle of Othea to Hector, or The Boke of Knyghthode, Translated from the French of Christine de Pisan with a Dedication to Sir John Fastolf, K.G. by Stephen Scrope, Esquire*, ed. George F. Warner (London: J. B. Nichols and Sons, 1904), provides an edition of the text, but the reader should be cautioned that the edition is hampered by typos, errors, and failures to mention dittography (many of which are remedied in Bühler's *Epistle* textual notes). Drimmer, "Failure before Print," 346–350, suggests that L may be Scrope's original copy for Fastolf and necessarily incomplete, in performance of the penury that, alongside the injunctions to moral virtue in the text, was intended to persuade Fastolf to relinquish his stepson's inheritance. Textually, L contains too many scribal errors to be plausible as Scrope's original, but Drimmer's theory could apply to its lost exemplar. On the fraught relationship between Scrope and Fastolf, see Jonathan Hughes, "Stephen Scrope and the Circle of Sir John Fastolf: Moral and Intellectual Outlooks," in *Medieval Knighthood IV: Papers from the Fifth Strawberry Hill Conference 1990*, ed. Christopher Harper-Bill and Ruth Harvey (Woodbridge, UK: Boydell Press, 1992),

109–145; and "Scrope, Stephen (1397–1472)," in *Oxford Dictionary of National Biography* (Oxford 2004), http://www.oxforddnb.com/view/article/66283.

13. Warner in Scrope, *Epistle*, ed. Warner, xx, speculates that the scribe intended to provide the Wycliffite English translations. This seems unlikely because of the number of times that he begins to copy the Latin, but at least one of Christine's French scribes had a similar impulse: the Cologny-Geneva Bodmer MS 49 translates the Latin into French (and also simplifies Christine's complex French). On Bodmer, see Jacqueline Cerquiglini-Toulet and Hélène Basso, *Epître d'Othéa: Coffret en 2 volumes* (Geneva: Fondation Martin Bodmer, 2008).
14. See also Bühler's observations in Scrope, *Epistle*, xxi–xxv. Bühler dismisses L as the most corrupt and incomplete (it does have substantial lacunae), but his purpose is to justify his choice of S as the base manuscript for his edition (ibid., xxiv); in my view, L's readings remain relevant to our exploration of the transmission of Scrope's text itself. Meanwhile, M exhibits many unique variants that suggest scribal substitutions of new English phrases for existing English phrases, independent of the French original, so I consider it less authoritative in some instances than Bühler.
15. Bühler, in Scrope, *Epistle*, xxv–xxvi, refers to Laud misc. 570 as a "sister-manuscript" copied from Scrope's source; Laud misc. 570 contains errors and variants, such as eyeskip or doublets, that are not transmitted by Scrope, so it was clearly not his exemplar. See also Scott, *Later Gothic Manuscripts,* vol. 1, 265. As Drimmer, "Failure before Print," 358, points out, the fact that Fastolf commissioned a French copy after Scrope's translation suggests Scrope's lack of success.
16. The most convenient access to these unique readings is found by consulting Gabriella Parussa, ed., *Christine de Pizan: Epistre Othea* (Geneva: Droz, 1999), which contains an appendix of textual variants, though some variants also appear in footnotes to the text if Parussa has emended the Harley 4431 reading.
17. See, e.g., Bühler's comments in Scrope, *Epistle*, xxix. In defense of the Babyngton manuscript and the Wyer translation, both translators relied on source manuscripts that vary significantly from Harley 4431, so their translations may be quite close to their source yet still not resemble the Queen's Manuscript. Note: Babyngton can be identified only as the copyist of the unique translation in British Library Harley MS 838; he is unlikely to be the translator; see *Bibell*, xxxi, lxii–lxiii. On the translations' relationship to French manuscripts, see Schieberle, *Feminized Counsel*, 168–191, and "*The Lytle Bibell of Knyghthod*, Christine de Pizan's *Epistre Othea*, and the Problem with Authorial Manuscripts."

18. For details on Scrope's formative years, his employment in his stepfather's household, and the inheritance that was never relinquished during Fastolf's lifetime, see Hughes, "Stephen Scrope," 109–146.
19. See Jane Chance, "Gender Subversion and Linguistic Castration in Fifteenth-Century English Translations of Christine de Pizan," in *Violence against Women in Medieval Texts*, ed. Anna Roberts (Gainesville: University Press of Florida, 1998), 161–194, at 168–169; Dhira B. Mahoney, "Middle English Regenderings of Christine de Pizan," in *The Medieval Opus: Imitation, Rewriting, and Transmission in the French Tradition: Proceedings of the Symposium Held at the Institute for Research in the Humanities, October 5–7, 1994, at the University of Wisconsin Madison*, ed. Douglas Kelly (Amsterdam: Rodopi, 1996), 405–427, at 407–409; and Nancy Bradley Warren, *Women of God and Arms: Female Spirituality and Political Conflict, 1380–1600* (Philadelphia: University of Pennsylvania Press, 2005), 58–86.
20. Jennifer Summit, *Lost Property: The Woman Writer and English Literary History, 1380–1589* (Chicago: University of Chicago Press, 2000), 73–74. Of course, the prologue to the Duke of Berry (the one to which Scrope had access) also lacks the discussion of Christine's lineage and her name, and it also presents her as the compiler of the volume, a term that in both French and English could refer to the actual writing itself or just the act of collecting others' writings.
21. *Feminized Counsel*, 158–159. See also Desmond, "Reading and Visuality," 104; and Laurie Finke, "The Politics of the Canon: Christine de Pizan and the Fifteenth-Century Chaucerians," *Exemplaria* 19 (2007): 27–31. On presentation portraits that feature patrons, not authors, see Michel-André Bossy, "Arms and the Bride: Christine de Pizan's Military Treatise as a Wedding Gift for Margaret of Anjou," in *Christine de Pizan and the Categories of Difference*, ed. by Marilynn Desmond, Medieval Cultures 14 (Minneapolis: University of Minnesota Press, 1998), 236–256, at 237–240.
22. Desmond, "Reading and Visuality," 108–109.
23. Schieberle, *Feminized Counsel*, 165.
24. Ardis Butterfield, "Rough Translation: Charles d'Orléans, Lydgate, and Hoccleve," in *Rethinking Medieval Translation: Ethics, Politics, Theory*, ed. Emma Campbell and Robert Mills (Suffolk, UK: D.S. Brewer, 2012), 204–225, at 206.
25. Bühler, in Scrope, *Epistle*, xxiii n., observes that Scrope and all three of his scribes also erroneously represent the names of Marcisus (Narcissus), Percival (Perseus), Oan (Pan), and Colus (Eolus).

26. All quotations are from Scrope, *Epistle,* ed. Bühler, unless otherwise noted. I have regularized word divisions, used i/j and u/v according to modern usage, and distinguished "thee" from "the." All italicizations represent my emphasis.
27. I present the S and L pronouns; Bühler's edition uses the M readings.
28. In the French, "serpent" can be masculine or feminine, according to the *Dictionnaire Moyen Français,* but Christine's text specifies "la serpent" here (versus "le serpent" when she refers to Cadmus in Ch. 28).
29. Bühler's edition suggests that he considers M's readings to be evidence that Scrope translated correctly and the S and L scribes introduced identical corruptions. I find it more likely that S and L record the original reading and M an independent correction.
30. See Millard Meiss, "Atropos-Mors: Observations on a Rare Early Humanist Image," in *Florilegium Historiale: Essays Presented to Wallace K. Ferguson,* ed. J. G. Rowe (Toronto, Canada: University of Toronto Press, 1971), 151–159. Both the Queen's Manuscript, London, British Library Harley 4431, and Paris, BNF MS fr. 606, among others, contain illuminations of Christine's unmistakably female Atropos. Laud misc. 570 correctly contains the feminine past participle "nottee," which suggests the likely accuracy of Scrope's source.
31. Meiss, "Atropos-Mors," notes that Christine's image is unusual; in the English literary context, such as Chaucer's *Pardoner's Tale,* Langland's *Piers Plowman,* and Lydgate's *Pilgrimage of the Life of Man,* Death is masculine.
32. This "*Et*" is unique to Laud misc. 570 and was probably in the manuscript source Laud misc. 570 and Scrope shared, leading to Scrope's "Bothe."
33. Ovid, *Metamorphoses,* trans. Stanley Lombardo (Indianapolis, IN: Hackett, 2010), 2.593–635.
34. Scrope misapprehends "*N'occis*" [do not kill] as the imperative of "*noter*" (Bühler, in Scrope, *Epistle,* 160n).
35. The only manuscript variant affecting pronouns is the L reading "this jurneye" instead of "his journay" in l. 27. Laud misc. 570 does omit "*case*" and records "*avancie*" instead of "*avanciee.*"
36. In at least one instance, Scrope strangely prefers "it" to choosing a gendered pronoun: regarding Aurora, he translates "*Aurora . . . c'est une deesse*" and "*elle rejoyssoit tous*" (Laud misc. 570, fol. 56v–57r; cf. Christine, *Epistre,* 261, l. 8, 262, ll. 12–13) as "Aurora . . . it is a goddesse" and "it rejoiced all those" (Scrope, *Epistle,* 56, ll. 2–3, 7).
37. *Bibell,* 73–74.
38. Scrope, *Epistle,* 27, l. 29 (perhaps by confusing French "*fist*" [to make] with a term for fiercely; cp. Christine, *Epistre,* 17.4), and 44, l. 13 (Scrope either mistranslates "*reclamer*" [to invoke/ask for help], which he

correctly translates three times in the *glose* and *allegorie*, or recasts the *texte* in the same model as those that establish an exemplar and enjoin the reader to remember or think on that person). There are many other similar errors, e.g., in translating Chapter 13's verb "livrera" [provided/delivered], which describes Minerva's provision of Hector with armor, Scrope uses "signed" in the *texte* but "delivered" in the *glose* and *allegorie*. Bühler's glossary in Scrope, *Epistle*, 225, expresses uncertainty about Scrope's choice of "signed," suggesting that he must mean "assigned" or "attested"; MED, *signen*, v., def. e, indicates that "signen of" could mean "provide, allot," but the only example is Scrope's, making that definition potentially suspect as the rationalization of an error.

39. Desmond, "Reading and Visuality," 112, 116, initially reads Scrope's broadening of Christine's original as a move towards a gender-neutral translation but ultimately sees it as a failed effort because the work ends with the Sybil, an image of exclusively female wisdom.
40. See, e.g., Roberta Krueger, "Christine's Anxious Lessons: Gender, Morality, and the Social Order from the Enseignemens to the Avision," in *Christine de Pizan and the Categories of Difference*, ed. Marilynn Desmond (Minneapolis: University of Minnesota Press, 1998), 16–40; Judith Ferster, *Fictions of Advice: The Literature and Politics of Counsel in Late Medieval England* (Philadelphia: University of Pennsylvania Press, 1996); and Richard Firth Green, *Poets and Princepleasers: Literature and the English Court in the Late Middle Ages* (Toronto, Canada: University of Toronto Press, 1980).
41. In, *Feminized Counsel*, 181–186, I note that this idea is latent in Christine but brought to the fore by the *Bibell* translator.
42. Neither of these changes can be explained by eyeskip, which is often the culprit in such omissions.
43. In all three manuscripts, Eolus' name is misspelled as "Colus," so it is also possible that the M scribe might have attempted to make sense of the error by constructing a goddess rather than a god.
44. There is also an unusual alteration to a statement by Augustine in Chapter 94, which should indicate that when *we* speak wisely, the words come from God, not ourselves, and when *we* endure adversity, the strength comes from God, not ourselves; M alone refers to when *he* speaks or *he* endures, referring back to Augustine instead of the reader (Laud misc. 570: "*nous parlerons . . . nous endurons*"). I can fathom no purpose for excluding women, here, though the alteration could have that effect.
45. For example, M records "worthinesse" for "hardynes" at *Epistle*, 43, l. 5 (Laud misc. 570: "*hardement*"); it offers "bene full" rather than "the victorye" at *Epistle* 104, l. 11 (Laud misc. 570: "*victoire*"); and it has

"undir that tre" for "undir the laurere" at *Epistle,* 106, l. 18 (Laud misc. 570: "*soubz le lorier*"), among other similar substitutions.

46. There are also basic reading errors too numerous to list, but, for example, Scrope's seemingly strange reference to the frail vessel in which "the liif is inne al nakid" (*Epistle,* 27, l. 20) results from reading "est sa vie contenue" [his life is contained] (Christine, *Epistre,* 227, ll. 26–27) as "est sa vie toute nue"; in translating "Sur toute riens toute ta vie" [Above everything all your life], Scrope apparently confuses "vie" [life] with a form of "voir" [to see], producing "that though maist see with ighe" (Christine, *Epistre,* 229, l. 4; Scrope, *Epistle,* 29, l. 15).
47. In legal proceedings of the fourteenth and fifteenth centuries, cases were conducted in French or English and translated simultaneously into Latin. Certain bureaucrats would be accustomed to such instantaneous translation and make errors like Scrope's all the time. See, e.g., M. T. Clanchy, *From Memory to Written Record: England 1066–1307,* 3d ed. (Wiley-Blackwell, 2013), 199–225; and W. M. Ormrod, "The Use of English: Language, Law, and Political Culture in Fourteenth-Century England," *Speculum* 78 (2003):750–787, esp. 775–776 and n. I am grateful to Linda Mitchell for suggesting the parallel to court records.
48. See Desmond, "Reading and Visuality," 101–103, for one reading of Scrope's translation as an intensely personal and emotional project.
49. Gibbs, "Christine," 407.

WORKS CITED

Manuscripts

Cambridge, St. John's College MS H.5.
London, British Library Harley 4431.
New York, Pierpont Morgan Library MS M 775.
Oxford, Bodleian Library MS Laud misc. 570.
Paris, BNF MS fr. 606.
Warminster, Longleat Library and Archives, MS Longleat 253.

Additional Sources

Anon. *The Epistle of Othea to Hector: A "Lytil Bibell of Knyghthod" Edited from the Harleian Manuscript 838,* ed. James D. Gordon. Philadelphia: University of Pennsylvania, 1942.

Bossy, Michel-André. "Arms and the Bride: Christine de Pizan's Military Treatise as a Wedding Gift for Margaret of Anjou." In *Christine de Pizan and the Categories of Difference,* ed. Marilynn Desmond, 236–256. Medieval Cultures 14 (Minneapolis: University of Minnesota Press, 1998).

Brown, Cynthia J. "The Reconstruction of an Author in Print: Christine de Pizan and the Fifteenth and Sixteenth Centuries." In *Christine de Pizan and the Categories of Difference*, ed. Marilynn Desmond, 215–235. Medieval Cultures 14 (Minneapolis: University of Minnesota Press, 1998).

Butterfield, Ardis. "Rough Translation: Charles d'Orléans, Lydgate, and Hoccleve." In *Rethinking Medieval Translation: Ethics, Politics, Theory*, ed. Emma Campbell and Robert Mills, 204–225. Cambridge, UK: D.S. Brewer, 2012.

Cerquiglini-Toulet, Jacqueline and Hélène Basso, *Epître d'Othéa: Coffret en 2 volumes*. Geneva: Fondation Martin Bodmer, 2008.

Chance, Jane. "Gender Subversion and Linguistic Castration in Fifteenth-Century English Translations of Christine de Pizan." In *Violence against Women in Medieval Texts*, ed. Anna Roberts, 161–194. Gainesville: University Press of Florida, 1998.

Christine de Pizan, *Christine de Pizan Epistre Othea*, ed. Gabriella Parussa. Geneva: Droz, 1999.

Clanchy, M. T. *From Memory to Written Record: England 1066–1307*, 3d ed. Chichester, UK: Wiley-Blackwell, 2013.

Desmond, Marilynn. "Reading and Visuality in Stephen Scrope's *Translatio* of Christine de Pizan's *Epistre Othea*." In *Thresholds of Medieval Visual Culture: Liminal Spaces*, ed. Elina Gertsman and Jill Stevenson, 95–122. Woodbridge, UK: Boydell Press, 2012.

Drimmer, Sonja. "Failure before Print: The Case of Stephen Scrope." *Viator* 46 (2015): 343–372.

Driver, Martha W. "Christine de Pisan and Robert Wyer: *The .C. Histoires de Troye*, or *L'Epistre d'Othea* Englished." *Gutenberg-Jahrbuch* 72 (1997): 125–139.

Ferster, Judith. *Fictions of Advice: The Literature and Politics of Counsel in Late Medieval England*. (Philadelphia: University of Pennsylvania Press, 1996).

Finke, Laurie. "The Politics of the Canon: Christine de Pizan and the Fifteenth-Century Chaucerians." *Exemplaria* 19 (2007): 27–31.

Gibbs, Stephanie V. "Christine de Pizan's *Epistre Othea* in England: The Manuscript Tradition of Stephen Scrope's Translation." In *Contexts and Continuities: Proceedings of the IVth International Colloquium on Christine de Pizan (Glasgow 21–27 July 2000), Published in Honour of Liliane Dulac*, ed. Angus J. Kennedy et al., vol. 2, 397–408. Glasgow: University of Glasgow Press, 2002.

Green, Richard Firth. *Poets and Princepleasers: Literature and the English Court in the Late Middle Ages*. (Toronto, Canada: University of Toronto Press, 1980).

Hughes, Jonathan. "Stephen Scrope and the Circle of Sir John Fastolf: Moral and Intellectual Outlooks." In *Medieval Knighthood IV: Papers from the Fifth Strawberry Hill Conference 1990*, ed. Christopher Harper-Bill and Ruth Harvey, 109–145. Woodbridge, UK: Boydell Press, 1992.

———. "Scrope, Stephen (1397–1472)." In *Oxford Dictionary of National Biography*. Oxford: Oxford University Press, 2004. http://www.oxforddnb.com/view/article/66283.

Krueger, Roberta. "Christine's Anxious Lessons: Gender, Morality, and the Social Order from the Enseignemens to the Avision." In *Christine de Pizan and the Categories of Difference*, ed. Marilynn Desmond, 16–40. Minneapolis: University of Minnesota Press, 1998.

Mahoney, Dhira B. "Middle English Regenderings of Christine de Pizan." In *The Medieval Opus: Imitation, Rewriting, and Transmission in the French Tradition: Proceedings of the Symposium Held at the Institute for Research in the Humanities, October 5–7, 1994, at the University of Wisconsin Madison*, ed. Douglas Kelly, 405–427. Amsterdam: Rodopi, 1996.

Meiss, Millard. "Atropos-Mors: Observations on a Rare Early Humanist Image." In *Florilegium Historiale: Essays Presented to Wallace K. Ferguson*, ed. J. G. Rowe, 151–159. Toronto, Canada: University of Toronto Press, 1971.

Mombello, Gianni. *La tradizione manoscritta dell' "Epistre Othea" di Christine de Pizan: Prolegomeni all'edizione del testo*. (Torino: Accademia delle scienze, 1967).

———. "Per un'edizione critica dell'*Epistre Othea* di Christine de Pizan." *Studi Francesi* 25 (1965): 1–12.

Nuttall, Jenni. "Margaret of Anjou as Patron of English Verse?: The *Liber Proverbiorum* and the *Romans of Partenay*." *Review of English Studies* 67 (2016): 636–659.

Ormrod, W. M. "The Use of English: Language, Law, and Political Culture in Fourteenth-Century England." *Speculum* 78 (2003): 750–787.

Ovid, *Metamorphoses*, trans. Stanley Lombardo. Indianapolis, IN: Hackett, 2010.

Schieberle, Misty. *Feminized Counsel and the Literature of Advice in England, 1380–1500*. Turnhout, Belgium: Brepols, 2014.

———. "*The Lytle Bibell of Knyghthod*, Christine de Pizan's *Epistre Othea*, and the Problem with Authorial Manuscripts." *Journal of English and Germanic Philology* (forthcoming).

Scott, Kathleen L. *Later Gothic Manuscripts, 1390–1490, A Survey of Manuscripts Illuminated in the British Isles*, vol. 1, 264–266. London: Harvey Miller, 1996.

Scrope, Stephen. *The Epistle of Othea to Hector, or The Boke of Knyghthode, Translated from the French of Christine de Pisan with a Dedication to Sir John Fastolf, K.G. by Stephen Scrope, Esquire*, ed. George F. Warner. London: J. B. Nichols and Sons, 1904.

———. *Stephen Scrope: The Epistle of Othea*, ed. Curt F. Bühler, Early English Text Society, o.s. 264. Oxford: Oxford University Press, 1970.

Summit, Jennifer. *Lost Property: The Woman Writer and English Literary History, 1380–1589*. Chicago: University of Chicago Press, 2000.

Warren, Nancy Bradley. *Women of God and Arms: Female Spirituality and Political Conflict, 1380–1600*. Philadelphia: University of Pennsylvania Press, 2005.

Anne of Cleves in Book and Manuscript

VALERIE SCHUTTE

Anne of Cleves is perhaps the least known of King Henry VIII's six wives. She is the sole subject of only three scholarly works,[1] and one recent study of the queens of England describes Anne as a "non-event."[2] She is certainly lost among studies of literature and humanism associated with Henry VIII and his wives.[3] James Carley, in his important work on the books associated with Henry and his six consorts, mentions her in a single sentence, while Jane Seymour is mentioned twice, and Henry's other four wives are given entire chapters.[4] Anne is overshadowed by the literary production, exceptional educations, or the interest in books and manuscripts of Catherine of Aragon, Anne Boleyn, and Katherine Parr. Anne may not have contributed to the *Book of Common Prayer* as Katherine Parr did, or been a patron of humanism like Anne Boleyn and Catherine of Aragon, but her impact on Tudor literature should not be ignored or relegated to one sentence.[5] However small Anne of Cleves's footprint was on Tudor literary culture, she does not deserve to be overlooked in studies of Henry VIII and his wives. This essay explores the extant books that mention Anne, were dedicated to her, or were written about her to show how she was represented in Tudor books and manuscripts.

This essay will offer the first compilation of books associated with Anne of Cleves. Although these books are few, this study is important; Anne of Cleves should not simply be passed over because she was queen for only six months. The sparse evidence left behind regarding Anne does not give any indication if and to what extent Anne read and used printed books and manuscripts herself. While this may make Anne unremarkable from Carley's perspective, she was still used and represented in books, primarily as a political tool. Books associated with Anne reveal that contrary to the case with Henry's other five wives, Henry's marriage to Anne was anticipated because Henry and Anne's marriage took nearly two-and-a-half years of negotiations, and so authors were able to mention that anticipation in their texts. Also, these texts show that there was international interest in Anne's marital situation and annulment and that she was remembered in publications within the half-century after her death. Books associated with Anne indicate that as a foreign bride she was well liked, eagerly awaited, and not religiously polemical, even though the myth still prevails that Anne was chosen for her and her family's Lutheran beliefs.

Anne of Cleves, daughter of John III, Duke of Cleves, and his wife Maria, arrived in England on December 27, 1539, after lengthy marriage negotiations and numerous weather delays. On New Year's Eve of that year, Anne and Henry had their fateful first encounter, in which Henry dressed in disguise to meet his bride and then took immediate dislike to her appearance and her reaction to his advances. On New Year's Day, Henry was still reeling from the previous day's meeting and could not be bothered personally to give Anne the New Year's gift of furs that he had for her, instead having Anthony Browne deliver them to Anne.[6] Her marriage to Henry did not take place until January 6, 1540, nearly one week after the New Year's festivities.

Both the timing and the brevity of Anne and Henry's marriage contributed to the paucity of evidence regarding Anne's association with and possible ownership of books. New Year's was the most common time for offering gifts to the monarch, and with Anne and Henry's marriage taking place immediately after New Year's of 1540 and being annulled prior to the following New Year, there would have been no celebratory occasion to present Anne with books during her marriage.[7] Anne never had the opportunity to develop her patronage of English books, nor was she one who would receive books and pass them to others to spread literacy, learning, and religious doctrine. Moreover, there is no evidence indicating that books were given to Anne after her marriage, so if any were, they were not recorded or were given to her privately. Nor does her will mention any ownership of books to bequeath to friends or members of her household.[8]

None of this is surprising, as Anne knew no English until she began her journey to England to marry Henry, so she may not have been able to receive and read the vernacular books that were becoming popular in England at that time.[9] Importantly, as noted by Carley, the timing of the Cleves marriage was one of relative religious stability in England; Henry's collection always grew most rapidly when he needed information from books to support his religious position. During his first annulment he acquired many books, as he also did when he intercepted several books during the dissolution of the monasteries. Throughout his marriage with Anne of Cleves, Henry had no need to acquire books rapidly, leaving even less opportunity for books to be owned by them together or bound with both of their initials or insignia.[10] All that is extant to suggest that Anne owned any books at all is a five-line inscription by Anne to Henry in a Book of Hours.[11] This article discusses that inscription by Anne as well as how Anne was written about in sixteenth-century books.

Anne in Book Dedications to Henry VIII

Henry VIII received at least sixty printed book dedications and numerous manuscript dedications. During his marriages, it was not uncommon for books to be jointly dedicated to Henry and his current wife, and even one of his children, as was the case with Giles Duwes's dedication in *An introductory for to lerne to rede, to pronounce, and to speake Frenche*, dedicated to Henry VIII, Queen Anne Boleyn, and Princess Elizabeth.[12] Other books simply replaced the name of one queen with another as Henry remarried, which was the case for an English-language Bible in which Henry and Anne Boleyn were the dedicatees in the first edition, and Henry and Jane Seymour were the dedicatees in the next edition.[13] Henry received two printed book dedications that mentioned Anne of Cleves, yet neither was dedicated to them jointly. Rather, both allude to the Cleves marriage.

Retha Warnicke shows that Henry's marriage to Anne of Cleves followed common protocol for an international royal marriage, but this marriage was unique for Henry, as Anne was the only foreign bride for whom he negotiated.[14] Although Catherine of Aragon was Spanish, she had previously been married to Arthur, Henry's brother, and had been in England for seven years before Henry married her. All of Henry's other brides were English ladies whom Henry courted personally rather than through his ambassadors. Therefore, Henry's two-and-a-half-year search for a bride offered a unique situation within England. It allowed for those seeking patronage and position to appeal to Henry for a place or wage to serve Henry's new bride. It also created excitement in England in anticipation of a more public marriage celebration than with Henry's third wedding.[15]

In this light, Richard Taverner dedicated his translation of *An Epitome of the Psalmes* to Henry VIII in 1539 and mentioned Henry's upcoming nuptials but did not mention the bride by name.[16] Taverner was a devoted translator and reformer. He was associated with Thomas Cromwell, with whom he began a professional relationship in the early 1530s, and went on to act as Cromwell's chief propagandist for religious reform.[17] In his dedication to Henry, Taverner writes of how he had previously worked for the Lord Privy Seal, Thomas Cromwell, but that three years ago, he entered

Henry's service and since then had been employed to do translations and other exercises. Taverner explains that he knows his translation is rude, but as Henry is a good king, Taverner hopes Henry will accept the translation, which will in turn increase its readership. As for Anne of Cleves, Taverner hopes God will:

> sende you the thynge that the most wyse kynge Salomon esteemed for the swetest and beste porcion of mans lyfe, and for a treasure inestimable, that is to wyte, a prudent and wyse lady to your maiesties wyfe and to our youre moost addicte subiectes Quene, whyche accordynge to the voyce of the prophete, maye be as a frutfull vyne in your maiesties house, furnyshed wyth chyldren lyke olyue braunches rounde about your graces table.[18]

Taverner continues that God has already heard his prayers and that "thys lady moost excellent" is "in iorney readye to be transported into your graces realme."[19] Taverner then wishes Anne a safe and speedy journey so that she arrives when Henry is ready for her. He concludes by wishing Anne will be pleasing to both Henry and his people.

Taverner, as an instrument of both Cromwell and Henry, appears to have had much information regarding the Cleves marriage; he anticipates Anne's arrival and wishes that she will give Henry both happiness and more heirs. Although the allusion to Anne is brief, this dedication is important because it shows the connection between Taverner, Cromwell, Anne, and Henry and accurately depicts layers of patronage at work. Henry was a patron of both Cromwell and Taverner. Cromwell previously employed Taverner and was the chief commissioner of the Cleves marriage. Taverner was instructed by Cromwell to translate this text and chose to present it to Henry and allude to his upcoming nuptials. Ultimately, Cromwell was executed due in part to his orchestration of the Cleves marriage. In the dedication it is not clear if Taverner is praising Henry's upcoming marriage because he thinks it will reap better rewards for himself or because Cromwell wants him to offer support for the match in print. No matter what, things did not work out the way Taverner thought God had planned them.

Walter Delaine, or Galterum Deloenum, as he signed in Latin, presented Henry a New Year's gift of a Latin New Testament in 1540.[20] Printed by John Mayler, it was the first separate Latin New Testament printed in England. Delaine's dedicatory preface to Henry is a staggering twenty leaves (forty pages) in Latin and is dated December 1539, very shortly before Anne arrived on English soil. On the first folio of the dedication, Delaine explains why he undertook the writing of this text and chose to dedicate it to Henry, citing that "nunc nouis nuptiis parare," or that Henry was preparing for the upcoming nuptials.[21] Anne is not mentioned by name, but the fact that Henry was engaging in a publicized, foreign marriage allowed Delaine to offer his New Testament as both a New Year's gift and a wedding present. Twice in the dedication Delaine calls himself Henry's "biblioscopum," or biblioscoper (the definition is unclear but is not the same as a librarian; perhaps it means one who searches for specific books), suggesting that Delaine and Henry already had an existing relationship having to do with the acquisition of books. But this dedication was a further attempt to gain Henry's patronage and support for a Latin New Testament.[22] This is another example of how the lengthy negotiations for the foreign marriage to Anne of Cleves allowed clients to appeal to Henry for patronage not only by offering him a gift but also by wishing him well in his upcoming marriage, an opportunity not afforded with Henry's other marriages. In these two dedications to Henry, Anne was welcomed as Henry's new bride, though not by name but in idea, and represented as a source of happiness for a king who thus far had had matrimonial troubles.

Books Dedicated to Anne of Cleves

During Anne's time in England, she was the recipient of two printed book dedications.[23] While neither of these dedications proves that Anne owned either of these books or that she had any hand in their production, they do suggest that Anne was an important figure in England and perhaps was a rallying point for those who did not agree with Henry's religious position or treatment of women.

Sometime during her brief tenure as queen, Anne of Cleves received the dedication of Sir Thomas Elyot's *Defence of Good Women*.[24] Elyot was a clerk of the Privy Chamber but was relieved of his position because he did not support Henry's annulment of his marriage to Catherine of Aragon. While Elyot was a known sympathizer of Catherine's, he was distressed not so much by the annulment itself but by the fear that Henry was being tyrannical and placing himself above the commonweal in granting himself a divorce.[25] Later, Elyot was in the entourage of men and women who received Anne when she entered England, which most likely explains why he chose her to be the dedicatee of his book; most likely he gave this to her as a wedding gift so as to gain her favor and patronage.[26]

Defence was printed in two editions, the first in 1540 and the second in 1545, yet Elyot wrote it sometime between 1531 and 1538.[27] The dedication to Anne was not included in the 1545 edition. Elyot's book is often cited for the rhetorical similarities between his main character, Queen Zenobia, and Catherine of Aragon, both of whom were foreign and educated and who educated their children.[28] This is not the place to go into those comparisons;

note, though, that this is an example of "how one book could be adapted and dedicated to support many causes at the same time"; it was quite common for dedicators to use veiled criticism to both praise and critique a monarch's actions or lack thereof.[29]

In a standard format for early-modern book dedications, the dedication begins: "To the most noble and moste vertuouse princesse Quene Anne, wife vnto the moste excellent prynce our moste graciouse soueraygne lorde, kynge Henry the. VIII. Thomas Elyot knight desyreth all honour."[30] Elyot tells Anne that he has read of Queen Zenobia and has decided to translate her story into English so that it could be read especially by women, so they would be encouraged to "imbrace vertue more gladly."[31] While his idea that women needed their virtue fortified seems chauvinistic by modern standards, increasing one's virtue was a common theme among books directed to early-modern ladies, especially when dedicated to royal ladies, who were expected to serve as examples for other women.[32] However, Elyot equally sees his book as written for the benefit of men; he notes how many men rebuke women for no cause, yet when they need a woman for some reason, they offer her praises. Elyot decided to make a treatise defending virtuous women and settled on the story of Zenobia, the third-century empress of Palmyra who fought against Rome yet fostered great court culture.

After explaining why he chose the story of Zenobia and the dialogue format of his book, Elyot returns to Anne of Cleves, as he sees her as a model of virtue and nobility. He dedicates this book to her "humbly desurung your highnesse in suche wyse to accepte my good wyll and seruice and this littell warke as your owne."[33] He hopes that "vnder your gracis protection and sauour it may saufely passe through the daungerouse rase of dysdayne and enuy, and be receyued thankfully and ioyousely of al good women in this your noble realme."[34] Here, Elyot appeals to Anne to fulfill the traditional, queenly role of intercessor and supreme example for all women by accepting his book and then passing it along to others to be read.

However, there is one particular sentence of Elyot's dedication that makes it clear that he did not know Anne personally, but blindly addressed his dedication to her in hopes of patronage. At the very beginning of the dedication Elyot tells Anne that this book could be used to teach Englishwomen virtue and "shulde be radde in our owne language."[35] This sentence is odd, because Anne of Cleves barely spoke any English at the time of her wedding, and if Elyot was in the entourage that brought her from Cleves, he should have been aware of that. It is also evidence that perhaps Elyot did not customize his dedication to Anne. If Elyot first wrote his text sometime between 1531 and 1538, but it was not published until 1540, it could have initially contained a dedication to a different queen, and Anne's name was substituted in the dedication in the 1540 printing. Both of Henry's queens during the years 1531 to 1538 (Anne Boleyn, who reigned from 1533 to 1536, and Jane Seymour, who reigned from 1536 to 1537) were native English speakers, so the dedication and all of its vague references to Anne's virtue and intercessorial powers could have applied to one of these queens. In dedicating his book to Anne in 1540, Elyot was probably hoping for both patronage from his new queen and that her name would serve as an endorsement of his book.

The other book dedication Anne received is quite interesting because it was directed to her after the annulment of her marriage to Henry, suggesting that she must have retained some power, patronage, or popularity. In 1553, Thomas Becon wrote *The Pomaunder of Prayer*, one of several collections of prayers he authored, and dedicated it to Anne of Cleves; *Pomaunder* was not published until 1558, one year after Anne's death.[36] It is possible that Becon first gave Anne a presentation manuscript of his text in 1553, but there is no such version extant. *Pomaunder* was printed at least eight times between 1558 and 1578, proving his collection of prayers to be very popular.[37] The dedication to Anne was kept in all versions except for that printed in 1578.

Becon began his dedication to Anne, "To the moste honorable and vertuous Lady Anne of Cleue, her grace, syster to the hye and myghtye Prynce Wylliam Duke of Cleue."[38] This dedication followed trends often found in dedications to royal English women, in that the dedicator praises his subject and mentions one of her male relatives.[39] Becon mentions Anne's brother rather than Anne's former husband, as Anne's marriage was long over and Henry was deceased but her brother still wielded power in the duchy of Cleves. Additionally, Becon was an evangelical who at one time wrote books under the name Theodore Basil to conceal his identity, so he probably desired Anne's connection with Cleves and other German evangelicals, just as Cromwell did.[40] Becon even left England during Mary I's reign and perhaps thought Anne would be a supporter and ally. This shows that like Elyot, Becon must not have had a personal relationship with Anne, as Anne and Mary I were friends, and Anne was most likely a Roman Catholic or possibly a reformed Catholic herself.[41] There would have been other Englishwomen more sympathetic to reform who would have made better dedicatees, such as Catherine Brandon, Duchess of Suffolk.

He asks Anne to "contynue therfore (most honorable Lady) as ye haue godly begun, both you and all your faithful family to call on the glorious name of the Lord our God with feruent prayer."[42] In doing so, he says, God will be her "fauorable father and strong shilde," perhaps suggesting that Anne needed male protection within England that her brother could only give her at a distance.[43] Becon once more alludes to Anne's brother, asking God to "blesse you both" with long life and health.[44] He concludes his dedication by requesting that Anne look favorably on his book and use the prayers contained within it to continue her relationship with God. Again, there is no evidence that Anne owned this book or even sanctioned the use of her name in its dedication by supporting a presentation manuscript version first. And, depending on exactly when in 1553 he dedicated this book to Anne, Becon may have already been in exile and may have thought he could gain protection from the Duke of Cleves by speaking well of the duke's sister. Furthermore, the earliest known extant printed version of Becon's text is from 1558, one year after Anne's death, and the dedication was printed in that volume, which would have offered no patronage benefit from Anne but, again, may have earned patronage or protection from the duke. Becon's dedication represents Anne as a pious, virtuous, royal woman who embraced vernacular English prayer and should be respected for her relationship with God.

Both Becon's and Elyot's dedications to Anne appeared in books that were printed at least five years after they were first written, thereby leaving open the possibility that they were first given to Anne in a presentation manuscript that no longer exists or were perhaps printed in an earlier edition that is no longer extant, or even the possibility that these texts were first dedicated to a different woman and Anne's name was inserted in a later edition. Whatever was the case, in these two dedications to Anne, Elyot and Becon used Anne's name to give authority their texts and to make commentary upon the current religious and political situation within England. Elyot's book dedication serves as an example of a dedicator offering his book to a royal woman with the hopes of receiving patronage in return, while using the case of Zenobia to show his displeasure with Henry's marital politics. Becon addresses Anne as the sister of an evangelical duke, quite possibly so that the duke would look on him with favor during his exile from England. As with the other books associated with Anne of Cleves, these two dedications show that Anne was regarded as an important international figure even after her death.

Anne's Inscription to Henry VIII

The one book that can be confirmed as having been owned by or at least handled by Anne of Cleves is a 1533 Book of Hours in which she wrote an inscription to Henry VIII.[45] Currently held in the Folger Shakespeare Library, the volume is printed in Latin on vellum and has several illuminated woodcuts and initials. On the back flyleaf is inscribed, "I besiche your grace hub [humbly] when ye loke on this remember me. yo[u]r gracis assured anne the dowgher of cleues."[46] Retha Warnicke suggests that after their divorce, Henry continued to take care of Anne, providing for her financially and even visiting her, so Anne might have given this book to Henry as a sign of goodwill, as she may have even brought it with her from Germany.[47]

Warnicke's theory may be correct, but since the book has a date of 1533 and a publication place of Paris, Anne could have either brought it with her or purchased it in England, and she could have given it to Henry any time from 1540 to 1547. Quite possibly she gave it to the king after their divorce, as she signed it the "dowgher of cleues," indicating that she was not queen at the time she gave the book, strengthened by the fact that Anne was not fluent in English until after her divorce.[48]

Eamon Duffy notes that Books of Hours were frequently passed around families and acquaintances, so it would have been very acceptable for Anne to give Henry a Book of Hours as a gift and even more traditional for her to write an inscription to him in it.[49] As Books of Hours were so commonly owned, this does not really speak to Anne's personal reading interests, especially as it was noted by Nicholas Wotton in 1539 that Anne could only read German, but at least it does show that Anne had some interest in books and thought that a Book of Hours would be appropriate for a king who was head of both his church and his realm.[50]

Anne's *Remonstrance*

One surprising book associated with Anne of Cleves was not written by her, owned by her, nor dedicated to her. Rather, a mid-sixteenth century French book caused quite a stir in England when it repopularized the divorce of Anne and Henry. As evidenced by several letters dating from the latter half of 1541 and first few months of 1542, there was still discussion in Europe about the possibility of Henry VIII taking back Anne of Cleves. After February 13, 1542, the discussion only intensified as Henry's fifth wife, Katherine Howard, was executed. In a letter from Charles de Marillac, a diplomat from France at the English court, to Anne de Montmorency, a French diplomat, dated October 1, 1541, Marillac indicated that there was a rumor that Henry was about restore Anne as his wife, as there was already gossip of Katherine's indiscretion and indecent behavior.[51] Richard Pate also repeated talk from Brussels regarding Henry's unlawful repudiation of Anne and the desire by a kinsman of the Duke of Cleves to take retribution.[52]

In December 1541, at the same time as Katherine Howard's affairs were revealed to Henry, Richard Taverner, the author who had previously written the dedication to Henry VIII discussing Henry's upcoming marriage to Anne, repeated a rumor that Anne had recently given birth to a son whom she conceived with Henry during a visit to Hampton Court.[53] While this rumor circulated after Anne had recently been bedridden with a stomach sickness and not because those around her wished Henry to remarry her, it did nothing to dispel the possibility that Henry would remarry Anne because she had given him another male heir. In a letter dated February 25, 1542, written by Eustace Chapuys, ambassador to England, to Charles V of the

Holy Roman Empire, Chapuys finally dismissed the prospect of their remarriage as very unlikely.[54] However, the possibility of Anne's reinstatement as queen only became more sensationalized with the publication of *L'oraison et remonstrance de haulte & puissante Dame, Dame Marie de Cleues*, allegedly written by or produced for Anne of Cleves.[55] *L'oraison* explicates the marriage of Henry and Anne, though the name "Marie" actually erroneously refers to Anne's mother's name in the title. This mistake, which was not corrected until 1561, must have cleared Anne of involvement in its production, for it is unlikely that she would not have used (or known!) her own name.[56]

On January 26, 1542, only eighteen months after Anne and Henry's divorce, William Paget, who served in several political and diplomatic positions under Henry VIII, Edward, and Mary, wrote a letter to Henry that mentioned an oration defending Anne of Cleves against Henry's repudiation of her.[57] Paget also sent a copy of the oration to Henry (in French) and asked if he should complain to the French king regarding its existence and try to discover the author.[58] One month later, on February 25, Paget wrote to the Privy Council that he had since spoken with King Francis of France about the book, as it was written in Anne's name, so it needed to be determined if she had any involvement.[59] Paget also wrote a separate letter to Henry after his meeting with Francis, dated one day later, and noted that the Privy Council was concerned about the book and had written to him to discover more about it and the people involved in its creation.[60]

Paget had recently discovered it was written by the abbot of Irvy, Jean de Luxembourg, later bishop of Pamiers in France.[61] Paget reported that in the meeting with Francis he asked Francis to suppress the book, yet Francis acted as though he had never heard of it. Francis promised Paget that he would suppress the printing and order extant copies to be destroyed, and also suggested that the Duke of Cleves could not have given his blessing to this book because Anne was still young and of childbearing age, so he would not ruin her chances of making another political marriage. Paget assured Francis that Henry had acted according to God's law and so he would not take Anne back. This correspondence suggests that this book was first produced some time in 1542, probably in direct response to the trial and execution of Katherine Howard. Yet the exact date of its first edition is unknown, and the first extant edition is dated 1547, after the deaths of both Henry and Francis.[62] So perhaps Francis really did suppress the book.

After its first mention in 1542, *L'oraison* was printed in at least nine editions: French editions appeared in 1547 and 1549, and Italian editions appeared in 1558, 1561, 1562, 1569, 1575, 1584, and 1741. *L'oraison* has largely been ignored since 1741. It was discussed by William Dunn Macray in 1880 and in two modern biographies of Anne, both of which cite Macray's article rather than check the source itself.[63] Yet, while Macray decries the limited use of this book and suggests that it should be understood as evidence of foreign interest in Anne, he, too, misses the full extent of the printed appearances of the volume; Macray identifies only two French versions and one Italian edition.

It is with Macray's analysis of Luxembourg's motivations for creating *L'oraison* that his essay shows its age and greatest inaccuracies. Macray speculates that because Anne was a Lutheran, all Roman Catholics in England were glad to see her marriage to Henry dissolved. So Macray suggests that Luxembourg wrote his text not to defend Anne, especially as he did not even call her by the correct name, but rather to deepen a rift between Henry and other European reformers.[64] Macray goes so far as to suggest that Luxembourg hoped to incite anger in Henry for the ill-fated match, thereby causing him to get rid of Cromwell, who organized the marriage, thus removing from court one of the greatest advocates for reform.[65] This seems like a very sophisticated plan for a bishop in France, and one would think he would be sure to supply the details of Henry and Anne's relationship correctly, including her name. As has since been suggested by Anne's biographers, Anne was not a Lutheran but a Roman Catholic: her mother was a devout Roman Catholic and Anne's only educator, though Anne's father, like Henry VIII, preferred reformed Catholicism and did not recognize the authority of the pope.[66] So Luxembourg could have intended his text to be a defense of Anne if contemporaries were aware of her religious preferences. Most likely, Luxembourg wrote his oration as a refutation of Anne and Henry's annulment, as the text is full of biblical information stating that God can approve and disapprove of marriages. It is not clear if he wanted to defend Anne personally, though the text does tie in nicely with Katherine Howard's execution and the possibility that Henry would remarry his fourth wife.

The earliest extant printed edition of *L'oraison* appears to have come from the press of Nicolas Paris in 1547.[67] Paris was Luxembourg's private printer at the monastery, hence the place of publication on the colophon states La Rivou, or the Cistercian house of La Rivoir.[68] After Nicolas Paris's edition in 1547, the tract seems to have gained infamy outside of the monastery and was reprinted in the city of Paris in a 1549 edition and at least two different 1552 editions.[69] It was printed in Italy, in Italian translation, in 1558.[70] The Italian translation is entitled *Repudio della reina Maria D'Inghilterra.*

However, the history of Luxembourg's text after the 1558 Italian edition is unclear. According to the online catalogue of the British Library, the library has in its holdings a copy of the 1547 edition, a copy of the 1549 edition, and two copies of the 1558 Italian edition. The catalogue also lists in its holdings six more Italian editions, printed in 1561, 1562, 1569, 1575, 1584, and 1741, all with titles beginning with *Repudio della reina Maria*. However, when one retrieves the physical volumes, one finds that these six books are not *Repudio* but are six editions of Francesco Sansovino's *Diverse orationi volgarmente scritte da molti huomini illustri de tempi nostri.*[71]

As it turns out, *Repudio* was not reprinted by itself in those six editions of the sixteenth and eighteenth centuries but was one of the orations included in Sansovino's collection of famous orations. The British Library catalogue mistakenly lists each of the reprintings of *Repudio* as separate volumes while making no mention that they are printed within Sansovino's compilation. This mistake goes all the way back to the 1883 *British Museum Catalogue of Printed Books.*[72]

According to Paul F. Grendler, Sansovino was an Italian author/translator/compiler of popular histories.[73] *Diverse orationi volgarmente scritte de molti huomini illustri de tempi nostri* is just one book of orations that he "collected, revised, and corrected," based on short histories written by others. *Diverse orationi* was printed in 1561 and 1569; it was also printed with a variant title in 1562, 1575, and 1584—*Delle orationi volgarmente scritte da molti huomini illustri de tempi nostril*—and as *Delle orazioni* in 1741.[74] In all six editions, Sansovino included *Oratione d'Anna reina d'Inghilterra,* or *Anna reina per lo ripudio suo* as it was titled in the tabula, finally correctly attributed to Anne of Cleves, even though it was well known by that time that Anne had nothing to do with the text. Besides the title's naming Anne correctly as the wife of Henry, Sansovino added an introductory paragraph for the text and removed all mention of Luxembourg as the actual author of the text, perhaps to give it more authority as having come straight from Anne.

The introductory paragraph is as follows:

> Henrico Ottauo Re d'Inghilterra, tolta la quarta moglie, che fu questa Anna sorella del Duca di Cleues, & effendoli venuto uoglia de repudiarla, per tor la quinta, & la sesta, come egli fece, la Reina veduta la sua volonta, disse la presente Oratione, nella qual si tratta s'egli fa bene, o no, a lasciar la sua legittima moglie per torne vn'altra.
>
> [Henry, the eighth King of England, removed his fourth wife, who was Anna, sister of the Duke of Cleves, and having then come to her to repudiate her, for his fifth and sixth [wives], as he did, the Queen obeyed his will and said this present Oration, in which case it is good or not to leave his legitimate wife for another one.][75]

What is most interesting about this introductory paragraph is Sansovino's assertion that Anne "disse la present Oratione,"—that Anne *said* this present oration upon her divorce, anticipating that Henry was leaving her for his next wife. So not only did Sansovino eliminate any mention of Luxembourg; he presented this oration as having been said by Anne. During the half-century immediately following Anne's divorce and for at least two centuries after, this oration was passed down in Italian historiography as factual.[76] This fake supplication to Henry VIII, rather than actual biographical information, was represented as Anne's heartfelt desire to remain Henry's wife. In England, while Anne remained popular after the divorce, she faded into relative obscurity after her death, yet in Italy she had an afterlife as a slighted woman who only did right by her husband yet was repudiated anyway.[77]

Anne continued to garner international interest after her death, as evidenced by a letter from an English ambassador to the Holy Roman Emperor Ferdinand I, in which he noted that there was a woman in Saxony claiming to be Anne of Cleves, who had fled from England seeking refuge in Saxony. Once it was determined that the woman was not Anne, she was imprisoned and died in 1560.[78] Perhaps Anne was lucky she was slighted, as things tended not to turn out well for Henry's other wives, even his sixth, Katherine Parr, who outlived Henry but died in childbirth the following year.

The oration most likely had great appeal because it was written in the form of a "personal appeal" by Anne and depicted her as grief-stricken by her removal as Henry's wife because she came to him from a foreign land prepared to be his lawful and obedient wife.[79] "Anne" professes that she has love only for Henry; she was never precontracted in marriage to another, as a precontract was used as one of the reasons legitimizing their divorce, and she goes on to address Henry's council as to why it is against God's laws for Henry to have repudiated her. While Henry may not have found that portion of the text offensive, he certainly would have considered the rest to be: it declares that Henry sought to marry Anne, so he should maintain his end of the marriage contract. Moreover, "Anne" knew that Henry had a poor reputation in Europe for being brusque and temperamental, yet Anne defended his previous actions and agreed to marry him anyway.

For Luxembourg, what is most egregious is that Anne willingly entered into marriage with Henry, did not commit any wrongdoings against her husband, and married Henry with good intentions, yet Henry repudiated her, thereby breaking her heart and showing himself to have weak morals. Now, what are Anne's options as a divorced woman living in a foreign country relying on the goodwill of her former husband? "Anne" concludes by leaving her fate in Henry's hands, reassuring him of her love, and making one final appeal to Henry's Privy Council to guide him to doing what is right. Rather than focusing on Anne personally, the text is more concerned that Henry has broken the sanctity of marriage. Macray is probably correct in surmising that feelings displayed by Anne in this text reflected reactions of those abroad: Henry repudiated his fourth wife hastily; had a disturbing reputation for acting rashly regarding women; marriage was a religious act sanctioned by God; and Henry had the opportunity to make things right with his fourth wife and with God by taking Anne back.

Even if not correctly cited by Macray or the British Library, Luxembourg's oration about Anne of Cleves had an enduring appeal that kept Anne relevant and made her an example for Roman Catholic Europe to show the extent of Henry VIII's immoral and heretical religious and marital choices. Not only did this oration create and solidify Anne's foreign reputation as a jilted wife who desperately wanted nothing more than to please her former husband, it also contributed to Henry's already poor reputation among European Roman Catholics, perhaps even going so far as to damage Elizabeth's reputation as the Protestant offspring of Henry, when in reality Anne and Elizabeth remained on good terms after Anne and Henry's marriage ended. That does not quite explain why Luxembourg's text was printed eleven times, but it does show that Anne continued to be of interest on the Continent as a royal woman in her own right, particularly as the title of the oration always reflected her queenly status, even once she was divorced and demoted to the rank of the king's sister. As with the books dedicated to Anne and the books dedicated to Henry that mentioned Anne, she was used in this oration to make a political statement regarding Henry VIII and England.

Conclusion

This essay makes clear that Anne of Cleves was used politically in books and manuscripts, though there is little evidence that she read them herself. Much as the name of a dedicatee could be invoked in a dedication without her prior knowledge or consent, these sources indicate that Anne's name was invoked by others for several reasons. In the two dedications to Henry VIII, Anne's personage, though not her name, is invoked by two dedicators both to praise Henry for his upcoming nuptials yet also to encourage Henry to patronize them for offering him their New Year's and marital blessings. In the dedications to Anne, her own name is invoked to give authority to the texts written by Becon and Elyot, yet in the case of Elyot, her name may have been cited to divert attention from his actual intention, which was to chastise Henry for repudiating his first wife. The inscription by Anne is the exception to this. Here Anne employs her own name and the royal status she had before her marriage to Henry to remind him that while she remained loyal to him after their marriage, she was still titled in her own right. Finally, in *L'oraison et remonstrance*, Anne's name was invoked for nearly two centuries as a Continental attempt to belittle Henry's authority and religious changes, publicizing his faults as a husband and ultimately indicating his faults as a monarch.

Anne was the perfect queen to write about because she was the only one whose marriage to Henry ended amicably (besides Katherine Parr), and she was his last surviving wife, living until 1557. Moreover, Anne had both Protestant and Roman Catholic ties; she was most likely a Roman Catholic herself, yet she hailed from a duchy that was part of Germany and had links to reform. Therefore, Anne could be supported by all causes and religious sects as a slighted wife who had to endure a brief marriage and repudiation by a heretic (for some) or a monarch who failed to implement reform fully (for others). In manuscripts and printed books, Anne's name is invoked to find favor with close male relatives, to give authority to the contents of specific books, and finally as a rallying point for anyone displeased with Henry VIII and the English religious settlement.

Independent Scholar

APPENDIX

Editions of *Remonstrance* and *Repudio*

Universal Short Title Catalogue. http://www.ustc.ac.uk/.
L'oraison et remonstrance. La Rivoir: Nicole Paris, 1547. Four extant copies, held in the British Library at C.55.c.8.
L'oraison et remonstrance. Paris: vend Arnoul L'Angelier, 1549. One extant copy, held in the British Library at C.55.a.2.
L'oraison et remonstrance. Paris: Christophe Foloppe, 1552. One extant copy.
L'oraison et remonstrance. Paris: pour Charles L'Angelier, 1552. One extant copy.
Repudio della Reina Maria. Bologna: per Antonio Giaccarelli& Pellegrino Bonardo, 1558. Thirteen extant copies.
Diverse orationi. Venice, 1561. Twenty-seven extant copies.
Delle orationi. Venice, 1562. Thirty-eight extant copies.
Diverse orationi. Venice, 1569. Thirty-seven extant copies.
Delle orationi. Venice, 1575. Forty-six extant copies.
Delle orationi. Venice, 1584. Forty-four extant copies.
Delle orazioni. Lione [Lyon], 1741. Beyond the purview of the USTC.

British Library. https://www.bl.uk/.
L'oraison et remonstrance. Nicole Paris, 1547. Call number C.55.c.8.
L'oraison et remonstrance. Paris: A. L'Angelier, 1549. Call number C.55.a.2.
Repudio della reina Maria. Bologna: A. Giaccarelli& P. Bonardo, 1558. Two copies, call numbers C.33.b.16 and G.1263.

Repudio della reina Maria. No publication information other than the date of 1562. Call number 835.f.6.(1.). Note says it is in Sansovino's book.
Repudio della reina Maria. No publication information other than the date of 1569. Call number 835.f.5. No mention of Sansovino.
Repudio della reina Maria. No publication information other than the date of 1575. Call number 835.f.7. No mention of Sansovino.
Diverse orationi. Venice, 1561. Call number C.66.c.22.
Delle orationi. Venice, 1562. Call number 835.f.6.(1.).
Diverse orationi. Venice, 1569. Two copies, call numbers 835.f.5. and 835.f.4.
Delle orationi. Venice, 1575. Call number 835.f.7.
Delle orationi. Venice, 1584. Call number 72.i.25.
Delle orazioni. Lione, 1741. Call number 12301.m.21.
None of the listings for Sansovino mention any connection to *Repudio della reina Maria.*

British Museum Catalogue of Printed Books Supplement: K–Kyshe. London: William Clowes and Sons, 1903.
All the museum's titles authored by Jean de Luxembourg are listed on page 389.
The 1547 edition is at call number C.55.c.8.
The 1549 edition is at call number C.55.a.2.
The 1558 Italian edition with *Repudio della reina* title is at call number C.33.b.16.
A 1562 edition is at call number 835.f.6.(1.). Noted as another edition of the Italian version, yet with a variant short title, *Oratione di Anna Reina per lo ripudio suo.*
A 1569 Italian edition is at call number 835.f.(5.). No information given other than year and size.
A 1575 Italian edition is at call number 835.f.(7.). No information given other than year and size.

British Museum Catalogue of Printed Books Supplement: A–Academies. London: William Clowes and Sons, 1900.
Sources associated with Anne of Cleves in the museum's holdings are listed on pages 98–99.
The 1547 edition is at call number C.55.c.8.
The 1549 edition call number C.55.a.2.
The 1558 edition. Two copies are listed, both of which have the same call numbers today.

The 1562 edition is listed as a second edition of the 1558 Italian *Repudio* with a variant short title, *Oratione di Anna Reina per lo ripudio suo* (the same as given in the 1903 catalogue), yet the listing also says, "See Sansovino (f.) Delle oration volgarmente scritte, etc. pt. 1."

The 1569 and 1575 editions are listed as other editionsof the 1562 edition. All three with the same call numbers as they still have today so the 1562, 1569, and 1575 editions are all considered later editions of the Italian version of *Repudio*, possibly with different titles.

British Museum Catalogue of Printed Books: ALT–AMT. London: William Clowes and Sons, 1883.

The four Italian editions are listed on pages 78–79.

The 1558 edition is named as *Repudio della reina* with current call number; no indication that the other three editions are related to *Repudio.*

The 1562 edition is named as *Oratione di Anna Reina per lo ripudio suo.* Also cross-referenced: "See Sansovino (F.) Delle oration volgarmente scritte ... parte prima, etc. Pt. 1."

The 1569 edition is named as *Oratione d'Anna Reina (per lo ripudio del marito).* Also cross-referenced to Sansovino.

The 1575 edition is named as *Oratione por lo ripudio suo.* Also cross-referenced to Sansovino.

For all, the call numbers have never changed.

NOTES

1. Elizabeth Norton, *Anne of Cleves: Henry VIII's Discarded Bride* (Stroud, UK: Amberley, 2010); Retha M. Warnicke, *The Marrying of Anne of Cleves: Royal Protocol in Early Modern England* (Cambridge, UK: Cambridge University Press, 2000); and Mary Saaler, *Anne of Cleves: Fourth Wife of Henry VIII* (London: Rubicon Press, 1995). Anne features in several biographies that address all six wives of Henry VIII, such as David Loades, *The Six Wives of Henry VIII* (Stroud, UK: Amberley, 2011); David Starkey, *Six Wives: The Queens of Henry VIII* (New York: HarperCollins, 2003); and Alison Weir, *The Six Wives of Henry VIII* (New York: Grove Press, 1991).
2. David Loades, *The Tudor Queens of England* (London: Continuum, 2009), 112. Loades says of Anne, "As a Queen, Anne had been a non-event . . . she was a diplomatic footnote, and is remembered best for her quite spectacular ignorance of matters sexual."
3. In James McConica's seminal study on English humanism, Anne is mentioned in one sentence and only for her marriage to Henry. James

McConica, *English Humanists and Reformation Politics under Henry VIII and Edward VI* (Oxford: Clarendon Press, 1965), 175. Maria Dowling, *Humanism in the Age of Henry VIII* (London: Croonhelm, 1986), 238, notes (incorrectly) that no books were dedicated to Anne except for one after her death, concluding that Anne had no real relevance to English humanism.

4. James Carley, *The Books of King Henry VIII and His Wives* (London: British Library, 2004), 108.
5. Micheline White, "Pray for the Monarch: The Surprising Contributions of Katherine Parr and Queen Elizabeth I to the Book of Common Prayer," *Times Literary Supplement*, April 3, 2015, 14–15; Maria Dowling, "Anne Boleyn as Patron," in *Henry VIII: A European Court in England*, ed. David Starkey (London: Collins and Brown Limited, 1991), 107–111; Dowling, *Humanism*, 219–247.
6. Norton, *Anne of Cleves*, 62.
7. Felicity Heal has recently published on gift-giving in England. See esp. Felicity Heal, "The Politics of Gift-Exchange under the Tudors," in *The Power of Gifts: Gift-Exchange in Early Modern England* (Oxford: Oxford University Press, 2014), 87–120.
8. Anne's will is reprinted in Agnes Strickland, *Lives of the Queens of England from the Norman Conquest*, vol. 5 (Philadelphia: George Barrie & Sons, 1902; reprint of 1844 edition), 96–98. However, portions of the will were not included by Strickland, and she also embedded her own commentary, such as making note that Anne gave a jewel to the future Queen Elizabeth.
9. Norton, *Anne of Cleves*, 10–11.
10. Carley, *Books of Henry VIII*, 34.
11. Folger Shakespeare Library, HH115/27. STC 15982. Anne's inscription to Henry is on the back flyleaf and is discussed further below.
12. Giles Duwes, *An Introductory for to Lerne to Rede, to Pronounce, and to Speake Frenche Trewly, Compiled for the Right High, Excellent, and Most Vertuous Lady, the Lady Mary of Englande, Doughter to our Most Gracious Souerayn Lorde Kyng Henry the Eight* (London: Thomas Godfray, 1533[?]). STC 7377.
13. Bible, trans. Miles Coverdale (Cologne: E. Cervicornus and J. Soter, 1535), ii.r. STC 2063.
14. See Warnicke, *The Marrying of Anne of Cleves.*
15. Norton, *Anne of Cleves*, 47.
16. Wolfgang Capito, *An Epitome of the Psalmes, or Briefe Meditacions vpon the Same with Diuerse Other Moste Christian Prayers*, translated by Richard Tauerner (London: R. Bankes, 1539). STC 2748.

17. Andrew W. Taylor, "Richard Taverner," *Oxford Dictionary of National Biography*. (online)
18. Capito, *Epitome*, fol. 4r.
19. *Ibid.*, fol. 4r–4v.
20. *Nouum Tesamentum*, trans. Walter Delaine (London: John Mayler, 1540). STC 2799.
21. *Ibid.*, a.3.r.
22. *Ibid.*, title page and a.3.r.
23. Valerie Schutte has previously published on the dedications to Anne of Cleves. See Schutte, *Mary I and the Art of Book Dedications: Royal Women, Power, and Persuasion* (New York: Palgrave Macmillan, 2015), 22, 25–30.
24. Sir Thomas Elyot, *Defence of Good Women* (London: Thomas Berthelet, 1540). STC 7657.5.
25. Greg Walker, *Writing under Tyranny: English Literature and the Henrician Reformation* (Oxford: Oxford University Press, 2005), 124–125, 135.
26. Gabriele Stein, *Sir Thomas Elyot as Lexicographer* (Oxford: Oxford University Press, 2014), 5.
27. William St. Clair and Irmgard Maassen, eds., *Conduct Literature for Women, 1500–1640*, vol. 2 (London: Pickering and Chatto, 2000), 201. The 1540 edition exists in only one extant copy held at the Huntington Library and has frequently been missed in previous scholarship on Elyot: Huntington Library, Rare Books, call number 88302. Foster Watson, ed., *Vives and the Renascence Education of Women* (New York: Longmans, Green & Co., 1912).
28. See Watson, *Vives and the Renascence*, 211–212; Stanford Lehmberg, *Sir Thomas Elyot: Tudor Humanist* (New York: Greenwood Press, 1960); Greg Walker, *Persuasive Fictions: Faction, Faith and Political Culture in the Reign of Henry VIII* (Aldershot, UK: Scolar Press, 1996), 181, 184–192; Constance Jordan, "Feminism and the Humanists: The Case for Sir Thomas Elyot's Defense of Good Women," in *Rewriting the Renaissance: The Discourses of Sexual Difference in Early Modern Europe*, ed. Margaret Ferguson, Maureen Quilligan, and Nancy Vickers (Chicago: University of Chicago Press, 1986), 242–258; J. Christopher Warner, *Henry VIII's Divorce: Literature and the Politics of the Printing Press* (Woodbridge, UK: Boydell Press, 1998), chap. 3.
29. Schutte, *Mary I*, 27.
30. Elyot, *Defence* (1540), A.ii.r.
31. Ibid.
32. Schutte, *Mary I*, 49–50. Juan Luis Vives, *A Very Fruteful and Pleasant Boke called the Instruction of a Christen Woman*, trans. Richard Hyrde

(London: Thomas Berthelet, ca. 1529). STC 24857. Vives's book is perhaps the most famous text that advocates for the necessity of female virtue.

33. Elyot, *Defence* (1540), A.iii.v.
34. Ibid.
35. Ibid.
36. Seymour Baker House, "Thomas Becon," *Oxford Dictionary of National Biography*.
37. I do not have access to the 1558 edition, so all quoted text comes from the 1561 edition. Thomas Becon, *The Pomaunder of Prayer* (London: John Day, 1561). STC 1746. Editions of *Pomaunder* were printed in 1558, 1561, 1563, 1565, 1566, 1567, 1570, and 1578.
38. Becon, *Pomaunder*, A.ii.r.
39. Schutte, *Mary I*, 47–48.
40. Seymour Baker House, "Thomas Becon," *Oxford Dictionary of National Biography*.
41. Norton, *Anne of Cleves*, 11, 37–38.
42. Becon, *Pomaunder*, A.iii.r.
43. Ibid.
44. Ibid.
45. Folger Shakespeare Library, HH115/27. STC 15982.
46. Folger Shakespeare Library, HH115/27, back flyleaf.
47. Warnicke, Marrying of Anne of Cleves, 252.
48. Carley, *Books of Henry VIII*, 108. Norton, *Anne of Cleves*, 46, 63, 74, 100.
49. Eamon Duffy, *Marking the Hours: English People and Their Prayers* (New Haven, CT: Yale University Press, 2006, 2011), 23–25.
50. In a letter dated August 11, 1539, Nicholas Wotton wrote to Henry VIII that Anne was educated by her mother and could read and write only German. British Library, MS Cotton Vitel. B xxi, fol. 186.
51. James Gairdner and R. H. Brodie, eds., *Letters and Papers, Foreign and Domestic, Henry VIII, Volume 16, 1540–1541* (London: Her Majesty's Stationery Office, 1898), entry 111.
52. *Ibid.*, entry 122.
53. *Ibid.*, entry 1414.
54. James Gairdner and R. H. Brodie, eds., *Letters and Papers, Foreign and Domestic, Henry VIII, Volume 17, 1542* (London: Her Majesty's Stationery Office, 1900), entry 124.
55. *L'oraison et remonstrance de haulte & puissant Dame, Dame Marie de Cleues* (La Riuou:Nicole Paris, 1547[?]). Marie was mistakenly used in the title instead of Anne.
56. William Dunn Macray, "The 'Remonstrance' of Anne of Cleves," *Archaeologia* 47 (1883):249–264, 251.

57. Gairdner and Brodie, *Letters and Papers Volume 17,* entry 55. Entry 56 gives the name of the printed edition of the tract on Anne of Cleves and suggests it was first printed in 1542 in France. It is unclear whether Paget sent Henry a manuscript or a printed edition.
58. No copy of the book appears to have been kept in Henry's libraries. James P. Carley, ed., *The Libraries of King Henry VIII* (London: British Library, 2000).
59. Gairdner and Brodie, *Letters and Papers Volume 17,* entry 126.
60. *Ibid.,* entry 128.
61. Sometimes also known as Joannes or John de Luxembourg.
62. William Dunn Macray suggests that the book Paget sent back to England was a manuscript copy, but there is no proof that it was manuscript or print. Macray, "Remonstrance," 251.
63. *Ibid.,* 251. Norton, *Anne of Cleves,* 123–124. Warnicke, *Marrying of Anne of Cleves,* 247–248.
64. Macray, "Remonstrance," 253.
65. *Ibid.,* 263.
66. Norton, *Anne of Cleves,* 11, 37–38. Even Strickland identified Anne as a Catholic. Strickland, *Lives,* 96.
67. On the copy held in the British Library, Marie has been crossed out in red ink and replaced with Anne. British Library, C.55.c.8.
68. Macray, "Remonstrance," 253.
69. *L'oraison et remonstrance de haulte & puissant Dame, Dame Marie de Cleues* (Paris: A. l'Angeliér, 1549). British Library, C.55.a.2; *L'oraison et remonstrance de haulte & puissant Dame, Dame Marie de Cleues* (Paris: Christophe Foloppe, 1552); *L'oraison et remonstrance de haulte & puissant Dame, Dame Marie de Cleues* (Paris: Charles L'Angelier, 1552).
70. *Repudio della Reina Maria D'Inghilterra* (Bologna, Italy: per Antonio Giaccarelli& Pellegrino Bonardo, 1558). Holdings in British Library at G.1263 and C.33.b.16.
71. Francesco Sansovino, *Diverse orationi volgarmente scritte da molti huomini illustri de tempi nostril* (Venice, 1561). Sansovino's text went through six editions (1561, 1562, 1569, 1575, and 1584, which were printed in Venice, and one edition in 1741 that was printed in Lione (Lyon)The references for the six volumes in the British Library are Sansovino, *Diverse orationi,* Venice, 1561, call number C.66.c.22; Venice, 1562, call number 835.f.6.(1.); Venice, 1569, call numbers 835.f.5 and 835.f.4; Venice, 1575, call number 835.f.7; Venice, 1584, call number 72.i.25; Lione, 1741, call number 12301.m.21.
72. See "Appendix: Editions of *Remonstrance* and *Repudio*" below.
73. Paul F. Grendler, "Francesco Sansovino and Italian Popular History, 1560–1600," *Studies in the Renaissance* 16 (1969):139–180.

74. Francesco Sansovino, *Delle orationi volgarmente scritte da molti huomini illustri de tempi nostril* (Venice: 1562). This information pertains only to *parta prima* of Sansovino's text. He also published a second part that featured different biographies of famous and historical people.
75. My translation.
76. For an examination of Italian interest in Tudor England, see Michael Wyatt, *The Italian Encounter with Tudor England: A Cultural Politics of Translation* (Cambridge, UK: Cambridge University Press, 2005).
77. Norton, *Anne of Cleves,* 111, 165.
78. This event is recounted in *ibid.,* 163–164. The ambassador's letter to Emperor Ferdinand can be found in Victor von Klarwill, ed., *Queen Elizabeth and Some Foreigners: Being a Series of Hitherto Unpublished Letters from the Archives of the Hapsburg Family,* trans. T. H. Nash (London: Bodley Head, 1928), 121–122.
79. Macray, "Remonstrance," 254.

WORKS CITED

Manuscripts

British Library
Call number 72.i.25.
Call number 835.f.4.
Call number 835.f.5.
Call number 835.f.6.(1.).
Call number 835.f.7.
Call number 12301.m.21.
Call number C.33.b.16.
Call number C.55.a.2.
Call number C.55.c.8.
Call number C.66.c.22.
Call number C.66 d.6.
Call number G.1263.
MS Cotton Vitel. B xxi, folio 186.
Folger Shakespeare Library, HH115/27. STC 15982.
Huntington Library, Rare Books, call number 88302.

Primary Sources

Becon, Thomas. *The Pomaunder of Prayer.* London: John Day, 1561. STC 1746.

Bible. Trans. Miles Coverdale. Cologne: E. Cervicornus and J. Soter, 1535. STC 2063.

Capito, Wolfgang. *An Epitome of the Psalmes, or Briefe Meditacions vpon the Same with Diuerse Other Moste Christian Prayers.* Translated by Richard Tauerner. London: R. Bankes, 1539. STC 2748.

Duwes, Giles. *An Introductory for to Lerne to Rede, to Pronounce, and to Speake Frenche Trewly, Compiled for the Right High, Excellent, and Most Vertuous Lady, the Lady Mary of Englande, Doughter to Our Most Gracious Souerayn Lorde Kyng Henry the Eight.* London: Thomas Godfray, 1533(?). STC 7377.

Elyot, Sir Thomas. *Defence of Good Women.* London: Thomas Berthelet, 1540. STC 7657.5.

Gairdner, James, and R. H. Brodie, eds. *Letters and Papers, Foreign and Domestic, Henry VIII, Volume 16, 1540–1541.* London: Her Majesty's Stationery Office, 1898.

———. *Letters and Papers, Foreign and Domestic, Henry VIII, Volume 17, 1542.* London: Her Majesty's Stationery Office, 1900.

L'oraison et remonstrance de haulte & puissant Dame, Dame Marie de Cleues. La Riuou: Nicole Paris, 1547(?).

L'oraison et remonstrance de haulte & puissant Dame, Dame Marie de Cleues. Paris: A. l'Angeliér, 1549.

L'oraison et remonstrance de haulte & puissant Dame, Dame Marie de Cleues. Paris: Charles L'Angeliér, 1552.

L'oraison et remonstrance de haulte & puissant Dame, Dame Marie de Cleues. Paris: Christophe Foloppe, 1552.

Nouum Tesamentum, trans. Walter Delaine. London: John Mayler, 1540. STC 2799.

Repudio della Reina Maria D'Inghilterra. Bologna, Italy: per Antonio Giaccarelli & Pellegrino Bonardo, 1558.

Sansovino, Francesco. *Diverse orationi volgarmente scritte da molti huomini illustri de tempi nostril.* Venice, 1561.

Sansovino, Francesco. *Delle orationi volgarmente scritte da molti huomini illustri de tempi nostril.* Venice, 1562.

Vives, Juan Luis. *A Very Fruteful and Pleasant Boke called the Instruction of a Christen Woman.* Trans. Richard Hyrde. London: Thomas Berthelet, ca. 1529. STC 24857.

Secondary Sources

Baker House, Seymour. "Thomas Becon." In *Oxford Dictionary of National Biography*. http://www.oxforddnb.com/

British Museum Catalogue of Printed Books: ALT–AMT. London: William Clowes and Sons, 1883.

British Museum Catalogue of Printed Books Supplement: A–Academies. London: William Clowes and Sons, 1900.

British Museum Catalogue of Printed Books Supplement: K–Kyshe. London: William Clowes and Sons, 1903.

Carley, James. *The Books of King Henry VIII and His Wives*. London: British Library, 2004.

———, ed. *The Libraries of King Henry VIII*. London: British Library, 2000.

Dowling, Maria. "Anne Boleyn as Patron." In *Henry VIII: A European Court in England*, ed. David Starkey, 107–111. London: Collins and Brown, 1991.

———. *Humanism in the Age of Henry VIII*. London: Croonhelm, 1986.

Duffy, Eamon. *Marking the Hours: English People and Their Prayers*. New Haven, CT: Yale University Press, 2006; 2011.

Grendler, Paul F. "Francesco Sansovino and Italian Popular History, 1560–1600." *Studies in the Renaissance* 16 (1969): 139–180.

Heal, Felicity. "The Politics of Gift-Exchange under the Tudors." In *The Power of Gifts: Gift-Exchange in Early Modern England*. Oxford: Oxford University Press, 2014.

Jordan, Constance. "Feminism and the Humanists: The Case for Sir Thomas Elyot's *Defense of Good Women*." In *Rewriting the Renaissance: The Discourses of Sexual Difference in Early Modern Europe*, ed. Margaret Ferguson, Maureen Quilligan, and Nancy Vickers, 242–258. Chicago: University of Chicago Press, 1986.

Lehmberg, Stanford. *Sir Thomas Elyot: Tudor Humanist*. New York: Greenwood Press, 1960.

Loades, David. *The Six Wives of Henry VIII*. Stroud, UK: Amberley, 2011.

———. *The Tudor Queens of England*. London: Continuum, 2009.

Macray, William Dunn. "The 'Remonstrance' of Anne of Cleves." *Archaeologia* 47 (1883): 249–264.

McConica, James. *English Humanists and Reformation Politics under Henry VIII and Edward VI*. Oxford: Clarendon Press, 1965.

Norton, Elizabeth. *Anne of Cleves: Henry VIII's Discarded Bride*. Stroud, UK: Amberley, 2010.

Saaler, Mary. *Anne of Cleves: Fourth Wife of Henry VIII*. London: Rubicon Press, 1995.

Schutte, Valerie. *Mary I and the Art of Book Dedications: Royal Women, Power, and Persuasion*. New York: Palgrave Macmillan, 2015.

St. Clair, William, and Irmgard Maassen, eds. *Conduct Literature for Women, 1500–1640*. Vol. 2. London: Pickering and Chatto, 2000.

Starkey, David. *Six Wives: The Queens of Henry VIII*. New York: HarperCollins, 2003.

Stein, Gabriele. *Sir Thomas Elyot as Lexicographer*. Oxford: Oxford University Press, 2014.

Strickland, Agnes. *Lives of the Queens of England from the Norman Conquest*. Vol. 5. Philadelphia: George Barrie & Sons, 1902; reprint of 1844 edition.

von Klarwill, Victor, ed. *Queen Elizabeth and Some Foreigners: Being a Series of Hitherto Unpublished Letters from the Archives of the Hapsburg Family*, trans. T. H. Nash. London: Bodley Head, 1928.

Walker, Greg. *Persuasive Fictions: Faction, Faith and Political Culture in the Reign of Henry VIII*. Aldershot, UK: Scolar Press, 1996.

———. *Writing under Tyranny: English Literature and the Henrician Reformation*. Oxford: Oxford University Press, 2005.

Warner, J. Christopher. *Henry VIII's Divorce: Literature and the Politics of the Printing Press*. Woodbridge, UK: Boydell Press, 1998.

Warnicke, Retha M. *The Marrying of Anne of Cleves: Royal Protocol in Early Modern England*. Cambridge, UK: Cambridge University Press, 2000.

Watson, Foster, ed. *Vives and the Renascence Education of Women*. New York: Longmans, Green & Co., 1912.

Weir, Alison. *The Six Wives of Henry VIII*. New York: Grove Press, 1991.

White, Micheline. "Pray for the Monarch: The Surprising Contributions of Katherine Parr and Queen Elizabeth I to the Book of Common Prayer." *Times Literary Supplement*, April 3, 2015, 14–15.

Wyatt, Michael. *The Italian Encounter with Tudor England: A Cultural Politics of Translation*. Cambridge, UK: Cambridge University Press, 2005.

Contrary Virtues and Apostles' Names in San Marino, Huntington Library MS HM 142

MARTHA RUST

San Marino, Huntington Library MS HM 142 has acquired fame in these pages and elsewhere for being the work, in part, of the prolific Dutch scribe who identifies himself on the last leaf of this manuscript as T. Werken, adding the date 1467 (f. 60).[1] Classified by Julia Boffey as an anthology of works for religious and spiritual instruction, this handsomely produced volume aptly reflects late fifteenth-century reformed lay piety by balancing emotive meditations on the passion with catechetical versifications of basic prayers and elements of the liturgy as it appears in books or hours.[2] In the first category, the manuscript preserves a witness to "O Vernicle" (*NIMEV* 2577), the Middle English poem on the instruments of the Passion; in the second, it gathers together Lydgate's verse calendar (*NIMEV* 1721), his verse paraphrases of the Pater Noster and Ave Maria (*NIMEV*s 2711 and 1045), two verse litanies (*NIMEV*s 914 and 1831), and Richard Maidstone's verse paraphrase of the Penitential Psalms (*NIMEV* 1961). Latin texts in the collection include the Psalter of St. Jerome, the Psalms of the Passion, the Litany of the Virgin, and a suffrage for St Erasmus, at the foot of the page upon which Werken has inscribed his colophon.

Given the orthodox character of this collection of mostly vernacular works, the texts written in a contemporary hand on its first back flyleaf make a fitting epilogue, for they comprise a miniature summa of the Christian faith, in the form of almost all of the lists that comprised the program of lay education set out in Canon 9, *Ignorantia sacerdotum*, of the Lambeth Council of 1281.[3] On the recto of the leaf we find, in a first column, the seven deadly sins, the seven works of mercy, the Ten Commandments, and the seven sacraments. In a second column, the articles of faith are given, in the form of the Apostles' Creed. On the verso of the leaf we find the Pater Noster, the Ave Maria, and the creed again. Beyond these core works, the recto also lists the five senses, and the verso preserves three common prayers: *In manus tuas*, *Confiteor*, and *Misereatur*.[4] While this flyleaf attests to the enduring stability of the Lambeth Council's prescribed lists as a group, red-ink elaborations on two of the lists, added by the same hand, offer examples of the magnetic attraction these canonical lists exerted on a wide variety of complementary enumerations of concepts, which tended to be quite variable. The two lists on this flyleaf that exemplify this phenomenon are the list of sins, which is matched to a list of habits and qualities by which they are vanquished, and the Apostles' Creed, articles in which are matched to apostles' names.

As Morton Bloomfield makes clear in his history of the seven deadly sins, the lists of seven virtues and seven sins developed independently of each other, which explains, as he puts it, "the great difficulty medieval writers faced when ... they attempted to oppose the virtues and vices."[5] Indeed, the cardinal virtues, comprising the four classical—prudence, justice, temperance, and fortitude—and the three evangelical—faith, hope, and charity—do not map onto the sins in any logical way at all. A response to the misfit between these two categories was the development of a variety of schemes of *remedia* for the sins, or, as Richard Newhauser terms them, "contrary virtues."[6] Some of these schemes acquire a level of canonicity of their own, while others seem to be a mix and match of several. The paired sins and *remedia* in the Pater Noster table in the Vernon Manuscript exemplify the latter category; in the first are pairings in the Wheel of Seven that frequently appears in the collection of diagrams known as the *Speculum Theologiae*.[7]

The pairings on our flyleaf in HM 142 show some affiliations with the Wheel of Seven: in particular, they share the motif of the virtues vanquishing the sins, but as Newhauser notes, that figuration is as old as the list of the seven deadly sins itself.[8] In the specificity of its lexicon, the contrary virtues on our flyleaf seem most closely aligned with the scheme of oppositions that Robert Grosseteste (c. 1175/1179–1253) sets forth in his *Templum Dei*, a pastoral manual whose popularity is evinced by its "hundred or so" witnesses surviving from the thirteenth to the fifteenth centuries, in addition to numerous extracts.[9] Our flyleaf list may constitute, if not an extract, then at least a reflection of the ongoing influence of Grosseteste's work. The two virtues that are rendered as phrases that capture the spirit but not the letter of those on Grosseteste's list—*gaudendo de boni alterius* (joy in another's good) and *continuam in bonis operis* (perseverance in good works)—suggest the influence of a sermon or perhaps the writer's own expansion on these topics.

Sins	ST Wheel[10]	PN Table	Templum Dei	HM 142
Superbia (Pride)	*Lorica humilitatis* (Breastplate of humility)	*Humilitas* (Humility)	*Humilitas* (Humility)	*Vincitur per humilitatem* (Vanquished by humility)
Invidia (Envy)	*Scutum compassionis* (Shield of compassion)	*Caritas* (Charity)	*Hilaritas* (Joy)	*Gaudendo de bono alterius* (Joy at another's good)
Ira (Wrath)	*Gladius pacientie* (Sword of patience)	*Pax* (Peace)	*Paciencia* (Patience)	*Vincitur per pacienciam* (Vanquished by patience)
Accedia (Sloath)	*Calige alacritatis* (Boots of alacrity)	*Leticia spiritualis* (Spiritual joy)	*Occupacio* (Bona opera)[11] (Good Works)	*Per continuam boni operis* (By perseverance in good works)
Avaricia (Avarice)	*Galea largitatis* (Helmet of generosity)	*Paupertas spiritual* (Poverty of spirit)	*Largitas* (Generosity)	*Per largitionem et sapienciam* (By generosity and wisdom)
Gula (Gluttony)	*Lancea sobrietatis* (Lance of sobriety)	*Mensura et sobrietas* (Measure and sobriety)	*Abstenencia* (Abstinence)	*Vincitur per abstienciam* (Vanquished by abstinence)
Luxuria (Lust)	*Baltheus castiatis* (Belt of chastity)	*Castitas* (Chastity)	*Continencia* (Continence)	*Vincitur per castitatem* (Vanquished by chastity)

Turning to the second set of red-ink additions on this flyleaf, we find an outcropping of another long and intriguingly tangled tradition: the legend that the apostles composed the Apostles' Creed, each individual apostle contributing one of its requisite twelve articles. The earliest attestation of the legend, in the *Expositio Symboli* of Rufinus (340/345–410), narrates the apostles' meeting after Christ's ascension to compose the creed, stating that each apostle contributed one clause but stopping short of associating each apostle with his specific contribution.[12] That elaboration seems to have begun with two sermons among Augustine's suppositious works, which also sowed confusion over which article was the responsibility of which apostle since the two sermons assign them differently.[13] In his 1953 essay "The Apostles and the Creed," Curt F. Bühler initiated a cottage industry devoted to tracking the appearances of the story from its origins through many early print books, which yielded three dozen or so instances and fourteen different pairings of apostles and articles, none of which matches the pairings in HM 142.[14] Making a telling context for the example in HM 142, many of the texts on Bühler's list into which the story had been incorporated were works of lay religious instruction, including *The Book of Vices and Virtues* and the *Ayenbite of Inwyt*.[15] It had even found its way into a copy of the *Ignorantia sacerdotum* itself (in Oxford, Bodleian Library MS Lat. th. c. 57, f. 16v). Along these lines, Mary Teresa Brady also discovered the legend in *The Pore Caitif*.[16] James D. Gordon contributed still more instances to the growing list, including four Middle English poems (*NIMEV*s 311, 1374, and 2700).[17] Gordon also solved the riddle of the variations in how the articles of the creed are divided out among the apostles, noting that all assign apostles to articles following (roughly) the order in which they appear in Matthew 10.2–4, Acts 1.13, or the canon of the Mass (in the section that begins *Communicantes*).[18]

This brings us back to our creed in HM 142. Its ordering of the apostles follows the order of the canon of the Mass, the order that is also followed by *The Book of Vices and Virtues*, *Ayenbite of Inwyt*, and, among works Robert R. Raymo also added to the list, *Speculum Vitae* and *A Myrour to Lewde Men and Wymmen*.[19] It should also be noted that in HM 142, the creed with its interpolated apostles' names is given the title "Simbolum," the term used by Rufinus, Pseudo-Augustine, Augustine, and a series of later commentators. According to Rufinus, the apostles gave the creed this name because of the double meaning of the Greek word "symbol." As he explains,

> Symbol in Greek can mean both "token" and "collection," that is, a joint whole to which several persons contribute. This is what the Apostles did in the case of our formulary, each contributing the clause he judged fitting. At the same

> time, it gets the name "token" or "watchword" from the fact that in those days, as the Apostle Paul vouches and as is testified in Acts, numerous vagabond Jews posing as apostles of Christ were going about preaching, their motive being the desire for gain, or gluttony.... The Apostles therefore prescribed the creed as a badge for distinguishing the man who preached the truth about Christ in harmony with their rule.
>
> (Symbolum enim Graece et indicium dici potest et conlatio, hoc est quod plures in unum conferunt. Id enim fecerunt apostoli in his sermonibus, in unum conferendo unusquisque quod sensit. Indicium autem uel signum idcirco dicitur, quia illo in tempore, sicut et Paulus apostolus dicit et in Actibus apostolorum refertur, multi ex circumcisis Iudaeis simulabant se esse apostolos Christi, et lucri alicuius uel uentris gratia ad praedicandum proficiscebantur.... Idcirco igitur istud indicium posuere, per quod agnosceretur is qui Christum uere secundum apostolicas regulas praedicaret.)[20]

Since none of the Middle English works uses this key term, it would appear that our writer was working from a Latin source, as he did with the contrary virtues. And since the order follows that of the Mass, perhaps he was himself a priest, or a scribe associated with one.

Intriguingly, an inscription on an early page in HM 142 records the name of a priest. Written in a fifteenth- or sixteenth-century hand, it reads, "Pray for ser Thomas Ware prieste."[21] As H. C. Schulz notes, we have a possible candidate for this personage in the form of the Thomas Ware who was the guardian of the Danvers chest at the University of Oxford in 1513.[22] That same Thomas Ware went on to have an illustrious career at Oriel College; indeed, according to G. C. Richards and H. E. Salter, "Ware had been the most important person in College for years" at the time of his appointment as its provost in 1530, a post he held until 1538.[23] While it is impossible to know who added the material to the leaf we have been considering, its erudite character lends additional support to the notion that the Thomas Ware of HM 142 and the Thomas Ware of Oriel College were one and the same person, which would place the manuscript in Oxford near to the time of its production. In turn, the very idea that the additions to two commonplace lists may admit to such differentiations as erudite or not erudite demonstrates the interpretive value of such ubiquitous yet highly diversified flyleaf additions.

New York University

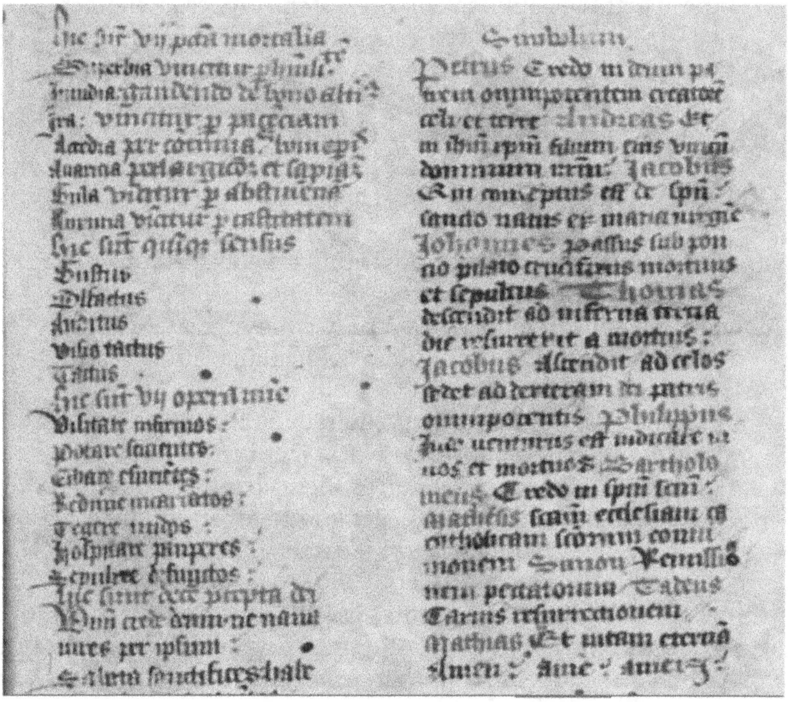

Figure 1. HM 142, f. 61 (detail), The Huntington Library, San Marino, California

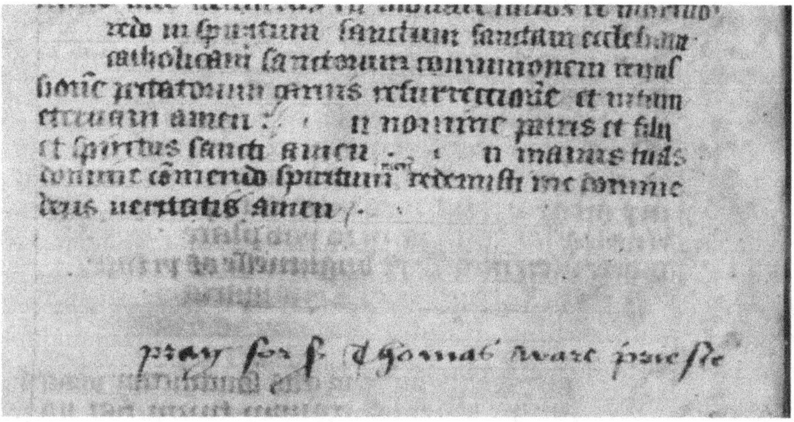

Figure 2. HM 142, f. 14v (detail), The Huntington Library, San Marino, California

NOTES

1. See Daniel W. Mosser, "Longleat House MS 30, T. Werken, and Thomas Betson," *Journal of the Early Book Society* 15 (2012): 319–335; and Joel Fredell, "Design and Authorship in the *Book of Margery Kempe*," *Journal of the Early Book Society* 12 (2009): 1–28, at 22, n. 16, which refers the reader, in turn, to R. A. B. Mynors, "A Fifteenth-Century Scribe: T. Werken," *Transactions of the Cambridge Bibliographical Society* 1 (1949–1953): 97–104. The most thorough study of HM 142 as a whole is still that of H. C. Schulz, "Middle English Texts from the 'Bemet Manuscript,'" *Huntington Library Quarterly* 3 (1940): 443–465. The entire manuscript has recently been made available online in the Huntington Digital Library (http://hdl.huntington.org/).
2. Julia Boffey, "Middle English Lyrics and Manuscripts," in *A Companion to the Middle English Lyric*, ed. Thomas G. Duncan (Cambridge: D. S. Brewer, 2005), 1–18, at 11. On English lay piety in the late fifteenth century as "reformed," see the introduction to Shanon Gayk's *Image, Text, and Religious Reform in Fifteenth-Century England* (Cambridge: Cambridge University Press, 2010), 1–14.
3. Also included in Canon 9 but not listed here were the *virtutes principale*: prudence, justice, temperance, fortitude, faith, hope, and charity. For the text of the Canon, see F. M. Powicke and C. R. Cheney, eds., *Councils and Synods, With Other Documents Relating to the English Church* (Oxford: Clarendon Press, 1964), 2. 900–905. In stating that these additions are contemporary to the manuscript, I follow C. W. Dutschke, *Guide to Medieval and Renaissance Manuscripts in the Huntington Library* (San Marino: Huntington Library Press, 1989), 194. Schulz sees the leaf as a later addition to the volume ("Middle English Texts," 451).
4. *In manus tuas* comes from Psalm 30; the complete line is *In manus tuas Domine, commendo spiritum meum. Redemisti me, Domini Deus veritatis* (Into thy hands I commend my spirit: thou hast redeemed me, O Lord, the God of truth) (Ps. 30.6). The first half of the line is recorded in Luke as Christ's last words, *Pater, in manus tuas commendo spiritum meum* (Father, into thy hands I commend my spirit) (23.46), and features in the Mass for Wednesday of Holy Week as well as in the series of Christ's seven last "words" (or phrases) from the cross, which structure a series of prayers that frequently appear in books of hours. The complete psalm also appears in books of hours as one of the Psalms of the Passion. For the text of the prayers, see *Horae Eboracenses*, ed. Christopher Wordsworth, Surtees Society 132 (Durham: Andrews, 1920): 141–142. The *Confiteor* and *Misereatur* are said at the beginning of the Mass. For the texts, see *Missale Ad Usum Insignis Et Praeclarae Ecclesiae Sarum*, ed.

Francis Henry Dickinson (Oxford: Burntisland, 1861–1863), vol. 1, col. 580. An English version of the *Confiteor* is given in Thomas Frederick Simmons, *The Lay Folks' Mass Book: Or, The Manner of Hearing Mass: With Rubrics and Devotions for the People*, Early English Text Society o.s. 71, (London: N. Trübner, 1879), 8–10.

5. Morton W. Bloomfield, *The Seven Deadly Sins: An Introduction to the History of a Religious Concept with Special Reference to Medieval English Literature* (East Lansing: Michigan State College Press, 1952), 67.
6. Bloomfield, *The Seven Deadly Sins*, 67. Richard Newhauser, "Preaching the 'Contrary Virtues,'" *Mediaeval Studies* 70 (2008): 135–162, at 136.
7. For a study of the history of this collection, including color plates, see Lucy Freeman Sandler, *The Psalter of Robert de Lisle in the British Library* (London: Harvey Miller, 1983), 23–27; plates 2–10, 14–15, and 24–25; and appendix 2. For a digitized version of the collection, see "*The Speculum theologiae* in Beinecke MS 416" (http://brbl-archive.library.yale.edu/exhibitions/speculum/). An earlier Wheel of Sevens seems to have circulated independently, on which, see Laura Cleaver, "From Codex to Roll: Illustrating History in the Anglo-Norman World in the Twelfth and Thirteenth Centuries," *Anglo-Norman Studies* 36 (2013): 69–90, at 81–83; and Marco Rainini, "Symbolic Representations of the *Lord's Prayer* in the Twelfth Century," in *Le Pater noster au XIIe siècle: lectures et usages* (Turnhout: Brepols, 2015): 157–186, and 167–175.
8. See Newhauser, "Preaching the 'Contrary Virtues,'" 136 and 143, where he discusses respectively the work of John Cassian and Evagrius Ponticus. Earlier than they was Prudentius, but his famous combat did not involve the canonical seven deadlies. Bloomfield, *The Seven Deadly Sins*, 64–65.
9. James McEvoy, *Robert Grosseteste* (New York: Oxford University Press, 2000), 142. The work is edited in Joseph Goering and F. A. C. Mantello, Robert Grosseteste, *Templum Dei: Edited from MS 27 of Emmanuel College Cambridge* (Toronto: Pontifical Institute of Medieval Studies, 1984). Goering and Mantello note that the work was the source for the Middle English poem *The Clensyng of Mannes Soule* (8).
10. Transcribed from New Haven, Beinecke Library MS 416. The sins appear in the order pride, avarice, envy, wrath, sloth, gluttony, and lust. English translation by Sam Spears, "The Wheel of Sevens," in *The Speculum theologiae in Beinecke MS 417* (Yale University, 2006), http://brbl-archive.library.yale.edu/exhibitions/speculum/.
11. "Bona opera" is given as the "medicine" for *debilitas* in another table in the *Templum Dei.* See Goering and Mantello, 38.
12. Rufinus, *Expositio Symboli*, ed. Manlius Simonetti, in *Tyrannii Rufini Opera*, Corpus Christianorum Series Latina 20, 1961, 127–182. English

translation by J. N. D. Kelly, in *Rufinus, A Commentary on the Apostles' Creed* (Westminster, MD: Newman Press, 1955). The earliest extant witness to the *Expositio* is Torino, Biblioteca Nazionale Universitaria G.V.26 (s. vi–vii). It was copied throughout the Middle Ages and was the first text printed in Oxford (1478, *STC* [2nd ed.] 21443). For a reprise of the manuscript tradition, which adds to Simonetti's list, together with a study of the Oxford edition, see A. C. De La Mare and Lotte Hellinga, "The First Book Printed in Oxford: The *Expositio Symboli* of Rufinus," *Transactions of the Cambridge Bibliographical Society* 7 (1978): 184–244. Augustine repeats the story in his *Sermo de Symbolo, PL* 40.1189–1202, at 1189–90.

13. Pseudo-Augustine, *De Symbolo IV, PL,* 39.2188–90; and *De Symbolo V, PL* 39.2190–91.
14. Curt F. Bühler, "The Apostles and the Creed," *Speculum* 28 (1953): 335–339. Bühler quotes a passage by Montague Rhodes James from 1930 that refers to an unspecified example of this tradition in stained glass (335). For a more recent and detailed study of the tradition in stained glass, see Madeline Harrison Caviness, "Fifteenth-Century Stained Glass from the Chapel of Hampton Court Herefordshire: The Apostles' Creed and Other Subjects," *Walpole Society* 42 (1968–1970): 35–60, especially appendices 1 and 2. For yet another iconographic tradition, that associated with the *Credo* of Jean de Joinville (1224–1317), see Lionel J. Friedman, *Text and Iconography for Joinville's Credo* (Cambridge, MA: Mediaeval Academy of America, 1958).
15. *The Book of Vices and Virtues,* ed. W. Nelson Francis, Early English Text Society o.s. 217 (London: Oxford University Press, 1942), 6–9. *Dan Michel's Ayenbite of Inwyt, or, Remorse of Conscience,* ed. Richard Morris Early English Text Society o.s. 23 (London: Trubner, 1866), 11–14.
16. Mary Teresa Brady, "The Apostles and the Creed in Manuscripts of *The Pore Caitif,*" *Speculum* 32 (1957): 323–325.
17. James D. Gordon, "The Articles of the Creed and the Apostles," *Speculum* 40 (1965): 634–640.
18. See William Maskell, ed., *The Ancient Liturgy of the Church of England, According to the Uses of Sarum, Bangor, York, & Hereford, and the Modern Roman Liturgy* (London: Pickering, 1846), 87.
19. *Speculum Vitae,* 1230–1452. Ed. Ralph Hanna, *Speculum Vitae: A Reading Edition,* Early English Text Society o.s. 331 (Oxford, Oxford University Press, 2008), 44–51. *A Myrour to Lewde Men and Wymmen,* 81–83. Ed. Venetia Nelson, *A Myrour to Lewde Men and Wymmen: A Prose Version of the Speculum Vitae, ed. from B. L. MS Harley 45,* Middle English Texts 14 (Heidelberg: Carl Winter, 1981). For still more works, see Robert R. Raymo, "Works of Religious and Philosophical Instruction," *A Manual*

of the Writings in Middle English 1050–1500, vol. 7, gen. ed. Albert E. Hartung (New Haven: Connecticut Academy of Arts and Sciences, 1986), 2255–2378 and 2467–2582, at 2283 and 2511–2512.

20. Rufinus, *Expositio Symboli,* 2.15–26, ed. Simonetti; trans. Kelly, 30. For a discussion of Rufinus's faulty philology and later commentators' use of the term *symbolum,* see Kelly, *Rufinus,* 101–102, n8.
21. Dating of the hand from Dutschke, *Guide to Medieval and Renaissance Manuscripts,* 194.
22. Schulz, "Middle English Texts from the 'Bemet Manuscript,'" 444; and see Joseph Foster, *Alumni Oxoniensis: The Members of the University of Oxford 1500–1714* (Oxford, 1891), s.v. "Ware, Thomas." On the Danvers chest and similar medieval endowments established for the University of Oxford, see T. H. Aston and Rosamond Faith, "The Endowments of the University and Colleges to circa 1348," in *The History of the University of Oxford,* gen. ed. T. H. Aston, *Volume I: The Early Oxford Schools,* ed. J. I. Catto (Oxford: Clarendon Press, 1984), 265–310, at 276–277 and 283.
23. G. C. Richards and H. E. Salter, eds., *The Dean's Register of Oriel 1446–1661* (Oxford: Clarendon, 1926), 82.

Another Woman Reader of John Gower's *Confessio Amantis:* Jacquetta of Luxembourg and Cambridge, Pembroke College MS 307

SARAH WILMA WATSON

At the end of Book 1 of John Gower's *Confessio Amantis,* a woman counsels a prideful and impulsive king toward humility and reason. In this story, usually called "The Tale of Three Questions," a young woman named Peronelle helps her father, a knight, answer three riddles posed to him by the king. Peronelle answers the questions wisely, and the king, impressed, says that he would marry her if she were the daughter of a peer. Instead, he offers her a gift of her choice. Peronelle immediately requests that the king increase her father's property holdings, and he does so, thus raising her father to the standing of a peer. Peronelle reminds the king of his words and asks that he honor them. Delighted with her beauty and wit, the king marries her.[1]

In this story, the young woman, Peronelle, carefully manipulates a delicate situation to achieve an outcome that benefits herself, her family, the king, and the community at large. She convinces the king to privilege humility over pride and reason over impulse, leading him to promote rather than destroy one of his most valuable and loyal servants, her father. The king's reasonable action enhances his reputation for fairness and stability among his people, and his marriage to Peronelle establishes a continuing opportunity for good counsel.

John Gower's *Confessio Amantis* is filled with stories addressing the topic of good governance. While Book 7 is the only section of the work that explicitly addresses the education of kings and princes, the poem as a whole could be considered a manual of political advice. The other seven books concern *self*-governance, detailing how an individual must conquer the seven deadly sins. This personal control is framed as an important precursor to successful political governance. Gower uses exemplary stories to illustrate how successful or failed self-control translates into good or bad kingship.[2] In some stories, as in "The Tale of Three Questions," women are presented as the force that guides male rulers toward this type of self-governance.

As Misty Schieberle argues in her monograph *Feminized Counsel,* the subordinate positon of women made them less threatening to the dominant order and provided women with a unique opportunity to counsel men in power.[3] As Peronelle explains to her father in "The Tale of Three Questions":

> For yit par chaunce I may pourchace
> With som good word the kings grace
> Your lif and ek your good to save.
> For ofte schal a womman have
> Thing which a man mai noght areche.[4]

While the king might perceive the advice of a knight to be critical or treasonous, the counsel of a powerless woman like Peronelle is nonthreatening. The king can change his actions in response to her words without losing his sense of authority. Examples of counseling women like Peronelle abound in the *Confessio Amantis.* Women address husbands, fathers, and sons; they advise kings, knights, and emperors. While the figure of the counseling woman is not uncommon in medieval literature, Schieberle argues that women in Gower's poem are presented as successful *political* advisors with surprising frequency.

Given the emphasis on governance in the *Confessio Amantis* and the examples of counseling women, it should not surprise us that a number of powerful medieval women owned copies of Gower's poem.[5] Joyce Coleman convincingly argues that Philippa of Lancaster, the daughter of John of Gaunt and the wife of the king of Portugal, was the patron of a Portuguese translation of the *Confessio Amantis.* The translation was likely produced in the late fourteenth or early fifteenth century by a servant in Philippa's household named Robert Payne.[6] Coleman further suggests that Philippa may have commissioned a Castilian *Confessio* as a gift for her sister Catherine, wife of Enrique III, king of neighboring Castile. The extant Castilian version was produced from a Portuguese copy of the *Confessio* rather than an English copy.[7] As María Bullón-Fernández observes, the political content of the *Confessio* may have been useful to both Philippa and Catherine, given their proximity to seats of European power. The material in the book provided a woman with political advice to pass on to her husband and sons and prepared her to rule should the occasion arise, as it did for late-medieval queens such as Isabel of Bavaria and Margaret of Anjou.[8]

Martha Driver has uncovered a third powerful woman reader of Gower's *Confessio Amantis.* Driver argues that Pierpont Morgan Library MS M.126 was made for an aristocratic female patron at the court of Edward IV, quite likely his queen, Elizabeth Woodville. Driver dates this copy of the *Confessio* to after Edward's IV ascension in 1461 and cites several notations made by the scribe Ricardus Franciscus that may point to Elizabeth as the intended owner of the manuscript. The most convincing of these notations is an inscription that reads "*vive la belle,*" perhaps a playful reference to Elizabeth's name, which was sometimes written as "Isabella."[9] The decoration of M.126 may also connect the codex to Elizabeth. Sonja Drimmer suggests that the red flowers at the base of the opening page may be identified as red carnations or gillyflowers, a floral emblem associated with Elizabeth.[10] Like Philippa and Catherine, Elizabeth was the wife of a king. As the consort of Edward IV, a new ruler inaugurating Yorkist control, Elizabeth may have found the political counsel in the *Confessio Amantis* especially useful.

In what follows, I would like to add a fourth woman to this group of powerful female readers of Gower's *Confessio,* a woman who bore a close relationship to Queen Elizabeth Woodville: her mother, Jacquetta of Luxembourg. Jacquetta owned and marked Cambridge, Pembroke College MS 307, a first-recension manuscript of the *Confessio Amantis.* She wrote her personal motto, "*sur tous autres*" (above all others), and her name, "Jaquette," three times in the margins of the manuscript, leaving a testament to her ownership and use of this copy of Gower's poem. Although Jacquetta's signatures in Pembroke 307 were noted by Kate D. Harris in 1989,[11] Jacquetta's inscriptional practice has not been considered at length or placed in the context of the growing body of scholarship on Gower's *Confessio* and powerful women readers.[12]

Like the other known women owners of the *Confessio,* Jacquetta was involved in politics for most of her life. In 1433, at the age of seventeen, she left her home in the Burgundian Low Countries to become the wife of a powerful English nobleman. Her new husband, John of Lancaster, Duke of Bedford, was the brother of King Henry V and had been named the Regent of France in 1422. The duke's marriage to Jacquetta was intended to bolster the alliance between England and the dukes of Burgundy during the Hundred Years' War.[13]

Though initially used as a passive pawn to secure foreign support, Jacquetta quickly became a political player in her own right. Described by a contemporary chronicler as "lively, beautiful, and gracious," Jacquetta wasted no time integrating herself into the royal court of her new home.[14] Within a month of arriving in England, Jacquetta became an English citizen, and less than a year later she was given the robes of the Order of the Garter. Although her husband died only eighteen months after their marriage, Jacquetta chose to remain in England and continued to style herself the Duchess of Bedford for the rest of her life.[15]

Perhaps in an effort to remain powerful and autonomous, Jacquetta chose as her second husband not a duke but a lowly knight named Richard Woodville. According to a contemporary chronicle, the marriage was contracted through Jacquetta's "own free will" and was loudly lamented by her relatives, who believed Richard to be "inferior to her first husband and to herself in regard to birth."[16]

In 1463, some twenty-five years after her controversial marriage to Richard Woodville, Jacquetta engineered another unexpected union—this time between her eldest daughter, Elizabeth Woodville, and the new king of England, Edward IV. This successful political maneuver, termed witchcraft by several medieval chroniclers, propelled the Woodville family to a position of high favor and influence at the English court.[17]

At some point during her eventful life, Jacquetta acquired and signed the copy of John Gower's *Confessio Amantis* noted above: Cambridge, Pembroke College MS 307. Jacquetta's copy of the *Confessio* is one of twenty-eight first-generation manuscripts of Gower's poem. These manuscripts, produced before 1425, are of a remarkably consistent format and quality. They are spaciously written on good parchment, usually by a single professional London scribe, and feature similar programs of illustration and decoration. Pembroke 307 is one of the largest and finest of the first-generation manuscripts, measuring over 400 millimeters high and including rich illuminations.[18]

It is very likely that Pembroke 307 came to Jacquetta through her first husband, John, Duke of Bedford. The manuscript is one of several *Confessio Amantis* manuscripts associated with the Lancastrian royal family. San Marino Huntington MS E1 26 A 17 was likely a presentation copy given to the Duke of Bedford's father, Henry Bolingbroke, later Henry IV.[19] Oxford, Christ Church MS 148 has a coat of arms associated with Thomas, Duke of Clarence, Bedford's elder brother, and Bodley 294 bears the motto and *ex libris* mark of Humphrey, Duke of Gloucester, Bedford's younger brother.[20] While Pembroke 307 does not include Bedford's arms or motto, it bears important stylistic connections to the Bedford Hours and Psalter (British Library, Additional MS 42131), which Bedford commissioned around 1420.[21] The scribe of Pembroke 307 also ties the manuscript, if not directly to the Duke of Bedford, at least to other members of the Lancastrian court, including Henry V and William de la Pole.[22] These pieces of information and the presence of Jacquetta's signature in the manuscript strongly suggest that Pembroke 307 was commissioned by, or at least owned by, the Duke of Bedford.

Jacquetta inscribed Pembroke 307 three times, using her motto and name to express her ownership of and engagement with this impressive codex. On folio 125r, Jacquetta wrote her personal motto *"sur tous autres"* (above all others) and her name "Jaquette" along the outer margin in a large script perpendicular to the main text (Fig. 1). The signature is decorated with two framing flourishes and a scroll on the descender of the "q." The large size, sideways orientation, and decoration of this motto-name pair and its placement at the midpoint of the manuscript may suggest that it is an ownership mark. The text on the corresponding page is part of Book Five (Avarice) and details the sins of stealth and pilfering. The first and third marks left by Jacquetta are found on the right-hand margin of folio 51v near the beginning of Book Three (Wrath) and on the lower margin of folio 141r in Book Six (Gluttony) (Fig. 2). Both are smaller than the middle mark but similarly include Jacquetta's motto and name. They appear in parallel to the text (rather than perpendicular) and may be interpreted as some kind of annotation, perhaps signaling Jacquetta's interest in a particular passage of text.[23]

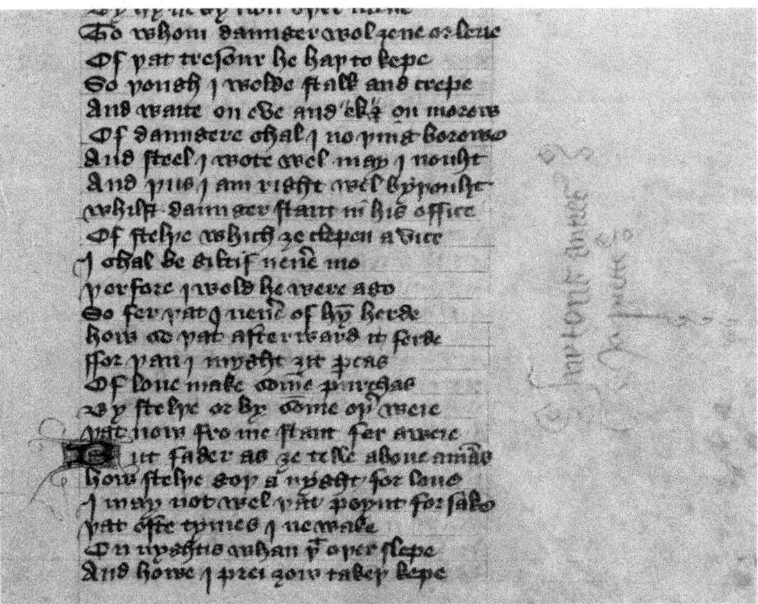

Figure 1. Cambridge, Pembroke College MS 307, folio 125r (By permission of the Master and Fellows of Pembroke College, Cambridge).

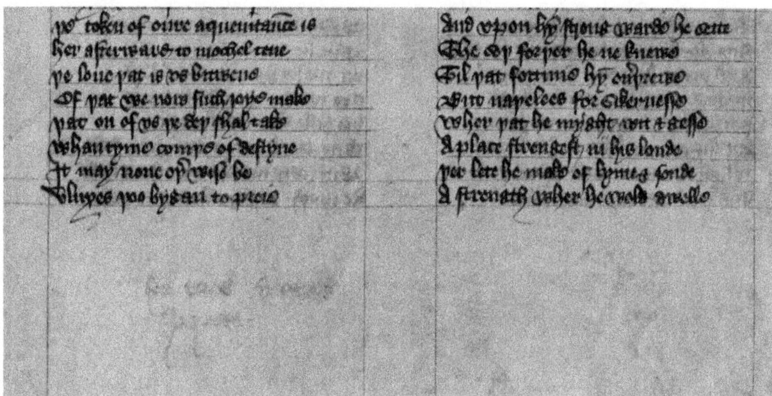

Figure 2. Cambridge, Pembroke College MS 307, folio 141r (By permission of the Master and Fellows of Pembroke College, Cambridge).

While ownership marks are often found on the flyleaves of late-medieval books, Jacquetta's repeated act of inscription, placed at different points in the manuscript in a very consistent form, is somewhat unusual. In Pembroke 307, Jacquetta seems to develop a system of personalized annotation, using her motto-name pair rather than anonymous check marks, Xs, or manicules, to note various points in the text. These multiple personal marks suggest that that Jacquetta not only owned but also *used* her copy of Gower's poem.

So, why might Jacquetta have found the *Confessio Amantis* useful? First, Gower's poem may have given Jacquetta special insight into the recent political history of England. Jacquetta's book belongs to an early recension of *Confessio* manuscripts in which Gower declares that he is writing "A book for King Richardes sake."[24] Around 1392, Gower rededicated his poem to Henry of Lancaster, Earl of Derby and the future King Henry IV.[25] Although Richard II was not deposed until 1399, it would seem that Gower "saw the writing on the wall." Gower's revised prologue is an excellent example of the subtle rhetorical dance necessary for navigating a power shift. We cannot know whether Jacquetta was aware of this alternative prologue, but the reference to King Richard in her copy of the *Confessio* would have reminded her that the current Lancastrian dynasty was fresh and potentially unstable.

This knowledge of political history could have helped Jacquetta to react swiftly when the Yorkists overthrew the Lancastrians in 1461. Despite her family's strong Lancastrian ties, Jacquetta immediately shifted her political fealty, pledging loyalty to the new Yorkist king, Edward IV, and appearing before him with her daughter Elizabeth to plead for the release and pardon of her husband and son. Edward granted her request, perhaps because Richard

Woodville was a minor, nonthreatening knight, perhaps because Jacquetta possessed important ties to Burgundy, or perhaps, as once chronicler notes, because he found her daughter Elizabeth beautiful.[26] Whatever the reason for the king's decision, Jacquetta was instrumental in preserving her family from social and political ruin.[27]

It may have been at this moment of uncertainty that Jacquetta marked a passage in the *Confessio Amantis* concerning the instability of Fortune. Her motto and name appear on folio 141r in the midst of the "Tale of Ulysses and Telegonus," at the bottom of a column of lines describing the dream that predicts Ulysses' change in fortune. The passage begins:

> Bot Fortune is of such a sleythe,
> That whan a man is most on heyhte,
> Sche makth him rathest for to falle:
> Ther wot no man what schal befalle,
> The happes over mannes hed
> Ben honged with a tender thred.[28]

This tidy maxim may have resonated with Jacquetta's experience of political upheaval as she witnessed the fall of Henry VI and the rise of Edward IV.

Following this momentous power shift, it would seem that Jacquetta was determined not just to survive but to rise with Edward IV to the top of Fortune's wheel. Starting in 1461, Jacquetta placed her daughter Elizabeth in the path of the young king, and in 1464, Edward IV married Elizabeth in a secret ceremony at the Woodville family house at Grafton. According to several records, only Jacquetta, a priest, and a few servants were present at the ceremony, and one chronicler suggests that Jacquetta brought about the union by witchcraft.[29] When the marriage was made public, many of Edward's supporters were surprised and angry to find that the king had married the widow of a lowly Lancastrian knight rather than pursuing a marriage alliance with France. While medieval chroniclers perhaps overemphasize or misrepresent Jacquetta's actions, modern historians agree that Jacquetta played an important role in bringing about the union.[30] When considering Jacquetta's involvement in this unlikely turn of events, one is tempted to recall the clever trick of the young woman in "The Tale of Three Questions." Like Peronelle, Elizabeth married a king despite her inferior social status.

Following Elizabeth's marriage to Edward IV, Jacquetta remained at her daughter's side. She was present at Elizabeth's coronation in 1465, regularly dined with the king and queen between 1466 and 1467, and attended Elizabeth's churching after the birth of her first daughter in 1466. In October

1470, when Edward IV was temporarily overthrown, Jacquetta accompanied her daughter and grandchildren when they fled to sanctuary at Westminster. She was presumably also present at the birth of Elizabeth's first son, the future Edward V, who was born at Westminster in November.[31] Jacquetta was thus close to Elizabeth during her early years as queen, perhaps offering her daughter support and advice as she navigated the political and personal complexities of queenship.

As noted above, Elizabeth Woodville owned a copy of Gower's *Confessio Amantis,* now Morgan Library MS M.126. Can Elizabeth's ownership of the *Confessio* be connected to her mother's possession of the same text? A direct link between the two manuscripts seems unlikely. Martha Driver, who has performed spot transcriptions of M.126, finds it to be a very close copy of Oxford, Fairfax MS 3 with some variants consonant with Oxford, Bodley 902.[32] Pembroke 307 and M.126 also exhibit very different programs of illustration—Jacquetta's *Confessio* includes two miniatures, whereas Elizabeth's *Confessio* originally had 106 miniatures, ninety-seven of which survive.[33] However, although Pembroke 307 may not have served as a copytext for M.126, it is still possible that Jacquetta's ownership of the *Confessio* influenced her daughter's possession or use of the same text. Pembroke 307, a stunning book, could have inspired the production of a new, even more lavish copy of the *Confessio Amantis* for Elizabeth. Jacquetta's reading of the *Confessio* might also have prompted imitative reading in her daughter. If Elizabeth Woodville wished to be a skilled politician like her mother, reading the *Confessio Amantis* would have been a good place to start. While such suggestions must remain in the realm of speculation, historical records place these two women readers of Gower in close physical, personal, and political proximity.[34]

In John Gower's poem, the *Confessio Amantis,* Jacquetta of Luxembourg may have found a guide to political history and a manual of political strategy. Though Jacquetta was not the spouse of a king, she was the wife of a regent during her first husband's lifetime, a favorite of Queen Margaret of Anjou during Lancastrian rule, and the mother of the queen consort during Yorkist rule. Subtle political maneuvers were Jacquetta's bread and butter, and the *Confessio,* with its tales of political negotiations and exemplary counseling women, could have provided a useful resource.

The physical inscriptions left by Jacquetta in Pembroke 307 make her interaction with the *Confessio* astonishingly "live." Whereas other copies of the *Confessio* were custom-produced for powerful women, Jacquetta personally modified a preowned manuscript that came into her possession.

Though not specifically designed for Jacquetta, Pembroke 307 and the text it contained attracted Jacquetta's attention and prompted her to leave marginal annotations.[35] Whether Jacquetta consulted the *Confessio* for political advice, moral guidance, entertainment, or some other purpose, her annotations provide remarkable evidence of a late-medieval woman reader engaging directly with Gower's text.

Haverford College

Acknowledgments

I am grateful to Martha Driver for offering me a number of helpful comments and references following the presentation of a version of this piece at the 2017 Early Book Society conference in Durham. I am also grateful to Erika Harman for reading a draft of this essay and giving many helpful remarks.

NOTES

1. John Gower, *The Confessio Amantis*, ed. Russell A. Peck, with Latin translations by Andrew Galloway, 3 vols. (Kalamazoo, MI: TEAMS, Western Michigan University Press, 2002–2004), vol. 1, bk. 1, ll. 3067–3446.
2. On self-governance and kingship in Gower, see Russell A. Peck, "The Politics and Psychology of Governance in Gower: Ideas of Kingship and Real Kings," in *A Companion to Gower*, ed. Siân Echard (Rochester, NY: D.S. Brewer, 2004), 215–238.
3. Misty Schieberle, *Feminized Counsel and the Literature of Advice in England, 1380–1500* (Turnhout, Belgium: Brepols, 2014), esp. 1–20. See also Misty Schieberle, "'Thing Which a Man Mai Noght Areche': Women and Counsel in Gower's *Confessio Amantis*," *Chaucer Review* 42.1 (2007): 91–109.
4. Gower, *Confessio*, bk. 1, ll. 3203–3207.
5. While I discuss only fourteenth and fifteenth-century women owners of Gower in this article, a productive study might be made of sixteenth-century women owners of Gower. Kate D. Harris draws attention to at least two such women. An early sixteenth-century inscription in Pierpont Morgan MS M.126 (a copy of Gower's *Confessio Amantis*) reads "grace seyton made thys." Oxford, Fairfax MS 3, another copy of Gower's poem, was signed by Isabel Fairfax (née Thwaites) in the early sixteenth century. Kate D. Harris, "Ownership and Readership Studies in the Provenance of the Manuscripts of Gower's *Confessio Amantis*," D.Phil. thesis (1993), 116, 122.

6. Joyce Coleman, "Philippa of Lancaster, Queen of Portugal—And Patron of the Gower Translation?" in *England and Iberia in the Middle Ages, 12th–15th Century*, ed. María Bullón-Fernández (New York: Palgrave Macmillan, 2007), 135–165. See also Robert F. Yeager, "Gower's Lancastrian Affinity: The Iberian Connection," *Viator* 35 (2004): 483–516.
7. Coleman, "Philippa," 156.
8. María Bullón-Fernández, "Translating Women, Translating Texts: Gower's 'Tale of Tereus' and the Castilian and Portuguese Translations of the *Confessio Amantis*," in *John Gower: Manuscripts, Readers, Contexts*, ed. Malte Urban (Turnhout, Belgium: Brepols, 2009), 109–132.
9. Martha Driver, "Women Readers and Pierpont Morgan MS M. 126," in *John Gower: Manuscripts, Readers, Contexts*, ed. Malte Urban (Turnhout, Belgium: Brepols: 2009), 71–107. It is worth noting that Ricardus Franciscus marked another Middle English manuscript with the name of a female patron. British Library, Harley MS 4012, a book of Middle English religious tracts in prose and verse, was produced in the 1460s by Ricardus Franciscus for Anne Wingfield Harling. On fol. 51r, Ricardus has added the name "Ane" to a bescrolled ascender. The manuscript also bears an inscription that reads: "Thys ys the boke of dame anne wyngefeld of ha[r]lyng." See Anne M. Dutton, "Piety, Politics, and Persona: MS Harley 4012 and Anne Harling," in *Prestige, Authority and Power in Late Medieval Manuscripts and Texts*, ed. Felicity Riddy (York: York Medieval Press, 2000), 133–146.
10. Sonja Drimmer, "The Visual Language of the Vernacular Manuscript Illumination: John Gower's *Confessio Amantis* (Pierpont Morgan MS M. 126)," 2 vols. Diss. Columbia University (2011), 176–179. See also Ann F. Sutton and Livia Visser-Fuchs, "The Device of Queen Elizabeth Woodville: A Gillyflower or Pink," *Ricardian: Journal of the Richard III Society* 11.136 (1997): 17–24.
11. Kate D. Harris, "Patrons, Buyers and Owners: The Evidence for Ownership and the Role of Book Owners in Book Production and the Book Trade," in *Book Production and Publishing in Britain 1375–1475*, ed. Jeremy Griffiths and Derek Pearsall (Cambridge, UK: Cambridge University Press, 1989), 171. See also Harris, "Ownership," 141–144.
12. In addition to the articles by Coleman, Bullón-Fernández, and Driver noted above, Katherine Lewis is currently preparing an article on women's interest in Gower, especially high-status women, in a forthcoming volume of historians' perspectives on Gower. On gender and power in Gower more generally, see Amanda M. Leff, "Writing, Gender, and Power in Gower's *Confessio Amantis*," *Exemplaria* 20:1 (2008): 28–47;

and María Bullón-Fernández, *Fathers and Daughters in Gower's Confessio Amantis: Authority, Family, State, and Writing* (Rochester, NY: D.S. Brewer, 2000).

13. Lucia Diaz Pascual, "Jacquetta of Luxembourg, Duchess of Bedford and Lady Rivers (c. 1416–1472)" *Ricardian* 21 (2011): 67–91.
14. "*Frisque, belle, et gracieuse.*" Enguerran de Monstrelet, *La chronique d'Enguerran de Monstrelet, en deux livres, avec pièces justificatives 1400–1444*, ed. L. Douët-d'Arcq (Paris: Mme. ve. J. Renouard, 1857–1862), vol. 5, 55.
15. Diaz Pascual, "Jacquetta," 69–72.
16. "*Sa franche voulenté*"; "*au regard du linage il n'estoit point pareil à son premier mari, le reégent, ne à elle.*" Monstrelet, *La chronique*, vol. 5, 272.
17. Diaz Pascual, "Jacquetta," 80–86.
18. Derek Pearsall, "The Manuscripts and Illustrations of Gower's Works," in *A Companion to Gower*, ed. Siân Echard (Rochester, NY: D.S. Brewer, 2004), 73–97.
19. Harris, "Ownership," 124–125.
20. Pearsall, "Manuscripts," 95.
21. The borders in the two manuscripts are very similar, and the two miniatures in Pembroke MS 307 were likely produced by an artist named Johannes, who also worked on the Passion miniatures in Add. 42131. Another detail that draws the manuscripts together and perhaps signals Bedford's interest in or awareness of Gower is an author portrait of Gower found on fol. 209v of Add. 42131. The portrait relates to other depictions of the writer and is accompanied by an inscription, "Gower," within the initial itself. Harris, "Ownership," 149.
22. The scribe is termed the Petworth scribe. He produced British Library, Sloane MS 3501, *The Master of Game*, an English translation of Gaston's *Livre de Chasse* dedicated to Bedford's elder brother Henry V, and British Library MS Arundel 119, a copy of Lydgate's *Siege of Thebes* commissioned by William de la Pole. Linne R. Mooney, "Vernacular Literary Manuscripts and Their Scribes," in *The Production of Books in England 1350–1500*, ed. Alexandra Gillespie and Daniel Wakelin (Cambridge, UK: Cambridge University Press, 2011), 202.
23. The signatures are very difficult to make out. Harris describes the inscriptions as "erased." Harris, "Ownership," 141.
24. Gower, *Confessio*, vol. 2, l. 24.
25. Russell A. Peck, "Introduction," in Gower, *Confessio*, vol. 1, 36.
26. The chronicler Jean de Wavrin notes that at the time of Rivers's pardon, "*le roy Edouard lenamoura telement que oncques puis nen polt oster son ceur*" [the king Edward had become so enamored with her (Elizabeth) that

he could never again free his heart]. *Recueil des croniques et anchiennes istories de la Grant Bretaigne par Jehan de Waurin*, ed. William Hardy (London: Longman, Green, 1891), vol. 5, 352–353.

27. Diaz Pascual, "Jacquetta," 80–83.
28. Gower, *Confessio*, vol. 3, bk. 6, ll. 1509–1514.
29. Some years later, the chronicler Robert Fabyan asserts that, "the kinge was enchuted by the duchesse of Bedford." Robert Fabyan, *The New Chronicle of England and France,* (London, 1516, repr. 1811), 654.
30. Diaz Pascual, "Jacquetta," 80–86.
31. Ibid., 83.
32. Martha W. Driver, "More Light on Ricardus Franciscus: Looking Again at Morgan M. 126," *South Atlantic Review* 79.3–4 (2014): 20–35.
33. Pearsall, "Manuscripts," 89.
34. The whereabouts of Pembroke 307 between Jacquetta's death in 1472 and the early sixteenth century are unknown. The manuscript bears the ownership inscription of Sir John Mundy, a goldsmith and alderman living in London at the beginning of the sixteenth century. How the book passed from Jacquetta to Mundy is unclear. Harris, "Ownership," 145–146.
35. Jacquetta also owned and annotated British Library Harley MS 4431, a collected works of Christine de Pizan. Her motto and name are found on the front flyleaf of the manuscript. Her name appears in the margins of three additional pages (fols. 51v, 52v, and 115v), and her motto appears on fol. 387r. Jacquetta also owned and signed British Library, Cotton MS Otho D II, an early fifteenth-century collection of travel accounts. The flyleaves and margins of this manuscript were lost in the Cotton fire of 1731, but a catalogue of the library produced by Thomas Smith in 1696 notes of Cotton Otho D II: "Liber iste, elegantissimus figuris illuminatus, olim pertinebat ad D. Jaquettam Luxemburgican, Ducissam Bedfordia, ut illa propria manu in fine libri testator." [This book, illustrated with most elegant figures, was once connected to Jacquetta of Luxembourg, Duchess of Bedford, as her own hand in the margin of the book testifies]. Thomas Smith, *Catalogus librorum manuscriptorum Bibliothecae Cottonianae,* 74 (translation mine). For a list of Jacquetta's possessions at the time of her death in 1472, see Diaz Pascual, "Jacquetta," 87–89. For a consideration of Jacquetta as a reader of Harley 4431, see Sarah Wilma Watson, "Jacquetta of Luxembourg—A Female Reader of Christine de Pizan in England," *Women's Literary Culture and the Medieval Canon* (Surrey Blogs, February 27, 2017), https://blogs.surrey.ac.uk/medievalwomen/2017/02/27/jacquetta-of-luxembourg-a-female-reader-of-christine-de-pizan-in-england/.

Punctuating Malory's *Morte Darthur*

HELEN COOPER

My interest in the punctuation of Sir Thomas Malory's *Morte Darthur* goes back to the mid 1990s, when I started work on a slightly abridged, modern-spelling edition of the work for Oxford World's Classics.[1] That series is aimed directly at modern readers, and Malory's is, I believe, the earliest text they have produced that is not either a translation or a full linguistic modernization. In addition to modernizing the spelling, my own edition provides a short glossary of frequent words and further foot-of-page glossing where either the words or the syntax of the original present difficulties. There were a good number of cheap modern-spelling editions of William Caxton's version available, so producing another seemed rather pointless; and in addition, the best text, and one step closer to Malory's original, is now accepted as being the Winchester manuscript (London, British Library Add. 59678; hereafter W). W had provided the basis for Eugène Vinaver's *Works of Sir Thomas Malory* in its three successive editions and for the single-volume student edition, but for reasons of copyright I could not take my text direct from those. Neither Stephen H. A. Shepherd's edition[2] nor P. J. C. Field's mighty new edition[3] had yet been published, so I worked directly from the facsimile of W edited by N. R. Ker.[4] The manuscript is now available online, and is available both on the British Library website and, in much higher quality, on the website of The Malory Project.[5] My aim was to keep as close to the original as possible while making the work as accessible as possible: in effect, as accessible to a modern audience as W would have been to its original readers.

As everyone who has edited any Middle English texts knows, accessibility involves punctuation, that largely invisible but always crucial modern addition to a medieval text. A single glance at W in comparison with any of its modern editions shows one immediate major difference: the manuscript presents its text in solid blocks unbroken over several folios, whereas those other editions supply both paragraphing and modern punctuation—conventions of presentation that modern readers require. Editions of Caxton's text, like their original (hereafter Cx), by contrast typically supply no paragraphing within the chapters: a presentation that Vinaver justifiably deplores in his second and third editions, where he paragraphs more extensively than in the first, since lack of paragraphing obscures a "vital aspect of the work," that is, "the substitution of dialogue for narrative."[6] Caxton breaks up his text into chapters that are smaller and therefore more reader-friendly than W's more widely spaced divisions, which are indicated by large capitals; but he bases his chapter divisions in the first instance on the breaks indicated in W, and does so by the same means of *litterae notabiliores* very similar in appearance to those in the manuscript. Both W and Cx supply punctuation, but their differences from modern conventions, from the absence of paragraphing and the nonexistence of speech marks to the lack of clear differentiation between what we would think of as periods, semicolons, and commas, tend to make for as much difficulty in readability as does the fifteenth-century spelling. In his edition, Vinaver supplies punctuation in a way he thought would best bring out the structure and cadences of Malory's work:

> Punctuation can do more than clarify his meaning: it can help to bring out the rhythm and movement of his prose. The frequent occurrence of compound sentences strung together by innumerable *and*'s is apt to obscure the fact that Malory's favourite period is a short one, falling into not more than three parts, and that, although he sometimes uses a wider pattern, his natural preference is for crisp and compact construction. Punctuation can make this apparent and so reveal the real cadence of Malory's sentences.[7]

This is true, and important; but while noting that "light punctuation has been adopted," which in practice often means added, Vinaver does not note how closely his basic punctuation conforms to that of the manuscript: it seems he arrived at a similar point to the scribes by his own route. I was struck, however, when I was working on the World's Classics edition, how well W's punctuation translated into modern conventions to produce a text that flowed – that did indeed bring out the cadences of Malory's sentences—and I attempted to reproduce that as far as possible, even while modern requirements of familiarity required additions. Stephen Shepherd, in his Norton edition, is equally faithful to a modernized version of W's punctuation; his edition is indeed in many ways the most faithful to the manuscript that we have, including, for instance, his use of a gothic typeface for proper names to indicate W's rubrication. Field does not describe his policy on punctuation, though he does not stray far from the manuscript (or from Vinaver). He reserves a direct reproduction of W's and Cx's original punctuation, in the form of double and single slashes, in citations from the original texts in the apparatus.

W and Cx do however use significantly different forms of punctuation, the most obvious of which is that W punctuates principally with double slashes (//) whereas Cx uses single slashes only (a form of the *virgula suspensiva*), and the two have different functions.[8] The double slash is a normally a form of paraph mark;[9] alongside its single slashes, Cx uses a different form of paraph mark (C), a form he also uses before his "capitulum" headings, but he uses it much more sparingly than W's double slashes.[10] To keep the distinctions clear, this article continues to refer to those marks as single slashes, double slashes, and paraph marks. Malcolm Parkes notes that the double slash often served as an indication to the rubricator to insert the more formal kind of paraph mark, but also that "it was often left to fulfil the function of the paraph itself."[11] Those different usages of punctuation in turn point to the fact that W and Cx are not merely using different symbols for the same effect, but are actively punctuating by different means and for different purposes. This difference calls into question Field's comment that W's double slashes "may be prompts for the later insertion of paraph marks that were never supplied"[12] (which, given their frequency, would be impractical), and which is also at odds with Parkes's categorization of the double slash as a form of paraph mark in its own right. Shepherd's practice of supplying the more familiar modern form of paraph mark, the pilcrow (¶), for W's double slashes may be technically correct, but it has the disadvantage of further defamiliarizing the text, of reducing its accessibility. The scribes of W did not use the more formal paraph symbol; and in the form used by Cx (C) those symbols are much more thinly spaced than W's double slashes, usually (but not consistently) serving as chapter subdivisions.[13]

At first glance, to readers unfamiliar with the punctuation used in both texts, the differences in practice between the manuscript and the print (most obviously, the use of double versus single slashes) do not look very significant. The hypothesis—the argument—of this paper is however that those disparities signal a much larger difference: that W is a text punctuated to facilitate reading aloud, whereas Caxton follows a practice closer to that established for Latin texts. To put it another way, W is written with the reader in mind, whereas the print is text-based or producer-based. That distinction between two basic kinds of punctuation has been described in various ways, all of which find an echo in the differences between W and Cx: rhythmical as opposed to logical; rhetorical as against grammatical; elocutionary or interpretative as against structural; or punctuating for the narrative as against punctuating for the syntax.[14] In the only detailed study of W's punctuation, D. Thomas Hanks and Jennifer L. Fish explore its rhetorical potential, noting in particular how "intensely audience-centred" it is, and how it compels readers themselves "to construct the syntax" in the very act of reading.[15] Cx by contrast largely constructs the syntax for its readers by its frequent use of virgules, single slashes, to mark off clauses, as was done in Latin, sometimes reinforcing them with a following small capital. Its practice is not altogether consistent, and it will at times print a complex sentence largely undivided, but there is still a clear difference from W. W does not uses single slashes, and the major scribe, Scribe A, uses as his own lighter mark of punctuation simply a small capital (smaller, that is, than the *litterae notabiliores* that mark new narrative sections); Scribe B's practice is largely the same, but with some differences as discussed below. These small capitals are markedly less intrusive and less frequent than Cx's virgules, but they provide W with a sufficient hierarchy of marked pauses that is dominated more by the movement of the narrative than by the syntactic unit. The small capital is not generally considered as a feature of punctuation,[16] but it very clearly acts as such in W. These features together mean that when the texts are read aloud, the manuscript produces a smoother and more nuanced reading than the print, in that its punctuation follows more the rhythmical and rhetorical patterns of the text. All premodern vernacular texts were likely to have been read out to a group rather than as a silent individual act, or at least to have been written with such presentation in mind; and not least for a work of prose fiction such as the *Morte*, "reading aloud" seems a much more accurate and natural term than "oral delivery," with its implications of at least some degree of memorization or performance. Individual silent reading gradually became more widespread with the introduction of print, but Malory's text reads as if he was sounding it out to himself in the very process of composition, and the manuscript preserves more of that process.

This is a proposition that is difficult to explain or justify on paper. Rhetorical punctuation requires the intonations of the speaking voice, which cannot be reproduced in print. One needs, moreover, to read one's self into W's rhythms sufficiently to overcome the immediate oddity—the non-recognizability in modern terms—of its punctuation, for even though one can give approximate modern equivalents of medieval punctuation marks, they do not work in quite the same way. Both texts employ a hierarchical range of marks indicating varying degrees of separation, but not only do the form the marks take differ, but they impose different movements on the texts themselves. The nearest modern equivalents for each text are something like this:

Winchester

small capital: semicolon or period
// (paraph mark): period, paragraph break, speech mark, marker for shift of direction
S (*littera notabilior*): style of large capital used to indicate a significant change of subject; much more thinly spaced than Cx's chapter divisions.

Caxton

/ (virgule): comma, semicolon, period
/ followed by small capital: period, speech mark
C (paraph mark): paragraph
S (*littera notabilior*): style of large capital used to open a chapter, often with a significant change of subject

At the cost of some repetition, a quick summary of the punctuation practices in each version of the text may be helpful. W has no close equivalent to a modern comma. This might appear confusing, as pauses have to be deduced from the movement of the text itself; but in a process of reading aloud, hesitations over that movement are in practice very rare. W's lightest form of punctuation does not involve any punctuation mark at all, but just the use of the small capital as a sense break roughly equivalent to a modern semicolon or period; it often introduces a conjunction such as "And" or "So," in a further cue from the text. More complicated is the multiple function of W's double slash //, the paraph mark noted by Parkes as indicating a final pause. When it functions as equivalent to a modern paragraph, it works both backwards and forwards, just as modern justified texts mark the end of a paragraph by a short concluding line and the start of the next by an indentation. W's double slash is normally followed by a small capital, so marking it out as stronger than a small capital alone. When the double slash is used for speech, parallels with modern speech marks are often misleading. It is most consistently used as an opening speech mark; it usually appears again at the end of a speech, but it is often omitted there if what has just been said is closely linked to what follows—if, that is, there is no shift in the direction of the narrative, for instance with a question and its reply. It can, for the equal but opposite reason, appear in the middle of a speech if the speaker moves on to a different subject, or a different aspect of the same subject. In these cases, it serves as an indicator to a reader that a shift in intonation is required; but to keep the reader on track, it is consistently followed by a repetition of the speaker's name, for example a second "seyde the kynge." Those repetitions appear awkward in modern terms, but they make excellent sense as aids to a reading aloud.

Cx's commonest punctuation mark, and his only frequent one—much more frequent than anything in W—is the single slash, the *virgula suspensiva*. This is described by Parkes as being used "to mark the briefest pause or hesitation in a text. Usually it marks the end of a *comma* [i.e., a division of a *colon* followed by a minor disjunction of a text where it may be necessary to pause], but in some fourteenth-, fifteenth- and sixteenth-century copies it could be used for all pauses except the final one."[17] This description refers primarily to Latin practice, but it broadly fits Cx's usage too: the virgulae mark syntactic units, often individual clauses though sometimes a run of several together, reinforced by small capitals for such matters as speech indicators. The practice is not, however, consistent, even for speeches.

Within the limitation of soundless print, an extract chosen at random from the manuscript and printed versions will go some way towards demonstrating the differences in the methods of punctuation. (The randomness is, I think, important, as it avoids the possibility of special pleading.) The passage in question is from the episode where Guinevere is accused by Sir Mador of murdering his kinsman Sir Patryse with a poisoned apple at the dinner she had organized for the knights, starting where those who had been at the dinner are dispersing. I have expanded contractions (mostly for þ-words, much more common in W than in Cx); I have followed W's pattern of capitalization for the "Sir" preceding a proper name, though the pattern appears random (Cx normalizes it to lower case); and I have represented W's rubrication of proper names by italics (no equivalent in Cx). W reads as follows (end of fol. 412r–413r), in a passage in the hand of Scribe A—and it should ideally be read aloud. Superscript letters refer to the following notes; repeated letters refer back to an earlier comparable usage.

And euery knyght yode where hym liked //[a] So whan the kyng and the quene were togydirs the kynge asked the quene how this case befelle Than[b] the [quene] seyde Sir[c] as Iesu be my helpe she wyst not how nother in what manere[d] // Where ys Sir *Launcelot* seyde kynge *Arthure* And he were here he wolde nat grucche to do batayle for you Sir[b,c] seyde the quene I wote nat where he ys but hys brother and his kynessmen deme that he be nat within thys realme // That me repentith seyde kyng *Arthure* for and he were here he wolde sone stynte thys stryfe //[e] Well than I woll counceyle you seyde the kyng[f] that ye go vnto sir *Bors* and pray him for to batayle for you for Sir *Launcelottis* sake and vppon my lyff he woll nat refuse you for well I se seyde the kynge that none of the iiii and xxti knights that were at your dyner where sir *Patryse* was slayne woll do batayle for you nother none of hem woll say well of you and that shall be grete sclaundir to you in thys court[g] [corruption in text] but now I mysse Sir *Launcelot* for and he were here he wolde sone putte me in my hartis ease // What[e] aylith you seyde the kynge that ye can nat kepe sir *Launcelot* vppon youre syde for wyte you well seyde the kynge who that hath sir *Launcelot* vppon his party hath the moste man of worship in thys worlde vppon hys syde Now[h] go youre way seyde the kynge vnto the quene and requyre Sir *Bors* to do batayle for you for sir *Launcelottis* sake // So[i] the quene departed frome the kynge and sente for sir *Bors* into the chambir and whan he cam she besought hym of succour // Madam seyde he what wolde ye that I ded for I may nat with my worship haue ado in thys mater because I was at the same dyner for drede ony of tho kyghtes wolde haue you in suspeccion // Also[e] madam seyde sir *Bors*[f] now mysse ye Sir Launcelot for he wolde nat a fayled you in youre right nother in youre wrong // for[j] whan ye haue bene in right grete daungers he hath succoured you And now ye hath dreuyn hym oute of thys countrey by whom ye and all we were dayly worshipped by hym Therefore madam I meruayle how ye dar for shame to require me to do ony thynge for you In so muche ye haue enchaced oute of your courte by whom we were up borne and honoured // Allas fayre knyght seyde the quene I put me hole in your grace and all that ys amysse I woll amende as ye woll counceyle me And[k] therwith she kneled downe vppon bothe hir kneys and besought Sir *Bors* to haue mercy uppon her other[l] ellis I shall haue a shamefull dethe and therto I neuer offended//

a Lighter than the paraph mark that Cx gives here, this double slash, followed by "So –" and the change of grammatical subject, is sufficient to alert a reader to the new narrative direction.
b The capital marks the change of speaker, but the close connection between Arthur's question and Guinevere's reply means a double slash is unnecessary.
c The start of the speech is sufficiently indicated by the capital for "Sir" and by the word itself.
d The shift from direct speech to indirect is not broken by any punctuation: the underlying thought is continuous.
e The double slash in mid-speech marks a new direction in the speaker's thought: in this first instance, the moment when Arthur turns from voicing his thoughts to addressing Guinevere.
f The repetition after a double slash of "seyde" plus the speaker keeps the reader informed that the speaker is not changing.
g The long run of unpunctuated text after the second "seyde the king" has its movement governed by the clause indicators, "that... that... where... for... nother... that".
h The small capital is sufficient here as Arthur is continuing with his interrogation of Guinevere.
i The double slash and the capital mark a new direction in the narrative; Cx gives a chapter break here.

j The double slash without a following capital is unusual, but "f" may just be a scribal variant on the usual capital form ff-. It signals a light change of intonation, as do the capitals marking off the equivalent of sentences in the rest of Bors's speech.
k The queen's kneeling continues the line of narrative indicated by her speech, therefore no double slash is necessary.
l The shift from indirect to direct speech does not require a punctuated pause (cf. d above).

In that passage, there are ten instances of the double slash and nine independent small capitals that serve as punctuation (i.e., excluding such things as their use for proper names). Cx by contrast provides one chapter division; two paraph marks, one followed by a small capital and one not; and forty single slashes,[18] of which thirteen are followed by small capitals and 27 are not. Those thirteen include one ambiguous case, a clause starting with "I" where the capital would be required anyway. Apart from mid-clause instances of "I" and the quasi-proper nouns "Realme" and "Courte," there are no small capitals without a preceding virgule. The most obvious difference between the texts is thus the much denser use of punctuation in Cx; less immediately obvious, but just as important, is the failure of many of these marks to provide a clear hierarchy of inflections and pauses of the kind required for reading aloud. Cx's version of the same passage, from the middle of Book XVIII chapter iv to the start of chapter v, reads as follows.[19]

and euery knyghte wente where it liked hem / ¶[a] So whan the kynge and the quene were to gyders / the kynge asked the quene how this caas bifelle / the quene ansuerd / so god me help I wote not how nor in what maner / where is sir launcelot said kyng Arthur / and he were here he wold not grutche to doo betaille for yow /[b] Sire sayd the quene I wote not where he is / but his brother and his kynnesmen deme that he be not within this Realme / that[c] me repenteth sayd kyng Arthur / For[d] and he were here / he wold soone stynte this stryf / Thenne I wille counceyle yow sayd the kynge [corruption in text here] and vnto sire Bors that ye wil doo bataille for her for sir launcelots sake / And vpon my lyf he wille not refuse yow / For wel I see said the kynge that none of these foure and twenty knyghtes that were with you at your dyner where sir Patryse was slayn that wille doo batail for yow nor none of hem wille saye well of yow[e] / and that shalle be a grete sklaunder for yow in thys Courte / Allas[f] said the quene and I maye not doo with all but now I mys sir launcelot / for and he were here / he wold putte me soone to my hertes ease / ¶[g] what eyleth yow said the kynge ye can not kepe sir launcelot vpon your syde / for wete ye wel sayd the kynge who that hath sire Launcelot vpon his partye / hath the moost man of worship in the world vpon his syde / Now goo your way said the kynge vnto the quene / and requyre sir Bors to doo bataille for yow for sire launcelots sake

¶ Capitulum quintum[h]/

SOo[i] the quene departed from the kynge / and sente for sir Bors in to her chamber / And whan he was come she besought hym of socour / Madame said he / what wold ye that I dyd / for I maye not with my worshyp haue adoo in this mater by cause I was at the same dyner for drede that ony of tho knyghtes wold haue me in suspecyon / Also[j] madame said sir Bors now mys ye sir launcelot / for he wold not haue fayled yow neyther in ryght nor in wronge / as ye haue wel preued whan ye haue ben in daunger / and now ye haue dryuen hym oute of this countrey / by whome ye and alle we were dayly worshypped by / therfor madame I merueylle how ye dar for shame requyre me to doo ony thynge for yow in soo moche ye haue chaced hym oute of your countrey / by whome we were borne vp and honoured / Allas fayr knyghte sayd the quene I put me holy in your grace / and alle that is done amys / I will amende as ye wille counceyle me / And[k] therwith she kneled doune vpon bothe her knees / and besought sir Bors to haue mercy vpon her / outher[l] I shall haue a shameful dethe and therto I neuer offended /

a One of Caxton's thinly scattered paraph marks, here signaling a significant change of scene and another stage of the narrative: a kind of lesser chapter division.
b The run of virgules up to this point give no sense of the hierarchy of pauses required between the grammatical units, until the final virgule plus small capital for the start of Guinevere's following speech; the effect is consequently jerkier than in W.
c The virgule signals the following new clause but without a following small capital to distinguish it immediately as a new speech. W provides a double slash before its capitalized "That."
d The stronger breaks that follow, marked by a single slash and following capital (/ For, / And etc.), come mid-speech, though the sense runs on directly from what has just been said; other examples occur throughout the extract.
e The run of unpunctuated syntactic units is less usual in Cx than in W: perhaps here, as sometimes in Latin, because they are all grammatically dependent on a single verb, "see." Other examples occur in Bors's speeches below.

f The virgule plus capital here signals a new speaker; this is Cx's commonest practice, but a virgule without a capital is also widespread, as with the king and queen's first passages of direct speech above, and at c.
g The paraph mark signals a new speaker, but it is not followed by a capital, and there is no significant break in the sense or narrative direction.
h One of the additional chapter breaks inserted in Cx where W offers only a double slash.
i This is Cx's standard typography for starting a new chapter. W uses similar *litterae notabiliores* for its more widely separated narrative divisions.
j The capital marks a new direction in the same speech, hence also the repetition of the speaker's name.
k The virgule plus capital here signals the transition from speech back to narrative.
l Unlike in W, a punctuation mark is used to indicate the shift between reported and direct speech, as also in the queen's first speech at the start of the extract.

That the two texts offer different methods of punctuation is evident; the next question must be whether anything can be deduced about Malory's own practice from those differences, and any answer must be much more hypothetical. Scribe A is not, of course, the only copyist at work on W; if Scribe B, who is generally taken to have been the secondary one, followed exactly the same practices as his senior, then the evidence for their reproducing what they found in their exemplar would be strengthened. It has, however, been widely accepted that that exemplar was not Malory's original, so even if the scribes of W were faithful to their copy, that would not clinch the case for the punctuation being Malory's. Moreover, Caxton is known to have had a second manuscript in his workshop, and that could possibly have already contained a more grammatically based punctuation for him to reproduce. The case for Caxton's punctuation being his own, however, is strengthened by the fact that its features as demonstrated in his edition of the *Morte* are also found in his prints of other comparable prose works, though the evidence is not entirely consistent. His *Chronicles of England,* in its first 1480 edition, starts off on the first page of its main text using small capitals and puncti but not virgules; but those already begin to appear on the verso of that folio, and they become more frequent as the volume progresses. The edition also uses paraph marks for chapter subdivisions in a manner comparable to the *Morte.*[20] *Charles the Grete,* published in the same year as the *Morte* (1485; *STC* 5013) and closer to it in genre, shows a practice almost identical to the *Morte,* with an abundance of single slashes with or without following capitals, and the occasional mid-chapter paraph mark.

If W does contain evidence for Malory's own punctuation, it would lie in the closeness of the practices of its two scribes: the more similar they are, the more likely they are to be following what they found in their exemplar, which, holograph or not, would at least be one degree closer to Malory. The evidence here is suggestive, but not quite conclusive. Scribe B copied folio 35r, folios 45r to 191r, and folios 229v to 346v. On both folios 35r and 45r, Scribe A copies the first few lines as if to provide a model for Scribe B to follow, but on those folios Scribe B departs from Scribe A's punctuation practice in his frequent use of punctus. These are usually but not always followed by small capitals, and there are some independent small capitals without a preceding punctus: the punctus, in other words, functions in the same way as Scribe A's double slash.[21] Towards the end of folio 45r, Scribe B does begin to introduce the double slash alongside the punctus, though somewhat sparingly; but the double slash becomes increasingly common as he continues to copy, and the punctus becomes correspondingly rarer. He abbreviates more heavily than Scribe A, especially for þ- words; and he also uses the double slash very generously for hyphenation. His copying of the Roman War section uses the double slash to mark a number of the original alliterative lines, though that is to be expected since they tend to be syntactic units. This passage comes from folios 77v to 78r :

> // yet he shappis at sir *Arthure* but the kyng shuntys a lytill and reches hym a dynte hyȝe uppon the haunche And ther he swappis hys *Genytrottis* in sondir//[22] Than he rored and brayed and yet angurly he strykes and fayled of sir *Arthure* and the erthe hittis that he kutte into the swarffe a large swerde length and more // than the kynge sterte up vnto hym and raught hym a buffette and kut his baly in sunder that out wente the gore that the grasse and the grounde all foule was begone // Than he kaste away the clubbe and caughte the kynge in his armys and handeled the kynge so harde that he crusshed his rybbes //[23]

A more direct comparison with Scribe A's work may be made by a folio such as 120r, a passage in the "Tale of Sir Gareth" that includes quite a lot of conversation, where the double slashes are frequent and serve the same function as those in the passage from the accusation of Guinevere quoted above; and that practice continues into Scribe B's extended later stint on the "Tristram." He is, however, more sparing with independent small capitals (the only one used in the passage above is for "And ther he swappis ... "), but more prolific with them after a double slash. If any tentative speculation can be offered based on this, it would be that Scribe B started out on both folios

35r and 45r using his own punctuation practice, which differed from both his exemplar and Scribe A, but then altered that practice to conform more closely to Scribe A's. It may be that that change was at Scribe A's request; but my own cautious inference would be that the increasing consistency in Scribe B's later practice results from his following at least the double slashes that he finds in his exemplar, whether at A's behest or on his own initiative, and that he accustomed himself as he progressed to a more faithful reproduction of what he found in front of him.

This article does not make any claim to being the final word on its subject. Much more remains to be done on Caxton's punctuation practices, not least in relation to his French and Latin sources; on the two scribes of Winchester; and on the punctuation of manuscripts of other fifteenth-century English prose texts. Only then will it become possible to offer a clearer hypothesis about how Malory himself shaped his text, and whether he did so by grammatical principle or by its sounding in the mind and voice.

University of Cambridge

NOTES

1. *Sir Thomas Malory: Le Morte Darthur: The Winchester Manuscript,* ed. and abridged by Helen Cooper, Oxford World's Classics (Oxford: Oxford University Press, 1998).
2. Sir Thomas Malory, *Le Morte Darthur,* ed. Stephen H.A. Shepherd (New York: Norton, 2004).
3. *Sir Thomas Malory: Le Morte Darthur,* ed. P.J.C. Field (Cambridge, UK: D.S. Brewer, 2013).
4. Sir Thomas Malory, *The Winchester Malory: A Facsimile,* intro. N.R. Ker, EETS s.s. 4 (1976).
5. The Malory Project, directed by Takako Kato and designed by Nick Hayward (http://www.maloryproject.com/). I have worked from both this and Ker's EETS facsimile for this article.
6. *The Works of Sir Thomas Malory,* ed. Eugène Vinaver, 3rd ed. revised by P. J. C. Field (Oxford: Clarendon Press; New York: Oxford University Press, 1990), cxxiv.
7. Ibid.
8. I have worked primarily with the facsimile with introduction by Paul Needham, *Le Morte d'Arthur / Sir Thomas Malory, printed by William Caxton 1485* (London: Scolar Press, 1976), supplemented by the EEBO copy (*STC* no. 801); the Malory Project has a digital facsimile in progress.

9. The double slash also serves as a hyphen when a word is divided at the end of a line; these are not counted in the analysis that follows.
10. On the forms and terminology for punctuation, see M.B. Parkes, *Pause and Effect: An Introduction to the History of Punctuation in the West* (Aldershot, UK: Scolar Press, 1992), 301–307.
11. Ibid., 305; and on the history of the double slash as an independent mark, ibid. 107. He gives an illustration of this usage from a prose text of the *Brut* closely contemporary with W, ibid. 208, pl. 28, with commentary on 209.
12. Field, ed., *Le Morte*, xliii.
13. The paraph marks have been extensively studied by Takako Kato, *Caxton's* Morte Darthur: *The Printing Process and the Authenticity of the Text,* Medium Ævum Monographs NS XXII (Oxford: Medium Ævum Monographs, 2002).
14. The emergence of punctuation, and especially in relation to reading aloud, is outlined by Henri-Jean Martin, *The History and Power of Writing,* trans. Lydia G. Cochrane (Chicago: University of Chicago Press, 1994), 56–58.
15. D. Thomas Hanks, jr., and Jennifer L. Fish, "Beside the Point: Medieval Meanings vs Modern Impositions in editing Malory's *Morte Darthur,*" *Neuphilogische Mitteilungen* 3rd ser., 98 (1997): 273–289 (274). They do not note W's contrast with Cx.
16. Hence Hanks and Fisher's characterization of W as being largely unpunctuated: the absence of distinctive punctuation marks is not at all the same as an absence of signals for pauses or changes of intonation, which are largely carried by these small capitals.
17. Parkes, *Pause and Effect,* 307 (and see 302).
18. This count excludes the virgule following the chapter number and the final one.
19. This is sig. Uiiii^{v}-v^{r} of the print (image 366 on EEBO).
20. *STC* 9991; the main text (beginning on sig. a1) is preceded by an unnumbered contents list.
21. Scribe B does, however, divide words at the end of a line much more frequently than Scribe A, and uses the double slash as equivalent to a hyphen. A further difference from Scribe A is B's greater readiness to use abbreviations.
22. The rarity of the errors by either scribe in rubricating proper names might suggest that it is itself a practice that they already found in their exemplar; but Scribe B's infamous misunderstanding here of "genytrottis" as a proper name requiring rubrication would potentially call into

question the possibility that that might have been Malory's own practice. Malory would hardly have made the mistake himself, though a puzzled scribe might have added it as an extra to what was in his exemplar.

23. The heavy editing of this section of the text in Cx prevents any direct comparison.

De Worde's Edition of Trevisa's Translation of *De proprietatibus rerum* (c. 1495) and its Relationship to MS Plimpton 263

A. S. G. EDWARDS

Wynkyn de Worde's edition of John Trevisa's Middle English translation of Bartholomaeus Anglicus's *De proprietatibus rerum* was published about 1495 (STC 1536; Duff 40).[1] Part of the interest in the printing of this text lies in the unusual fact that its manuscript setting copy survives.[2] It was established over sixty years ago by R. W. Mitchner that de Worde's edition was largely based on New York, Columbia University MS Plimpton 263.[3] But some aspects of the relationship between this manuscript and de Worde's printed text invite fuller examination than they have received.

De Worde did not follow his copy text invariably. This is particularly so at the beginning of his work, where, in a radical intervention, he replaces the "Prohemium" and text of Book I, which comprises twenty-one chapters in his copy text and in other manuscripts, with a "Prologue of the translator" and a new Book I that consists of a single chapter followed by a summary of the following Books II to XIX. In total, the Prologue and Book I in de Worde's edition amount to about 2,400 words. It is only with the beginning of Book II at the start of a new quire that compositor's marks start to appear in the Plimpton manuscript.[4]

De Worde's decision not to follow his setting copy at the start of his edition has not been the subject of much discussion. Mitchner reports simply that "there are no markings in Book I of the MS. text, of course, because de Worde does not print that book; he offers instead a paraphrase of the material in it, plus some moral reflections of his own."[5] His comment is compressed in the modern edition of Trevisa's translation, which simply reports, "[de Worde] abridges and paraphrases Book I."[6] There has not been any further consideration of the issue apart from the observation of Sue Ellen Holbrook that "the version [in de Worde] differs so considerably that the possibility of another source altogether should be investigated, as should be de Worde's reasons for preferring it."[7]

There is no textual relationship between the version of Book I that de Worde printed and the form of this book that appears in the manuscripts of the *De proprietatibus*. As a preliminary to suggesting why this is the case, it is necessary to describe the opening and closing sections of de Worde's edition of Trevisa's Bartholomaeus Anglicus translation.

The physical features of these sections can be briefly described. The opening quire, quire A, of which only Aii and Aiii are signed, comprises the title page (Ai); Trevisa's prefatory verses (Ai^{v}); and "Prologue of the Translatour" (Aii^{r}–^{v}). The "Prologue" is followed by a woodcut (Aiii; Hodnett 1298) and the heading "Incipit liber .i. de. trinitate & de capitulis istorum librorum sequencie," a title that does not have any parallel with that in any of the surviving manuscripts. The text of Book I extends from Aiii to Av, ending at the top of Av. These leaves have the running title "Liber Primus." They are followed (Av^{r}–^{v}) by a summary of the next eighteen books. The next leaf in the copies that I have examined marks the start of quire B, a quire of eight leaves; this quire gives details of the number of chapters in each Book. The next quire, b, is the beginning of Book II and is of six leaves; from the next quire (c) the quires are generally, but not invariably of eight leaves. The final quire (oo) is six leaves, the first four of which are signed. The text of Book XIX ends on the recto of signature ooiiij; signatures ooiiij^{v} to oov^{v} have the verse "Prohemium Bartholomei | de proprietatibus rerum." Signature oovi repeats the xylographic title page; signature oovi^{v} has Caxton's device.

Both the first and last quires, quires A and oo, suggest that there were some problems with the printing of these sections of the text, seemingly involving initial miscalculations over how much copy would be available. As the description above indicates, the first quire (A) contains text on only five leaves.[8] The fact that the first four leaves of quire oo are signed suggests that it had been initially envisioned as a quire of eight leaves, although there is nothing after the sixth leaf. And the title "Prohemium" for the verses on signatures ooiiij^{v} to oov^{v} in the final quire suggests that these were originally intended to precede the beginning of de Worde's text, not conclude it. It seems that at both the beginning and end of his edition de Worde had some difficulties in accurately assessing the space required for copy for those sections of his text that are unique and found himself with blank leaves, A6 and oo7 to oo8. Such facts suggest that de Worde was not in possession of a complete copy text when he began the casting-off process. It may also be that in addition to not coming from the Plimpton manuscript, copy for these quires did not come necessarily from the same source or at the same time.

Certainly the verse "Prohemium" was clearly composed specifically for this edition. It mentions "Roger Thorney mercer," the apparent commissioner of the edition, as well as "William Caxton first printer of this boke," and the paper maker "John Tate the yonger." It consists of thirteen rhyme royal stanzas, and extends over three pages as set up in quire oo. That the "Prohemium" is printed at the end of the book suggests that it was received after copy for the prologue and Book I and was too long to be accommodated on the final leaf of quire A, which consequently had to be left blank, and the verses repositioned to the very end of the volume.

The problems with the "Prohemium" may have been caused by the late and overlong arrival of copy, which required its repositioning to a point in the book different from that originally envisaged. The problems with the Prologue and Book I may have been caused by the absence of any copy at all. The most likely reason for the omission of the text of the Prologue and Book I as these appear in the Plimpton manuscript is that de Worde never received them. The Plimpton manuscript amounts to nearly four hundred large leaves, copied in double column. It could not have been cast off for setting and distribution in a bound form. Indeed, it is possible that it had never been bound when de Worde got it.[9] Since it would have come into the printing shop in quires, it may be that the early quires, either inadvertently or because the owner of it for some reason did not wish them to be used, were not handed over to de Worde's press to be set. With such a large manuscript in disbound form, such confusions about the storage and distribution of manuscript copy would be possible.

In the absence of the Prologue and Book I, de Worde had to commission new copy for these parts of the text. This may have led to a decision to begin setting with Book II (which, as noted above, starts a new quire), while waiting for copy for Prologue and Book I to be prepared. The copy he received for Book I did not run to a complete opening quire, but was too long to leave sufficient space for the "Prohemium" verses, hence the blank, often canceled, A6.

One objection to this hypothesis might seem to be the presence in de Worde's edition, on signature A1v, of the prefatory Middle English verses (*NIMEV* 664.3) that appear in the majority of the manuscripts. Since these verses occur on the opening leaf of the text in Plimpton, the failure to follow Plimpton for the Prologue and Book I might seem to require a different hypothesis. For why would de Worde print these verses but then abandon his copy text for what follows?

One possibility is consistent with the hypothesis advanced above. The recto of the opening leaf in Plimpton, which contains the verses and the start of the Prologue,[10] has an elaborate full-page border. Because of its decoration, such a page (and by extension the quire of which it was a part) might have been initially set aside in the printing house to ensure that it did not get stained or marked up.[11] If so, then it may have become mislaid, so that its contents were not available for the preparation of Book I.

The prefatory verses comprise twenty-four lines in couplets. There are over twenty orthographic (but not substantive) differences between Plimpton and de Worde's printed text of these lines. Either the text was modified in de Worde's house by editor or compositor or he had a different source.[12]

A factor that may bear on what happened is the decision to print these verses on the verso of the title page. An examination of the rest of his incunabular output suggests that elsewhere de Worde very rarely included verse in this position or saw the verso as a place to start a text.[13] I can identify only seven other publications in which de Worde begins a text on the verso of a title page: *The Assembly of Gods* [1498] (Duff 253; STC 17005); Lydgate, *the Chorle and the Byrde* [1497?] (Duff 259; STC 17011); William Lyndewode, *Constitutiones prouinciales ecclesiae anglicanae* (Duff 279; STC 17103); Clement Maydeston, *Animaduertandum . . . magister Clerke correctonis* (Duff 296; STC 17726); John Stanbridge, *Paruula* (Duff 342; STC 23163.7); *Here Begynneth a Lytell Treatise for to Lerne Frensshe* (Duff 407; STC 24866); and *A Lytell Treatyse That Sheweth How Every Man & Woman Ought to Faste on ye Wednesday* (Duff 413; STC 24224). A number of these are small books, ranging from four (*Lytell Treatyse That Sheweth*) to six (Stanbridge) to eight (Lydgate's *Chorle and the Byrde*) to twelve (*Lytell Treatise for to Lerne Frensshe*) to sixteen (*Assembly of Gods*) leaves, where space constraints seem likely to have been the determining factor in where the text began.

Only two, Clement Maydeston (168 leaves) and William Lyndewode (226 leaves), are substantial books, both in prose. Such evidence suggests that de Worde did not as a rule like to begin a text on the verso of the title page. But in this instance he may simply have had no other option. The most economical assumption seems to be that the mislaid verse passage in Plimpton was received or recovered only at a very late stage in the production process, after the rest of the first quire had been set, when the only available space was on the verso of the title page. If so, then the changes between Plimpton and de Worde's text are the result of editorial or compositorial interventions.

If de Worde had rediscovered the early quire of the Plimpton manuscript at a late point in the preparation of his edition, the differences in length between the versions of the Prologue and Book I in Plimpton and those that de Worde had commissioned and (presumably) had already set up, along with the rest of the text, would have left him with the only option of including the verses in an unusual position. It seems that like the "Prohemium," the Prologue and Book I of de Worde's 1495 edition were specifically done for this edition.

This is not the only point where it has been claimed that de Worde departs from his setting copy. It has been stated that de Worde's edition was "conflated in part (Books III chapter 23 to V chapter 38, and Books V chapter 40 to VI chapter 14) with another manuscript that closely resembled (but was not [BL Harley 4879])."[14] The Plimpton manuscript has no printer's marks on folios 32 to 66 and 71 to 84, the leaves containing these parts of the text. But it seems open to question whether de Worde actually used a different manuscript for these parts of his edition. Examination of the printed variants in Volume I of the Clarendon edition of *On the Properties of Things* reveals relatively few unique variants in de Worde's edition that could support the assumption that he used a different manuscript for these passages.[15] Nor is there any real evidence in the printed variants to suggest a relationship between de Worde and BL Harley 4879, the manuscript held to "closely resemble" de Worde's text for these sections.[16] The most likely explanation for the absence of printer's marks in these sections of the Plimpton manuscript is that de Worde, for whatever reasons, had a copy made of them, which was then used as setting copy.

The printing of de Worde's edition of Trevisa's translation of the *De proprietatibus rerum* seems to have involved a number of distinct problems in the treatment of its setting copy. The arguments outlined above may provide the most economical way of accounting for the printing of the beginning and end of this text.[17]

University of Kent and University College, London

APPENDIX: DE WORDE'S PROLOGUE AND BOOK I

De Worde's version of the Prologue and Book I have never been printed in their entirety or original form.[18] In what follows, the abbreviated forms in the printed text have been silently expanded except for the ampersand; "y^{e}" is rendered as "the"; "w^{t}" as "with"; "y^{t}" as "that"; the nasal contraction has been expanded as "–n-" or "–m-";[19] light punctuation has been added; de Worde uses virgules or periods to mark the ends of sentences irregularly and occasionally uses the colon in ways that do not accord with modern usage; orthography and capitalization have been preserved. The paragraphing is that of the original. No emendations have been made for sense.

[Aii^ra] Prologue of the Translator

True it is that after the noble & experte doctryne of wyse & well lernyd Philosophers lefte & remaynyng with vs in wrytyng we knowe that the propritees of thynges folowe & ensewe their substaunces. Herfore [*sic*] it is that after the ordre and the distinccioun of substaunces the order and the distynccyon of the propritees of thynges shal be and ensewe. Of the whiche thynges this werke of all the bokes ensewynge by the goode grace, helpe & assystence of almighty god is compyled & made. Merueyle not the witty & eloquent reders that I, thynne of wytte and voyde of cunnynge, haue translatid this boke from latin into our vulgayre langage as a thynge profitable to me & perauenture to many other whyche vnderstonde not latyn nor haue not the knowlege of the proprytees of thynges. Whiche thynges ben approued by the bookes of grete & cunning clerkes and by the experience of moost witty and noble Phylosophres. Alle thyse propritees of thynges ben full necessary and of grete value to them that wyll or be desyrous to vnderstonde the obscuretees or derknesse of holy scriptures whiche be yeuen to vs vnder fygures, vnder parables & semblaunces, or liklihodes of thynges naturelles and artyfycelles.

Saynt Denys that grete philosopher & solempne clerke to his boke namyd of the heuenly Ierarchies of Aungelles testyfieth and wytnesseth the same sayenge in this manere: What so euer ony man wyll coniecte, feyne, ymagyne, suppose, or saye it is a thynge impossyble that the lyghte of the heuenly dyuyne clarete couerte & closid in the deyte or in the god[**Aii^rb**]hede sholde shyne vppon vs yf it were not bi the dyuersitees of holy couertures. Also it is not possyble that oure wytte or entendement myghte ascende vnto the contemplacyon of the heuenly Ierarchyes immaterielles yf our wytte be not ledde by some materyell thynge: as a man is ledde by the honde soo by thyse fourmes visibles our wytte maye be led to the consyderacyon of the gretnesse or magnytude of the moost excellent bewteuous clarete dyuyne & Inuysyble. Reciteth this also the blessyd appostle Poul in his epistles, sayeng that by thise thynges visybles whyche ben made and ben visible man maye se and knowe by his Inwarde syghte Intellectuall the diuyne celestyall and godly thynges whiche ben Inuisibles to this our naturall sighte. Deuowte doctours of Theologye or dyuinyte for this consyderacyon prudently and wysely rede and vse natural philosophye & morall, and poetes in ther ficcions & feyned Informacyons vnto this fyne or ende so that by the lyklyhode or simylitude of thynges visybles our wit or our vnderstondynge spirytuelly bi clere and crafty vtteraunce of words may be so well ordred and vttred that thyse thynges corporelles maye be cowplid with thynges spyrytuelles and thyse thynges visybles may be conioyned with thynges Inuysybles. Excyted by thyse causes to the edifyenge of the people conteyned in our crysten faith of almyghty Cryst Iesus whose maieste diuyne is Incomprehensyble and of whom to speke it becomyth noo man but with grete excellent worshyppe and honoure and wyth an Inwarde dredefull fere. Loothe to offende I purpose to say somwhat vnder the correccyon of excellent lerned doctours & [**Aii**va] wyse men what euery creature reasonable ought to byleue in this oure blessyd christen faythe.

[**Aiii**] Woodcut [Hodnett 1298]

Incipit liber .i. de. trinitate & de capitulis istorum librorum sequencie

[**Aiii**ra] The fader the son the holy ghost be thre persones by personall proprytees but thabsolute propritees be commune to all thre persones but some of thyse [**Aiii**rb] proprytees ben more appropred to oone than to one other. As thus power is appropryd to the fader. To the sone wysdome is attrybute. And to the holy ghost is attrybute grace. [**Aiii**va] The fader is god, the sone is god, the holy ghost is god. And thise thre persones be not thre goddes but one very god euerlastynge, one essence or one beyng euer perdurable or durynge wythout mesure, not chaungeable. Almyghty, one substaunce and in one nature symple. The fader is of no thynge precedent, the sone is of the fader, the holi ghost is of the fader and of the sone, procedynge wythoute begynnynge of tyme and wythout ende. Thyse thre persones ben one substaunce togider wyth one perdurabilyte togider and one is egall to the tother in all manere of perfeccyon and eche one is Omnypotent or almyghty, and one begynnynge of all thynges, create of noothynge, or made of ony thynge, creatour of all creatures, visybles or Inuysibles, spyrytuelles or corporelles. The whyche creatour by a myghty vertue fro the begynnynge of tyme creat togyder the creature angelyke and the worldly nature of no thynge or of no matere precedent. This creator thenne made man and nature humayne comune to the fyrste tweyne natures, for man is of body corporall and of soule he is made spyrytuall. From this holy trynyte all confusion and all myxcion of persones is voyded, for the fader is another, the sone is another, the holy ghost is another, nor the fader may not be the sone nor the holy ghost, nor the sone maye not be the fader, nor the holy ghost. Nor the holy ghost maye not be the fader nor the sone but to thyse thre persones is one essence or beynge and one nature commune, the whyche is the begynnynge of alle thynges, and out of this begynnynge ther is no begynnyng. Thyse thre persones be one god one essence, Indyuysible or vnable [**Aiii**vb] to be dyuyded: one substaunce and one nature. The fader is no gretter nor of gretter power than is the sone nor than the holy ghost is, for the vnyte of the dyuyne essence or being is egall or lyke in power to the fader, to the sone, and to the holy ghost. And this holy trynyte is one god, the fyrste begynnynge wythout begynnynge not creat, nor engendryd, not passible nor mortall, mighty of power to make all thynges wythout nombre and wythout ende, fountayne of all godenesse and of all vertue, whyche by hys symple knowlege knoweth al thynges present & to be and may do euery thyng that he woll doo; but he wyll not do euery thyng that he may doo for he myght dystroye alle the worlde and yet he woll not do it. How be it that this dyuyne essence or beynge maye not be perfyghtely knowen nor comprised by ony resonable and mortall creature yet there is not ony mortall persone hauynge the vse of dyscrecyon but that he woll confesse there is a god whyche is the cause and begynnynge of all thynges. How be it there is no man of suche wytt and humayne vnderstondynge that can suffycyently serche or fynde what thyng god is properly after the gretnesse of his moost excellent maieste but oonly the fader, the sone, the holy ghost be one trynyte in one vnite, one unyte in nature and in essence one trinyte in persones thre, so named trynyte, as one vnyte of persons thre whiche be vnyed togider in one nature. Vnder this fourme rehercyd it suffyceth to euery cristen creature to knowe the trynyte and in especyall to theym whyche ben of the lay see or state.

The knowlege of the names of god is not required as necessari to eueri man [**Aiv**[ra]] to knowe for thei ben many in nombre. And eueri name that is of god it sheweth or signyfieth the goodly essence or beyng or it sygnyfieth the godly or diuyne perfeccyon or it shewyth the dyuyne or godly persones. The name signyfienge or betokenynge the dyuyne essence or beynge ben callid names essencialles. The names whyche betoken or sygnyfye dyuyne or godly perfeccyon ben callyd names perfeccionalles. The names shewynge, betokenynge, or specyfyenge the godly or dyuyne persones be namyd personalles or vocinalles. Thyse thre maneres of names be dyuyded in to many other maneres of names whyche of necessitee ben to be lernyd of thyse grete and cunnynge doctours of theologye or of diuynyte, whyche ben to vs, or of ryht oughte to be, techers and prechers of the worde of god incarnat and to shewe vs ensample of good lyfe bi theyr virtuous liuynge and euer to be stronge & myghty and redy dfendours [*sic*] of our cristen fayth and of holy chirche bi their excellent perfyghte science and cunnynge. It is ryghte necessary to vs that lyue in thys our crysten faythe to truste truely and stedfastly to byleue that the sone of the fader of heuen whiche is withoute begynnyng coeternall to his fader and to the holy ghost by the hole concent of thys blessyd trynyte and one vnyte and by the cooperacyon of the holy ghost he entred into the wombe of the moost pure, moost intemerate, moost immaculate, moost clene, moost vertuouse, moost humble, and moost meke vyrgyne Marye in whom was neyther spotte nor ryuyll of synne after the salutacyon of Gabriel the archangel whan she had answerde thyse words of mekenesse: Beholde and se [**Aiv**[rb]] I am the handmayde of the lorde; be it doo to me after thy worde. Thus thys blessid sone of god not leuynge or forsaking the godhede toke mankynde vnto the godhede and is perfyghte god, one with his fader in godhede; he is also perfyghte man and in his manhede he is lesse than his fader is. And in his manhede he is in hebrewe namyd Iesus in the tonge greke he is called Sother and in latin he is called

Saluator. And euery name of thyse thre in our langage is to saye a sauyour. He is also namyd Emanuel whiche name by Interpretacyon in our langage is to say god is with vs. After his moost blessyd natyuyte he proued in his humanite that he was perfyghte god for he cowde all scyence without ony techer. He also chaungyd pure water in to wyne He gaue syghte to the man that was borne blynde. He sayd openly to the Iewes and to the Pharisees: I whyche speke to you am the begynnyng. He fedde many thousandes of people wyth few looues of brede & wyth fewe fishes. The wynde & the see obeyed to his commaundement. He reysed Lazar fro dethe to lyfe whyche was foure dayes deed and stynkynge in his graue. In thyse and in many moo excellent myracles he shewed that he is perfyght god. He also shewed that he is perfyght man. For he ete and dranke and slepte and soo toke encrease in nature as man dooth. He wepte, he fastyd, he suffryd all the miseries and wrecchidnesse of man excepte synne. Yt lyked hym to fulfyll, to perfourme, and to accomplysshe all the words that holy Patriarkes and Prophetes had vttred and spoken of hym longe tofore or he toke oure humanytee. And soo to fulfylle the prophecyes he [**Aiv**[va]] suffred that his humayne nature shold be taken by the kyssynge of his vnkynde discyple and moost horrible traytour Iudas. And by the cruell persecucyon of the Iewes after many punycyons they blasfemyng god tofor Pilate cried vengably, crucyfye, crucifye him, and so vnder Pounce Pilate he suffryd to be crucyfyed and vpon the crosse he deyed in his humanyte and was enterid or buried. And notwythstondy-nge that his sepulcre or graue was seelyd and syned & kept with knightes, yet the thyrde day by his godhede or dyuynyte he rose in his humanite and at .xl. day ensewyng he ascended in to heuene and sitteth there att ryghte honde of his fader. And he fro thens perfyghte god and perfyghte man is to come and to iuge the lyuynge and the deed. In the deed is vnderstonde the body whyche hath be mortall. And in the lyuynge is vnderstonde the soule whyche is spirytuall and Inmortall. Tofore this Iuge Cryste Iesus whyche is god and man syttyng in his trone of Iugement all resonable creatures shall stonde. And he shall sette alle rightfull on his ryght syde and all vnryghtfull on his lefte syde and all shall be Iuged after theyr actes or dedes, and after theyr thoughtes as they haue ben guyded in theyr bodyes, well other euyll. Thenne the good shal haue blysse eternal and all the euyll accursed shal haue and suffre euerlastyng payne. Wherfore euery crysten man and woman haue thys blessyd trynyte, the fader, the sone, the holy ghost stedfastly grounded in their fayth as one perfyghte vnyte. To this vnyte in trynyte and to this trynyte in on unite mankynde be neuer vnkynde, for this blessyd Iesus oure sauyour the se[**Aiv**[vb]]conde persone of the trynyte whyche with his fader and wyth the holy ghost is on god, one essence, and one vnyte whyche Iesus also of his Infynyte goodnesse, of his excellent pite, & of his moost plenteuouse mercy, suffryd pacyently moost horryble payne and passyon and dethe in his humanyte for to redeme al mankynde. And for this his Indicible, or not able to be spoken and Inenarrable, or not able to be talkyd or tolde, grete excellent and myghty kyndnesse he desyreth of man but this yeft saying thus: Geue me thy herte and it suffyseth to me.

Man yf thou loue almyghty god thou bileuest and trustest in god.And thy true and stedfaste bileue is but a thynge deed wythoute good werkes. Herfore [*sic*] euery man and woman doo euer good dedes and haue good thoughtes, and that thy langage be good. And in case that bi humayne fragilyte or freyltee thou trespas ayenst the commaundement of almyghty god yet se that thou dispayre not for the good lorde of his habundaunt grace hathe gyue a lawe for trespassours in thys present lyfe, that is to saye contrycyon confessyon and satisfaccyon. And euery resonable creature takynge this way maye be sure that almyghty Cryst Iesus, very god and man, is medyatour in his perfyghte humanytee to the hyghest and moost blessyd and Inestymable dyuynyte or deyte for all mankynde.

Syth it is peryllouse to euery erthely man and in especyall to him that hath a thynne wytte and lytyll cunnynge as I knowe that I haue, to wade depe in thyse materes of dyuynyte And also thise proprytees of thynges ben dyuyded in to .xix. bokes Wherfore I woll commytte the correcion of thyse bokes to the wyse [**Av**[ra]] vnderstondynge and noble and gentyll dyscrecyon of the reders. And thus we wol fynysshe and make an ende of this matere and shall shewe compendyously the content of euery boke of this present volume. And after to procede to the chapytours of the same.

The fyrste boke conteyneth the table wyth the Chapytours of euery of thyse xviij. bokes folowyng for this table with this forsayd matere in the whyche matere the names of god essencialles, perfeccyonalles, and personalles ben declared suffycyently for our byleue.

The seconde boke treateth of the proprytees of angelles good and euyll...

NOTES

1. STC and Duff date it "[1495]." *Catalogue of Books Printed in the XVth Century Now in the British Library BMC Part XI* ('t Goy Houten, Netherlands: Hes & De Graaf, 2007) dates it "[*c.* 1496]" on 200; for discussion of the dating, see 201.
2. There are very few instances where such copy texts survive in English printing; eight are identified in Margaret Lane Ford, "Author's Autograph and Printer's Copy: Werner Rolewinck's *Paradisus conscientiae*," in *Incunabula: Studies in Fifteenth-Century Books Presented to Lotte Hellinga*, ed. Martin Davies (London: British Library, 1999), 109–128, in Appendix I: "A Provisional List of Recorded Fifteenth-Century Printer's

Copies, with Selected Literature," 119–125, nos. 17, 18, 23, 26, 28, 29, 30, and 33; the Bartholomaeus is no. 28; see further, Lotte Hellinga, "List of Printer's Copy Used in the Fifteenth Century," in *Texts in Transit* (Leiden, Netherlands: Brill, 2014), 67–101. For a further example, see Daniel Wakelin, "Caxton's Exemplar for *The Chronicles of England*?" *Journal of the Early Book Society* 14 (2011): 75–113; and Lotte Hellinga, "Caxton's *Chronicles of England* and Its Printed Copy," *The Library* 7th ser., 18 (2017): 316–324.

3. See R. W. Mitchner, "Wynkyn de Worde's Use of the Plimpton Manuscript of *De proprietatibus rerum*," *The Library*, 5th ser., 6 (1951–1952): 7–18. It has been stated that this manuscript "was obtained for [de Worde's] use through the good offices of Roger Thorney, mercer": see M. C. Seymour, ed., *On the Properties of Things: John Trevisa's Translation of* Bartholomaeus Anglicus De Proprietatibus Rerum, 3 vols. (Oxford: Clarendon Press, 1975–1988), 3.21. There is no evidence for this; de Worde states in his "Prohemium" that his edition was printed "at prayer and desire | Of Roger Thorney mercer."
4. They begin on fol. 13v, the start of de Worde's quire *b*.
5. Mitchner, "Wynkyn de Worde's Use," 9.
6. Seymour, *On the Properties*, 1.41. "A Note on the Text" (1.xi–xii) mentions de Worde's edition and discusses its departures from Plimpton in parts of Books III–VI but not the question of Book I.
7. Sue Ellen Holbrook, "A Medieval Encyclopedia 'Renewed by Goodly Printing': Wynkyn de Worde's English *De proprietatibus rerum*," *Early Science & Medicine* 3 (1998): 119–156, 132 n. 54.
8. I have not made a full census of surviving copies; but a number do lack A6, including those in Pierpont Morgan Library, Huntington, Princeton University, both copies in the Bodleian Library, Cambridge University Library, Chicago, Newberry Library, and the John Rylands Library of the University of Manchester.
9. The earliest record of a binding on this manuscript comes in the description in its sale: Christie's, May 15–18, 1925, lot 371, where it is described as bound in "18th century stamped russia." On the contemporary tendency not to bind medieval manuscripts, see Jean Vevrin, "'Quaderni simul ligati': Recherches sur les manuscrits en cahiers," in *Of the Making of Books: Medieval Manuscripts, Their Scribes and Readers: Essays Presented to M. B. Parkes*, ed. P. R. Robinson & Rivka Zim (Aldershot, UK: Scolar Press, 1997), 64–70.
10. The opening quire of Plimpton is a separate booklet containing the table of chapters; see Ralph Hanna and Thorlac Turville-Petre, eds., *The Wollaton Medieval Manuscripts* (York, UK: York Medieval Press, 2010), 125.

11. Another factor may have been that the opening leaf as it now exists has suffered considerable damage to the upper and outer margins. If it was in that state in 1495, then the owner may have been reluctant to have it sent to the printing shop but had a copy made.
12. The treatment of these verses in the modern critical edition is open to some skepticism; very few variant readings are recorded. It is not noted there that the text of the version in Cambridge University MS Ii. V 41 is printed in Rossell Hope Robbins, ed., *Secular Lyrics of the XIVth and XVth Centuries* (Oxford: Clarendon Press, 1952), 94–95; this contains a number of substantive variants not noted in the modern edition (I, 40). Other manuscripts do not seem to have been collated at this point.
13. I take these figures from E. G. Duff, *Printing in England in the Fifteenth Century: E. Gordon Duff's Bibliography with Supplementary Descriptions, Chronologies and a Census of Copies*, ed. Lotte Hellinga (London: Bibliographical Society, 2009).
14. Seymour, *On the Properties*, 1.xi.
15. See Hellinga, *Catalogue of Books Printed in the XVth Century*, 201. If the variants printed in the Clarendon edition are a reliable guide, unique variants from de Worde appear at the following points: 125/12, 126/9, 126/27, 141/13, 143/13, 158/26, 160/20, 165/24, 166/18, 168/3, 169/5, 172/15, 175/12, 176/31, 181/1, 183/4, 184/15, 184/27, 185/9, 186/15, 201/33, 202/28, 205/1, 221/26, 222/13, 225/11, 229/13, 237/1, 238/24, 241/1, 241/17, 244/16, 248/10, 250/20, 252/1, 252/9–11, 260/24, 264/11, 265/11, 265/22, 266/32, 267/2, 272/16, 273/27, 273/33, 277/1, 279/3, 279/22, 280/6, 283/32, 284/28, 285/6, 285/18, 286/8, 287/14, 288/3, 289/15, 289/35, 290/1, 290/27, 291/10, 296/31, 298/11, 298/25, 299/10, 299/26, 302/32, and 304/14. This is not a large number, just over forty, in a span of about 180 pages of text, particularly since a number involve the simple omission of single words.
16. Agreements between de Worde's edition and this manuscript against all the other witnesses as recorded in the Clarendon edition are few over the same long section of text; they occur only at 129/4, 129/5, 129/10, 134/16, 135/5, 147/34, 150/20, 156/33, 160/1, 164/8, 165/11, 185/24, 211/18, 220/21–22, 225/22, 245/4–5, 263/33, 265/28, 287/27, 292/22, 304/20, and 310/6.
17. I am indebted to Professor Julia Boffey both for the use of her notes on the Plimpton manuscript and for comments on a draft of this paper.
18. De Worde's "Prologue of the Translator" is printed in part, in regularized form, in Charles W. Dunn and Edward T. Byrnes, eds., *Middle English Literature* (New York: Harcourt, Brace, Jovanich, 1973), 491–492.
19. Occasional otiose nasal contractions have been ignored.

Caxton at Work: How the Temporale of the *Golden Legend* Was Made

JOHN SCAHILL

Concerning his *Golden Legend* (henceforth GoL), William Caxton states:

> I had by me a legende in Frensshe, another in Latyn and the thyrd in Englysshe, whiche varyed in many and dyuers places, and also many hystoryes were comprysed in the two other bookes whiche were not in the Englysshe book; and therfore I haue wryten one oute of the sayd thre bookes.[1]

This leaves much to be explained. It is true that he used the *Légende dorée* (henceforth LgD),[2] the *Legenda aurea* (henceforth LgA)[3] and the *Gilte Legende* (henceforth GiL)[4], except in the set of Old Testament legends, which draw on none of those texts.[5] But by what process would an author who is primarily a printer rather than a literary artist or scholar combine three lengthy sources? His statement indicates a desire for comprehensiveness, leading to the conflation of parallel versions, but detailed analysis will show that this is not exactly what Caxton did.

It has been difficult to investigate Caxton's authorial procedures in the absence of a scholarly edition of GoL, of the relevant (c) version of LgD, or (until recently) of any version of GiL. A parallel text of a sample section—the opening of the "Dedication of a Church," chosen at random, though with a qualification indicated below—allows us to analyze his methods (see Appendix 1 below).

An inspection of the parallel text shows how close the three are, so that for the most part there is no way of deciding which of the earlier texts was the source of GoL, except for the numerous cases where the English versions have identical lexemes while LgD has a synonym of different etymology: the first line alone provides *chirche* versus *eglise* and *halowed emonge/amonge* versus *celebre entre*. There is just one unique agreement between the English texts that arguably extends to structure and meaning (see the passage labeled **ii** in Appendix 1 below).

On the other hand, there are sufficient places (marked in bold) where GoL and LgD agree against GiL to confirm that the French text was also a source.[6] In a minority of cases, GoL's word is not GiL's but an anglicization of the one in LgD; thus *memoire* instead of *mynde*, *sacrefyeng* instead of *hal-winge*, *coueryng* instead of *helinge*. Some of these adoptions led Caxton into notable innovations. The meanings "paint, sculpt, decorate" are attested for the French *imaginer* (see the passage labeled **i** in Appendix 1 below) but are not recorded for *imagine(n* in the *Middle English Dictionary* or the *Oxford English Dictionary*.[7] Nor is *Signyficatly* (see the passage labeled **iii** in Appendix 1 below) recorded in either dictionary, and this adverbial formation of the very rare adjective *significate* would appear to be a calque on the word in LgD. (In both these cases, the GiL reading is a conjectural emendation, on the basis of its French source.) It may be that further lexical divergences between the English texts have in fact been prompted by LgD, in that GoL uses its habitual equivalents for French words, such as *bycause that* for *pour ce que* and *ought to* for *doit* (as opposed to *for that* and *shulde* in GiL). When LgD and GiL differ in syntax or meaning, GoL regularly sides with the French; thus *to the sight* in contrast to *whanne we see*, *that which* in contrast to *yef she*, or *we haue* in contrast to *she is sent*.

GoL, then, is not simply the fusion of LgD and GiL that Caxton's statement might imply. LgD provides the framework, and GiL is primarily a lexical resource.

What of Caxton's third claimed source, the LgA? Evidence for its use is scanty, even when LgD and GiL are both unsatisfactory. Thus, the puzzling *admyracion* (see the passage labeled **iv** in Appendix 1 below) is reproduced from LgD, in disregard of the correct reading, *adiuratione*, available in LgA.[8] (GiL, lacking any equivalent, would have been no help here.) Similarly, the obscure *But in this* (see the passage labeled **vi** in Appendix 1 below) is retained; consultation of LgA would have yielded the more meaningful *et infra*,[9] continuing the quotation from Hugh of St. Victor. The obscure sentence *She breketh . . . good maners* (see the section labeled **vii** in Appendix 1 below), no easier in LgD or GiL, has evidently not been checked against the clearly superior reading of LgA, *Frangis vocem, frange et voluntatem, servas* *consonatiam vocum, serva concordiam morum.*[10] On the other hand, *offyce* (see the section labeled **v** in Appendix 1 below), which has no equivalent in LgD or GiL, may have been prompted by *orationes* in LgA.[11]

From this evidence, it can be hypothesized that Caxton worked from LgD but that GiL was available for simultaneous consultation, and where it ran closely parallel to LgD—as it generally did—it was drawn upon for lexis. This extends the existing view of Caxton as a translator whose vocabulary was largely a passive reproduction of that of his sources:[12] having GiL simultaneously available freed him from the need to translate vocabulary at all, though he sometimes derived his lexis from the French, as well as his structures. In addition, there are idiosyncratic expansions and condensations as well as occasional consultation of the Latin. Caxton's stated desire for comprehensiveness is reflected in the passages shared by GoL and LgD with no equivalent in GiL.

This handling of sources is typical of the Temporale from the fourth text, "Epiphany," onwards. The evidence for this claim will be set out in the edition in preparation, which will also identify some exceptions, notably original additions by Caxton and passages in which LgA is the immediate source.

The first three texts, however, are different. For the second, "Nativity," GoL follows LgD in giving a version abbreviated to about one third the length of that in GiL and LgA, and use of GiL seems impossible to demonstrate, in spite of occasional agreements in wording. In the next, "Circumcision," the situation is reversed: GiL is abbreviated to about one third the length of the other texts, and again, connections between the two English versions are hard to identify. But in the first, "Advent," the versions mostly do run parallel, yet the opening section (see Appendix 2) shows that the position is quite different from that found in "Dedication of a Church."

In this parallel text, much more is bolded to indicate that GoL and LgD agree against GiL, meaning that GoL's source can only have been LgD. (The several places where they preface the vernacular version of a quotation with the Latin version, omitted in GiL, are less significant.) It is likely that GiL was consulted: the first line has a phrase (see the passage labeled **viii** in Appendix 2 below) that appears to come from it (and has no equivalent in LgA), while in the section labeled **ix** in Appendix 2 below, LgD has a lengthy paraphrase (the first part omitted here), for which GoL, like GiL, has a briefer substitute, though its wording could also be derived from LgA, *ibi enim solummodo est eruditus.*[13] Other unique lexical agreements between the English texts are not frequent or remarkable enough to exclude the kind of coincidences likely when two translators work on very similar originals. Perusal of the three texts suggests that GiL did not furnish the near-continuous gloss of LgD that Caxton found so convenient in later sections such as

"Dedication of a Church." The risks involved in the lack of an English crib are suggested by the passage labeled **x** in Appendix 2 below: GoL uses much of the lexis of LgD but loses track of the sense, perhaps because GiL offers no equivalent. (In the French, as in the original Latin, Christ redeems people from subjection to the law, whereas in the English version he redeems them in order to make them subject to the law.)

These findings cast some light on a related question. If Caxton had before him GiL, itself based on LgD and LgA, why did he make a new English version drawing on the same sources? Two answers have been proposed. Manfred Görlach postulates that Caxton either discovered the GiL only after he had started on his own translation or wanted to make something new,[14] while George Painter supposes that he found out about the GiL only after he had completed his own translation.[15] On the evidence set out here, Painter's view cannot be correct. Görlach's first proposal could be right: the similarities between the English versions in "Advent" are scanty, and compelling evidence for the use of GiL exists only from the fourth legend, "Epiphany," onwards. Alternatively, GiL may have become available at an early stage, but Caxton, having embarked on a translation of LgD, did not yet find it useful. The GiL text in "Advent" does indeed match LgD less neatly than it does in "Dedication," suggesting greater divergence between the (c) version of *Légende dorée* and the earlier versions, among which was the principal source of GiL.[16] More detailed conclusions on this point require further study of the genesis and development of the (c) version, not to mention a readily available text. The absence from GiL of texts for Resurrection and Corpus Christi, included in both LgD and GoL, might have been an additional factor; but perhaps, having started with LgD as his main source, Caxton simply modified his procedures rather than transform them, so as to avail himself of the lexical resource that GiL offered.

University of Technology, Sydney

APPENDIX 1

The Dedication of a Church

GoL sig. d8va–e1ra
LgD 362ra–362va
GiL 959/1–961/63

GoL The dedicacion of the chirche is solempnly halowed emonge the other feestes of the chirch, and
LgD *La dedication de leglise est solempnellement celebree entre ces autres festes de toute leglise et*
GiL The dedicacion of the chirche is solempnely halowed amonge all other festes of the Chirche and

and bycause that it is double chirche or temple, that is to wete materiall and spyrytuell, and therfor it
pour ce que il est double eglise ou temple/ Cest assauoir materiel et espirituel et pour ce est il
for that the double feste of the chirche or temple, that is to saie materiall or spirituel, and therfor it

is to be seen shorthly of the dedicacion of this double temple. As to the dedicacion of the
a veoir briefment de la dedicacion de ce double temple Quant a la dedicacion du
is to be seen shortly of the dedicacion of this temple that is double. As to the dedicacion of this

temple materyall, iij thynges ben to be considered: first wherfor it is halowed or dedicate, secondly
temple materiel *trois choses sont a considerer premierement pourquoy il est dedie ou sacre/ Secondement*
materialle temple, three thinges be for to be considered; furst wherfor it is dedied or sacred, secoundely

how it is halowed, **thirdly by whom it is halowed. And bycause that ij thynges ben in the**
comment il est sacre/ ***Tiercement par lesquelz il est sacre/ Et pour ce que deux choses sont ou***
how it is sacred.

chirche that ben halowed, that is the aulter and the temple, therfor it is first to be seen how the aulter is halowed.

temple qui sont sacrees/ Cest lautel et le temple/ pour ce est il premierement a veoir comment lautel est sacre

The aulter is first halowed for thre thynges. First, to make sacrefise to God, as it is said
Lautel premierement est sacre a trois choses premierement a sacrefier aux dieux/ si comme il est dit
The auuter is furst sacred to .iij. thinges; furst for to sacrifie to God, as it is saide
(Genesis viij), "Noe edyfyed first an aulter to Our Lord and toke of all the birdes
en genesi ou .viij^e^. chappitre/ Noe ediffia premierement vng aurel a nostre seigneur & prinst de tous les oiseaulx
in Genesy in the .viij. chapitre: "Noe edified furst an auuter to oure Lorde and toke of all the briddes

and of all the beestes of the world and offred them vpon the aulter." And the sacrefise that we make vpon þe aulter
et de toutes les bestes du monde et loffrit sur lautel/ Et ce sacrefice que nous faisons sur lautel/
and all the bestes of the worlde and offered hem up on the auter." And that sacrifice that we do upon the auuter

is the body and blood of Ihesu Crist that we sacrefye in **memoire** of the passion of Our Lord,
cest le corps et le sang ihesucrist que nous sacrefions en ***memoire*** *de la passion nostre seigneur*
is the bodi and the blode of Ihesu Crist that we sacrifice in **mynde** of the passion of our Lorde

after þat he commanded vs and said, "Doo ye this in my **memorye**." We haue iij **memoryes**
selon ce que il nous commanda et dist faictes le en mon ***memoire****/ Nous auons trois* ***memoires*** *de*
after that he vs recomaunded and saide: "Dothe this in **mynde** of me." We haue thre **myndes** of

of the passion of Our Lord. Þat one is the mynde of the passion [of hym] **that we haue in wrytyng,**
la passion nostre seigneur Lune memoire est la passion ***que nous auons en escript/***
the passion of oure Lorde: that one mynde is the passion of oure Lorde;

and that other **ymagyned**[i] in figure and þat is **to the sight**. **For** th'ymage of Ihesu Crist, and of the
et lautre ***ymaginee*** *en figure et cest quant* ***au veoir car*** *limage de ihesu crist et les*
that other is [ymagined] in figure, and that is **whanne we see** the ymage of Ihesu Crist and

other ymages that ben in the chirche for the remembraunce of **Ihesu Crist** and of his sayntes, **is** for to **moeue**
autres ymages qui sont en leglise a la remembrance de ***ihesu crist*** *et des sains* ***est*** *pour* ***esmouuoir***
other ymages that be in the chirche in rememberaunce of **God** and of his seintes for to **stere**

þe deuocion of the people. Thise ben **also** as þe bookes of the laye peple and thise ij **memoryees** ben
la deuoucion des gens/ se sont ***aussi*** *come les liures es layes gens/ & ces deux* ***memoires*** *ne sont*
the deuocion of the peple, for thei be as bokes to lay men, and these two **myndes** be

but one. The second **memorye** is in worde, **that is** the **Passion** of Our Lord prechid, and this mynde is
que vng/ La seconde ***memoire*** *si est en parolle* ***cest*** *la* ***passion*** *ihesu crist preschie/ et ce memoire*
but one. The seconde **mynde** is but one in worde, and that is the **passinge** of Ihesu Crist preched, and that mynde

is as to the heeryng. The thirde mynde is the passion of Our Lord transfigured into this sacrement,
se fait quant a loyr/ Le tiers memoire si est la passion ihesucrist transfiguree en ce sacrement
is made to the heringe. The thridde mynde is the passion of Ihesu Crist transfigured in this sacrement

which is verily the soule, body and blood[ii] of Ihesu Crist, and this mynde is as to þe tastyng. And
qui est vraiement a[m]e ou corps et ou sang de nostre seigneur/ & ce memoire est fait quant au goust Et
that is verily soule, body and blode of Ihesu Crist, and this mynde is made as to the taste. And thanne

yf the passion of Ihesu Crist whiche is wreton enbraceth þe **talente**, and **that which** is prechid enbraceth it
se la passion ihesu crist qui est en escript embrase ***lentalentment/*** *et* ***celle qui*** *est preschee lembrase*
yef the passion of Ihesu Crist that is wretin embrasith the **will** and **yef she** [be] preched enbr[a]se hym,
yet more, moche more ouht this **sacrement** enflamme, in whiche it [is] enprynted so **signyficatly.**[iii]
encore plus/ *trop plus fort la doit enflamber ce* ***sacrement*** *on quel elle est emprainte si* ***signiffiement/***
thanne moche more strongely shulde enflawme this in whiche she is enprentid so **signifi**[**auntli**].

Secondly, as for to calle þe name of Our Lord, wherof is said (Genesis *xij*), "Abraham edefyed
Secondement a appeller le nom de nostre seigneur et de ce dist la genesi ou .xij. chappitre abraham ediffia
Secondely for to calle the name of oure Lorde, and of that saithe the Genesy in the .xij. chapitre: Abraham edified

an aulter to Our Lord." And this inuocacion or callyng ought to be made after þat th'appostle saith
vng autel a nostre seigneur/ et ceste inuocacion our appel doit estre faicte selon ce que lapostre dist
an auuter to our Lorde [...]" And this vocacion or callynge shulde be called and made after that the apostle saithe

to Thymothee, or by prayers made **by admyracion**[iv] for to take away þe euyllis fro vs, or by orysons made
a thimotees ou par prieres qui sont faictes ***par admiracion*** *pour oster les maulx ou par oroisons faictes*
to Timotheus, or by praiers that be made for to take away eueles, or by orisones made

to gete the goodes, **or by requestes made** t'encreace **the goodes** and to kepe them. The first
pour impetrer les biens/ ***ou par les requestes faictes*** *pour* ***les biens*** *accroistre et garder/ La premiere*
for to gete goodes and for to encrece **hem** and for to kepe hem. The furst

that is made vpon the aulter is said proprely a messe, bycause that Ihesu Crist is sente fro heuen. And

qui est faicte sur lautel est proprement ditte messe/ pour ce que ihesucrist y est enuoie du ciel/ Et
that is made upon the auuter is properly saide the masse, for that Ihesu Crist is sent fro heuene. And

this worde messe proprely is said of sendyng, and to the messe Ihesu Crist is sente from his Fader
messe proprement est ditte denuoier et la messe ihesucrist est enuoie de son pere
messe is properly saide for to sende, and atte the masse Ihesu Crist is sent from his fader,

and sacreth the same hoste. For first **we haue** hym fro hys Fader sent to vs by his incarnacion, and
et sacre celle meisme hostie [. . .] / Car premierement du pere ***auons*** *par incarnacion/ et*
and sacred that same oste, "[. . .] for furst **she is sent** from the fader to vs by incarnacion, and

after sent of vs to his Fader by hys Passyon. **And first he began to be with vs by sacrefyeng**, and we with hym
puis fuit enuoiee de nous au pere par passion/ ***Et premierement il commencha a estre auec nous par sacrefiement****/ et nous auec lui*
sethe it is sente of vs **by halwinge**." And we therewith

by this oblacion that he praye for vs. And it is to wete that the messe is songen in thre langages,
par celle oblacion qui prie pour nous Et est assauoir que la messe est chantee en trois langaiges/
bi that oblacion that praiethe for vs. And it is to wete that the masse is songe in thre langages,

that is, in Greek, in Hebrew and in Latyn; **and is for to represente the tytle whiche was sette**
cest en greec en hebrieu/ et en latin/ ***et est pour representer le tiltre qui fut mis***
that is in Grewe, Ebrwe and Latin,

on the crosse in his gloryous Passion, whiche was in Greek, Hebrew and Latyne, and also for
sur la croix et sa glorieuse passion qui estoit escript en grec/ en ebrieu & en latin*/ et aussi pour*
and also for

to signefye that alle maner langage ought to preyse God. The tongue Latyn is th'offyce,[v] gospell and pystell, **and the songe.**
signifier que tout langaige doit louer dieu/ la langue latine est les euuangilles les epitres ***et le chant***
to signifie that alle langages shulde preise God. The tonge of Latin is the pistoles and the gospeles;
In Greek is the kyryes whiche ben said ix tymes, that we may come to the ix ordres of angellis.
le grec est la quirielle qui est dicte par noeuf fois/ si que nous puissons paruenir aux noeuf ordres des angelz/
the Grewe is the *kyries* that is saide .ix. tymes so that we may come to the. ix. ordres of aungeles;

The Hebrew is *alleluya, sabaoth* and *osanna*. Thirdly, it is halowed for to synge on. And herof saith
lebrieu est lalleluya sabaoth et osanna/ Tiercement il est sacre pour chanter et de ce dist
of the Ebrw is the Alleluya, Osanna and Sabaoth. Thriddely it is sacred for to synge, and therof saithe

the Book of Ecclesiaste (the xlvij chapitre), "**He ordeyned them power** ayenst theyr enemyes and made them
le liure ecclessiaste ou .xlvij[e]. chappitre ***il lui ordonna puissance*** *contre les ennemis et le fist*
the boke of Ecclesiaste in the .xlvij. chapitre: "**Ho yaue hem might** ayenst the enemyes and made hem

to be put away **fro aboute** the aulter, and made the syngers to synge and to gyue swete melodyes
oster ***denuiron*** *lautel et fist chanter les chantres et donna doulce melodie*
to be putte awey from the auuter and made the syngers to synge, and thei yaue a suete melodie

in theyr sowne," and said melodyes in **plurel nombre**. After that Hugo de Sancto Victore saith,
en leur son/ et dit melodies en ***plurel*** *selon ce que hue de saint victor dist*
in her sowne." And he saithe melodyes in **wepinge** after that Hugo de Sancto Victore saithe

ther ben thre sownes that make thre melodyes, for ther is a sowne by smytyng, by wynde
trois manieres de sons sont qui font trois melodies/ car il est son par ferir/ par vent

thre manere of sownes ther ben that maken .iij. melodies. There is a sowne by smitinge, by wynde,

and by songe; the touchyng or smytyng **apparteyneth** to the harpe, and the wynde to th'organes,and the voys to the songe.
et par chant/ le bouter ou ferir ***appartient*** *a la harpe et aux orgues le souffler et a la voix le chant*
and bi synginge. The touchinge and the smitynge **longith** to the harpe, and to orgonis the blowing, and to the voys the syngynge.

And this concordaunce of songe may be assygned to the concordaunce of good
et ceste concordance de chans peult estre assignee a la concordance de bonnes
And this concordaunce of singinge may may be assigned to the concordaunce of good

maners, for as to the touchyng of th'arpe, it may be reported to the werke of the handes, and
meurs/ Car au toucher de la harpe len peult raporter leuure des mains/ & au
maners, for in the touchinge of the harpe men maye reporte the werke of the honde, and in the

blowyng of th'organes to the deuocion of the thought, and the songe of the voys to the prechyng of the word of God.
sonffler des orgues la deuocion de pensee/ et au chant de la voix la monicion de la polle/
blowinge of orgones the devocion of the thought, and to the songe of the voys the techinge of the worde;

But in this,[vi] "What proufyteth the swetnes of the **voys** wythout the swetnes of the herte? She breketh
mais en ce que prouffite la doulceur de la ***voix*** *sans la doulceur du coeur/ Elle cassa*
but in that, what profitithe the suetnesse of the **songe** withoute the suetnesse of the herte? She brekithe

the voys, but the wyll kepeth the concordaunce of the voys and of good maners"[vii]
la voix/ mais la voulente garde la concordance des voix et la concordanc[e] des bonnes meurs
the voys, but the wille kepithe the concordaunce of the voys and the concordaunce of good maners

APPENDIX 2

Advent

GoL sig. a1ra–a1va
LgD 5ra–5rb
GiL 973/1–974/36

GoL The tyme of th'Aduent or comyng of Our Lord[viii] **into this world is halowed in holy chirche**:
LgD ***LE temps de laduent*** *est dit pour laduenement nostre seigneur ihesucrist* ***au monde/*** *et* ***est celebre en leglise***
GiL The comyng of oure Lorde that is called Advent is made

the tyme of iiij wekes **in betokenyng of iiij** dyuerse **comynges. The j was whan he cam and**
pour quatre sepmaines/ ***en signifiant quatre aduenemens/ Le premier fut quant il vint et***
by .iiij. wokes to **signifie that there be .iiij. comynges. The furst coming is**

apierid in humayn nature and flessh. **The ij is in the herte and conscyence. The iij is at the deth.**
saparut en *char* ***humaine/ Le second est en coeur et en conscience/ Le tiers est a la mort/***
in flesshe, **the secunde in dethe, the thridde in thought**,

The iiij is at last iugement. The last weke may vnnethe be accomplissed, for the glorye of the sayntes
Le quart est au iugement/ La derraine sepmaine peut peu estre acomplie/ Car la gloire des sains
the fourthe in iugement. And the last woke is vnnethe <ende>d for that the glorie of seintes

whiche shal be yeuen **at the last comyng** shal neuer ende ne fynysshe. And **to this signyfyaunce**
qui est donnee ***ou darrain aduenement*** *ne sera iamais terminee/ Et* ***a celle signifiance***
that shall be youe hem **that last Sonday** shall neuer faile. And **therfor**

þe first responce of the first **weke** of Aduent hath iiij verse, to rekene *Gloria patri et filio* for one,
le premier respons de la premiere ***sepmaine*** *de laduent/ a quatre verses/ a comp-*

ter gloria patri/
the furst response of the furst **Sonday** of Advent, for to acounte the *Gloria patri,* conteinithe .iiij. verses

to the reporte of the iiij wekis. And howbeit that there be iiij comynges of Our Lord,
a rapporter a .iiij. sepmaines/ *Et ia soit ce quil y ait .iiij. aduenemens/*
to that ende to signifie the forsaid .iiij. cominges. And though it be so that there be .iiij.comynges,

yet þe chirche maketh **mencion** in especial but of tweyne, þat is to wete **of that** he cam in **humayne**
touteffois leglise par especial fait ***mention*** *de deux Cest assauoir* ***de celuy*** *de* ***humaine***
yet the Chirche makithe speciall **mynde** but of .ij., that is to saie of the comynge in

nature to the world and of þat he cometh to the iugement and dome, as it **apperith** in th'offyce of
nature au monde/ et de celui au *iugement/ ainsi quil* ***appert*** *en loffice de*
flesshe and of the iugement so as it is in the Office

the chirche of this tyme. And therfor the fastynges **that ben in this tyme ben of gladnes** and of ioye in one partie,
leglise *de ce temps/ et pour ce les ieunes* ***qui y sont/ sont de leesse*** *et de ioie en partie/*
of that tyme. And for this cause the faste **of Aduent hathe** sum parte of ioye

and that other partie is in bitternesse of herte. Bycause of the comyng of Our Lorde
et les autres sont de amertume de coeur/ *pour la cause de laduenement*
and sum of wepinge, for by the comynge

in our nature **humayne they ben** of ioye **and gladnes**; and bycause of the comyng **at þe day of** iugement
en char ***humaine elles sont*** *de ioie* ***& de leesse/*** *pour la cause de laduenement* ***au iour du*** *iugement*
into flesshe the faste is saide of ioye, and by reson of the coming **in** iugement

they be of bitternes and heuynes. As towchyng the comyng of Our Lord in our bodyly flessh,
elles sont damertume et de tristresse/ *En tant que a laduenement en char humaine*
the fast is [sai]de of wepinge. [. . .] And unto cominge into flesshe

we may considre thre thynges **of this comyng. That is to wete th'oportunyte,** the necessyte
nous pouons considerer *trois choses* ***de cest aduenement/ cest assauoir le oportunite/*** *la necessite/*
it may be saie thre thinges: the furst is [the] **couenablete** of the cominge and the necessite

and the **vtylyte. The oportunyte of comyng is taken by the reson** of the man that first was
et le ***vtilite/ Le oportunite de ve[ni]r est prinse pour la raison*** *de lomme qui premierement fut*
and the **profit. The couenablete is vnderstode furst of the partie** of the man that was furst

vaynquysshyd in the lawe of **nature** of the defaulte of the knowlege **of God, by whiche**
vaincu *en la loy de* ***nature*** *de la deffaulte de la congnoissance* ***diuinne/ de quoy***
ouercome in the lawe of **kinde** by defauute of goodly knowlache. **For in tho dayes**

he fyll in to euyll errours, and therfore he was constrayned to **crye to God,** [. . .] "Lord gyue lyght
entre mauuaises erreurs ***il*** *tresbuscha/ & pour ce il fut constraint de* ***crier a dieu/*** [. . .] *Sire enlumine*
thei fill in right wicked erroures of idolatrie, and therfor he was constreined **to saye**: "Lorde yeue light

to myn eyen." After cam the lawe **of God, whiche hath gyuen commandement** in whiche
mes yeuix/ que ie te puisse congnoistre/ Apres vint la loy ***de dieu qui a donne commandement/*** *en laquelle*
to myn eyen." And after that [come] the lawe that comaundithe in whiche

he **hath ben** ouercome of **impuissance**, as first he **hath** cryed, "Ther is non þat fulfilleth but that
il ***a este*** *vaincu de* ***impuissance/*** *comme premierement il* ***eust*** *crie/ il nest nul que acomplisse mais qui*
[he] **was** ouercome by **non power** as he **before** criethe and saithe: "There is none that fulfellithe but here is that

comandeth." For ther he is only taught but[ix] not delyuerd fro synne ne holpen
commande [. . .] Et seulement il fut ensignie par le commandement/ mais pour ce ne fut il point de pechie deliure ne aidie
comaundithe." And this he is only taught, but he is not deliuered fro synne, nother holpe

by grace, and therfore he was constrayned to **crye**, "Ther laketh non to **comande** but ther is none that
par grace/ Et pour ce fut il constraint de ***crier*** *il est bien qui* ***commande/*** *mais il nest qui*
by [any] grace for to do well, and therfor was he con[s]treined for to **saie and chaunge his spekinge**: "There is none that

accomplisheth the commandement." Thenne cam the Sone of God in tyme whan man was
acomplisse le commandement/ *Doncques vint le filz de dieu ou temps quil affreoit quant lhomme fut*
comaundithe but that **fulfellithe**." And thanne come the sone of God couenably whanne man had be

vaynquysshid of ygnorance and **impuissaunce, to þ[at]** yf he had so comen tofore perauenture man
de ignorance et ***impuissance conuaincu/ ad ce que*** *se il feust deuant venu/ par auenture il*
ouercome with ignoraunce and **vnmight, for** yef he had come before perauenture man

myght saye þat by his owne merites he myght haue be **saued**, and **thus he had not be bounde to yeld**
eust peu dire que par ses merites il euist este ***sauue/*** *et* ***ainsi il nen euist este point te[n]u de rendre***
wolde haue saide that he had be **heled** by his propre merites and **by that he shulde not take**

thanks to God. The ij thynge þat is shewd vs of this comyng is the necessyte
graces a dieu/ La seconde chose qui nous est moustree de cest aduenement est la necessite
his medicine aggreably. Secondely she is vnderstonde

by **reson** of the tyme, of whiche th'appostle **Poul** speketh (*ad Galatas* the iiij chapitre): [. . .]
pour la ***raison*** *du temps du quel lapostre saint* ***pol*** *parle ad galatas ou .iiije. chappitre/* [. . .]
bi the **partie** of the tyme wherof the apostle saith to the Galathas in the .vij. chapitre:

"**Whan the plenitude** or ful tyme **of the grace of God was ordeyned, thenne he sente his sone þat**
Quant la plenitude *du temps* ***de la grace de dieu ordonnee/ Adont il enuoia son filz qui***
"He came in the plente of tyme."

was God and sone of the virgyne and wyf, whiche was made subget to the lawe. To that þat they be subget
fut fait dieu et filz de la vierge femme qui se fist subgect a la loy/ ad ce que ceulx qui sont subgectz

to þe lawe he bought hem agayn, and were receyued sones of God by grace of adopcion."[x]
a la loy il les rachettast et feussent receuz filz de dieu par grace de adoption

NOTES

1. GoL, sig. *2vb. GoL (ISTC ij00148000; BMC XI 144) is currently available only in modernized form. Mayumi Taguchi, Satoko Tokunaga, and I are preparing an edition of the Temporale and Old Testament for the Early English Text Society, and this article depends on that collaborative work. The text, edited with modern punctuation and word division, is based on a copy in Cambridge University Library, Inc.2.J.1.1 [3781], and we are grateful to the Department of Rare Books and the Syndics of Cambridge University Library for the provision of high-resolution images and also for a transcription provided by Early English Books Online (EEBO-TCP Phase I). Some grounds for the assumption that Caxton is in fact the author are set out in John Scahill, "Caxton's *Golden Legend*: How Many Translators?," in *Language Contact and Variation in the History of English*, ed. Yoko Iyeiri, Lawrence Schourup and Mitsumi Uchida (Tokyo: Kaitakusha, 2017), 3–22.
2. The precise source is version (c) of the *Légende*, which differs markedly from the only modern edition, Brenda Dunn-Lardeau, ed., *Jacques de Voragine: La légende dorée* (Paris: Honoré Champion, 1997). This is based on an early printed edition which has undergone some correction from the Latin. Version (c) is represented here by the probable actual source, a Low-Country print (ij00151500) in a diplomatic transcription, apart from the expansion of abbreviations and the correction within square brackets of a few misprints. The folio numbers have been obtained by adding four (for the preliminary leaves) to the numbers visible in the British Library copy (IC 50152). On the versions, see further Richard Hamer, "From Vignay's *Légende dorée* to the Earliest Printed Editions," *Le moyen français* 32 (1993): 71–81.
3. Cited from Bruno W. Häuptli, ed., *Jacobus de Voragine: Legenda aurea* (Freiburg, Germany: Herder, 2014), though Caxton's text would seem to have differed appreciably from any of the modern editions.
4. Cited from Richard Hamer, ed., *Gilte Legende* Early English Text Society 327, 328, 339 (Oxford: Oxford University Press, 2006–2012).
5. The discussion in this paper therefore concerns the Temporale only. Preliminary observations suggest that the remaining component of GoL, the Sanctorale, is for the most part similar to the Temporale in its genesis.
6. Words unique to just one of the texts are less indicative of their interrelationships; GoL in particular shows a fondness for slight expansions. Omissions of longer passages not present in all three texts are marked by [. . .]. Underlining has occasionally been used to indicate the scope of the passage under discussion.

7. H. Kurath, S. M. Kuhn, et al., eds., *The Middle English Dictionary* (Ann Arbor: University of Michigan Press, 1952–2001), http://quod.lib.umich.edu/m/med/. *The Oxford English Dictionary: Second Edition on CD-ROM (v.4.0)* (Oxford: Oxford University Press, 2009).
8. Häuptli, *Legenda aurea*, 2408.
9. Ibid., 2408.
10. Ibid., 2410.
11. Ibid., 2408.
12. See N. F. Blake, "Caxton's Language," *Neuphilologische Mitteilungen* 67 (1966): 122–132, 125.
13. Häuptli, *Legenda aurea*, 78.
14. Manfred Görlach, *The South English Legendary, Gilte Legende and Golden Legend*, Braunschweiger Anglistische Arbeiten 3 (Braunschweig, Germany: Technische Universität Carolo-Wilhelmina, 1972), 89.
15. George D. Painter, *William Caxton: A Quincentenary Biography of England's First Printer* (London: Chatto and Windus, 1976), 145.
16. The discussion in Hamer, *Gilte Legende*, III, 2–3, taken together with his "From Vignay's *Légende dorée*," implies that the exemplar belonged to the (a) version but may, like the (b) version, have contained the *Festes nouvelles*. There is sufficient similarity between these versions and (c) to account for the sporadic lexical agreements, against GoL, between GiL and LgD.

Notes on the Early Modern Additions to an Italian Fourteenth-Century Book of Hours

CAROLINE KONCZ

The art historian Ernst Gombrich described doodles as symptomatic of the desire to create, despite skill level.[1] When a person doodles, Gombrich argues, he or she does not try to master the art of drawing. Instead, Gombrich views the illustrative act as a product of tedium.[2] In the late medieval and early modern periods, doodling was likely practiced by people across the social spectrum, from famous artists to bored scribes.[3] Many scholars have recently analyzed the scribbles of early modern notaries, whose written records contain a variety of "doodles" in their margins.[4] However, not all images made by the untrained hand were thoughtless drawings done to occupy a bored mind. The term "doodle" is inherently dismissive. How do we know when something was a "doodle" as opposed to when it was something more meaningful? Given recent interest in the personalizing and annotation of medieval and early modern books in the work of Kathryn Rudy and many others, this unpublished set of leaves is an addition to the corpus of surviving examples of works whose illustrations were made in multiple periods by several hands.[5]

The Ohio State's Rare Books and Manuscripts Library contains fourteen leaves from a now-fragmented Italian Book of Hours. These pages are illustrated with what some might consider doodles—drawings that lack finish, finesse, or seemingly even a purpose, and as such, have not been the object of any serious study. The manuscript was likely produced near the end of the fourteenth century; the leaves are decorated with images which were added at least a century later, probably in the early sixteenth century. This essay aims to address why these pictures were drawn in the manuscript and what sort of meaning might be found in them. While they could be referred to as doodles—the bored marks of an amateur artist—I will describe them as illustrations or images. I believe they relate to the content and function of the book in which they are found. The images are tantalizing and vague, managing to seem both unique and idiosyncratic but also somehow rote and unremarkable. Indeed, it is their allusive form and meaning that drew me towards them.

Although Ohio State's library owns fourteen folios of the manuscript, which are all illustrated on the recto of the page, I will be looking more closely at only four of the leaves that contain the most interesting and unique images. I briefly studied the other leaves and believe that their illustrations have similar goals to the ones I focus on here but leave them to further scholarship.[6] I refer to the Latin found on the recto and verso of the four pages as well as their images. By comparing the text to the images, I argue that these marginal illustrations contain thematic links to the text. It is likely they were made purposefully by a later owner of the Book of Hours, serving both as idiosyncratic decoration for the individual's prayer book as well as documentation of the person's spiritual meditations and aspirations. While sharing some of the function and meaning of medieval marginalia as these are usually understood, the illustrations in these manuscript leaves differ from those more usually found in Books of Hours due to the extended time gap between the leaves' initial creation and their later decoration.[7]

Each of the fourteen fragmented pages of the disassembled prayer book measures 193 by 143 millimeters. Both recto and verso contain twelve lines of text from different sections of the Book of Hours.[8] Each page's recto includes vibrant and colorful decorations covering two of the four margins. Folio 85 recto, for instance, includes a branch of blooming flora along the right margin shaded with various pinks, yellows, and greens (Fig. 1). In the center of the bottom margin, the amateur illustrator places a circular image filled with a blue cross, which is also found on several other of the leaves in Ohio State's collection.[9] The images on the recto of the folios do not appear to be the product of an illuminator from the late fourteenth century.[10] At the earliest, these additional pictures were added around 1500, and could even be dated as late as the seventeenth century. Curators at Ohio State's library support a later dating.[11]

We can only speculate about who might have made these marginal illustrations, or exactly when or where they were produced, but we can try to understand why these images were subsequently drawn in by an untrained hand. According to Kathryn Rudy, medieval manuscripts, including Books of Hours, did not remain in one unchanged condition throughout their

tentib; effecti sunt. Ecce
parturit iniusticiam.
concepit dolorem et pe-
perit iniquitatem.
Lacum aperuit et ef-
fodit eum: et incidit i
foveam quam fecit. Co-
vertetur dolor eius
i caput eius: et i ver-
ticem ipsius iniqui-
tas eius descendet.
Confitebor dno se

Figure 1. Columbus, The Ohio State Rare Books and Manuscript Library, MS 157, fol. 85r. Photograph courtesy of the Ohio State Rare Books and Manuscript Library.

existence. Rather, they were "open objects": many owners would change their prayer books by adding both images and texts, even by inserting supplementary pages.[12] Because these books had many users over a long period, altering Books of Hours was a way for a manuscript to remain relevant and special to its later owners.[13] Rudy emphasizes that subsequent owners decorated their manuscripts as an act of personalization, whether the illustrations were made by themselves or commissioned from hired hands. Nearly anyone could have personalized a Books of Hours with images, especially with access to pattern and model books.[14] However, I doubt that the illustrator of the Ohio State manuscript copied the images directly from a pattern book as the iconography seems too unusual. Instead, I argue that the images the artist chose to place in the text appear as though they were very personal and conscious decisions.

When contemplating fragmentary folio 89 recto, the viewer beholds a page that at its apex contains a beautifully elaborated red "M" initial, which dates to the period of the manuscript's initial medieval production (Fig. 2). On the right side of the folio, the early modern illustrator paints a tree branch with budding leaves of green, contrasting nicely with the large red letter to its left. Below the text, the amateur artist depicted an ambiguous object, which appears to be unfinished rather than washed with color as are many of the other illustrations found in these pages.[15] Thus, this leaf best shows the artist's working method: the artist drew in the pictures, outlined the images in brown ink, and colored them in accordingly. As to the identity of the unfinished object in the drawing, it is difficult to say for certain what is being illustrated. Although it looks similar to a cooking pot, the two holes on top may represent the filling hole and wick of an oil lamp.[16] Next to this object, our artist depicts a cross placed in a circle, partially colored in blue.

The page's text is from the Office of the Dead, Lesson Three, which contains verses from Job 10: 8–12.[17] On this page, the text from Job reads:

> Thy hands have made me, and fashioned me wholly round about, and dost thou thus cast me down headlong on a sudden? Remember, I beseech thee, that thou hast made me as the clay, and thou wilt bring me into dust. Hast thou not milked me as milk and curdled me as cheese?[18]

The text leads the viewer back to the unfinished oil lamp. By considering the lamp's materiality, practical use, and possible symbolic value, we can comprehend why the owner of the text drew it. This specific type of oil lamp, made from clay, links to Latin "lutum," which is found in the center of the page.[19]

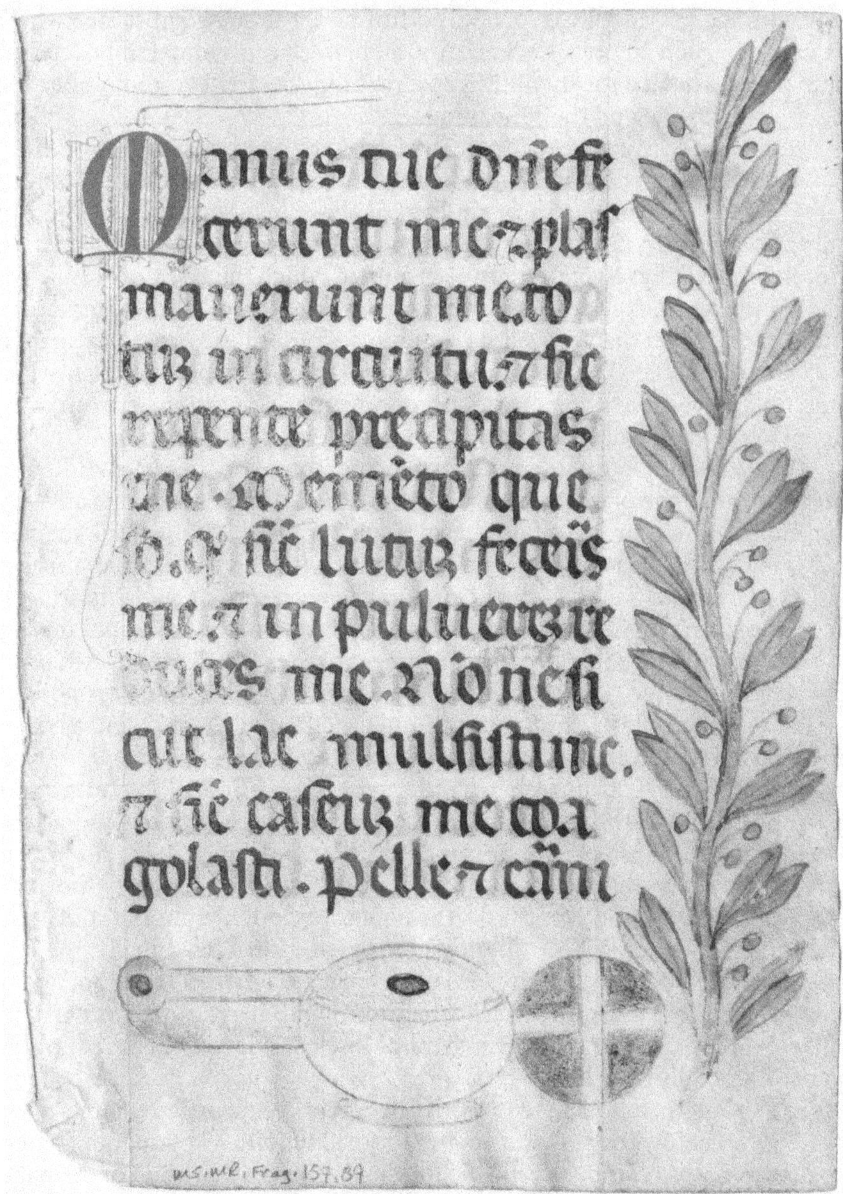

Figure 2. Columbus, The Ohio State Rare Books and Manuscript Library, MS 157, fol. 89r. Photograph courtesy of the Ohio State Rare Books and Manuscript Library.

Furthermore, clay could be produced from oil, the same substance which is burned in such an object.[20] Perhaps, then, the lamp's materiality acted as a mnemonic device for the illustrator, helping the artist to remember the verses on the page and their meaning.

Beyond serving as a tool for memorization or place finding, the oil lamp could also more generally have reflected the amateur artist's meditations upon the verses. The illustrator could easily have handled such an object in daily life. The artist might have used it publicly to provide light on an altar in church or privately to give light to the room in which the Book of Hours was read.[21] Further, the oil lamp could have acted as a symbol for the illustrator's ruminations upon the verses. Like Job himself, the sinful artist was shaped like clay by the hands of God and would one day be brought to dust.[22] The lamp thus serves as a fitting metaphor for one's short duration here on earth; the oil in the lamp will only burn for so long before extinguishing.

What can we make of the rest of the images found on the page? Although the meaning of the plants is more enigmatic (and doodles of plants are very common in the margins of medieval manuscripts), I would still suggest that one could at least associate the imagery with the verses thematically. As Lucy Freeman Sandler argues, marginalia with secular subjects are still able to contain religious meaning.[23] Since the verso of the page contains no illustrations, the text here too might connect to the illustrations drawn onto the recto. On 89 verso, Job continues, crying out to God, "Thou hast clothed me with skin and flesh: thou hast put me together with bones and sinews: Thou hast granted me life and mercy, and thy visitation hath preserved my spirit."[24] This text suggests why the artist drew a flourishing branch on the right margin of the recto. Rather than being there for pure decoration, these flora could instead symbolize the budding life and mercy for which the worshipper is grateful. Instead of drawing a human figure or self-portrait to represent this joy and gratitude, the illustrator looks to another of God's creations to symbolize his or her own bones and sinews.[25] Finally, the circular object embellished with a cross and placed between the branch and lamp can be more straightforwardly read as a symbol of the amateur artist's faith. I will look at the cruciform symbol in closer detail where it appears again on the following leaf.

Like 89 recto, folio 137 recto contains carefully drawn illustrations from life (Fig. 3). Below the text, the amateur artist includes a bouquet of golden flowers, perhaps blooming yellow daffodils, while the right side of the page displays a yellow-gold lidded vessel set atop a broken column, marked again with the circular cruciform symbol.[26] Before describing these objects, I would first like to turn to the text. The verses that accompany the images again derive from the Office of the Dead. From the Vespers section of the book, Psalm 129: 2–6 states:

uocez depcatõis mẽ
Si iniquitates ob
ſuãueris dñe. dñe
quis ſuſtinebit
Quia apud te p
piciacio eſt. ⁊ prop
t legez tuaz ſuſti
nui te dñe Sub
ſtinuit aĩa mẽam
uerbo eius. ſpera
uit aĩa mẽa in dño
A cuſtodia mat

Figure 3. Columbus, The Ohio State Rare Books and Manuscript Library, MS 157, fol. 137r. Photograph courtesy of the Ohio State Rare Books and Manuscript Library.

> If thou wilt observe iniquities O Lord: Lord who shall endure it? Because with thee there is pitifulness: and for thy law I have expected thee O Lord. My soul hath stayed in his word: my soul hath hoped in our Lord.[27]

The verso of the page continues the psalm, calling for mercy and redemption for Israel and its evils. I offer two possible readings of the golden vessel. On one hand, it could depict a funerary urn that is placed upon a fragmented pedestal. If the object is read as an urn, then the cross marking the column below would symbolize the remains as a Christian's. As such, the artist depicts the ultimate result of humanity and its sins—death. These drawings then point to the mortality of man and his necessity to lean upon God. Stamping the monument with the sign of the cross, the illustrator shows that it is only God's mercy that allows this Christian to hope for life after death. In this instance, the flowers too can be read as memorial, placed perhaps before the grave of the artist's loved one.

However, the object's form is ambiguous; it could also be read as a pyx or ciborium.[28] In this instance, the cross placed below, which is composed within a circle, might be read as the host, similar in size and shape to the Sacramental bread.[29] If the artist intended this, I would still argue that these doodles reflect upon the page's text. In this case, the illuminator illustrates God's own response to the psalmist's cries for mercy. Contemplating the verses, the artist depicts the symbols of the Eucharist, representative of Christ, who ultimately paid for man's sins. Moreover, placing these sacramental instruments atop a broken column further emphasizes the power of Christ. In the sixteenth century, statues placed atop columns still held idolatrous connotations.[30] Perhaps to displace these anxieties, the illustrator instead places a ciborium atop a broken column. Rather than depicting a statue of Christ, then, the artist instead draws a representation of the actual body of Christ (after being blessed by a priest) that is elevated. Ultimately, then, this image could be read as a Christian triumph over the law, represented below as the column, broken for evermore.[31]

Turning to another section of the illustrator's prayer book, folio 143 recto, we find a page from the Hours of the Cross (Fig. 4). The text here describes the excruciating ordeals of Christ's Passion:

> At the third hour of the day they crucify him cry,
> In a purple robe clad him more to mock thereby,
> Piteously his head was pricked with the crown of thorn,
> To the place of pain his cross was on his shoulders born.[32]

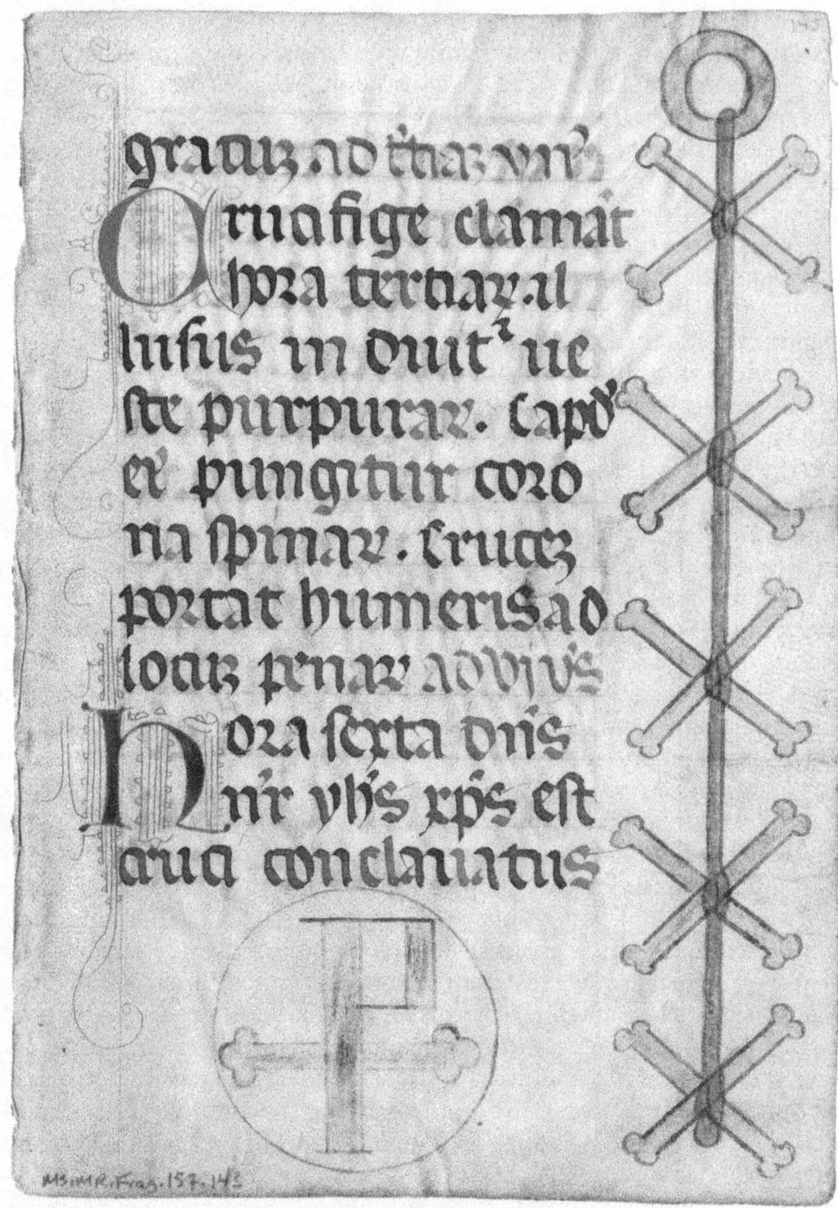
gratiaz. ad tciaz. vus
Crucifige clamat
hora tertiay. Il
lusus in duit ve
ste purpurey. Capud
eius pungitur coro
na spinay. Crucez
portat humeris ad
locuz penay. Ad vius
Hora sexta dnus
nr ihs xps est
cruci conclauatus

MS.MR.Frag.157.143

Figure 4. Columbus, The Ohio State Rare Books and Manuscript Library, MS 157, fol. 143r. Photograph courtesy of the Ohio State Rare Books and Manuscript Library.

The artist does not depict Christ in the flesh, placed upon the cross with a crown of thorns; a convincing figural illustration like this may have been beyond the artist's skill. Instead, the illustrator decorates the page with what appears to be a red leather thread that hangs from a golden loop. Attached to this string are a series of ten bones, grouped into sets of two, placed diagonally against one another, forming X's that are evenly placed down the vertical plane. If a viewer turns her head slightly to either side, she would find that these bones too make signs of the cross. The artist could be depicting Christ and the Passion through these bones, which recall the body while not directly representing it.[33] Furthermore, the bones evoke the image of a religious relic the artist might have viewed in his or her local parish.[34]

In addition to the string of bones that can be interpreted as relics or crosses, we again find a cruciform symbol below. Choosing blue to shade in the figure, the illustrator decides to combine the form of the cross along with the initial P. This initial could possibly stand for the family's name, for it appears on folios 44, 86, and 128 rectos. If the "P" is the family's initial or monogram, it would be consistent with the late medieval and early modern practice of adding monograms, initials, and coats of arms to one's prayer books to express personal possession.[35] Another possible interpretation of the P marked with a horizontal band might be that it represents the Chi Rho symbol, making up the first two letters of Christ's name. Although the Chi symbol is not accurate in the circle, it can be correctly found on the right side of the page, depicted five times in a column. This again would lead us back to readings and interpretation of the text on the page that describes the Passion of Christ.

The final folio that I would like to examine is 150 recto, the sole page that depicts a human figure (Fig. 5). This leaf's text comes from the Seven Penitential Psalms, which worshippers often prayed from when resisting the desire to sin.[36] Along with an image of a vertical tree branch holding acorns below the text, the artist depicts an illustration quite strikingly different from the rest of the manuscript illustrations.[37] In a semi-circle, the illustrator draws what appears to be a building, perhaps even a furnace or oven, made of brick or stone. Inside the shape, through a window, or opening in the furnace or oven, there is an androgynous, hairless, and nude figure crowned by a halo, surrounded by fire. The figure's arms are crossed over the chest so it is difficult to discern its sex. Although we should be able to see the person's genitalia, the flames of reds, oranges, and yellows burn, extending out just below the navel. The fire fans around the figure, appearing wing-like in its spread.

Who is this figure trapped in the flames? Why is he or she nude, and where exactly is he or she placed? The image seems to refer to text from Psalm 37: 15–18:

> Because in thee O Lord have I hoped: thou shalt hear me O Lord my God. For I have said, lest sometimes my enemies rejoice over me: and whilst my feet are moved, they spoke great things upon me. Because I am ready for scourges: and my sorrow is in my sight always.[38]

On the back of the page the psalm continues, "Because I will declare my iniquity: and I will think for my sin."[39] The last few lines of this text are most interesting in comparison with the image of the figure in flames. The psalm states that the writer of the verse is prepared to be punished, for he or she knows his or her guilt. To depict someone, then, who was prepared to suffer, it would make sense that the artist would illustrate a figure who went through trials or persecution for faith, yet ultimately triumphed. Although I am not certain who this figure in the flames is, I believe that there are several possibilities, which are open to interpretation.

Because the figure has a halo, he or she is holy. Looking to the Bible first for possible examples, we find reference to three men, Shadrach, Meshach, and Abednego, from Daniel 3:19–30, who faithfully enter a furnace, refusing to worship the gods of Nebuchadnezzar.[40] While they are in the flames, a fourth figure miraculously appears, resembling a god. Since the three men are virtually untouched by the fire (they come out with every hair on their head intact, their clothing untouched), could the figure depicted on the leaf then be the fourth individual who materializes in the fiery furnace? I would not discount this reading, but I wonder if the artist instead illuminated here a martyred saint, a figure who once put hope in God when enduring hardships at the hands of enemies, as in Psalm 37. If so, this image of a burning, haloed figure may be evocative of a saint's martyrdom.

The only saint that I have found to be associated with an oven or furnace is Saint Victor of Milan, a Roman soldier who was martyred at the turn of the fourth century CE. Although he was ultimately beheaded, several sources have mentioned his being severely tortured beforehand, including being flung into a flaming oven.[41] Furthermore, St. Victor is usually recognizable as a Roman soldier on horseback or with an oven containing fiery flames.[42] While I have found no other saints burnt alive in an oven or furnace, I have discovered several others burnt at the stake or at least associated with flames.[43] A particularly interesting account is the martyrdom of Saint Polycarp, a bishop from Smyrna who refused to stop practicing Christianity in Imperial Rome. According to early Christian chronicles, Polycarp was also set to be burned at the stake, but when the fire lit, it formed a space around him, like a wall or narrow chamber. Furthermore, the saint's body was not burned but was rather like "bread in the baking or gold and silver refined in a furnace."[44]

Figure 5. Columbus, The Ohio State Rare Books and Manuscript Library, MS 157, fol. 150r. Photograph courtesy of the Ohio State Rare Books and Manuscript Library.

It is plausible that the illuminated figure in the flames is a rendition of either Polycarp or Victor. However, because of its bizarre iconography, the illustrator of the Ohio State manuscript was more likely inspired by multiple martyrdom images of saints set on fire. Although the figure's iconographic ambiguity makes me hesitant to identify it as a specific religious figure, I maintain that the person drawing the haloed body was responding to the religious verses. In doing so, the artist illustrated the Psalm and created a powerful and praise-worthy image. The figure in the illustration is shown in flames but is faithful to God.

The illustrations in this prayer book are not thoughtless scribbles, but reflect instead the meditations of a devout individual. It seems that the person who received a once imageless Book of Hours seized upon the opportunity to decorate it, adding unique and personal images to the manuscript pages. The annotated prayerbook, after all, was a tactile way to access prayer and meditations on God. These illustrations might not exhibit the highest level of artistic skill, but they are nevertheless done with care and consideration. The owner of the book took time with the washes, carefully coloring in the lines, and choosing the pigments for their beauty and naturalistic qualities. While much of the marginalia drawn on the leaves could be viewed as purely decorative—as a doodle—a closer look at the text and its relation to the images raises questions about this assumption. I have no doubt that the later owner who decorated the pages wanted the manuscript to be pleasing to the eye. Ultimately, these illustrations display the work of a Christian artist who meditated upon the Word not only through the eyes and mouth, but also with drawings by hand.

The Ohio State University

NOTES

1. Eric Johnson and the Ohio State Rare Books and Manuscript Library graciously allowed me to access and reproduce these images of the manuscript. I also thank Eric for his time and expertise and for introducing me to the leaves. Additionally, I thank Martha Driver and the Early Book Society for letting me present this paper in a sponsored session at Kalamazoo in 2018 and for the inspiring feedback from the audience. Lastly, this project would not have been possible without the advice, guidance, editing, and encouragement from Karl Whittington at Ohio State. This paper began as a result of his stimulating graduate level course on medieval manuscripts taught at OSU in the Spring of 2017. I am especially grateful for his aid and deep commitment to his students.

2. Ernst H. Gombrich, "Pleasures of Boredom: Four Centuries of Doodle," in *The Uses of Images: E.H. Gombrich. studies in the social function of art and visual communication* (London: Phaidon, 1999), 212.
3. According to Giorgio Vasari, the great Cimabue and Giotto were known to have spent much of their youth doodling. Vasari recounts young Cimabue sketching "men, horses, houses, and diverse other things of fancy." In the "Life of Giotto," Vasari repeats the legend promulgated previously by Ghiberti in his *I Commentarii* that Cimabue found young Giotto in a field drawing a naturalistic representation of a sheep upon a rock. Impressed, he ended up taking the young child with him to train. Although we have no real evidence for Vasari's anecdotes about the artists' young lives, it is nevertheless compelling that his stories of artists always include this insistent urge to draw or doodle. Giorgio Vasari, vol. 1 of *Lives of the Painters, Sculptors, and Architects*, trans. Gaston du C. De Vere (New York: Alfred A. Knopf, 1996), 51, 97.
4. In her article, Carolyn Dean analyzes notarial doodles found in the Archivo Regional in Cuzco, Peru from 1630–1810. Challenging Gombrich's argument that scribal doodles were solely the result of the employee's boredom, her essay argues that these doodles had several other purposeful roles. Carolyn Dean, "Beyond Prescription: Notarial Doodles and Other Marks," *Word & Image* 25, no. 3 (2009): 293–316. Another essay similarly analyzes the erotic marginal doodles found on early modern ledgers in the Modena State Archive. Guido Guerzoni, "The erotic fantasies of a model clerk: amateur pornography at the beginning of the Cinquecento," in *Erotic Cultures of Renaissance Italy,* ed. Sara F. Matthews-Grieco (Burlington: Ashgate, 2010): 61–88.
5. Kathryn M. Rudy, *Piety in Pieces: How Medieval Readers Customized Their Manuscripts* (Open Book Publishers, 2016), accessed February 27, 2017 http://public.eblib.com/choice/publicfullrecord.aspx?p=4694636.
6. Although little is known about the provenance of the leaves, the fourteen fragments emerge from the modern practice of collectors' purchasing prayer books from the Middle Ages and cutting miniatures and single leaves out of the text to resell separately. This practice took off in the nineteenth century, around when "fake" manuscript pages also began to be sold for profit. Sandra Hindman, et al., *Manuscript Illumination in the Modern Age: Recovery and Reconstruction* (Evanston, IL: Northwestern University, 2001), xxiv–xxv.
7. For more on this, see Lilian Randall, *Images in the Margins of Gothic Manuscripts* (Berkeley: University of California Press, 1966), and Michael Camille, *Image on the Edge: The Margins of Medieval Art* (Cambridge: Harvard University Press, 1992).

8. For general scholarship on Books of Hours, see Roger S. Wieck, *Painted Prayers: The Book of Hours in Medieval and Renaissance Art* (New York: George Braziller, 1997), and *Books of Hours Reconsidered,* ed. Sandra Hindman and James H. Marrow (Turnhout, Belgium: Harvey Miller Publishers, 2013).
9. Varying forms of this image can be found on folios 41r, 46r, 63r, 89r, 98r, 98v, 135r, 137r, and 148r.
10. For a comparative example of a more typical kind of Trecento illumination, see Columbia University's Rare Book and Manuscript Library MS 12, F. 26.
11. In an email (2018), Eric Johnson, the curator of Ohio State's Rare Books and Manuscript Library, has also agreed with this dating of the late sixteenth or seventeenth century. For this dating, he takes into consideration the images' color, quality, and design.
12. Rudy, *Piety in Pieces,* 16.
13. Books of Hours were often passed down through one's family line. Christopher De Hamel argues that these prayer books were akin to domestic heirlooms, similar to genealogical books that recorded their family's heritage. Christopher de Hamel, "Books of Hours and the Art Market," in *Books of Hours Reconsidered,* ed. Sandra Hindman and James H. Marrow (Turnhout, Belgium: Harvey Miller Publishers, 2013), 44–46.
13. Wieck, *Painted Prayers,* 2–3.
14. Dean, "Beyond Prescription," 312.
15. A finished example of this object can be found on 41r, which is colored in with yellow and brown. It too has a dark hole in the object's center as well as one in the handle on its left.
16. This suggestion was proposed to me during the presentation of this paper at Kalamazoo's International Congress of Medieval Studies on May 11, 2018 in the Early Book Society's panel, "Personalization in MSS and Printed Books: Ownership Marks, Annotations, Emendations." The oil lamp depicted here appears most like examples found from the ancient Greek and Roman periods, produced out of terracotta. Due to its inexpensive material, it seems possible that the illustrator of this manuscript had a similarly constructed oil lamp made of clay.
17. This section of the book was often read for the souls of the deceased who were trapped in purgatory. Wieck, *Painted Prayers,* 117–118.
18. Translations from Glenn Gunhouse, "A Hypertext Book of Hours," accessed July 7, 2018, http://medievalist.net/hourstxt/home.htm. "Manus tuae plasmaverunt me et fecerunt me totum in circuitu et sic repente praecipitas me/ Memento quaeso quod sicut lutum feceris me et in pulverem reduces me / Nonne sicut lac mulsisti me et sicut caseum me coagulasti ..."

19. For more on clay oil lamps, see Eric C. Lapp, "Clay Lamps Shed New Light on Daily Life in Antiquity," *Near Eastern Archaeology,* 67, no. 3 (2004): 174–175.
20. According to *The Dictionary of Biblical Imagery,* the word "oil" itself is found almost two hundred times in the Bible. It is mentioned in both common and sacred contexts in the Old and New Testaments, such as fueling oil lamps. In Exodus 25:6, God informed Moses that olive oil for lamps would be an acceptable sacred offering for the Tabernacle. Leland Ryken, Kames C. Wilhoit, Tremper Longman III, *Dictionary of Biblical Imagery* (Downers Grove: InterVarsity Press, 1998), 603.
21. Although the illustrator of this Book of Hours might have used a candle rather than this antiquated object, the overall effect of each item is nevertheless the same.
22. In his book on the Gothic idol, Michael Camille also notes that the medieval artist was considered to be created by God, as if made from clay. Michael Camille, *The Gothic Idol: Ideology and Image-making in Medieval Art* (Cambridge: Cambridge University Press, 1989), 33.
23. Lucy Freeman Sandler, *Studies in Manuscript Illumination 1200-1400* (London: The Pindar Press, 2008), 92.
24. "Hypertext Book of Hours," "... carnibus vestisti me et ossibus et nervis conpegisti me / Vitam et misericordiam tribuisti mihi et visitatio tua custodivit spiritum meum."
25. In John 15: 5–8, Christ compares his followers to branches, referring to himself as the vine. Having been granted everlasting life, the Christian's branches flourish and produce fruit, as seen in the illustration with its green berries.
26. I have had trouble distinguishing exactly what type of flower this is. My best guess is that the artist was attempting to depict a daffodil, for the illustration mimics the flower's trumpet-like structure, also referred to as a corona. "How the daffodil got its trumpet," University of Oxford News, accessed May 23, 2018, http://www.ox.ac.uk/news/2013-02-19-how-daffodil-got-its-trumpet.
27. "Hypertext Book of Hours," "Si iniquitates observaveris Domine: Domine quis sustinebit? / Quia apud te propitiatio est: et propter legem tuam sustinui te Domine. / Sustinuit anima mea in verbo eius: speravit anima mea in Domino."
28. This idea was suggested to me by Drew Jones and Karen Winstead during a practice session for the Kalamazoo conference at Ohio State, organized through Ohio State's Medieval & Renaissance Graduate Association, 8 May 2018.

29. Aden Kumler also analyzes manuscript illustrations of the Eucharist in *Translating Truth: Ambitious Images and Religious Knowledge in Late Medieval France and England* (New Haven: Yale University Press, 2011).
30. Included here are several texts that have been written concerning art and idolatry in sixteenth century Italy. These writings specifically address the anxiety that arose from columns topped with statues and other objects in the period. Michael Cole, "Perpetual Exorcism in Sistine Rome," in *The Idol in the Age of Art: Objects, Devotions, and the Early Modern World,* ed. Michael Cole and Rebecca Zorach (Burlington: Ashgate, 2009), 57–75, and Alexander Nagel, *The Controversy of Renaissance Art* (University of Chicago Press, 2011), 103–152. Michael Camille also addresses idols and columns in his book on Gothic idolatry. Camille, *Gothic Idol,* 197–203.
31. The column could also refer to Christ's flagellation during the Passion. Its broken state, then, might be interpreted as Christ's triumph over his torture and death. James Hall, 2nd ed. of *Dictionary of Subjects and Symbols in Art* (Boulder: Westview Press, 2008), 255–256.
32. "Hypertext Book of Hours":

    Crucifige clamitant hora tertiarum:
    Illusus induitur veste purpurarum:
    Caput eius pungitur corona spinarum.
    Crucem portat humeris ad locum poenarum.
33. Skulls and bones were also placed under the Cross of Jesus at times in Western art from the Middle Ages, according to Jennifer Speake. *The Dent Dictionary of Symbols in Christian Art* (London: JM Dent, 1994), 129.
34. Of course, no remains of Christ's physical body exist since his body and soul ascended to heaven, according to Christian doctrine. Nevertheless, contact relics of Christ were considered holy objects, such as the lance that pierced Christ's side.
35. Wieck, *Painted Prayers,* 17.
36. Ibid., 9, 91. The seven penitential psalms are psalms 6, 31, 37, 50, 101, 129 and 142.
37. Although I have investigated the religious symbolism of acorns for this specific illustration, I was unsuccessful at finding any connections. In this case, I must admit that some of the drawings found on the leaves may be either purely decorative or perhaps contain a more personal meaning to the illustrator.

38. "Hypertext Book of Hours," "Quoniam in te Domine speravi: tu exaudies Domine Deus meus. / Quia dixi, ne quando supergaudeant mihi inimici mei: et dum commoventur pedes mei, super me magna locuti sunt. / Quoniam ego in flagella paratus sum: et dolor meus in conspectu meo semper."
39. Ibid., "Quoniam iniquitatem meam annunciabo: et cogitabo pro peccato meo."
40. This identification was also suggested to me at the Kalamazoo panel, "Personalization in MSS and Printed Books."
41. Anna Jameson, vol. 2 of *Sacred and Legendary Art* (New York: AMS Press, 1970), 416.
42. Arthur de Bles, *How to Distinguish the Saints in Art by their Costumes, Symbols, and Other Attributes* (New York: Art Culture Publications, Inc., 1925), 152, 155.
43. Some of the saints that were burnt alive (although some were ultimately unharmed from this method of torture) include St. Afra, St. Apollonia, St. Christina, Sts. Cosmo and Damian, St. Ephesus, and St. Lucia. Ibid., 144. St. Anthony of Padua is also sometimes shown with fire since he is the patron saint of protection against the flame. George Ferguson, *Signs and Symbols in Christian Art* (New York: Oxford University Press, 1961), 41.
44. Polycarp's martyrdom is recounted and analyzed in Donald Attwater, "The Early Martyrs," *Life of the Spirit (1946-1964)* 11, 130 (not sure what these numbers are referring to?) (1957): 441–454, and M. Therese Lysaught, "Witnessing Christ in Their Bodies: Martyrs and Ascetics as Doxological Disciples," *The Annual of the Society of Christian Ethics* 20 (2000): 239–62.

The Contents of Vulgate Bibles Produced in England

RALPH HANNA

Anyone who has ever messed about in libraries, as opposed to just looking for a single text, will have run into a good many Latin Bible manuscripts. Excepting Books of Hours, they are about the most common surviving medieval books, and like Books of Hours, particularly complex ones. Indicatively, one medieval term for the Bible was *bibliotheca,* or "library," and these volumes contain, as everyone knows, a vast congeries of texts. Yet the overwhelming majority of the survivors one runs across in British libraries is pretty boilerplate, since they universally are a product of about seventy years' worth of thirteenth-century copying in Paris, northern France, and Oxford. This surge apparently filled the demand for Latin scripture for the remainder of the Middle Ages (late medieval Latin Bibles are rare indeed), and the manuscripts often show signs of up to three centuries of active use. These books, which have standardized formats for contents, size, mise-en-page, and most frequently, decorative styling (or consultative features), are the product of centralized mass-production.

As a result, cataloguing these books, especially in comparison to any other book with a comparable number of texts (folio collections of Augustine, for example), is a relative doddle. A typically succinct statement of the needful appears in the most extensive description of any Bible in Neil R. Ker's *Medieval Manuscripts in British Libraries.*[1] If one eliminates the fine print in the middle, to which I *am* going to return, Ker's account absorbs less than a page, and it really tells one all one needs to know to deal with this book. This, and absolutely nothing further, is the *cataloguing* model to which any biblical description should aspire; it is efficient, communicative, and provides all the necessary information. Anything further is supererogatory and confusing, and, in cataloguing—as my father used to say about some other subjects, mainly my youthful behaviors—*zuviel ist zuviel.*

That said, Ker's description offers hints about certain kinds of problems lurking inside "the common Parisian Bible" and its insular cousins. This is emphatically not, in concerted detail, the material for a catalogue description, where it will only create absolutely illegible clutter.[2] This material will allow one to note in descriptions proper only deviations from the expected. More importantly, such a separation of detail from a catalogue description will convert looking at Bibles into something like a proper book-historical investigation. Ultimately, that is a kind of study—I should imagine, a book-length one—different in mode and rhetorical kind from making a catalogue.

As I say, Ker's description offers hints of problems. All of them might be reduced to much the same single observation. The Bible is a text absolutely authoritative, and in certain accounts, at least the older portions of it directly conveyed by Yah. It carries within itself, as The Word, an absolute statement of its canonical status, of its utter completeness, and of its imperative exact reproduction as Word (Deut. 4:2).[3] That statement, ironically enough, was authored by the Temple scribes who had just finished substantially changing what they had received. But their guilty knowledge in reproducing a changed book—and they will have considered their work ameliorative, something better than what they had received—remained inherent in reproducing the Bible throughout the Middle Ages. The author, at least of the Hebrew, may have been Yah, but like every author, he depended upon errant, and engaged, human agents to get The Word out there.[4]

As a result, however similar they may initially appear, Latin Bibles hide large amounts of deviance—and deviance of a sort always available, as potential model, to other producers. By this, I am not referring simply to local textual readings—although there is plenty of mileage there. These are not limited to simple (and expected) scribal errors; it is very likely that the scribes responsible for copying Scripture took away bundles of quires and then returned them for new bundles. One cannot assume in advance that any single Bible actually represents the product of but a single exemplar (a production this extensive will have required multiples). Thus, copies of the work will, in all probability, show a range of shifting affinities with books with which there is no particular reason to believe them connected.

But there is yet more extensive variation among Latin copies, which Ker's introductory paragraph only signals. My general statements below are predicated upon a survey of what I imagine a representative sample of available insular Vulgates—nearly fifty relevant books, about half from Oxford libraries. I have either examined these books myself, or have derived information about them from fully descriptive recent catalogues. I have tried to limit my survey to books probably English, or early in England (which may imply special production to meet demands of English clients). In the notes I cite the evidence relevant to my general statements using the sigla I assign to each book in the Appendix below.

We all know (or think we do) that the canon of Scripture was settled long before Parisian Bibles were made. Not so. The optionals still appear in appendices in the rear of modern Vulgates (and in one case, in the text in the standard edition).[5] A very great many copies include, and in no predictable combination, 3 Ezra (in Vulgate contexts, Nehemiah = 2 Ezra; 4 Ezra is pretty universally appendix material); a prayer of Manasses at the end of 2 Chronicles; and a fifty-second chapter of Ecclesiasticus ("the prayer of Solomon," still printed as the text in the Stuttgart edition). Among later/modern biblical writings, the pseudo-Pauline epistle to the Laodiceans appears occasionally.[6]

But inclusiveness is not the only problem. Medieval Latin Bibles are capable of textual selectivity/deselection—and in shocking ways. A quite substantial number of Latin Bibles, a fifth of those I have surveyed, dispense entirely with that text most central to liturgical practice, the Psalter.[7] It is thoroughly possible that many clerical users of the Vulgate required no text of the Psalms, having absorbed it *auswendig* from its weekly liturgical repetition. Alternatively, these volumes may have been produced for individuals who had ready access to separate Psalters, perhaps in more extended volumes that also included their Books of Hours. Or these books may be the product of contracts for whole Bibles, with the Psalter deliberately made to be bound separately, perhaps for formal liturgical use.

That second prospect leads to a further observation about the codicological status of this biblical book in Latin tradition. It is very frequently bibliographically separate from the remainder of the full Bible manuscripts in which it is found, essentially a fascicular production. Moreover, in the construction of Latin Bibles, the end of the Psalter (and thus, its booklet), not the head of Matthew, is the traditional production break in making the book, the halfway point where two-volume Bibles universally divide (imitated in the juncture of Forshall and Madden's volumes 2 and 3).[8]

This separateness frequently appears to have been mandated by certain peculiarities of the text. Psalters, in Latin biblical tradition, have a special format shared with no other biblical book; uniquely, because they represent choral responsive singing, they have verses (other books did not until the sixteenth century), and the verses are quite emphatically set off in manuscript by some form of colored *littera notabilior* (and often by verse-ending line-fillers). (This will contrast with the in-chapter punctuation of the remaining books, which is by the period, sometimes marked with following red-slashed *littera notabilior.*) Moreover, while the Psalter might be optional only, sometimes, in the Latin tradition, it is extensive, and like the Stuttgart Vulgate, presents two of Jerome's translations in parallel.

Ker's ideal Parisian Bible also hides a variety of fairly predictable behaviors in Latin tradition of potentially wider impact. As one can see from Ker's account, the standard order of the Parisian biblical books differs from that familiar from modern printed Bibles. The conventional medieval order of Christian writings does not follow the fundamentally historical order enshrined in the modern text. Rather, it records, in a rough way, the historical order of biblical composition, the authors' proximity to the Incarnate, and the gospels are immediately succeeded by the Pauline epistles (which actually predate all the gospels, except perhaps Mark). The Acts of the Apostles is very nearly at the back of the book. Yet plenty of medieval Latin Bibles show variant orders here, and efforts at grouping the Christian historical accounts, i.e., moving Acts to follow John, the concluding gospel. But this transposition is not unproblematic, and book producers who front-load Acts most normally drag with it the Catholic epistles. In a few books I have looked at, even the Apocalypse comes along for this ride, and the last book of the full Bible is the epistle to the Hebrews.[9]

Moreover, the treatment of Acts is far from the only commonplace transposition of textual order available in Latin tradition. Tobit often does not precede Judith and Esther, but follows them. Moreover, the Maccabees often, like Acts, may appear substantially advanced from their customarily "intertestamentary" position, in this case also to emphasize their connections with other "historical" materials. This decision, probably inspired by some access to the *veritas Hebraica,* is accompanied by some quite substantial reorderings of the remainder of the "Old Testament."[10] The appendages to the prophecy of Jeremiah are potentially mobile, Baruch particularly so, in a very few books attached to Ezechiel. And Thessalonians, rarely only the first epistle, more normally both, occasionally appear before, rather than after, Colossians.[11]

If one returns to Ker's description of Lambeth Palace MS 1364, one finds that more than half his account is given over—so that Ker never has to do it again for any of the other Bible manuscripts he describes—to one feature of medieval Bibles (still selectively present in the standard Stuttgart Vulgate). The books include, widely dispersed through the text, a substantial amount of non-biblical material, basically exegetical instructions and historical contextualization of the biblical text. These materials are conventionally known as "Jerome's prologues," and as Ker lays them out, there are sixty-four of them, appearing at fixed points in the Vulgate text.[12]

If one thought the variations in content and order among manuscripts of an authoritative text, supposedly inviolable and invariate, were confusing, the prologues are more so. In Anglo-Latin tradition, the handling of less authoritative explanatory materials of clear human authorship appears thoroughly bewildering and various. The prologues to the biblical books turn out to be surprisingly malleable, and Ker's precise sixty-four-item account, while often followed, is very far from the whole story. There are, for example, prologues of some diffusion that not just Ker, but the expert F. Stegmüller, never saw—and for which, even after an assiduous bit of searching, I cannot offer a source. For example, there is a prologue to Zephaniah with the incipit, "Iosiam regem Iude cuius temporibus Sophonias prophetasse," or another to Haggai, "Moriente Dario rege Medorum et succedente in regno." In some manuscripts I have seen, they are hopefully ascribed to Jerome, but they certainly are not among the works printed as his; the first, at least, looks to me like an abbreviated paraphrase of material from Petrus Comestor's *Historia scholastica*.[13]

To begin with, the sixty-four seem to have been considered by Bible producers only a rough template. That is, most Anglo-Latin biblical books have most of them, and pretty invariably, in the expected places. But, given that these are exegetical/historical aids, and not Scripture, no copyist seems ever to have felt compelled to actually provide them all. Scribal practice suggests to me that one rule in play in producing Latin Bibles might be stated as, "One book, one prologue." For certainly, one universal in Bibles produced in England is the suppression of multiple prologues to the same book. This rule, of course, introduces its own small frisson, since, if someone is going to decide to suppress one prologue of two or three, obviously that person gets to choose which one ought to be omitted.

Ker's list of the standard prologues shows immediately where the problem areas might be expected to fall. Job, Joel, Amos, Jonah, Maccabees, and Matthew all have multiple prologues and thus are all prime candidates for modest excisions. In the case of Job and Matthew, where such streamlining is common, it is always the second prologue that is suppressed—although, confusingly, if typically, having suppressed RB 357 before Job, scribes are prone to add in extra materials, not part of the traditional sixty-four.[14] But, in the equally common case of reducing the prologues to the Maccabees, it is universally the first two prologues that are omitted, with only Stegmüller's RB 551 retained.[15] The minor prophets show a considerable amount of variation, complicated by a further feature I will mention in a moment; thus, various producers suppress Stegmüller RB 510 before Joel, yet others Stegmüller RB 511, and of the set before Amos, only Stegmüller RB 515 has anything like more or less universal transmission.[16]

Other commonplace suppressions are, in a general way, similar. That is, if the rule is "One book, one prologue," this might be perceived as having a corollary, "One prologue for each continuous biblical genre." One of the most commonly absent prologues is Stegmüller RB 327, to the continuation, 2 Chronicles; one might note that the Stuttgart Vulgate only nominally separates the traditional two books, in its rendition given the single title "Verba dierum." Or again, Ecclesiastes and Wisdom frequently lack prologues (RB 462 and 468, respectively); in this case, RB 457 serves as a general introduction to all the "Wisdom books."[17] But, at the same time, I would note that, confusingly enough, RB 468 to Wisdom offers one of the most common variants that neither Ker nor Stegmüller ever saw: a version with an extra sentence at the head, "Incipit quartus ordo eorum librorum qui in." This appears to have been derived from a rubric that in the *Patrologia Latina* rendition of the Vulgate introduces the book of Judith (28:1449n), and to have become absorbed into the subsequent text.[18]

Further, in many cases, English Vulgate manuscripts respect the Parisian instruction, "Prologue goes here," but they do not provide the standard Parisian text. The most ubiquitous example, to which I have already alluded, concerns the minor prophets. In my experience, this provision of materials occurs in Anglo-Latin Vulgates at least as frequently as does the received Parisian pattern, and perhaps more frequently. Certainly, beginning with Micah or Nahum, and in some Vulgates affecting the entire sequence from Obadiah on, English Bibles either supplement the standard prologues with, or offer in their stead, an alternate set of prologues. All these examples—extremely brief, three sentences at the most, and thus probably not construed as an exception to the "one prologue" rule—are indexed in Stegmüller. Although there is copious variation here (recall that my examples of prologues unnoted in Stegmüller are prefixed to prophets in this sequence), most usually English book producers offer materials they have gleaned from non-Vulgate Jerome sources. In this case, they simply lift the brief account of each prophetic book from Jerome's epistle 53, where he instructs Paulinus in the study of scripture (*Patrologia Latina* 22: 546–547).[19] So there is a richly various background in paratextual biblical materials.

As a consequence, although one respects Ker's presentation (and it offers an exemplary general guide), it is very far from the full story of Anglo-Latin Bibles. Fewer than a quarter of the books I have surveyed follow this model strictly, even for gross biblical contents (and ignoring whether the texts appear in Ker's order). Thus, no researcher should be either surprised or elated to discover minor variation or unindexed prologue materials. Whatever the appearance of uniformity (or of our conviction of the inviolable holy text), Anglo-Latin Bibles display all the quirks of transmission familiar in less august contexts.

Keble College, University of Oxford

APPENDIX

Manuscripts Consulted, cited by sigla in the notes

(All are from Oxford, unless stated otherwise)

All Souls College: A1 MS 1; A2 MS 2; A3 MS 3
Balliol College: B1 MS 1; B2 MS 330; B3 MS 348; B4 MS 351[20]
Bodleian Library, Digby MSS: Di MS 229
Christ Church: Ch1 MS 105; Ch2 MS 106; Ch3 MS 107; Ch4 MS 108; Ch5 MS 109; Ch6 MS 110; Ch7 MS 111
Dublin, Trinity College: D1 MS 35; D2 MS 36; D3 MS 37; D4 MS 38; D5 MS 40; D6 MS 41; D7 MS 42; D8 MS 43; D9 MS 44
Exeter College: E MS 45
Hereford Cathedral: H1 MS P.vi.4; H2 MS P.vii.1
Lincoln Cathedral: L1 MS 1; L2 MS 131; L3 MS 246
Magdalen College: M1 MS lat. 2; M2 MS lat. 108
Merton College: Me1 MS 7; Me2 MS 235
The Queen's College: Q1 MS 52; Q2 MS 55; Q3 MS 299; Q4 MS 358
St John's College: J1 MS 4; J2 MS 29; J3 MS 48; J4 MS 100; J5 MS 110; J6 MS 123; J7 MS 193; J8 MS 207
Worcester Cathedral: W1 MS F.162; W2 MS Q.83

NOTES

1. Completed by A. J. Piper, 4 vols. (Oxford: Clarendon, 1969–1992), now with a fifth volume of indexes, ed. I. C. Cunningham and A. G. Watson (Oxford; Clarendon, 2002), here the account of Lambeth Palace Library, MS 1364 at 1: 96–97. Contrast, for example, R. M. Thomson's description of the Augustine anthology, Merton College, MS 1, *A Descriptive Catalogue of the Medieval Manuscripts of Merton College, Oxford* (Cambridge: Boydell, 2009), 36.
2. I must acknowledge that, in spite of Ker's wisdom and authority, cataloguing since *Medieval Manuscripts* has often remained strangely impervious to his presentation. For one example of the tendency, (attempt to) consult Peter Kidd's illegible accounts in the web-mounted descriptions of Queen's College manuscripts; contrast the succinct, yet perfectly communicative treatment in Thomson's *Merton*. This essay will, at least, suggest that details rendered close to unrecoverable in descriptions like Kidd's, and telegraphically communicated in Thomson's, do conform to certain variously common patterns, even if not the expected "Parisian" model.

3. And cf. the reprise, at Apoc. 22: 18–19.
4. See the discussion of the textual aberrancy of commonly circulating Bibles in chapter 15 of "The General Prologue," in *The Earliest Advocates of the English Bible,* ed. Mary Dove (Exeter, 2010), 80/2802–11, 81–82/2846–62; Anne Hudson and Elizabeth Solopova, "The Latin Text," in Elizabeth Solopova, ed., *The Wycliffite Bible: Origin, History and Interpretation* (Leiden: Brill, 2017), 107–132 passim; and my "The Wycliffite Translators' Vulgate Manuscript: The Evidence from Mark," *Medium Ævum* 86 (2017), 60–90.
5. *Biblia Sacra, iuxta vulgatam versionem,* ed. Robert Weber et al., 4th edn (Stuttgart: Deutsche Bibelgesellschaft, 1994). The appendices, with most of these variant texts, appear at 1909–1976; the one bit accepted into the text at 1095.
6. 3 Ezra appears in fourteen of the books I have surveyed, A2 (uniquely, with 4–6 Ezra as well) A3 Ch5 Ch6 D2 D4 D5 D7 J6 J8 L3 M2 Q4 (and in Ch2 as a later addition). The prayer of Manasses occurs in seventeen copies, A1 A3 B2 B4 Ch1 Ch6 D9 Di J5 J6 J8 M1 M2 Me1 Q3 Q4 W1. Ecclesiasticus 52 ("the prayer of Solomon") is rather weakly attested, in the light of its inclusion in the standard text, in twelve copies only, B1 B4 Ch2 Ch3 Ch4 Ch5 D5 J4 J5 L2 Q2 Q4. The Pauline Laodiceans appears in only seven of the books, B4 D3 D7 D9 H1 J1 Q2.
7. The Psalter fails to appear in ten of the sampled books A1 B1 Ch6 Ch7 J4 J6 L1(?) M1 Q2 (added later in Di).
8. Josiah Forshall and Frederic Madden, eds, *The Holy Bible, Containing the Old and New Testaments,* 4 vols (Oxford: Clarendon, 1850). For an example of such a separate booklet and two-volume full Bible, see British Library, MS Royal 1 B.x (once property of John Dyggon, fifth recluse of Sheen) and J1. Dyggon's book also includes a parallel-text Psalter.
9. Acts alone follows John in J2 Q1. Acts and the Catholic epistles are advanced to this position in B1 D6 Di E H2 J6 M1 Q2 W2. And both Catholic epistles and the Apocalypse follow Acts here in Ch4 J3 J4 W1. In two aberrant instances, H1 L2, only the Catholic epistles appear in this position. After all, James, whose letter stands at the head, was "the Lord's brother," and the other authors among the apostles.
10. Tobit follows Judith and Esther in A1 B4 Ch4 D3 J2 J3 Q1 W2. In the "historical" handling of Maccabees, the books usually follow Esther, to be succeeded by prophets, Job, the Psalter, and "Wisdom books" (thus concluding with Ecclesiasticus). Examples of this order occur surprisingly frequently, in A1 Ch4 Di E J4 Q1 Q2 W2. The traditional *tanakh*/Hebrew whole Bible, imitated a bit inconsistently in such presentations, comprises three text blocks: the Pentateuch (*torah*), *nevim* ("prophets,"

including the last three books of the Octateuch), and *ketuvim* ("[miscellaneous] writings," beginning with Psalms and Job); cf. *Biblia Hebraica Stuttgartensia*, ed. A. Alt et al., 2nd edn (Stuttgart: Würtembergische Bibelanstalt, 1983).

11. Baruch, absent from A1 L1, precedes Lamentations in Ch2 J4, follows Daniel in Ch4, and is copied in two bits one displaced, in D6. Both letters to the Thessalonians precede Colossians in A2 Ch4 D5 H2 J3 J5, 1 Thessalonians only in J6.
12. For the partial modern reproduction of these, see, for example, *Bibla Sacra* 3–4, 285–286, 364–366, etc. Such paratextual materials are conventionally identified, as I will do here, by the numbers assigned each of the texts in F. Stegmüller, *Reportorium Biblicum Medii Aevi*, 11 vols. (Madrid: [Consejo Superior de Investigaciones Cientificas], 19[5]0–80) (hereafter RB); all the biblical materials and the prologues appear in volume 1.
13. "Josiam" appears as a second prologue, supplementing Ker's standard example (RB 534) or another, in Ch1 J2 Q2; cf. *Patrologia Latina* 198:1415–18. "Moriente," an acephalic version of the standard RB 538, appears in Ch1 Ch3 J2 Q2 W1 (and British Library, MS King's 2). A further example: Ch4 prefaces Obadiah, not with RB 519+517, but "Arguuntur illi qui populum domini persequentes"; it also appears as an additional prologue in the same position in J4.
14. RB 589, the second prologue to Matthew, is absent in about half the books surveyed, Ch1 Ch3 Ch7 D3 D6 D7 D8 D9 Di E H1 J1 J2 J3 J7 L3 M1 Me1 Me2 W2 (D5 lacks both prologues; L2 W1 substitute other materals; and A3 uniquely suppresses RB 590 instead). The second prologue to Job, RB 357, is completely lacking in fourteen books, A3 Ch2 Ch7 D3 D8 H1 J1 J2 J6 J7 L3 Me1 Q3 (neither prologue in B4); but in another nine instances, it is replaced by another text, usually RB 349 or 350 or some combination of both, in Ch1 Ch3 Ch4 D9 J3 L1 Q1 Q2 W1.
15. The first prologue to Maccabees, RB 547, is absent in more than half the copies, B1 Ch1 Ch2 Ch3 Ch4 D2 D7 D9 E J1 J2 J3 J7 L2 L3 M1 Me1 W2 (added later in Ch2, different materials supplied A2 A3); the second, RB 553, absent in all these, does not occur in Ch7 Me2 either (it again is a later addition to Ch2). Four manuscripts, D5 D6 Di H1, provide no prologue here at all.
16. RB 511 is lacking in Ch1 Ch2 (added later) Ch3 D5 D9 J2 J3 L1 L2 Q2, in the last, however, with non-standard prologues in its place. RB 510 does not appear in Ch2 E J1 L3 M1 Me1 Me2, and W1 suppresses both, although providing other materials here. In the case of Amos, the first

prologue, RB 515, is lacking only in Ch4 Ch7 J3 J4. RB 512 also occurs frequently, only absent in E L2 L3 M1 Me2 W1; but the third prologue, RB 513 is very widely suppressed, absent from Ch1 Ch2 (added later) Ch3 Ch4 Ch7 D6 D9 Di E J2 J3 J4 L1 L3 Me1 Me2 Q1 Q2 W1 W2.

17. RB 327 occurs in only a minority of volumes in the survey, absent from B4 Ch1 Ch2 Ch3 Ch4 Ch5 Ch7 D1 D3 D5 D6 D7 D8 D9 Di H1 J2 J5 J6 L3 M1 M2 Me2 W2 (its omission was remedied later in Ch2 Ch5). RB 462 to Ecclesiastes is lacking in A2 Ch2 (supplied later) Ch4 Ch7 Di D3 D9 E H1 J1 J2 J3 L2 L3 Me1 Q1 Q2 Q4 W1, and RB 468 to Wisdom in all these, excepting A2 J2 L2 W1, but it fails to appear in A3 D7 D8 M2 Q3 as well.
18. The expanded version, "Incipit," occurs in Ch1 Ch3 J2 J7.
19. This replacement/supplement series parallels Ker's prologues 33–39 and includes RB 525, 527, 529, 532, 535 (very occasionally 539), 540, 544 or 545, respectively. Versions of this sequence, either alone or as supplements, approach being the majority form in local Bibles, occurring in Ch1 Ch2 Ch3 Ch4 D5 D9 H1 J1 J2 J4 L1 L2 L3 Me1 Me2 Q1 Q2, portions only in A2 E W1 W2. In cases where the sequence extends back to Obadiah, RB 516 replaces RB 517, as in Ch1 Ch2 Ch3 D5 D9 J1 J2 J3 J4 J6 J7 L1 L2 Me1 Q1 Q2 W2.
20. These books, for which I rely upon R. A. B. Mynors, *Catalogue of the Manuscripts of Balliol College, Oxford* (Oxford: Clarendon, 1963), are not so fully described as the remainder of the books here, and the information presented might be taken as provisional.

A London Expatriate Scribe? John Vale in Portugal

JOE STADOLNIK

British Library, Additional MS 48301A is a late fifteenth-century manuscript compilation of copy-letters, London chronicle material, and political texts such as John Fortescue's *Governance of England* and John Lydgate's prose *Serpent of Division*.[1] Thanks to the scholarship of Anne F. Sutton and Livia Visser-Fuchs, we know a good many details about the life and career of its scribe, John Vale, who signs his initials *JV* four times in the manuscript.[2] Originally from Suffolk, Vale appears to have moved to London by 1463 when he appears in the will of a Bury St. Edmunds merchant as "Thomas Vale's son now dwelling at London with Thomas Cook."[3] Cook was a wealthy London draper, whose name appears throughout the letters collected in Vale's book. Vale worked for Cook in legal and secretarial capacities in the ensuing years, earning some trust and respect in local circles; by the late 1470s, contemporary documents styled him "gentleman of London" and often as the rather more genteel "John de Vale."[4] Upon Cook's death in 1478, Vale continued to act on behalf of Cook's widow Elizabeth in disputes with her son and Thomas's heir, Philip. Elizabeth, who had inherited the estates of her father Philip Malpas, later trusted "John Devale" to be an executor of her estate in an 1484 will and as feoffee of some Malpas lands in Essex.[5] Vale also appears to have subsequently maintained contacts with Cook's son-in-law, John Forster, a draper himself and inheritor of Malpas properties with his wife Joan *née* Cook. A later, nearly contemporary hand adds a list of tenants of one such Malpas property at the end of Additional 48301A, suggesting that the book passed from John Vale into the Forster household sometime after 1484.[6]

Apart from this miscellany of his own making, Vale owned at least three other miscellaneous books: an English scientific miscellany (Cambridge, Trinity College MS R.14.52), a religious miscellany in English and Latin (Worcester Cathedral MS F.172), and a verse compilation including works by Chaucer and Lydgate (British Library, Harley MS 2251). All three manuscripts were produced by the bookmaking operation of John Multon, a London stationer.[7] Multon also bequeathed a psalter to "John de Vale" in his 1475 will.[8] In London, Vale proved capable of cultivating valued working and social relationships with bookmakers like Multon as well as members of city's elite mercantile class, like Thomas and Elizabeth Cook and John Forster (himself a client of Multon). So established, John de Vale—draper's man of affairs, made gentleman of London, scribe, and reader—then disappears from the surviving documentary record by 1485: he left no sign of a will, or a widow, or children, in English sources.[9] What happened to him?

A Portuguese chancery document provides one possible account of John Vale's whereabouts later in life. In 1499, Dom Manuel of Portugal grants the status of *vizinho* in the town of Tavira in the Algarve to one "João da Vala, Englishman."[10] The document refers to this new *vizinho* by his name and nationality three times: "Joham da Vala imgres" twice in the text proper and once in the left margin.[11] *Vizinho* literally means "neighbor" in Portuguese, but here conveys a formal municipal standing with legal and commercial advantages. The king certifies João da Vala's right to "trade, sell, buy [tratar vemder comprar]" in the town and his enjoyment of all the honors, privileges, freedoms and customs afforded *vizinhos*, as well as his reciprocal obligations to pay any associated taxes and customs to the proper agents of the Crown there. Grants of *vizinhança* in Tavira like this are not regularly recorded in royal chancery registers; Dom Manuel does, however, extend the status of *vizinho* to one Diogo Pinto, called a "foreign merchant resident in Tavira," in 1518.[12] It could be that alien merchants like Pinto and Vale required royal certification to be confirmed as *vizinhos*, or sought it out for good measure.

Could João da Vala be John de Vale setting up shop in a coastal town in the Portuguese Algarve? An affirmative case can be made in terms general and particular. Tavira was not so remote from Vale's London in 1499 as one might guess. The Algarve was a productive agricultural region, and English merchants imported its fruit, wine, and dyes in quantity often via Lisbon and other Iberian ports.[13] Situated on the gulf of Cádiz, Tavira sat along a trading route routinely plied by English ships. The Middle English sailing directions in John Paston's book trace a voyage around the Cabo de São Vicente at the southwestern tip of Portugal, past Tavira and then Huelva,

Seville, and Sanlúcar de Barrameda in nearby Andalusia, before reaching the straits of Gibraltar.[14] Trade with Portugal at the time was growing more and more lucrative for London men in particular: Wendy Childs describes a "surge" in Anglo-Portuguese trade in the 1490s, one centered in London rather than in previously active ports like Southampton and Bristol.[15]

Vale's residence in Tavira by 1499 accords with what details we know of his biography.[16] We can only estimate his age at the time. He was "dwelling at London with Thomas Cook" by 1463, though we do not know under what terms he entered Cook's service or at what age. He may have been quite a young man, living with Cook to learn the trade at fourteen or so, and yet to make a name for himself (he was still "Thomas Valys son" in the will). Thus, in 1499, he was fifty years old at the youngest when he won the privileges of *vizinhança* in Tavira and set up well in the Algarve for a comfortable late career. There he could act as a factor for his English contacts: buying and selling goods on their behalf under favorable terms, or assuring safe receipt and dispatch of cargoes.[17] For adventurous Englishmen of Vale's position and skills, a stint abroad was a means of advancement in a mercantile career. It provided training in the craft, and opportunity to strengthen relationships with foreign brokers, one's clients back home, and other upwardly mobile Englishmen resident there. Vale may have already spent time in Iberia as a young man on behalf of Cook and the drapers, and sensed opportunity in a return in the late 1480s and 1490s. As for his means to make such a move, we know he came into some substantial seed money for his own investment in 1478, when Thomas Cook left him the sum of £50 in gratitude for his service. Cook also left Vale an annuity of four marks out of the profits of a London property. Elizabeth Cook granted him life interest in a shop on Bridge Street in London—prime retailing space—in her own will of 1484.[18] Vale had done quite well for himself then, and had both the acumen and the assets to make a move thereafter. If he had partners in his venture, they could shoulder a share of the costs incurred in sending a trusted and able man to act as their factor in the Algarve, a region of growing importance to London merchants. The newly-won privileges of a *vizinho* in 1499 in this export-rich region would have only improved Vale's position.

The most compelling case for John Vale's identity as the Englishman João da Vala in Tavira is founded on the many and particularly deep connections of the Drapers' Company with Portugal and Spain. Wendy Childs positively identifies more drapers trading with Spain than members of any other London company throughout the fifteenth century.[19] The draper and London mayor Bartholomew James seems to have been born in Portugal to an English father.[20] Other London drapers sailed the Iberian run, visiting Portugal and Andalusia to prosecute commercial interests. Wendy Childs finds John Bownde based in Andalusia for a time, traveling to Huelva,

Seville, and Sanlúcar.[21] George Bulstrode unsuccessfully courted a widow with sumptuous gifts he had bought in Andalusia in the 1480s; William Folkys had been "to Lisbon in his youth."[22] Thomas Howell, made a freeman of the company in 1506, spent twenty-six years shuttling between London and Seville, leading Childs to wonder if he simply preferred Andalusian life (a snowbird Londoner ahead of his time).[23] The gulf of Cádiz bustled with London drapers and their agents, with whom Vale might trade, cooperate, or entertain at Tavira to his advantage.

One draper stands out in the company for his Portuguese connections. Edward Brampton was born Duarte Brandão in Lisbon, a Jew and illegitimate son of a blacksmith's wife.[24] He moved to London in 1468, where he converted, with Edward IV standing as godfather. A man of many talents and Yorkist sympathies, Brampton was made a freeman of the draper's company in 1477, as Vale was managing Cook's affairs. Business was very good, good enough that Brampton could soon advance the Treasury a tidy sum of £700 for its debt to Spanish merchants in exchange for exemption from the wool custom on exports through Straits of Gibraltar.[25] England proved less hospitable to Brampton after the Yorkist defeat at Bosworth in 1485, and he returned to Portugal soon after. Back home, Brampton was renaturalized by successive favorable kings, and crucially, he set himself up in international trade as Duarte Brandão again. In 1487 he sold off extensive local holdings to buy exemption from customs on charcoal, wood, linen, and other commodities in Lisbon.[26] The careers of John Vale and Edward Brampton coincided at the London drapers' hall in the late 1470s through the early 1480s, and again when they moved from England to Portugal in the following decades just as Anglo-Iberian trade surged through London. In Tavira and Lisbon, João da Vala and Duarte Brandão could each capitalize upon their past English acquaintance. Vale could look to Brandão for credit and connections in a new country; Brandão had in Vale a dependable and enterprising agent posted in the Algarve, with intimate knowledge of Anglo-Iberian trade and, perhaps more importantly, the traders engaged in it.

Vale might have taken Multon's psalter with him to Portugal, but his four miscellanies have lingered on the shelves of English libraries. These he may have given away to friends and associates, or sold. The miscellany in his own hand, Additional MS 48301A, passed to the Forsters. Trinity MS R.14.52, his practical-scientific miscellany, has a later signature from a "Ri[?] Roos" on folio 271v.[27] One Robert Roos began an apprenticeship with the drapers in 1488; a number of Rooses were mercers.[28] There is an ownership inscription on the same page, "Iste liber constat Johannes Bampton." Two John Bamptons were mercers, earning their freedom in 1474 and 1480. Harley MS 2251, a manuscript apparently copied from a Shirley exemplar, landed in the hands of "Nycolas Sky*ner*" for a time, who signs the top margin of folio 9r. One Nicholas Skynner left a will in 1508 donating a "stondyng maser"—a standing bowl—to the merchant haberdashers' hall in Farringdon and a small sum to "Seint Austins," presumably the parish church of St. Augustine by St. Paul.[29] Harley MS 2251 then passed to the antiquarian John Stowe.[30] The whereabouts of Vale's religious miscellany, Worcester Cathedral Library MS F.172, are a mystery prior to its donation in the early eighteenth century.[31] On the whole, Vale's books changed hands among readers affiliated with the City's prestigious livery companies the drapers, mercers, and haberdashers, tracing out a network of literary exchange that mapped onto and across those of mercantile activity.[32]

If the *vizinho* of Tavira and the English scribe of Additional MS 48301A were one and the same man, then the life of João da Vala *olim* John Vale followed a course from childhood in Suffolk, through adulthood among the merchants of London, to resettlement in the Algarve. In Tavira, John Vale closed the fifteenth century like no other Lydgate scribe or reader of Chaucer whom we know of. The arc of this life, then, invites us to recalibrate our operative sense of the horizons of those Middle English scribes and readers who shared his metropolitan milieu.

Institute of Advanced Studies, University College London

Acknowledgments

The author is grateful to Anya Adair and Spencer Strub for reading over drafts of this paper, and to Professor Wendy Childs, who has fielded questions about the history of Anglo-Iberian exchange with extraordinary generosity.

NOTES

1. On this manuscript and its context, see Margaret Kekewich, et al., *The Politics of Fifteenth-Century England: John Vale's Book* (Stroud: Alan Sutton Publishing Limited for Richard III and Yorkist History Trust, 1995).
2. He signs "per me JV" in the margins of folios 94r and 119v, and "by me JV" at the end of two letters, both on folio 187v.
3. For those details see Sutton and Visser-Fuchs, "The Provenance of the Manuscript: The Lives and Archive of Sir Thomas Cook and His Man of Affairs, John Vale," *Politics of Fifteenth-Century England,* 73–126; 103.
4. He is referred to as a 'gentleman of London' in two chancery documents: Kew, National Archives, C1/54/131 and 66/400; cited in Sutton and Visser-Fuchs, "Provenance," 106.
5. Sutton and Visser-Fuchs, "Provenance," 99.

6. The list of tenants of Porter's Fee in Dagenham is on folio 188v of the manuscript. Porter's Fee passed from John Cook to his sister Joan Forster. The Forsters sold it to Avery Cornburgh in 1488; the Cornburghs sold it to one William Hussey in 1495. Ibid., 103.
7. On Vale's books, see ibid., 108–109. All three MSS are in the hand of a single scribe; Sutton and Visser-Fuchs strongly suggest that the scribe, known as the Hammond scribe, may very well have been Multon himself. Linne R. Mooney raises the possibility that John Vale, John Shirley, and the Hammond scribe were members of a common class of household clerks that enjoyed remarkable access to many and various copy-texts with which to compile books in "John Shirley's Heirs," *Yearbook of English Studies* 33 (2003): 182–198, 190. For an inventory of the Hammond scribe's output, see Mooney, "More Manuscripts Written by a Chaucer Scribe." *The Chaucer Review* 30, no. 4 (1996): 401–407, and "A New Manuscript by the Hammond Scribe Discovered by Jeremy Griffiths," in *The English Medieval Book: Studies in Memory of Jeremy Griffiths*, ed. A. S. G. Edwards, Vincent Gillespie, and Ralph Hanna (London: The British Library, 2000), 113–123.
8. Sutton and Visser-Fuchs, "Provenance," 108.
9. As Sutton and Visser-Fuchs observe, "No personal details about Vale have been discovered after the end of 1484 ... If Vale left a will it has not survived, and if he left a widow and children they have not been identified" (in "Provenance," 107).
10. Arquivo Nacional Torre do Tombo, Chancelaria de D. Manuel I, liv. 16, folio 16v.
11. By Portuguese chancery convention, Englishmen named John and Portuguese named João tend to be 'Joham' on paper. When authorizing an Englishman named John Redy to carry arms in 1462, Portuguese scribes styled him "Joha*m* Redy ingres"; John Collin [?], granted the same right in 1450, is "Joham Collim ingres." Arquivo Nacional Torre do Tombo, Chancelaria de D. Afonso V, liv. 9, folio 54v; ibid., liv. 11, folio 40r.
12. Chancelaria de D. Manuel I, liv. 44, folio 7v.
13. There is evidence for direct English trade links with Tavira specifically (such as a record of a shipload of fruit and wine arriving from Tavira in 1443) and with the Algarve more generally. On the 1443 shipment, see Wendy R. Childs, *Trade and Shipping in the Medieval West: Portugal, Castile, and England*, Textes et Études du Moyen Âge 70 (Porto: Fédération internationale des instituts d'études médiévales, 2013), 133. The *Christopher* of Bristol returned from an unnamed port in Algarve on December 11, 1480, laden almost entirely with dried fruit customarily enjoyed for Christmas, and three bags of "grain": probably *kermes vermilio*, a dye used to make luxury woolens; see E. M. Carus-Wilson,

The Overseas Trade of Bristol in the Middle Ages (Bristol: Bristol Record Society, 1967), 232.

14. On these instructions in British Library, Landsdowne MS 285, see Geoffrey A. Lester, "The Earliest English Sailing Directions," in *Popular and Practical Science of Medieval England,* ed. Lister A. Matheson (East Lansing: Colleagues Press, 1994), 331–368. These directions are lines 185–218. The text does not mention Tavira by name but describes a route by its coast.
15. Childs, *Trade and Shipping in the Medieval West,* 125.
16. There are indeed other contemporaneous John [de] Vales in records (a Gloucestershire fuller, clerks of Cambridge and Bristol), but most can be easily disqualified as the 1499 resident of Tavira, and none are so qualified as Cook's factotum, as I argue here.
17. On English factors and merchants in Iberia, see Childs, *Anglo-Castilian Trade in the Later Middle Ages* (Manchester: Manchester University Press, 1978), 184–187; *Trade and Shipping,* 119–120; Gordon Connell-Smith, *The Forerunners of Drake* (London: Longmans, Green and Co., 1954), 18–24.
18. Sutton and Visser-Fuchs, "Provenance," 106–107.
19. Childs acknowledges that this reckoning of the companies' relative engagement in Iberian trade is based on a "sample too small and incomplete for firm conclusion," yet maintains that it "seems clear enough that the drapers were the group most concerned with Spanish trade" (*Anglo-Castilian Trade,* 211).
20. Childs, *Trade and Shipping,* 206–207.
21. Childs, *Anglo-Castilian Trade,* 184 and 186.
22. On Bulstrode's extravagant courtship, see Sylvia L. Thrupp, *The Merchant Class of Medieval London* (Chicago: University of Chicago Press, 1948), 106–107, and Childs, ibid., 186.
23. On Thomas Howell, see Childs, ibid., 185, and G. Connell-Smith, "The Ledger of Thomas Howell," *The Economic History Review,* New Series, 3:3 (1951): 363–370, 365 and 370, and Heather Dalton, "Negotiating Fortune: English Merchants in Early Sixteenth-Century Seville," in *Bridging the Early Modern Atlantic World: People, Products, and Practices on the Move,* ed. Caroline A. Williams (London and New York: Routledge, 2009), 57–74.
24. For Brampton's life, see Rosemary Horrox, "Brampton, Sir Edward [Duarte Brandão] (c. 1440–1508), soldier and merchant," *Oxford Dictionary of National Biography,* https://doi.org/10.1093/ref:odnb/37218. See also Cecil Roth, "Sir Edward Brampton, alias Duarte Brandão: Governor of Guernsey, 1482–1485," *Report and Transactions of La Société Guernesiaise* 16, part II (1956): 160–170.

25. Roth, ibid., 164. Other occupations, however, often drew his attentions away from that business. He captained a Portuguese carvel against the Scots in 1481, and served from afar as governor of Guernsey from 1482 to 1485.
26. Ibid., 167.
27. Mooney, "More Manuscripts," 404.
28. For this information I rely upon the *Records of London's Livery Companies Online* (londonroll.org). Literary interests had a precedent in the Roos family: Thomas Roos, a mercer, listed a number of books in his possession in an 1433 will. See Kathleen L. Scott, "Past Ownership: Evidence of Book Ownership by English Merchants in the Middle Ages," in *Makers and Users of Medieval Books: Essays in Honour of A.S.G. Edwards*, ed. Carol M. Meale and Derek Pearsall (Cambridge: D.S. Brewer, 2014), 150–177, 172.
29. Kew, National Archives, PROB 11/16/541.
30. Mooney, "More Manuscripts," 404. One Nicholas Skynner of Multon is named in a 1499 Suffolk conveyance recorded in British Library, Stowe Ch 248. He appears in a prosperous and learned milieu—alongside with other men of East Anglian merchant families such as the Heyghams and the Dourants, and Cambridge clerks John Puregold and William Peper.
31. R. M. Thomson with Michael Gullick, *A Descriptive Catalogue of the Medieval Manuscripts in Worcester Cathedral Library* (Woodbridge, Suffolk: D. S. Brewer, 2001), 114–116.
32. For Vale's place in these London textual networks, see Julia Boffey, "London Books and London Readers," in *Cultural Reformations*, ed. James Simpson and Brian Cummings (Oxford: Oxford University Press, 2010), 420–437: 426–428; Sheila Lindenbaum, "London texts and literate practice," in the *Cambridge History of Medieval Literature*, ed. David Wallace (Cambridge: Cambridge University Press, 1999), 284–309, 303.

Two Manuscripts of the *Practica Phisicalia Magistri Johannis de Burgundia* and their Censorship

PATRICK OUTHWAITE

This article identifies two previously unknown early sixteenth-century manuscript copies of the Middle English translation of the *Practica phisicalia*, the recipe book of John of Burgundy (circa 1338–1390).[1] Both censor the same section of the text: that concerning the treatment of male genitalia. John of Burgundy, a professor of medicine from Liège, was a widely circulated and much translated author with an audience that included non-professionals and those informally trained.[2] Indeed, the practical character and vernacular language of the codices examined here suggest they were likely owned or used by barbers, or perhaps even by laymen or women. The post-production lives of these manuscripts register, through glossing and excising, a shift in taste and sensibility and a recognition that certain recipes were obsolete for post-medieval readers. This activity forms part of a trend in which early-modern medical practitioners became increasingly concerned with transmitting "decency" and obscuring the "obscene"—namely details of reproductive organs and vulgar language—in their works.[3]

Two manuscripts of the *Practica phisicalia*—London, Wellcome Library MS 406 and Montréal, Osler Library, Bibliotheca Osleriana 7591—have gone unacknowledged until now, presumably because they contain no reference to the title of the work or its author.[4] In fact, these details are only featured in one of the surviving manuscripts: London, British Library, Additional MS 33996.[5] The lack of such information in all but one copy has made it difficult for cataloguers to associate the *Practica* with John of Burgundy in the first place.[6] The most significant examination of the work was by Fritz Heinrich, who in 1896 produced an edition of the *Practica* using Additional MS 33996 as his base text.[7] Heinrich identified six manuscripts of the work, all of which are now held in the British Library: Additional MSS 3396 and 19674,[8] Harley 1600, Royal 17 A. III, and Sloane MSS 405 and 3153. A seventh manuscript, Oxford, Bodleian Library, Rawlinson D. 251, is discussed by M. Claire Jones in an unpublished thesis from 2000.[9]

To this list, we can now add London, Wellcome Library MS 406 (hereinafter "Wellcome") and Montréal, Osler Library, Bibliotheca Osleriana 7591 (hereinafter "Osler"). The recipes of the *Practica phisicalia* appear in these manuscripts alongside works not known to be composed by John of Burgundy, such as charms and poems that espouse the virtues of particular ingredients.[10] The manuscripts are very similar in their composition and layout. Each contains a condensed version of the *Practica*, leaving a number of the recipes wanting. The pages of Wellcome are 140 x 100 millimeters; Osler is slightly larger, at 201 x 130 millimeters. Both codices are relatively small, cheap productions composed of parchment in quires of eight (with one exception, as I shall discuss). Both were produced in the first quarter of the sixteenth century, featuring Anglicana and Bastard-Anglicana (*cursiva-antiquior*) hands. Osler is written in a single hand: a neat, fluid Anglicana with large looping ascenders and descenders. The titles for each recipe are written in a thick red *fere-textura* Bastard-Anglicana.[11] The main scribal hand of Wellcome is similar to the looping Anglicana of Osler. The distinctive features are its z-shaped **r** and backwards sigma-shaped **e**. However, the opening twenty-two folios, before the *Practica* begins, present a significantly neater and more disciplined Bastard-Anglicana on parchment of fairer quality than the rest of the codex. These folios include ornamental capitals in blue and red ink, with semi-vinet marginal decorations that are occasionally embellished with grotesque animal heads.[12]

Neither scribe relied on any other surviving copy as an exemplar. Osler has linguistic similarities to both Sloane 3153 and Royal 17 A. III, as shown in its spelling and use of thorn,[13] but it also contains a number of textual divergences that cannot be explained by scribal intervention or error. For example, in the recipe of an ointment "for the skaldyng of a mannes pyntell" (78),[14] Osler presents a sentence on the preparation of the ointment out of sequence. Instead of preparing the butter and herbs before placing the concoction in an earthen pot, as all the other manuscripts prescribe, Osler states: "take a new erthen potte & do in thys erbis & thi buttre when they be medlid." This is unlikely to be a scribal error, per se, as the sentence still makes syntactical sense and the final product would not be much affected; it merely means that the recipe is to be prepared in a different order.

Wellcome is linguistically close to Sloane 405[15] but features variant lines, such as this extra line in the recipe "for swellyng of a mannys pyntell" that does not feature in the other surviving manuscripts: "Anoþer take þe jus of planteyn [ribwort plantain or *plantago lanceolata*]."[16] It would be a stretch to suggest that both Osler and Wellcome are separate recensions of the *Practica*, but at the same time neither wholly conforms to any other surviving manuscript. These divergences are illustrative of Irma Taavitsainen's assessment of recipe books, which she argues are more "adaptable and flexible" than typical academic medical works. As a result, scribes and owners often adapted recipe books for their own ends instead of rigidly following an authoritative exemplar.[17]

Possibly the most significant commonality between Wellcome and Osler is that their sections concerning treatments for male genitalia have evidently been censored. Wellcome censors two recipes: "for swellyng of a mannys pyntell" (folio 35v) and "for scalding of a mannes pyntell" (folio 36r). In each case a reader has ruled through the word "pyntell" (penis) in the title with a thick black ink, so that only the tips of the ascenders and descenders are visible. "Pyntell" is replaced with the Latin equivalent, "veretrum," which is written in a more formal, laterally compressed *fere-textura*. Next to the annotation on folio 35v, a second, later hand has again written "veretrum."[18] Perhaps this annotator deemed the original gloss to be illegible, as this repeated word is thinner, with disconnected, set letters.[19] These glosses are written in an archaizing style by a post-medieval reader, in an attempt to mimic the other titles in the codex. This ostensible censorship does not extend to the recipes themselves, however, but only to their titles. The exchange of Middle English for Latin may very well have been because the word "pyntell" changed from a relatively neutral anatomical label in the sixteenth century to an obscenity in the late seventeenth century.[20] Presumably this censorship was intended for those thumbing through the manuscript looking for a desired text, as someone wanted to keep certain readers away (most likely laymen and particularly women) with an added level of mediation.[21]

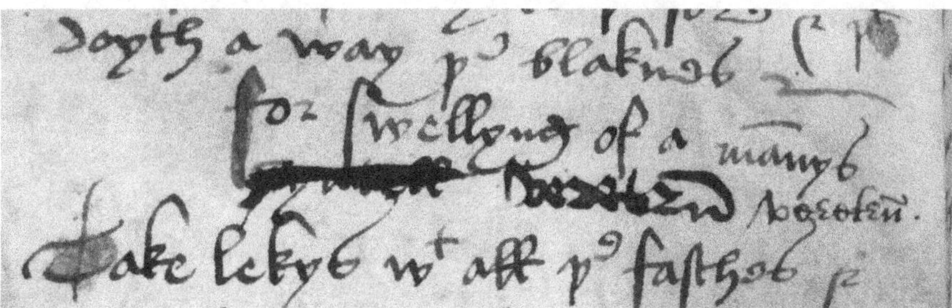

Figure 1. London, Wellcome Library MS 406, f. 35v 'For swellyng of a mannys veretrum'. Courtesy © Wellcome Collection.

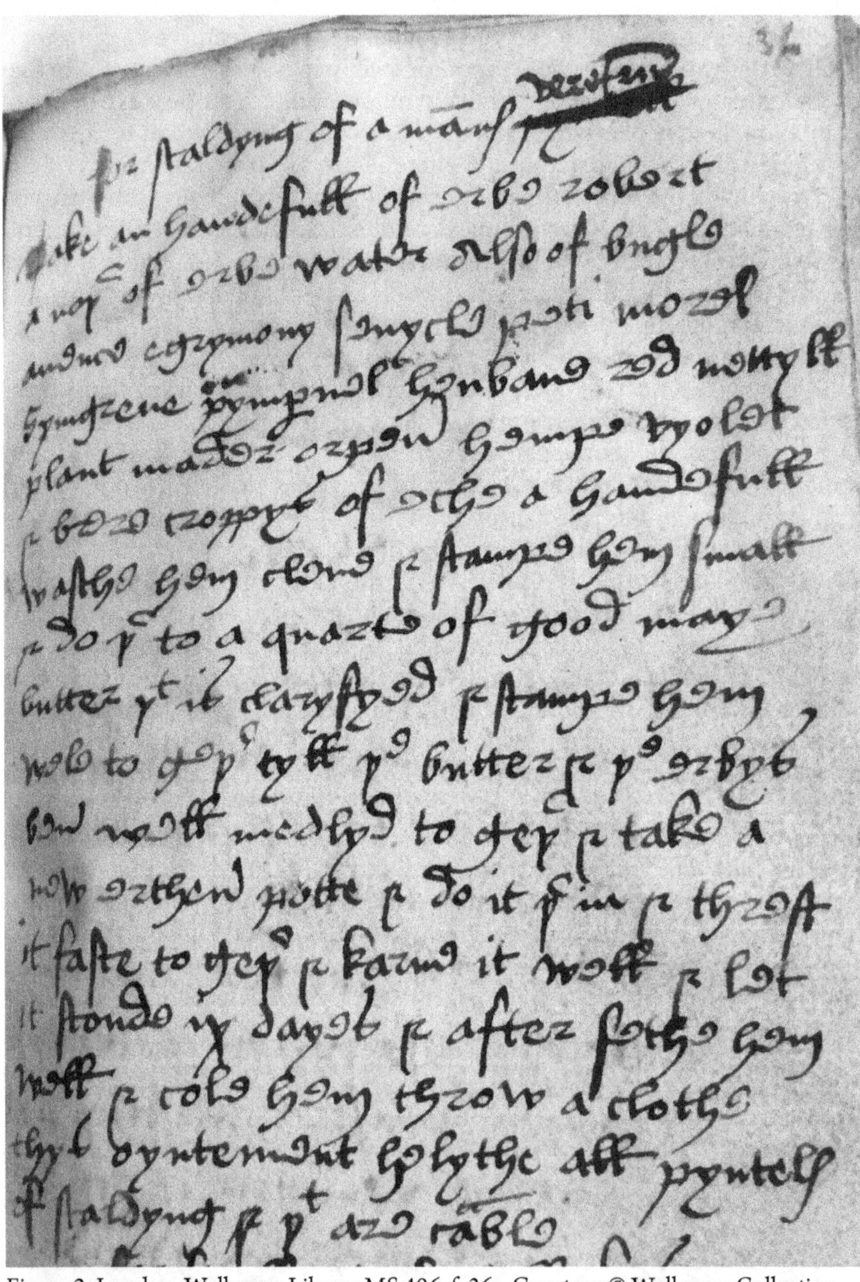

Figure 2. London, Wellcome Library MS 406, f. 36r. Courtesy © Wellcome Collection.

Osler does not obscure words, but excises recipes altogether. Two leaves are missing that must have contained almost all of the recipe "Ffor swellyng of ballokes" (only the title and five lines survive on page 78) and the entirety of the recipe "Ffor ache in mannes lendes [loins or genitalia]." We can be sure that two leaves are missing because the quire in which these recipes are partially contained (quire six of ten) is the only quire of six in the entire manuscript and remnants of the excised pages are clearly visible in the gutter. The missing leaves are likely not the result of wear, as this kind of physical intervention is exceptional in the manuscript, and elsewhere there is minimal damage. Furthermore, the remaining stubs show clear signs of excision with clean lines that must result from cutting.

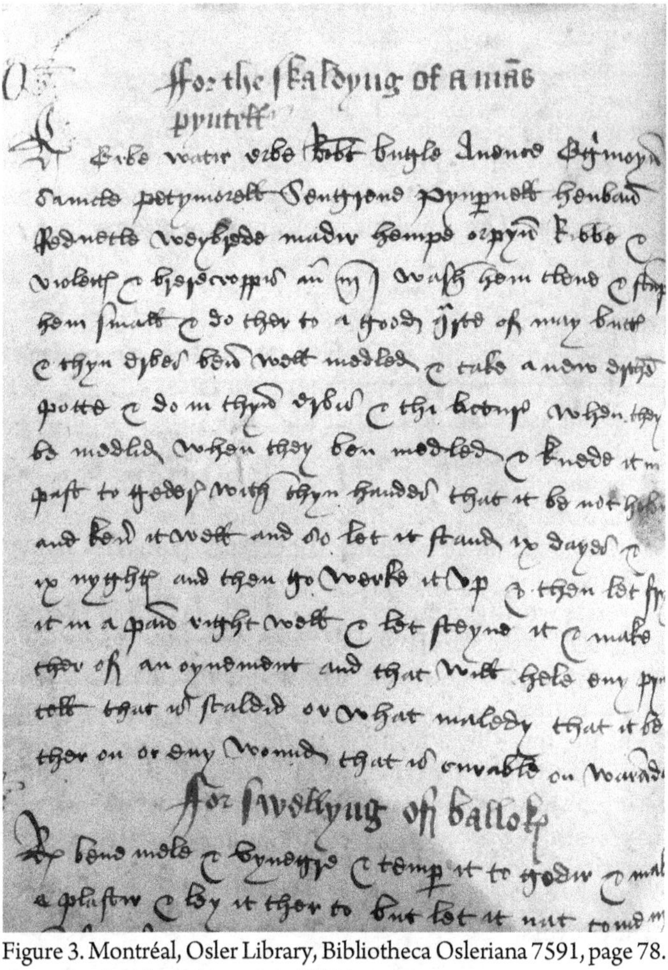

Figure 3. Montréal, Osler Library, Bibliotheca Osleriana 7591, page 78. Courtesy © Osler Library, McGill University.

Adding to this, the portions of the recipes concerning the penis and testicles that do survive are the only recipes in the entire manuscript that have manicules pointing to their titles, suggesting that they were at some point considered notable. It is possible that the two missing leaves were removed by a reader for ease of access in continued consultation of the recipe "Ffor ache in mannes lendes." Alternatively, the leaves may have been removed because the owner of the manuscript did not appreciate the attention that they received. The annotations in the manuscript, written in an eighteenth-century hand, add comments, modernize the spelling of certain words, and offer judgments on the effectiveness of recipes. The annotator inscribed his name at the beginning of the codex: "Ed. Cooper. 1726."[22] Next to a poem in tetrameter elsewhere in the codex, entitled "Ematites is the stones name," Cooper explains in a marginal note: "Ther [sic] is a specimen of the poetry in those / Days; bring the virtues of the lapis / Hamatitis set forth in stylish verse" (100). If Cooper appreciates the "stylish" verse so much as to comment on it, perhaps he was moved to expunge pages that he found uncouth or offensive in some way. Cooper did not view the entire codex as an archaic artifact, as his annotations suggest that he found practical use in some of the recipes. The excisions may represent an attempt to update the work for post-medieval readers, as evidently the removed recipes (if indeed he was responsible) were unnecessary for his use.

Clearly different forms of censorship are registered in the two manuscripts: one obscures the titles of two recipes and presents a desire for selective readership in the use of Latin; the other excises portions of the recipes themselves. Still, it is significant that the same section of the *Practica* is altered in both manuscripts. This is not merely coincidence, as nothing else in either manuscript is emended or removed. Osler and Wellcome reflect a trend that started in the early modern period, where authors and owners of manuscripts became concerned to obscure references to reproductive organs because they were considered indecent, and yet the manuscripts were still seen as worthy to preserve. Joan Cadden illustrates that physicians showed "signs of discomfort" when referring to sexual organs,[23] signs that the manuscripts in this study display in their physical alterations. Equally, as mentioned earlier, the discomfort could have been with the specific word "pyntell," as the term became a vulgar obscenity during the time that the annotations were made. Whether the instances of censorship were a matter of repressing distasteful material, excising the outdated and redundant, or a mixture of both, the physical interventions provide a clue as to how these codices continued to be relevant to post-medieval readers.

McGill University

Acknowledgments

I thank Michael Van Dussen and Faith Wallis for their invaluable comments and help in drafting this article. Thanks also to Elma Brenner and the staff of the Osler and Wellcome Libraries for granting me access to the manuscripts discussed.

NOTES

1. The precise date of composition is unknown.
2. Lister M. Matheson, "Médecin sans Frontières?: The European Dissemination of John of Burgundy's Plague Treatise," *ANQ: A Quarterly Journal of Short Articles, Notes and Reviews,* no. 18 (2005): 19–30.
3. Christine de Pisan and Bartholomaeus Anglicus were particularly concerned with avoiding the "naming of parts" because of the post-lapsarian connotations attached to sexual reproduction. See Michael Camille, "Obscenity Under Erasure: Censorship in Medieval Illuminated Manuscripts," in *Obscenity Social Control and Artistic Creation in the European Middle Ages,* ed. Jan M. Ziolkowski (Leiden: Brill, 1998), 148, 152.
4. The last leaf of Montréal, Osler Library, Bibliotheca Osleriana 7591, features a signature that is obscured by a tear in the parchment. All that remains is "Iohannes . . . ." It is conceivable that it once read "Johannes Burgundia" (104).
5. John of Burgundy identifies himself in some copies of his most famous work, *De epidemia,* as "John with the beard": "ego iohannes de burgundia, aliter dictus cum barba, civis Leodiensis et artis medicine professor" (Matheson, "Médecin sans Frontières?," 19).
6. This is reflected in the catalogue records, none of which supply the title, and only the record for Sloane 405 (as opposed to the manuscript itself) names "Johannes Burgundia" as the author. This is typical for recipe books. See Irma Taavitsainen, "Middle English Recipes: Genre characteristics, text type features and underlying traditions of writing," *Journal of Historical Pragmatics,* no. 2 (2001): 97.
7. John of Burgundy, *Ein Mittelenglisches Medizinbuch,* ed. Fritz Heinrich (Halle: M. Niemeyer, 1896).
8. Heinrich wrongly labels this manuscript as Royal 19, 674.
9. M. Claire Jones, "Vernacular literacy in late-medieval England: the example of East Anglian medical manuscripts" (PhD Thesis: University of Glasgow, 2000), 229–233.
10. See Tony Hunt, "The Poetic Vein Phlebotomy in Middle English and Anglo-Norman Verse," *English Studies,* no. 77 (1996): 311–322; Claudius F. Mayer, "A medieval English Leechbook and its 14th century

Poem on Bloodletting," *Bulletin of the History of Medicine*, no. 7 (1939): 381–391.

11. This hand is characterized by its two-compartment **a**, the **f** and tall **s** that do not regularly descend below the base line, and its semi-regular quadratus minims.
12. See folios 8r, 13r, 16v.
13. Heinrich, *Ein Mittelenglisches Medizinbuch*, 17–39.
14. Osler is paginated in a modern hand.
15. This is particularly reflected in the scribes' sparing use of thorns and yoghs. Wellcome chiefly uses thorns when the scribe runs out of space in a line. Cf. Heinrich, *Ein Mittelenglisches Medizinbuch*, 17–39.
16. Wellcome, f. 35v; Heinrich, *Ein Mittelenglisches Medizinbuch*, 126, line 21. The rest of the recipe conforms to Sloane 405.
17. Irma Taavitsainen, *Middle English Lunaries: A Study of the Genre*, Mémoires de la Société Néophilologique de Helsinki XLVII (Helsinki: Société Néophilologique, 1988), 116.
18. The annotator likely took his Latin translation from John Trevisa's translation of Bartholomaeus Anglicus's *De Proprietatibus Rerum*, which glosses "veretrum" with "pintle." Juhani Nori, *Dictionary of Medical Vocabulary in English, 1375-1550: Body Parts, Sicknesses, Instruments, and Medicinal Preparations, Parts I & II* (London: Routledge, 2016), 834.
19. There is insufficient evidence for dating these glosses, but it is clear that the annotations are later than the main hands of the codex.
20. The word was always somewhat impolite but it was commonly used in medical texts. By the seventeenth century, however, the term was con sidered to be a profanity only used by those lowest in society. See Eric Partridge and Paul Beale, *A Dictionary of Slang and Unconventional English: Colloquialisms and Catch Phrases, Fossilised Jokes and Puns, General Nicknames, Vulgarisms and Such Americanisms as Have Been Naturalised* (London: Psychology Press, 1984), 887; Michael Adams, *In Praise of Profanity* (Oxford: Oxford University Press, 2016), 41–2.
21. The codex and its censorship might suggest a domestic setting, where a paterfamilias would not wish his wife or daughters to stumble across this recipe. For discussion, see Irma Taavitsainen and Paivi Pahta, "Vernacularisation of Medical Writing in English: A Corpus-Based Study of Scholastics," *Early Science and Medicine*, no. 3 (1998): 160–7.
22. For provenance: William Osler, *Bibliotheca Osleriana: A Catalogue of Books Illustrating the History of Medicine and Science* (Montréal: McGill-Queen's University Press, 1969), 680.
23. Joan Cadden, "'Nothing Natural is Shameful': Vestiges of a Debate about Sex and Science in a Group of Late-Medieval Manuscripts," *Speculum*, no. 76 (2001): 66–71.

Dating by Ductus: Differentiating Pen Stroke from Pen Angle in the Construction of Anglicana "d"

AMY CONWELL

For some years Malcolm B. Parkes's *English Cursive Book Hands 1250–1500* has defined Anglicana as a cursive script[1] written in a rapid duct facilitated by curved, connecting strokes, which developed a distinct and dateable morphology in several letterforms, including the "d."[2] According to Parkes, the downstroke of the looped ascender of the "d" transitions between the end of the thirteenth and the beginning of the fourteenth century from a high-contrast diagonal (that is, wider than the vertical strokes, see Parkes's Plate 1 (i), late thirteenth century) to a relatively even stroke (proportional to the vertical strokes, see Parkes's Plate 1 (ii), mid-fourteenth century).[3] Parkes attributes this change in contrast to a change in pen angle, from "very oblique" to "almost upright":

> Scribes changed the angle of the pen from very oblique to almost upright. This is most immediately obvious in such details as the elimination of the heavy diagonal stroke in the looped ascender of d. The handwriting appears to be more vertical, and the strokes acquired added dimension.[4]

Some questions arise from Parkes's claim, which has been accepted by other paleographers and manuscript scholars. First, what does Parkes mean by "angle of the pen"? Does he mean the angle of nib cut?[5] The angle of pen shaft? The direction of stroke?

Parkes argues that in the second half of the thirteenth century, as subsidiary features of letterforms were exaggerated for "calligraphic effect," the duct slowed and the pen was held at an oblique angle, constructing heavy contrast in diagonal downstrokes (see the loop of the Anglicana "d").[6] In the beginning of the fourteenth century, as calligraphic reform reprioritized ease of writing and legible graphs, the duct quickened, and the pen was held at an upright angle, reducing the contrast in diagonal downstrokes. So, in the span of half a century, Parkes argues pen angle transitioned from about 45 degrees, or perhaps even 135 degrees,[7] to about 90 degrees. Is such a dramatic change in pen angle realistic? Is it possible to find the angle of the writing instrument in letterforms preserved on the manuscript page?[8] If so, do existing angles give evidence of this change in pen angle? If not, then what change in instrument or approach caused the attenuation of the downstroke of the Anglicana "d"?

This discussion takes a practical approach to the treatment of the Anglicana "d," drawing on the neglected study of calligraphy as craft. It involves some experiments that aim to recreate (as far as possible) scribal conditions to examine assumptions about the relationship between practice and purpose, input and output, conditions and style, in order to investigate how and why writing changes—what produces the new? Specifically, it seeks to test Parkes's claim that the attenuation of the downstroke of the Anglicana "d" followed on a change in pen angle and to challenge the assumptions behind this claim—assumptions about how paleography treats and relates to script, primarily as "image" and "visual model," as Parkes argues in his later text *Their Hands before Our Eyes*.[9] Although paleography's impulse to treat script as static facilitates ease of identification and dating, it privileges identification of received letterforms, the consolidation of any given script into a typeface, over investigation of "writing as a 'dynamic' process among, in competition with and as a constituent part of other social and cultural processes,"[10] and, thus, deprioritizes methodological inquiries that seek to break down script into process.[11]

I first tested the effect of changing pen angles on the Anglicana "d" in an experiment I devised as part of Professor John Haines's Spring 2015 course "Practical Palaeography" at the Centre for Medieval Studies at the University of Toronto.[12] I asked my classmates to draw "d's" at four different "increasingly upright" pen angles (30 degrees, 45 degrees, 60 degrees, and 75 degrees) with straight-cut nib quills in ink on a parchment-equivalent writing support secured to a writing surface angled at approximately 45 degrees.[13] If participants drew "d's" in the 45 degree quadrant with heavy contrast on the downstroke and progressed in the 75 degree quadrant to relatively even contrast, a one-to-one relationship between contrast and pen angle would be confirmed. However, when participants progressively moved their pens from oblique to upright (Fig. 1)—participants tended to hold their pens at a similar angle in each of the four quadrants (Fig. 2)—this change did not affect the width of the stroke. Rather, participants' "d's" spoke to Parkes's point that individual scribes write in hands that introduce "personal features which give some [scripts] a highly idiosyncratic character."[14] Despite participants' varying successes, the result of writing on non-lineated paper, inexperience with calligraphy, and/or miscommunicated instructions, their evenly weighted letters suggest that the degree of contrast in the loop of the Anglicana "d" does not correspond to pen angle alone. Are we forgetting other critical factors in the composition of stroke width?

Perhaps paleography's tendency to set retrospective alphabets to identify scripts and to study letters as received forms curbs methodological innovation. In the words of twenty-first-century scribe Cheryl Jacobsen:

> Palaeographers have for a long time studied the letters as given objects to be identified and classified and to assist in transcription and translation, but for some reason how it was done got overlooked or even (dare I say?) snubbed. Why aren't pen angle, pen width, or letter weight, common terms in manuscript study? Using these terms in conjunction with an effective and clear analysis would give scholars an excellent understanding of the character and process of a particular letter form.[15]

Jacobsen points to a blind spot in paleographical research. For expedience, and because it is the way things are done, scholars tend to base new ideas about the genesis of script and letterform on the work of past paleographers, their *auctoritates,* at the expense of other modes of curiosity. Bernhard Bischoff, Michelle Brown, Albert Derolez, Jane Roberts, and Linne Mooney, and craftspeople such as Marc Drogin base analysis, dating, and reconstruction of English scripts on Parkes's *English Cursive Book Hands 1250–1500.*[16] Parkes himself relies on terms (e.g., "oblique" and "pen angle") remembered from the work of paleographers such as Cyril E. Wright, Charles Johnson, Charles H. Jenkinson, Neil R. Ker, and Leonard C. Hector on documentary scripts.[17]

In *The Handwriting of English Documents,* Leonard C. Hector describes the Anglicana nib cut as oblique, "the quill was cut to an oblique edge, so that as long as the pen was held naturally and at a constant angle to the writing-surface the strokes it made were thick or thin according to the angle they made with this edge."[18] Hector asserts that together nib cut and pen angle account for the writing angle recorded on the page in entrance strokes and at the tops of minims. This follows on calligrapher Edward Johnston's oblique-cut nib theory in *Writing and Illuminating, and Lettering:*

> Most people are accustomed to holding a pen slanted away from the right shoulder. The nib therefore is cut at oblique angle to the shaft, so that, while the shaft is slanted, *the edge of the nib is parallel with the horizontal line of the paper,* and will therefore produce a horizontal thin stroke and a vertical thick stroke.[19]

As Johnston suggests, different nib angles can produce like letterforms. An oblique nib held at a straight angle and a straight nib held at a "slanted" angle can both produce "tilted" letters,[20] and an oblique nib and a straight nib can both produce "round, upright letters" (Fig. 3). Thus, the angle of the pen shaft, expressed on the writing support as the angle of the nib to the baseline, in combination with nib cut ultimately determines the angle of the writing instrument to the baseline.

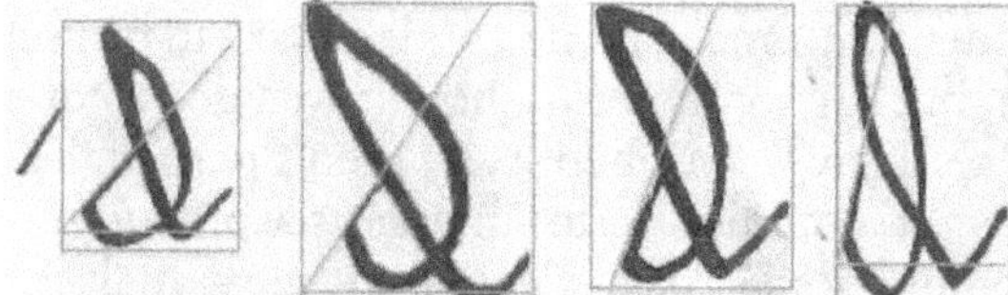

Figure 1: Left to right: 30° (47°), 45° (55°), 60° (70°), and 75° (77°). (Not to scale.)

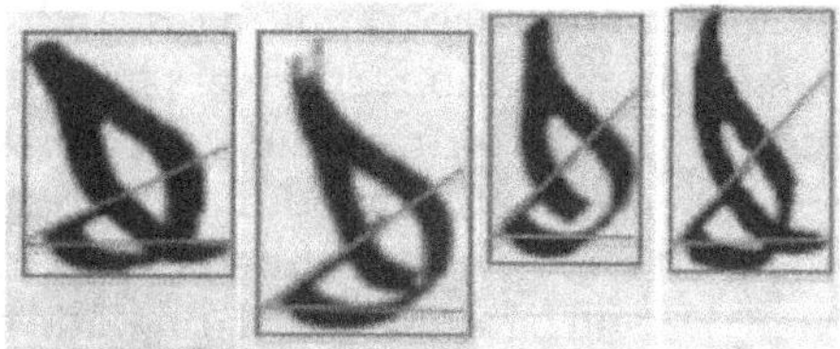

Figure 2: Left to right: 30° (29°), 45° (43°), 60° (52°), and 75° (53°). (Not to scale.)

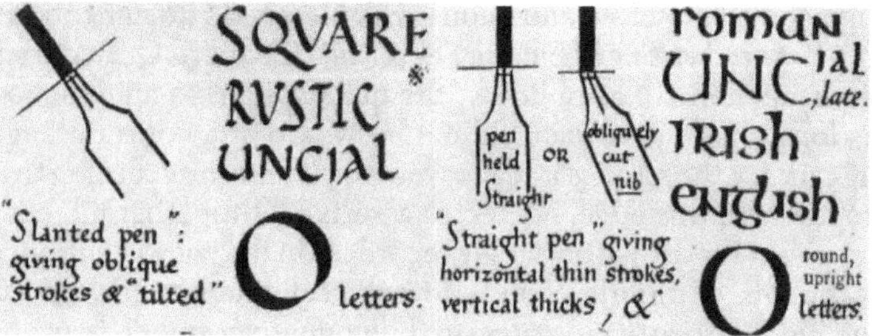

Figure 3: Aspect of "oblique" versus "straight" angle.

Since pens with nibs cut at the same oblique angle can draw diagonals of varying width depending on their shaft slant, and similarly, pens held at the same oblique shaft angle can draw diagonals of varying width depending on their nib cut, it would be difficult to isolate either from the angle of the writing instrument preserved on the manuscript page. However, Parkes takes his predecessors' constant "oblique" nib cut as a given and concludes variable shaft angle (shifting from "oblique" to "upright") is responsible for the change between the end of the thirteenth and the beginning of the fourteenth century in the downstroke of the Anglicana "d."[21] With nib cut held constant, we can see the effect of a changing shaft angle on this downstroke. For example, consider a pen with a straight-cut nib: if we angle the pen at 0 degrees (i.e., with the flat end of the nib parallel to the baseline) and draw a vertical line, the thickest part of the nib will pull down the thickest stroke the pen can produce (one nib width). If we angle it at 90 degrees (i.e., with the flat end of the nib perpendicular to the baseline) and draw a vertical line, the narrowest part of the nib will pull down the thinnest possible stroke.[22] As the pen angle moves from 0 degrees to 90 degrees, the flat end of the nib turns away from the direction of the stroke, reducing the surface area of the nib moving in the direction of the stroke, and thinning out the stroke. If the above example illustrates what Parkes means by "angle of the pen" (i.e., the slant of the pen *shaft* responsible for the angle of nib to baseline), then shifting it in an increasingly "upright" direction would reduce the width of the stroke.

Assuming a constant nib cut, such changes in the angle of the pen shaft would correspond to changes in the overall writing angle, the combined angle of shaft slant and nib cut that determine the angle of the writing instrument to baseline. Thus, to investigate Parkes's claim that a change in pen angle attenuated the downstroke of the Anglicana "d," I attempted to identify the overall writing angle in use in Parkes's plates. According to Jacobsen, this angle can "be seen in the writing itself in the ends of strokes and in the thickest part of a curved letter," which captures the "width of the nib of a broad-edged pen,"[23] that is, in the thickest and thinnest strokes of a letter. Using professional onscreen measuring tools, PixelStick and ScreenScales,[24] I delineated and measured the angle parallel to the thinnest strokes (the approach stroke at the lobe) for a selection of "d's,"[25] and I checked these angles against the serifs of neighboring minims and the opposite side of the lobe of the "d."[26] As a subscript of Gothic and a calligraphic script in its own right, Anglicana would have been written at a constant angle (of about 45 degrees), as Hector notes above. However, I found a range of angles in both plates and no indication of the writing angle changing, as it would if the shaft slant shifted from oblique to upright, from the end of the thirteenth to the middle of the fourteenth century, from Plate 1 (i): 31 degrees to 60 degrees (aside from one outlier, 31 degrees to 49 degrees) to Plate 1 (ii): 36 degrees to 45 degrees (Tables 1 and 2, right column).

If not pen angle, then what caused this visible diminution in the width of the diagonal downstroke? A freer style of writing? The fast cursive duct? As Jacobsen notes, as speed increases "there are fewer actual horizontal or vertical lines."[27] A reduction in nib width?[28] A deliberate change in pen pressure? Differences in fixation parameter? Fixation parameter, the degree to which the pen turns against the direction of the stroke, as demonstrated by Inkscape, a "professional vector graphics editor,"[29] controls the contrast in a script (Fig. 4). Fixation parameters range from a stable, constant pen angle to a flexible, yet still constant angle (the pen turns only "a little"), to a freely rotating angle (the pen is "always perpendicular to the stroke").[30] Thus, a fixed, constant pen angle (i.e., the pen does not turn against the direction of the stroke) might account for the high-contrast, calligraphic aspect (diagonals drawn at one nib width) of Parkes's Plate 1 (i), and a semi-fixed pen angle (i.e., the pen turns a little) might account for the mid-contrast aspect (diagonals drawn at or less than one nib width) of Plate 1 (ii). Although it might make sense to tie contrast to fixation, as I have shown, angles are ranging and inconstant in both plates—both likely have a semi-fixed pen angle—and fixation parameters may simply reflect a scribe's skill, experience, and/or writing conditions. So, then, if pen angles span a similar, flexible range in both plates, what accounts for the higher contrast in the diagonal downstrokes in Parkes's Plate 1 (i)?

To answer this question, I broke down, analyzed, and recreated my "d" letterform using Edward Johnston's seven-step method of script analysis (recommended by Jacobsen).[31] The method entails identifying (1) "weight of letter form," (2) "pen angle," (3) "geometric shape of letter," (4) "number of strokes," (5) "order of strokes," (6) "direction of stroke," and (7) "speed." The final five steps in this method were apparent or had already been satisfactorily worked out by others; however, the first two steps were unknown. To determine "weight of letter form," or the ratio of nib width to x-height (minim height), I needed to first identify either the nib width or the ever elusive "pen angle," which "can be seen after the fact by looking at the clear ends of strokes and axis of circles."[32] I took the median angle of both ranges in Parkes's plates (approximately 40 degrees) as the pen angle and used that to find the weight of the "d." A pen angled at 40 degrees draws its thickest possible stroke (one nib width) at 140 degrees (i.e., when the direction of the stroke is perpendicular to the pen angle), and I found (again, using PixelStick and ScreenScales) that the flourished "v" was the only letter in both plates containing a straight stroke at 140 degrees (Fig. 5). I measured

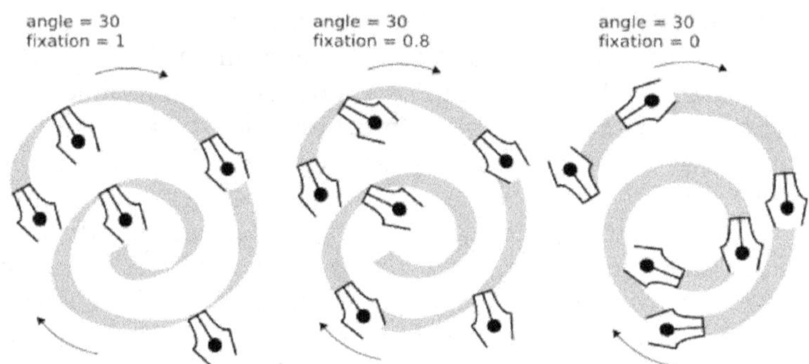

Figure 4: The effect of fixation on contrast.

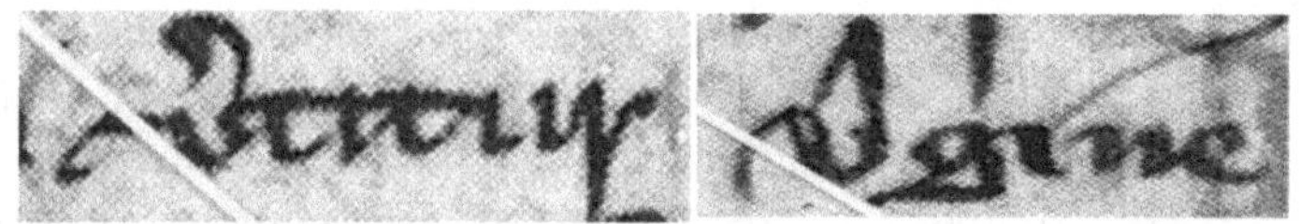

Figure 5: Plate 1 (i): *vertitur*, Plate 1 (ii): *virgine*. (Not to scale.)

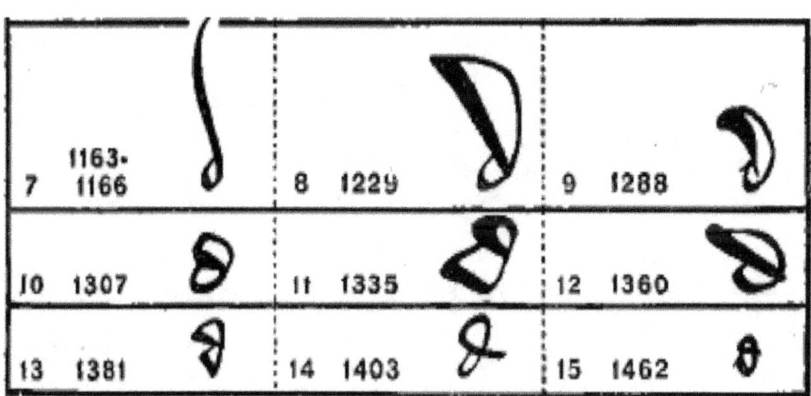

Figure 6: The oblique downstroke (8) curves (9, 10) then grows horizontal (12).

the width of the 140 degree stroke and the x-height of each word, and found that the nib width to x-height ratio for both plates is approximately 1:4 (i.e., minim height was approximately four times the width of the nib).[33]

Based on the information gathered from Johnston's work, I drew my guidelines[34] and then replicated the thirteenth- and fourteenth-century Anglicana letterforms outlined by Charles Johnson and Charles H. Jenkinson in *English Court Hand, A.D. 1066–1500* (see Fig. 2: 8, 9, 10, and 12).[35] Johnson and Jenkinson's 8 and 9 correspond to the predominant forms in Parkes's Plate 1 (i); 10 and 12 correspond to the predominant forms in Parkes's Plate 1 (ii) (Fig. 7 and 8). When studying and practicing the direction of the stroke, I noticed that the late thirteenth-century plate (i) tends to finish the stroke at the base of the lobe (pulling its stroke down diagonally at approximately 140 degrees, perpendicular to pen angle at 40 degrees), whereas the mid-fourteenth-century plate (ii) finishes the stroke at both the base and head of the lobe (pulling its stroke across horizontally at approximately 180 degrees and finishing it on an upward flourish, parallel to pen angle at 40 degrees). My experiments with the effect of this change in direction on the width of the downstroke of the loop of Hector's 10 (Fig. 8 [double pencil], Fig. 9 [quill and ink]) demonstrate the predictable fact that as the downstroke moves from parallel to perpendicular, the stroke is drawn not with the thickest part of the nib but with the thinnest, and the width of the stroke decreases. The change in the contrast of the diagonal downstroke of the Anglicana "d" does not reveal a change in angle of pen shaft (from "oblique" to "upright"), but rather a change in ductus (from a downstroke finished on a diagonal to a downstroke finished on a horizontal) on a more or less constant writing angle.

Figure 7: 8 (1229), 9 (1288), 12 (1360). Double pencil. (Not to scale.)

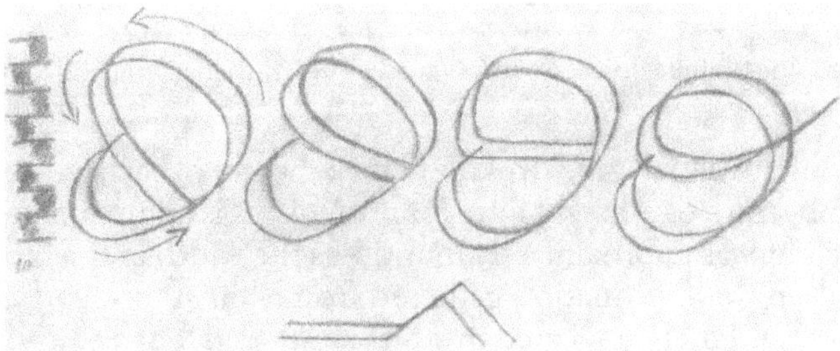

Figure 8: 10 (1307). Double pencil. (Not to scale.)

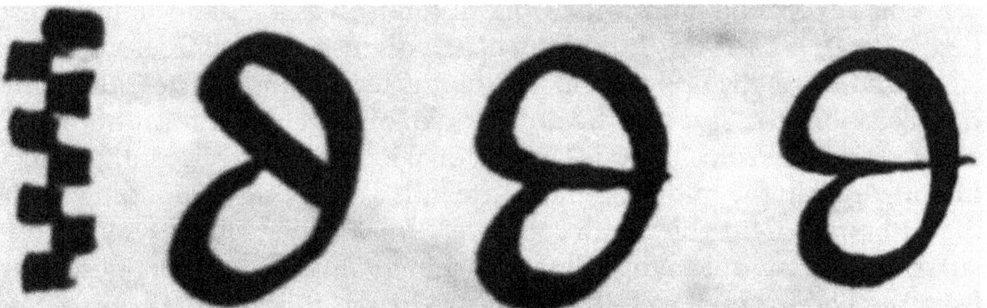

Figure 9: 10 (1307). Quill and ink. (Not to scale.) As the final downstroke moves from a diagonal to a horizontal, the flat end of the nib moves from parallel with to almost perpendicular to the direction of the stroke; the reduction in the surface area of the nib moving in the direction of the stroke reduces its width.

Plate 1 (i)					
"d's"		Perpendicular to thickest part of the stroke		Parallel to thinnest part of the stroke	
l.1	huiusmodi		50°		60°
l.6	dum		59°		37°
l.7	conditionem		45°		35°
l.7	quando		52°		49°
l.10	remedio		36°		35°
l.11	huiusmodi		54°		36°
l.12	ad		54°		46°
l.13	difficultate		66°		31°
l.17	domos		62°		44°
l.20	domos		55°		47°

Table 1: Pen angles in Plate 1 (i). (Not to scale.)

Plate 1 (ii)					
"d's"		Perpendicular to thickest part of the stroke		Parallel to thinnest part of the stroke	
l.2	comanda		33°		39°
l.2	de		69°		42°
l.6	dieu		48°		36°
l.7	dolour		72°		40°
*l*9	dame		82°		45°

Table 2: Pen angles in Plate 1 (ii). (Not to scale.)

This conclusion affirms the work of Johnson and Jenkinson in *English Court Hand, A.D. 1066–1500,* which, in a discussion of different forms of "d" found in English documents of the thirteenth and fourteenth centuries, describes the slope of the downstroke of the current form of the "d" as transitioning from "oblique" or diagonal in the early thirteenth century to horizontal in the middle of the fourteenth century, after rounding out in the latter part of the thirteenth century.[36] Now the question is why did this letterform round out? Why did the finishing point of the stroke raise itself from the base to the head of the bow? Why did the script take on a new style? My findings support the claim that as Anglicana became commonplace as a book script, the practice of cursive writing "contaminated" it: the two-stroke form of the "d" "with the loop turning to the left for increased cursivity" consolidated into a single stroke, as Jane Roberts argues in *Guide to Scripts Used in English Writings up to 1500,*[37] and the finishing point of the downstroke moved from the base to the head of the bow to simplify the writing process. That is, the script's calligraphic ideal gave way to changing production conditions and to the difference in speed and style of book as opposed to documentary writing.[38] This raises another question. Do paleographical forms inevitably change when scribal conditions do? If so, the new might be understood as the path of least resistance, as evolution rather than innovation. That, in turn, suggests that a letter's given form—the idea that there is constancy before there is change—is a paleographical fiction.

University of Toronto

Acknowledgments

I would like to thank Alexandra Gillespie for her guidance in preparing this article for publication and her keen editorial insight, and John Haines for his support in the early stages of this project and his comments on an early draft. Any errors are mine alone.

NOTES

1. Malcolm B. Parkes, *English Cursive Book Hands 1250–1500* (Oxford: Clarendon Press, 1969). Parkes, like Gerard I. Lieftinck, uses "cursive" to denote "a category of script with certain distinctive letterforms." Braxton Ross, "Review of *English Cursive Book Hands, 1200–1500,*" *Modern Philology*, 69.3 (1972), 250. See also Gerard I. Lieftinck, "Pour une nomenclature de l'ecriture livresque de la periode dite 'gothique'," in Bernhard Bischoff, Gerard I. Lieftinck, and Giulio Battelli, *Nomenclature des ecritures livresques du ixe au xvie siècle* (Paris: Service des publications

du Centre national de la recherche scientifique, 1954), 19 in Parkes, xiv, note 4. Lieftinck uses cursiva to indicate a category of Gothic script distinguished by a single-compartment "a," loops on ascenders, and descenders on "f" and "s." Jan W. Burgers, "Palaeography and Diplomatics: the Script of Charters in the Netherlands during the Fourteenth and Fifteenth Centuries," *Quaerendo* 38.1 (2008): 15–16.

2. These connecting strokes, "the finishing movement of one stroke and the approach movement to the next," appeared as single strokes on the writing support, and evolved into auxiliary letterforms (Parkes, xiv.)
3. The two facsimiles, Plates 1(i) and 1(ii), demonstrating this change span about 75 years and an entire subsystem of Gothic (Parkes, 1.)
4. Parkes, xv–xvi.
5. Nib cut can account for pen angle: "if the edge of the nib were cut at right angles to the shaft, obviously the horizontal stroke would not be thin, and the true thick and thin stroke would be oblique." Edward Johnston, *Writing and Illuminating, and Lettering,* 8th ed. (London: Spottiswoode, Ballantyne, 1917), 66, note 1. Parkes was aware of Johnston's work, citing it in his selected bibliography, although not in his footnotes.
6. Parkes, xv. Parkes follows Leonard C. Hector who argues in *The Handwriting of English Documents* that in the twelfth century "the perpendicularly ascending d of the orthodox text hand has been definitively replaced by the form in which the ascender is bent backwards." Leonard C. Hector, *The Handwriting of English Documents,* 2nd ed. (London: Edward Arnold, 1966), 55.
7. Both obtuse and acute angles qualify as oblique, "*Geom.* Of an angle: less than 180 degrees but not equal to a right angle" ("oblique, adj., n., and adv."). Oxford English Dictionary Online, March 2015, http://www.oed.com/view/Entry/129718?rskey=Uu0IZn&result=1&isAdvanced=falsel. While an obtuse angle would work with Parkes's backwards-slanting script theory, modern calligraphers suggest an acute angle would be more feasible for a right-handed scribe, "the most natural and traditional for right-handed calligraphy" ("Angle and Fixation," *Inkscape Tutorial converted from DocBook source by tutorial-html.xsl,* last modified April 30, 2005, http://www-mdp.eng.cam.ac.uk/web/CD/deskapps/inkscape/tut5.html.)
8. That is, is it possible to find the combined angle of the writing instrument (the angle of nib cut and shaft slant) in letterforms preserved on the manuscript page?
9. Malcolm B. Parkes, *Their Hands before Our Eyes: A Closer Look at Scribes,* The Lyell Lectures Delivered in the University of Oxford 1999 (Aldershot: Ashgate, 2008), 127–145, as cited in Daniel Wakelin, "Writing

the Words," in *The Production of Books in England 1350–1500,* edited by Alexandra Gillespie and Daniel Wakelin, 34–58, Cambridge Studies in Palaeography and Codicology (Cambridge: Cambridge University Press, 2011), 37–38.

10. Wakelin, "Writing the Words," 38.
11. This is not a new criticism. Albert Derolez raised similar concerns about the "crisis of palaeography" in his introduction to *The Palaeography of Gothic Manuscript Books: from the Twelfth to the Early Sixteenth Century,* "drawing attention to the problematic nature of the scientific status of the discipline and the weakness and fragmentation of its methodological assumptions." Albert Derolez, *The Palaeography of Gothic Manuscript Books: from the Twelfth to the Early Sixteenth Century* (Cambridge: Cambridge University, 2003), 7, as cited in Orietta Da Rold and Marilena Maniaci, "Medieval Manuscript Studies: A European Perspective," in *Writing Europe, 500–1450: Texts and Contexts,* edited by Aidan Conti, Orietta Da Rold, and Philip Shaw, 1–24, Essays and Studies 2015 (Cambridge: D. S. Brewer, 2015), 17–18, note 56. Da Rold and Maniaci echo Derolez's concerns in "Medieval Manuscript Studies: A European Perspective," arguing, "research in palaeography has long remained substantially faithful to methodologies of ancient and deep-rooted tradition, and poorly permeable to the application of new techniques of investigation" (Da Rold and Maniaci, 14.)
12. Thanks to my eleven classmates in Practical Palaeography, taught by Professor John Haines in Spring 2015 at the Centre for Medieval Studies at the University of Toronto. Thanks particularly to Ben Durham and Lane Springer for the collaborative pen-carving sessions and to Maria-Claire Apostoli for the use of her verdigris.
13. The "d's" were drawn according to modern calligrapher Marc Drogin's Gothic *Littera Bastarda* model. Marc Drogin, *Medieval Calligraphy: its History and Techniques* (Montclair: Allanheld and Schram, 1980), 155. The pens were turkey feather quills hand-carved according to the advice and YouTube demonstrations of modern calligrapher Dennis Ruud, who taught a Carolingian calligraphy workshop I attended in 2014 (Dennis Ruud, *How to Cut a Quill Pen,* 2011, https://www.youtube.com/watch?v=-qjIFKl522o, 9:37). The ink was handmade verdigris or Speedball super black calligraphy ink. The writing support was white Strathmore Parchment. The page was divided into quadrants marked with angle degrees and symbols. The writing surface was a clipboard. The writing surface angle was about 45 degrees, a comfortable writing angle used for Gothic scripts (Johnston, 61.)
14. Ross, 251.

15. Cheryl Jacobsen, "A Modern Scribe Views Scribes of the Past," in *Scraped, Stroked, and Bound: Materially Engaged Readings of Medieval Manuscripts,* edited by Jonathan Wilcox, Utrecht Studies in Medieval Literacy, 23 (Turnhout: Brepols, 2013), 81.
16. Bernhard Bischoff in *Latin Palaeography: Antiquity and the Middle Ages* cites Parkes's *English Cursive Book Hands 1250–1500* in support of his brief description of "anglicana." Parkes, *English Cursive Book Hands,* xiv, in Bernhard Bischoff, *Latin Palaeography: Antiquity and the Middle Ages,* translated by Daibhi O Croinin and David Ganz (Cambridge: Cambridge University, 1990), 142, note 106. Albert Derolez in *The Palaeography of Gothic Manuscript Books* in a "discussion of a wider European category he calls Cursiva Antiquior" argues "only Anglicana within this grouping, 'precocious and long lasting' and 'a highly idiosyncratic script' developed into 'a canonical book script'." Derolez, *The Palaeography of Gothic Manuscript Books,* 133–134 in Jane Roberts, *Guide to Scripts Used in English Writings up to 1500* (London: British Library, 2006), 161, note 2. Jane Roberts in *Guide to Scripts Used in English Writings up to 1500* categorizes and dates English cursive scripts according to the evolution of letterforms detailed by Parkes and others; she comments that the Anglicana "d," constructed in a single stroke, "derives from a two-stroke form with the loop turning to the left for increased cursivity" (Roberts, 162, 166–168.). Marc Drogin in *Medieval Calligraphy: its History and Techniques* misrepresents script categories. Drogin, citing Parkes, conflates Gothic cursive scripts from Bastard Anglicana and Bastard Secretary to Cadel Capitals into a single functional script that he calls Gothic Littera Bastarda (Drogin, *Medieval Calligraphy,* 64–67, 153–164.)
17. Parkes, *English Cursive Book Hands,* xiv–xvi. Parkes expands Neil R. Ker's formal book script "Anglicana" in *Medieval Manuscripts in British Libraries* into a subsystem of Gothic used in both books and documents, an Anglicana system that breaks down into Anglicana (the cursive scripts in England previously referred to as "Court Hands" or "Charter Hands"), Anglicana Formata (Ker's "Anglicana"), and Bastard Anglicana (scripts containing elements of both the cursiva and formata). Neil R. Ker, *Medieval Manuscripts in British Libraries,* i (Oxford: Oxford University, 1969), xi, in Parkes, *English Cursive Book Hands,* xvi, note 7.
18. Hector, 19.
19. Johnston, 65–66.
20. Johnston, 44.
21. Parkes's consideration of the combined impact of nib cut and shaft slant on the formation of strokes is evident in his definition of "duct." Parkes

defines duct as "the distinctive manner in which strokes are traced upon the writing surface: it represents the combination of such factors as *the angle at which the pen was held in relation to the way in which it was cut,* the degree of pressure applied to it, and the direction in which it was moved" (Parkes, *English Cursive Book Hands,* xxvi.) When we investigate pen angle, we investigate duct.

22. Jacobsen, 84.
23. Jacobsen, 83.
24. "Pixelstick," *Plum Amazing,* accessed April 19, 2015, http://plumamazing.com/mac/pixelstick; "Screenscales," *Talon-designs,* accessed April 19, 2015, http://sur.ly/o/talon-designs.net/screen_scales.htm/AA001290.
25. I first identified and extracted all variant forms of the Anglicana "d" in use in Parkes's plates, following on the example of Jean Preston and Laetitia Yeandle in *English Handwriting 1400–1650: An Introductory Manual.* Preston and Yeandle created alphabets, including all the variant forms of each letter, particular to hands in their manuscripts. This facilitated study of scripts' representative letterforms and demonstrated the particularities of any given hand. Jean F. Preston and Laetitia Yeandle, *English Handwriting, 1400–1650: An Introductory Manual* (Binghamton, NY: Medieval and Renaissance Texts and Studies, 1992). I pulled ten model "d's" out of the 39 Anglicana forms (44 total) in Plate 1 (i) (Table 1), and five model "d's" out of the 25 "d's" in 1 (ii) (Table 2). I then measured the pen angle used to draw each exemplar "d."
26. Pen angle can also be found in the angle perpendicular to the thickest strokes. Since there are fewer thick strokes, and Parkes's dating theory is tied to the relative width of the ascenders, I first analyzed the perpendicular angle. I used PixelStick ("Pixelstick," *Plum Amazing*) to draw lines parallel to the thickest part of each diagonal, lines perpendicular to those lines, and then horizontal lines ("the baseline" of the pen) through the intersection of the first two. I then used ScreenScales ("Screenscales," *Talon-designs*) to measure the delineated angles. Despite both scripts' visible inconsistencies, variations in the slope of the ascenders, in the height of the bows, and in the shape and size of the negative spaces, or counter shapes, inside the loops and bows, I was suspicious of the wide ranges of pen angles I found: Plate 1 (i): 36 degrees to 66 degrees, and Plate 1 (ii): 33 degrees to 82 degrees (Tables 1 and 2, left column). This wide range in pen angles may be due to the fact that the thickness of a given stroke does not only correspond to nib width; as Jacobsen warns, "extra pressure on the quill, which is easily applied, will yield an extra wide mark" (Jacobsen, 83). Moreover, the curving downstroke of the

ascender of the Anglicana "d" is not a true diagonal, and thus does not have one single pen angle perpendicular to it.

27. Jacobsen, 85.
28. As Michelle P. Brown notes in *Understanding Illuminated Manuscripts: A Guide to Technical Terms* under the entry for "pen," the wider the nib, the more calligraphic the script; "cursive (i.e., more rapidly written) scripts were generally produced with a thin pen and formal bookscripts with a broad pen." Michelle P. Brown, *Understanding Illuminated Manuscripts: A Guide to Technical Terms* (Malibu: J. Paul Getty Museum and British Library, 1994), 97.) Reduction in nib width would reduce contrast in a script at large, not in a single graph, so this cannot explain the attenuation in the downstroke of the Anglicana "d."
29. "Inkscape," *Inkscape*, accessed April 21, 2015, https://inkscape.org/en/.
30. "Angle and Fixation," *Inkscape Tutorial*; "Calligraphy Tool," *Inkscape*, accessed April 21, 2015, http://en.flossmanuals.net/inkscape/toolbox/calligraphy-tool/.
31. Jacobsen, 83–85. Edward Johnston's seven-step method of script analysis applied to the Anglicana "d" letterform: (1) the "weight of letter form," or ratio of the nib width to x-height, is 1:4. (2) The "pen angle" is 40 degrees. (3) The "geometric shape of letter" moves from an angular or ovular/vertically sloping shape to round/horizontally sloping shape. (4) The "number of strokes" needed to construct the letterform is one. (5) The "order of strokes" is not applicable since there is only one. (6) The "direction of stroke" is as follows: the stroke curves down and to the left from the top of the x-height, then curves to the right (forming the lobe), and then curves up and to the right, passes the top of the x-height, curves up and to the left, and then (now, further left than the entrance stroke) curves down and crosses over to the right side of the lobe of the d (closing the loop of the ascender). (7) The "speed" used to compose the letterform is a quick, cursive duct.
32. Jacobsen, 83–84.
33. Using this ratio, I determined that the guidelines used in Parkes's plates are proportional to the cursive guidelines Rosemary Sassoon recommends in *The Practical Guide to Calligraphy*: an x-height of about four nib widths, and capitals, ascenders, and descenders of up to eight nib widths. Rosemary Sassoon, *The Practical Guide to Calligraphy* (New York: Thames and Hudson, 1982), 41.
34. I drew guidelines for my two writing tools, a double pencil and a hand-cut quill. I placed a semi-translucent sheet of parchment over a lineated sheet of paper (guidelines for the baselines at 0 degrees and guidelines

for the pen angle at 40 degrees), secured both to my writing surface (clip board) angled at 45 degrees, and drew "d's" with my writing tool angled at 40 degrees.

35. Johnson and Jenkinson, *English Court Hand,* 11–12.
36. Charles Johnson and Charles H. Jenkinson, *English Court Hand, A.D. 1066–1500* (Oxford: Clarendon, 1915), 11.
37. Roberts, 166–168.
38. As Michelle P. Brown notes in *A Guide to Western Historical Scripts from Antiquity to 1600,* as documentary scripts were adapted for book use (from the late thirteenth century), "a predictable scenario of contamination of scripts occurs" and "'compromise' book hands increasingly supplanted the original *textualis* hierarchy in all but the most formal or conservative of works" (from the late fourteenth to sixteenth century). Michelle P. Brown, *A Guide to Western Historical Scripts from Antiquity to 1600* (Toronto: University of Toronto, 1990), 80–81.

Descriptive Reviews

MICHELLE P. BROWN, ILDAR H. GARIPZANOV AND BENJAMIN C. TILGHMAN, EDS.
Graphic Devices and the Early Decorated Book.
Boydell Studies in Medieval Art and Architecture.
Woodbridge, Suffolk: Boydell and Brewer, 2017.
xiv + 301 pp. 83 color plates.

The editors of this excellent and timely volume pose the study of graphigraphy, the analysis of the "graphic architecture" of the book in late Antiquity and the early Middle Ages, as an intellectual approach that is as relevant today as it was in the period of its conception. The stated aim of this collection of essays is to address the problem of how to "read" not only the hypo- or hypertextual signs of the early medieval text, but how to perceive mise-en-page through the lens of medieval reading communities that shared greatly varying levels and definitions of literacy. The wide range of graphic devices and the requisite methodologies for their interpretation are the focus of this collection. Embellished capitals, frames, diagrams, monograms, and monogrammatic initials are examined in the context of their often multivalent purposes. The graphic elements of the early medieval book are linked both backwards and forwards in time from late antique calligraphic culture to contemporary post-textual digital communication. This volume, part of the Boydell Studies in Medieval Art and Architecture series, directed by Julian Luxford and Asa Simon Mittman, is beautifully produced, with copious color plates on high-quality paper. It is a pleasure to peruse.

The first section of this volume examines the use of graphic devices in the early medieval codex in the context of a range of diverse cultures. Ildar H. Garipzanov traces the origin of sacred display lettering in early medieval books to late antique acclamatory monograms. David Ganz (*Monumenta*

Germaniae Historica) interrogates the word "character," found in both Greek and Latin, in the context of the description of script. Catherine E. Karkov examines decorated initials as places where script and abstract design intersect—and perhaps direct interpretation—while Eric Palazzo suggests that the shape of the initial "O" in contrasting liturgical contexts indicates their exegetical interpretation. Lawrence Nees examines quire marks in Latin manuscripts and end-of-verse indicators in copies of the Qur'an that appear overly embellished for their modest functions. He suggests that they may bear witness to an intersection of the graphic traditions of Eastern and Western manuscript traditions. Cynthia Hahn traces the use of the graphic symbol of the cross in early medieval Christian manuscripts through Insular and Merovingian books to the Carolingian period. She argues that the meaning of the cross as a Christian symbol is at this point symbolically loaded with Carolingian political inferences.

In the following section on Insular and Frankish manuscripts, Michelle P. Brown explicates the multivalent interpretations of the decorated incipit pages of the core survivals of the Insular world: the Lindisfarne and St. Chad Gospels and the Book of Kells, where word and image are fused. She finds cultural quotations of their forms in other manifestations of cultural practice and identity such as the physical structure of pilgrimage shrines. Tina Bawden discusses the topology of these decorated incipit pages in Insular and Carolingian examples in the context of the formality of the relationship between the letters and their frames. She suggests that medieval scribes exploited the liminal status of their art in creating initials and display letters that functioned in both visual topological and linear textual realms simultaneously. Benjamin C. Tilghman's chapter focuses on the graphic representation of the rending of Christ's garments of Mark 15:25 in the Book of Kells. Here both word and image reflect the essential process of the division of the garments themselves, and contemplation of the graphic art of script and illumination serves to encourage meditation on the interpretation of the passage in a broader Christian context.

Beatrice Kitzinger interrogates the possibility of "reading" patterned forms in contrast, and in compliment, to figural representations in ninth- and tenth-century Carolingian gospel books.

Leslie Brubaker's approach to graphic signs, frames, and initials in Byzantine manuscripts is similar to Kitzinger's in that the key to navigation of the text, and to the augmentation of its interpretation, is to be found in the marginal sigla that accompany the text. Brubaker perceives an understood glyphic hierarchy on the page that simultaneously directs and enhances the perception of the textual content. Kallirroe Linardou's examination of a deluxe edition of the *Praxapostolos* codex demonstrates how the complex graphic organization of this volume encourages multisensory interpretation.

Linardou argues that a sense of instantaneous perception could be enjoyed by the reader fluent in the language of aniconic illustration. David Ganz (Zurich) examines the transformational power of early medieval treasure bindings, as well as their relationship to the texts they contain. He argues that the enshrinement of the text within the treasure binding cued the use of specific materials and techniques. Figural images, diagrammatic schemes, and especially engraved letters enhanced the performativity of the text, and shifted its status to a more fluidly interpreted object. The final chapter in this book, by Herbert L. Kessler, demonstrates how graphic elements can alter and expand the interpretation of even the most conventional medieval figural representations.

This is a fascinating and beautifully produced book. It is most certainly a must for all research libraries that support scholarship on the late antique and early medieval book as well as the study of book history more generally. Linking early medieval graphigraphy to skills required of the twenty-first-century digital reader connects us to the reading experience of the past and to a future of shifting visual rhetoric.

Cynthia Johnston, Institute of English Studies, University of London

MARGARET CONNOLLY AND RALUCA RADULESCU, EDS.
Editing and Interpretation of Middle English Texts: Essays in Honour of William Marx.
Texts and Transitions 12.
Turnhout, Belgium: Brepols, 2018.
xix + 351 pp. 30 B&W illustrations and 2 color plates.

The scholarship of William Marx, honorand of *Editing and Interpretation of Middle English Texts,* has focused on the problems of editing and interpreting texts both as an editor himself and as general editor of the series Middle English Texts and the journal *Trivium.* Generally, an editor's task has been viewed as establishing a text as closely as possible to that assumed to have left the author. However, given that medieval scribes could freely adapt, extract, or redact Middle English texts, a modern critical edition of a text extant in several copies will reflect its editor's decision as to which copy has the best reading; his or her choices will thus offer an interpretation of the text that does not necessarily represent how it was received by its original readers. The contributors to this Festschrift have all addressed this problem.

After a short preface by Derek Pearsall and a general introduction by the editors, Margaret Connolly and Raluca Radulescu, focusing on Marx's own work as editor and his engagement with religious writings and chronicles, the fifteen essays that follow are organized under three headings reflecting his interests: "Interpreting the Textual Evidence," "Editing and Interpreting Chronicles," and "Editing and Interpreting Religious Texts."

For the first of these topics, A. S. G. Edwards, "Aspects of Method in the Athlone Edition of *Piers Plowman,*" offers a critical reappraisal of George Kane's editorial method in his treatment of the ABC versions of *Piers.* The next two essays examine the punctuation of medieval texts, showing how different uses of punctuation could affect the interpretation of a text or even the look of it on the page. Ronald Waldron, "Whose Punctuation Is It, Anyway? A Sampling of Some Manuscripts of the *Polychronicon*," compares and contrasts the punctuation of a short passage in the original Latin text as seen in Ranulph Higden's autograph manuscript (San Marino, Huntington Library, HM 132) with other copies of his chronicle and with manuscript copies of John Trevisa's English translation. Waldron's sampling reveals that the scribes felt under no obligation to copy their exemplar's punctuation. He suggests Higden was rubricator as well as scribe of Huntington, since the double virgule serving as a direction to supply a red paraph is frequently omitted.

Janet Cowen, "London, British Library, MS Additional 10304: Caesural Pause Marks—A Help to the Reader?" also examines the use of the virgule and concludes that in the unique manuscript of *On Famous Women*, a verse translation of parts of Boccaccio's *De mulieribus claris*, the scribe's use of the virgule is of only limited help to the reader in terms of rhythm and syntax; its consistent use, however, in defiance of phrase boundaries, helped to give a "Lydgatean look" to the page, since it gives the presentation of the verse a resemblance to Lydgate manuscripts.

Hans Sauer, "Binomials in the Middle English and Early Modern English Versions of Boccaccio's *De mulieribus claris*," studies the use of word pairs both in *On Famous Women* and in Henry Parker, Lord Morley's sixteenth-century prose translation of Boccaccio. Both English versions employ far more binomials than Boccaccio did; as their example demonstrates, such usage was an "ingrained stylistic trait" (91) with late-medieval and early-modern English authors and translators.

The next four contributions tackle the complicated textual histories of different chronicles. Erik Cooper, "The Case of the Cutting Copyist: Or, How London, British Library, MS Sloane 2027 of Robert of Gloucester's *Chronicle* Lost 4000 lines," studies the omissions made to Sloane's version of the *Chronicle* and finds it was edited by someone chiefly interested in the factual rather than the legendary history of England. Since other texts in Sloane are faithful copies, the scribe cannot be that editor. Andrew Prescott, "English Chronicle Narratives of the Rising of 1381," argues that one should not take accounts of the Peasants' Revolt at face value; instead they should be viewed as self-serving civic narratives, as writers such as those of the accounts in London Letter-Book H or the Middle English prose *Brut* were anxious to deflect allegations that upright citizens had any complicity in a yokels' revolt. Raluca Radulescu also considers the *Brut* in "The Middle English *Brut* Chronicles and the Modern Editor." Her paper is a "call to action" (169) for collaboration among scholars working on the manifold copies of the *Brut* to help establish its significance both in the history of ideas and in the English language, particularly in regard to the shaping of a political vocabulary. Julia Boffey, "Robert Fabyan's Two Hats: Compiling *the Great Chronicle of London* and *The New Chronicles of England and France,*" reiterates the tendency of authors and scribes to tweak the text of the *Brut* and London Chronicles to suit local or national interests. Differences between Fabyan's two histories in his accounts of the years 1439 to 1512 can hence be explained by the different audiences he envisaged for each: the *Great Chronicle* was intended for a London audience, the *New Chronicles* for a wider readership.

The third and final topic, editing and interpreting religious texts, is introduced by Oliver Pickering's essay, "Verse to Prose or Prose to Verse? A Problematic Text of *The Nine Points Best Pleasing to God,*" which provides a new edition from two manuscripts of a short devotional work extant in both prose and verse that treats the sequence of points in a different manner from other known versions. Susan Powell, "Further Thoughts on Editing the *Festial,*" offers a "medley of ideas" (211) occasioned by her further reading subsequent to her edition of John Mirk's *Festial.* New information leads to the interesting speculation that medieval fragments found in the Staffordshire Record Office might represent the remains of the Lilleshall Library, where Mirk was a canon. Margaret Connolly, "The Edited Text and the Selected Text and the Problem of Critical Editions," revisits her edition of *Contemplations of the Dread and Love of God,* another work with a complex manuscript tradition. As editor she worked with complete manuscripts of the text, but several chapters circulated independently. Such chapters have an "essentially different nature" (230) from the complete work, and their appearance in some of the earliest witnesses of *Contemplations* raises the question of whether they were simply extracts, adapted and shaped, or were written separately before becoming part of the whole. Veronica O'Mara, "Problems in Indexing and Editing Middle English Prayer as Illustrated by the Chester Processional Texts," discusses the difficulties faced by an editor of medieval prayers in deciding how far to go in trying to locate sources and find other copies to ascertain whether a prayer was unique or not.

The remaining contributions consider texts in early print. Mayumi Taguchi, "The Use of Sources in *The Historye of the Patriarks* and Caxton's *Golden Legend,*" shows how two translators of the *Legenda aurea* employed different sources to create their own versions of the *Legenda.* She notes that neither translator used the Wycliffite Bible as a source for biblical passages but produced their own versions, and wonders if this was due to the proscription against vernacular bibles in England. Martha Driver, "Revisiting *Nychodemus Goȿpell,*" shows and tells with ample illustrations the ways in which Wynkyn de Worde adapted the woodcuts used in Julian Notary's earlier edition of the text in his own. De Worde's use of the pictures guides the reader's interpretation of *Nychodemus Gospell* as primarily a dramatic text. In the final essay, John J. Thompson, "Reformations, Reading Practices, and Textual Afterlives: The Pseudo-Bonaventuran Tradition, *c*.1400–1600," contrasts the devotional reading of two families, that of Robert Thornton and the Roberts family of Willesden. He speculates on Thornton's motives in choosing to copy *The Privity of the Passion* rather than Nicholas Love's *Mirror of the Blessed Life of Jesus Christ* for family reading, despite Love's being a local author. The *Mirror* was more widely disseminated and continued to be popular in the sixteenth century, published by Caxton, Pynson, and de Worde, although the Roberts family owned a fine illuminated manuscript of the work in which the births of the owner's children and his death were recorded.

The Festschrift concludes, as is customary in such collections, with a list of Marx's own publications. His manifest interest in popular theology, chronicle writing, and editorial practice has been amply recognized by the insights afforded by this volume.

Pamela Robinson, Institute of English Studies, University of London

EMILY C. FRANCOMANO

The Prison of Love: Romance, Translation, and the Book in the Sixteenth Century.
Toronto: University of Toronto Press, 2018.
x + 320 pp. 30 figs.

Recent years have seen, certainly for French but also for other languages, a renewed vitality in studies of the transition of literary texts from manuscript to print. Those long-neglected but voluminous early-press versions of medieval epics and romances—reworkings, translations, *mises en prose*—are increasingly explored, enthusiastically, as in themselves worthy of literary analysis. The present book is a distinguished and lively addition to those explorations. The *Cárcel de Amor* was written by Diego de San Pedro in the 1480s as an entertainment for the court of Castile; briefly—the plot is very much convoluted—it is the touching story of a young man, Leriano, who dies, melodramatically, of love requited but unfulfilled. By 1492, in Seville, it had found its way into print, and being wonderfully of its time, it was resoundingly successful, not only in the Iberian peninsular, but as Chapter 2 shows, throughout Western Europe, with translations into Italian, French, and English.

This interesting book traces the *Cárcel*'s history across borders and time frames, focusing not just on textual adaptations and translations but also on its material history in manuscripts, incunabula, and early printed editions; because of this, and perhaps also because of so coherent a corpus, it makes an excellent lens through which to survey the book history of the transition from manuscript to print and the "sociology of texts" (the book is very much in the line of descent from D. F. McKenzie, Jerome McGann, and Roger Chartier).

The first chapter simply addresses the authorial and scribal dynamics of the society within which the *Cárcel de Amor* was created, and its reception particularly in the Iberian peninsular, focusing here on its first, Spanish, rewriter, Nicolás Núñez. Chapter 2 explores the translations made by Bernadí Vallmanya, Lelio Manfredi, François d'Assy, and Lord Berners and especially the paratextual apparatus that each of them introduces and that highlights the processes and procedures of translation—and its value. The third chapter turns to the toolboxes of the translators and what they tell us about the ideologies of vernacular-to-vernacular translation in the early modern period. Chapter 4 is devoted to the texts proper—the original, the reworkings, and the translations—to focus especially on the authors' and the adaptors' attention to and fascination with the written word: this is a text that prioritizes the written word, in letters particularly—and in which the hero Leriono dies, romantically, when he swallows his lady's letters. Chapter 5 surveys the profusion of printed books in which the *Cárcel de Amor* reached audiences all over Western Europe—what Francomano calls its "radiant diffusion"—and on what their different designs and formats can tell us about the readings of the publishers and the readership they targeted and reached.

Chapter 6 turns to the "visual rhetoric" of the different editions: lavishly illustrated with woodcuts, it focuses once again on the printers' and artists' insistence on the written and spoken word, and not only on publishers. Well into the age of print, in the 1520s, lavishly illuminated manuscripts or "luxury remediations" of the French translation were commissioned, and these are the subject of Chapter 7, again lavishly illustrated, alas only, but not unexpectedly, in black and white. The final Chapter 8 turns to a magnificent tapestry series from northern France or the Low Countries, produced also in the 1520s, and explores the way in which its three-dimensional character provides a quite different perspective on the romance. The book is completed with editions of the principal translators' paratexts, a listing of editions and known manuscripts of the romance, a highly up-to-date bibliography, and a useful index.

Francomano stresses throughout, rightly, the remarkable value of this abundance of different manifestations of this intensely "adaptogenic" romance to the student of the material history of the book. Her close attention to detail, her careful eye, her sheer enthusiasm—her notes are legion, but the book reads enjoyably—make this book a pleasure to read: it is also a model for the analysis of mushrooming textual traditions in the early modern period.

Jane H. M. Taylor, Durham University

RALPH HANNA

Patient Reading / Reading Patience: Oxford Essays on Medieval English Literature.
Exeter Medieval Texts and Studies.
Liverpool: Liverpool University Press, 2017. xii + 370 pp.

Ralph Hanna is so prolific a scholar that selecting essays for his latest collection cannot have been easy. *Patient Reading* follows on from *Pursuing History,* which appeared in 1996 and brought together work of the preceding dozen years. The sub-title of the new collection, *Oxford Essays on Medieval English Literature,* alludes to the span of time (and the environment) in which its constituent parts were written, namely since Hanna's appointment in 1997 to what became the Chair in Palaeography in that university.

The book comprises thirteen essays grouped into three sections, followed—unexpectedly—by a lengthy, previously unpublished excursus on *Piers Plowman* that begins provocatively (a favorite word of Hanna's), "This is the book I thought I never wanted to write" (271). Certain of the preceding essays are also new: "Vernacular Exegesis in Fourteenth-Century England" and "Performing Exegesis: Lyric and Sermon in Cambridge University Library, MS Gg.6.26," both within the opening section entitled "Language Barriers," and "John of Wales and 'Classicising Friars'" in the closing section entitled "Historicising the Archive," "archive" in the newish and very general sense (frequent in the book) of body of surviving historical materials. The second section, wholly containing previously published work, is "Nasty Books: Collection Procedures." The three groupings demonstrate Hanna's interest in the multi-language realities of medieval English literacy and his extensive knowledge of Latin "commentative" texts (a term that he prefers to the much narrower "exegetical"); his huge expertise in bibliographical book history ("how any text has come to be joined with others in a typically miscellaneous medieval book", [2]); and his achievements regarding the topography—the localization—of medieval books. In fact he characterizes the volume as "in the main, a sequence of local studies" (1), and maintains that he deliberately avoids "offering general pronouncements and global explanations", that the essays should be taken "merely as exemplifications of types of method" (2). This is, of course, too modest. As with the work of the late Ian Doyle, the revelatory demonstrations of the nature of the medieval books he discusses function as general principles for the rest of us.

The opening section seems deliberately designed to stress the lowly place of the English vernacular. After an introductory essay on "Literacy, Schooling, Universities," which valuably discusses Latin educational texts and points also to the prevalence of Anglo-Norman in grammar teaching, Hanna in effect downgrades medieval English by demonstrating that very often it exists only on the margins of a non-vernacular literate richness. He concentrates on sermon manuscripts, putting the scraps of English verse unearthed by the original compilers of the *Index of Middle English Verse* firmly in their place as no more than prompts or exempla for use during a preacher's oral performance. Two essays (including one of the new ones) are devoted to performing his own detailed commentative analysis of the Latin contents of Cambridge University Library, MS Gg.6.26—whose sermons contain a text of the well-known Middle English version of "Candet nudatum pectus" (*IMEV* 4088)—but, perhaps revealingly, he has in the end to admit the "expressive force" of that short lyric (89).

Hanna's conclusions can be controversial (thus he queries "the notion that there is a definable and discrete Middle English vernacular archive that one might prioritise," [61]), but his provocations are salutary. And when he turns to specifically English sermon materials, as in the new "Vernacular Exegesis in Fourteenth-Century England," he usefully contrasts the simplicity and lack of commentative ambition of the early fourteenth-century verse *Northern Homily Collection* with the sophistication of the three English prose sermons in Worcester Cathedral Library, MS F.10 (c. 1400), which he characterizes—like the Latin sermons that surround them—as "suggestively setting audiences on their way to the richness of non-biblical and non-English materials of all sorts" (45). The contrast is obvious, but Hanna's point is the scarcity of "fully commentative" fourteenth-century English texts.

The four essays in the second section are codicological in nature—"nasty books" they may seem, but not after Hanna's expert analyses of their make-up. The essay on the early thirteenth-century Lambeth Palace Library, MS 487 (published in the 2009 festschrift for Bella Millett) demonstrates in masterly fashion how its scribe added further English homiletic materials not originally planned and constructed quires of varying sizes to cope with these changes. "Producing Magdalen College MS lat. 93"—a book produced over two hundred years later—is a brilliant deconstruction of a miscellaneous Latin manuscript largely written by John Dygon, recluse of Sheen, uncovering layer after layer of archaeological strata. Hanna shows that the indexes appear to relate to other Dygon manuscripts and he concludes that MS lat. 93 may represent simply one collection of quires assembled at a late stage into this particular form. He comments along the way that while setting out in order the contents of the manuscript "may be appropriate for a catalogue, it has disadvantages when considering the book as a production" (109)—a preoccupation with the nature of manuscript cataloguing that he has more recently explored in an essay published in *The Library* in 2017. The two other pieces in this section in turn revisit and greatly extend discoveries first made by Kathleen Scott about manuscript English fragments now dispersed into separate bindings in the Rawlinson collection (placing their production in the context of the Mercers' Company in early sixteenth-century London), and analyze the household book (Bodleian Library, MS Lat. Misc. c.66) put together in the later fifteenth century by the Cheshire gentleman Humphrey Newton (demonstrating that he had some engagement with contemporary literary culture).

The subsequent section,"Historicising the Archive," begins with Hanna's classic 2003 British Academy lecture "Yorkshire Writers," showing that it was not so much the works of Rolle that were central to the religious literary culture of the region as the four long instructional English verse compositions *Speculum Vitae, Cursor Mundi,* the *Prick of Conscience,* and the *Northern Homilies.* Hanna's method here is to study the textual transmission of the poems via manuscript and scribal connections. The companion piece that follows, "Some North Yorkshire Scribes and their Context" (2008), has become equally well known for suggesting the minster town of Ripon as a possible centre of copying, partly for dialectal reasons. The amount of circumstantial supporting detail, especially about "Local readers, actual and putative," is more than impressive.

Two quite different essays then follow. "Dr Peter Partridge and MS Digby 98" somewhat resembles that on Humphrey Newton—one man and his manuscript—but Hanna historicizes Partridge precisely in the context of early fifteenth-century Oxford Lollardy, analysing Digby 98 to show that Partridge, in later life, almost certainly took action to suppress evidence of his earlier adherence to the cause. The essay was written for Anne Hudson's festschrift (2004). The new "John of Wales and 'Classicising Friars,'" in contrast, returns us to sermon materials and would have fitted better with the opening section of the book, were it not that Hanna is now concerned wholly with Latin. The essay takes issue with the exegetical scholar Beryl Smalley's dislike (in *English Friars and Antiquity*, 1960) of the use of classical sources in the sermons of fourteenth-century Oxford friars, showing that they were writing in the tradition established by their predecessor John of Wales. Hanna demonstrates that John's purpose was to provide effective preaching materials for others to use, including *similitudines* that he believed should be characterized by "their delightfulness and their memorability" (261).

After such a sequence of largely manuscript-based studies, the subsequent eighty-page literary and textual discussion of the figure of Patience in *Piers Plowman* comes as a surprise (though it fits better than some of the essays with the "Medieval English Literature" of the volume's subtitle). Comprising an explanatory preface, an "ideological prequel," a prologue, four numbered sections, and its own bibliography, it is indeed its own book, or at least booklet. There is, throughout, no doubt of Hanna's intense engagement with the text and his seriousness about language—this is truly, punningly, "patient reading"—but there is a feeling that the work has been included to demonstrate further this great scholar's versatility and because it could be. It does not fit well with the rest of the volume, and although it will no doubt be essential reading for students of *Piers Plowman* (section four comprises a more general consideration of the C Version revisions), explication of a difficult poem is not always made easier by Hanna's sometimes knotty prose. Book historians might have preferred further demonstrations of his incomparable ability to reconstruct the shape, size, and production methods of now dismantled manuscript volumes, as in "Unnoticed Middle English Romance Fragments in the Bodleian Library: MS Eng. poet. d.208," published in *The Library* in 1999. Hanna's longer-lasting legacy, one feels, will reside in penetrating codicological studies of this kind.

Oliver Pickering, University of Leeds

PHILIPPA HARDMAN AND MARIANNE AILES
The Legends of Charlemagne in Medieval England: The Matter of France in Middle English and Anglo-Norman Literature.
Cambridge, UK: D. S. Brewer, 2017.
471 pp. 5 B&W plates.

The Old French *chanson de geste* has not wanted for critical studies, starting with the *editio princeps* of the Oxford *Chanson de Roland* in 1836 and the earliest days of the discipline of romance philology in the following decades of the nineteenth century. Interest continues unabated, and the Société Rencesvals pour l'Étude de l'Épopée Romane is devoted largely to the genre (the medieval Spanish epic also falls within its purview). Anglo-Norman *chansons de geste* have not been neglected, being considered part of the epic corpus in the *langue d'oïl.* The relations between Continental and insular medieval French literature are still problematic from a scholarly point of view and still riddled with cross-Channel attitudes at a time when such issues ought to have been thoroughly resolved. Middle English manifestations of the so-called *matière de France,* which are usually consigned to the periphery of a catch-all genre of "Middle English romance," have not benefited from the same kind of persistent critical examination as the *chanson de geste.* Even with the realization that Middle English romance was not just a watered-down version of the great French texts but rather a corpus of texts translated (in all senses of the word) and remodeled for Anglophone audiences, the Charlemagne texts derived directly or indirectly from French models have never taken center stage.

It is the great virtue of this book not just to provide the first reexamination of the Middle English texts for many years but also to read them alongside Anglo-Norman *chansons de geste* as part of what could be considered post-Conquest insular epic production. While Marianne Ailes will no doubt have provided the most input on the Anglo-Norman side and Philippa Hardman on the Middle English, their collaboration is seamless, and their dual authorship is entirely successful. The two authors clearly read and commented extensively on each other's work.

One of the great paradoxes of French literary history is the transmission of the earliest Old French texts in insular copies. The preservation of the great French national epic *La Chanson de Roland* in Oxford, Bodleian Library, Digby 23 (England, s. $12^{2/4}$) has been a frequently silent embarrassment to Continental scholars, but Hardman and Ailes confront it head-on, arguing first (and obviously, although not to all) that Francophone literary culture was common to audiences and readership on both sides of the Channel for much of the Middle Ages, and second that its principal themes of religious warfare, Crusades, monarchy, and empire determine the choice and nature of the Charlemagne texts produced in both languages in England. Although thematic concerns function as common denominators in the individual chapters of this book, Ailes and Hardman are careful not to reduce their commentary to a simplistic demonstration of the predominance of shared themes.

A general introduction, "Charlemagne in England" (1–31), argues that the three strands of the tradition that seem to have appealed to insular audiences—presumably because they lend themselves to articulating the above-mentioned concerns—are those centered on Roland, Fierabras, and Otinel. The chapter titles give a good idea of the content of the book: chapter 1, "Acculturating Charlemagne: The Insular Literary Context" (1–31); chapter 2, "Charlemagne 'Translated': The Anglo-Norman Tradition" (32–155); chapter 3, "Charlemagne 'Appropriated': The Middle English Tradition" (156–220); chapter 4, "Re-Imagining the Hero: The Insular Roland and the Battle of Roncevaux" (221–263), chapter 5: "Re-Presenting Otherness: The Insular *Fierabras* Tradition" (264–345), chapter 6: "Re-Purposing the Narrative: The Insular *Otinel* Tradition" (346–401). A conclusion, "The Insular Afterlife of the Matter of France" (402–411), neatly ties up the various threads of the discussion.

In a sense, the notion of cultural encounters defines what this book is about. On one level, it relates to a central theme of the clash of religions and cultures and their expression within the texts, and on another, it articulates the acculturation and assimilation of the *matière de France* in both Anglo-Norman and Middle English in England, and to a minor degree, in Scotland. Once again, Hardman and Ailes are astute enough to show how insular Charlemagne texts are characteristically insular while at the same time retaining important links with the Continental corpus. It might be interesting to see where the Middle Welsh texts fit into this insular model.

The whole book is characterized by careful analysis of the central texts and the manuscripts that transmit them, all conveniently listed in an Appendix (412–417). Some texts will be unfamiliar while others are part of the canon: versions of the *Chanson de Roland,* the Pseudo-Turpin, *Fierabras* and *Otinel* in both languages, the Anglo-Norman *Destruction de Rome,* one Middle English and one Middle Scots Charlemagne poem (*The Sege of Melayne* and *The Taill of Rauf Coilyear*) with no evident French model. Some of the manuscripts are well-known indeed, and better than many of the texts they contain: the Oxford *Roland* manuscript, the Auchinleck manuscript, the Fillingham manuscript, the London and Hannover copies of *Fierabras* and the *Destruction de Rome,* and the London Thornton manuscript. An exhaustive bibliography (419–459) and an index (461–471) complete the volume.

This is a substantial and significant contribution to the comparative study of Anglo-Norman and Middle English narrative literature in a multilingual context. It will be the point of departure for anyone wishing to tackle the subject in the future.

Keith Busby, University of Wisconsin-Madison

MARY KANE and JANE ROBERTS, EDS.
Kane from Canada.
Tempe, AZ:
Arizona Center for
Medieval and Renaissance Studies, 2016.
284 pp. 45 illustrations, 2 family trees.

This is perhaps an odd book to be reviewed in an academic journal. Despite its cover (Piers with spade from Oxford, Bodleian Library, MS Douce 104), and its author, the pre-eminent *Piers Plowman* editor, George Kane, it says almost nothing about editing or *Piers* or academic life until the last two of the fifteen chapters. In these Kane takes the reader through his academic career from 1946 until his appointment to the Chair at King's College, London in 1965. The book is unfinished in practice (Kane's last teaching was at Chapel Hill 1977 to 1987), but in all important ways, it is finished. It was edited by his daughter, Mary, and his former colleague at King's, Jane Roberts, after Kane's death in 2008 at the age of 92.

As a first-year undergraduate at King's in October 1966, I attended at least one of George Kane's lectures (I was a very poor attendee at all lectures)—at least, only one is memorable to me, and I still empathize with my callow self, incredulous that a whole hour could be spent discussing whether "shepe" meant sheep or shepherd (l. 2 of the Prologue). The decision to review this book was perhaps therefore affected by filial piety, although my personal experience of George Kane was remote and cold—my Ph.D. was supervised, not by him, but by Ron Waldron, who told me recently that Kane passed to him students he had no particular interest in supervising himself. Therefore the fact that I can say, having read this book, that my empathy with George Kane and my respect for him are both immeasurably enhanced, and indeed that my respect for him is immeasurable, is not what I had expected when I first set about reading it.

In fact, the bulk of the book (written for his grandchildren as a record of their origins) deals with Kane's early life in Canada and his experiences as a prisoner of war fighting between 1940 and 1945. Again, that is not a subject to which this reviewer would be naturally drawn. It is, however, very well written, completely enthralling, and utterly honest. George Kane was born in Canada in 1916 and moved to England to work on his Ph.D. in 1938. He enlisted in the British Army (Artists' Rifles) on the outbreak of war in September 1939 and was captured in the defence of Calais the following year. For the next five years he recorded carefully, and then in this book re-examines minutely and with forensic honesty, his experiences, particularly in relation to his homosocial relationships, his own personal character and the intricate details of the attempts, of which he was always part, of himself and his fellow prisoners of war to escape from, respectively, Laufen, Oflag VIB Warburg, Oflag VIIB Eichstätt, and Oflag IXAH Spangenberg.

Kane's resourcefulness and fortitude were most likely established by his paternal ancestry in Ulster, his maternal ancestry in Lutheran Germany, his rural upbringing in Saskatchewan, his close and loving family, and his education by the Benedictine fathers of St Peter's Abbey. These in themselves may explain what the book reveals of a strong sense of duty, a hatred of indolence (in himself more than others), a determination to be usefully occupied, a love of study, a love of the practical outdoors, and a strong companionship with men and strong attraction to women. Since this review must concentrate on those aspects relevant to this *Journal*, rather than describing the impact of Kane's personal characteristics on his wartime experiences (although these form the most compelling chapters of the book), one can see his life of scholarship in all these traits.

It is clear that Kane the editor came about by chance. He came to England in 1938 to work, as he thought, on a Ph.D. on John Milton with C. J. Sisson at University College, London; passed on by Sisson to R. W. Chambers, he looked fruitlessly for a Milton supervisor until Chambers casually directed him towards his own work on *Piers Plowman*. Thus Kane found himself editing the last three passus of the B text. Interrupted by the war, he was compelled by his dogged sense of duty to complete the thesis (once his materials had been returned from Aberystwyth where they, with the English department, had gone for the duration of the war). Two sentences explain all about Kane as editor of *Piers Plowman* and as a man: "Over half a century I have from time to time bitterly regretted the luck that put the largest part of the burden of *Piers Plowman* editing on me, denying me studies that I loved and would have revelled in. But I have never been moved to hold this against Chambers; to have known him enriched my life" (79). In the war years, when books were sent to the prisoner of war camps, Kane read much. In particular he enjoyed reading all three books of the *Divina Commedia* with a fellow prisoner of war. The book parcel Chambers sent from England (Skeat's EETS *Piers Plowman*, Jusserand's *English Wayfaring Life*, Owst's *Literature and Pulpit*) remained untouched; *Piers* reminded Kane unhappily of his waiting Ph.D. and was anyway impossible to study without total uninterrupted concentration, and "with the best will in the world I could not force myself to be interested at that time in Jusserand's sturdy beggars and Owst's delinquent religious and mercenary friars" (184). Chambers's kindness ("unquestionably so intended") "should have directed me to examine my life constructively," but instead Kane turned to *Candide, Manon Lescaut, Les liaisons dangereuses*, and *La dame aux camélias*.

After the war it was imperative to complete the Ph.D. to salve Kane's conscience for his doctoral support by the Imperial Order of Daughters of the Empire, and that was done: "my thesis was slight, and I am not proud of it." His hope had been that with the Ph.D. he "could go back to Canada and my beloved Renaissance" (73). This did not happen, and he remained at UCL. Entirely inexperienced as an assistant lecturer in 1946, he taught himself the gamut of Middle English literature (and some Old English). In particular, at a time when philology was king, he had no philological background. Indeed, while he had loved French as a subject at school, "nothing...had prepared me for the dry-as-dust phonology" of Mildred Pope's *From Latin to Modern French*, which was used at his university in Canada, Northwestern. (Not that he hated languages, just "dry-as-dustness." His German, for example, had made him one of the "Germans" who were given speaking roles in attempted camp escapes.) His description of the post-war years demonstrates the ease of university life in those far-off days, the academic camaraderie of the few scholars in teaching positions in the few English universities with few students (mostly ex-servicemen and then ex-National Service men), and the chance and lucky happenstance that led people with flats or houses to let and jobs to offer to wish to give the housing and employment to George Kane. (Not just chance—people liked and trusted him.) There was also much time (again in those far off days when administrative duties were light) to work on *Piers Plowman*, first on the B text, then, when it became obvious that he needed to understand the A text (but the work of its editors, Chambers and J. H. G. Grattan, had lapsed beyond recovery), on the A text.

In 1955, Kane moved to the women's college, Royal Holloway, for ten years, and then, as noted above, to King's for about the same period. His reminiscences of the pleasant college life at Englefield Green, and of the years of his children's upbringing, are charming, and his recollections of colleagues and students are fair but frank—the only criticism is the occasional observation that certain friends and colleagues did not take their research to the stage of publication, a sin for which Kane himself could never be accused, having sacrificed himself for the tedium of editing: "the price has been high, thirty-five years of preoccupation at the expense of time that would otherwise have gone to more lively and exciting literary engagement" (250). Perhaps it is as a literary critic manqué that one must understand the editor Kane (for example, "it did not cross my mind that anyone at all well acquainted with the *Piers* poem could seriously propose that the sorry A text in MS Bodley 851 was an early form of the poem," [252]). The "preoccupation" was, however, alleviated by Kane's meeting with Talbot Donaldson, and the male camaraderie which comes across so clearly in his prisoner of war camp descriptions (and which he admits were partly the reason for his leaving Royal Holloway for King's) made his collaboration with Donaldson a pleasure: "I sacrificed a day with the Dictionary files [he was spending a month in New Haven working through the *Middle English Dictionary*] and in return acquired a collaborator as well as a lifelong friend" (253). The relationship was collaborative, but Donaldson had no manuscript experience and so became "a quick, apt pupil" (253) and a hard worker to Kane's brief: "The rich intellectual engagement I enjoyed during my twenty-five years of collaboration and association with Donaldson is, in retrospect, some recompense for the unquestionable drudgery of much of the editorial work" (263).

One is glad that George Kane found recompense for the emotional aridity of his scholarship. As his daughter says in her afterword: "His great loves were his immediate family, Canada and fishing, probably in that order" (282). It is clear to the reader of his book that *Piers Plowman* could not feature anywhere in a list of loves. But, thanks to this autobiography with its scrupulous lack of guile, the strength of George Kane's reputation can now lie not only in *Piers Plowman,* but in his honesty and integrity of character. His daughter's last words in this book are: "He was a father who was hard to like at times but always easy to love, respect and be proud of" (284).

Susan Powell, University of Salford (emerita), University of Leeds

OMAR KHALAF, ED.
Alexander and Dindimus, Edited from Oxford, Bodleian Library, MS Bodley 264.
Middle English Texts 55.
Heidelberg: Universistätsverlag Winter, 2017.
liv + 80 pp.

The most recent volume from the Middle English Texts series is unusual in a number of respects. Not only is it an edition of a text that is said to be one of the earliest examples of the Alliterative Revival, but it is also presented with copious illustrations, something that has not been the case with previous Middle English Texts volumes. Admittedly, the illustrations are not up to the normal high standards of current reproductions (something that the publisher could possibly consider), but it is still useful to have these nine plates, particularly as they are integral to the text, as the editor explains so carefully. Omar Khalaf's introduction to *Alexander and Dindimus* is finely judged, taking in the poem's somewhat complicated history, its language and localization, meter and rhythm, the illustrations, rubrics, sources, and fragmentary nature, alongside a creditable manuscript description.

The poem, known to many as *Alexander B,* is uniquely found in one manuscript, Oxford, Bodleian Library, MS Bodley 264, which otherwise contains a large core of profusely illustrated French poems on Alexander copied in France or Flanders in 1338. The English poem, alongside a French text on the travels of Marco Polo, was interpolated into the volume in the fifteenth century, possibly owing to the influence of one of the early owners, Anthony Woodville, Earl Rivers. Because it begins abruptly, the poem has long been thought of as fragmentary (a view endorsed by Khalaf) and related to the so-called *Alexander A* (or *Romance of Alisaunder*). It deals with an epistolary exchange between Alexander the Great and Dindimus (the king of the Bragmans), in which the latter represents the ascetic and the spiritual, and Alexander the materialistic and the worldly.

Following his careful manuscript description, Khalaf investigates the language rigorously, paying particular attention to dialectal stratification and concluding that the current text, in a South-West Midlands dialect, was transcribed by a Northern scribe and that

> [t]his contributed to the creation of a text where the linguistic features of the fifteenth-century English are not simply superimposed on the original substratum of the poem that belonged to a century before, but, on the contrary, they form a combination in which both phases of the English language are still recognizable, and are coherently amalgamated in a homogenous whole. [xxvii–xxviii]

In his discussion of meter and rhythm, he makes use of statistical analysis to show the stresses of the aa/ax alliterative pattern before moving on to a lengthy and very informative section on the illustrations (xxx–xxxvi), followed by a brief comment on the rubrics. In many ways the discussion of the illustrations is one of the most interesting parts of the introduction. The editor has gone into an unusual degree of detail to demonstrate his points and in so doing succeeds in clearly showing the subtle ways in which illustrations can serve to supplement the message of a medieval text. Khalaf works his way through the description of the nine images in which the illuminator sought to imitate (albeit not so successfully) the layout and composition of the French images in the rest of the volume. He then spends some time discussing the history of the left and right iconographical placing of figures (or places) in images, noting "the left-right opposition has been present in every culture since ancient times" (xxxiii) and that in the West it was systematized by Aristotle who thought that "the right side of the human body is warmer than the left, its blood purer, with more spirit and less water" (xxxiii). Indeed, heaven itself had its right and left sides, which led to the orientation of both church altars and buried corpses to face the right side—that is, to the east, with the west being the seat of Satan. From such minute analysis Khalaf is then in a very good position to demonstrate not only the importance of the placing of Alexander (the worldly and emotional) on the left and Dindimus (the spiritual and intellectual) on the right, but also the position of their feet (in Christian tradition, proper movement should take off from the right foot). In this way he is able to show clearly the significance of the left-right positioning in the individual illustrations and how they serve "to develop a narrative thread that is distinct from the written text" (xxxiv). This narrative thread developed in the illustrations therefore departs from the text but at the same time serves to draw "the reader's attention to some of the major themes developed in Alexander's and Dindimus's epistolary exchange such as kingship, ethics, and religion" (xxxv).

The poem is translated from the *Collatio Alexandri et Dindimi per litteras facta* (the Latin translation of one of the Greek texts from the "Indian treatises" branch of the Alexandrine tradition) found in the *Historia de Preliis Alexandri Magni*. According to Khalaf (xxxviii–l), there are three redactions of the *Collatio* (labeled respectively *Collatio I, II,* and *III*), and it had a wide and early circulation in Europe: for instance, Alcuin writes about sending a copy to Charlemagne, and there are forty-two extant manuscripts from medieval England that contain *Collatio I,* as well as various other texts, including forty-nine copies of Gower's *Confessio Amantis,* where it features as part of Book V. In his study of the sources, Khalaf provides detailed evidence that the text in Bodley 264 could have derived from a sub-branch of the tripartite division of the forty-two witnesses, represented by three manuscripts, albeit that "the English poem translates and paraphrases, without any apparent order, readings that are unique to *each* of the three manuscripts considered" (xlviii).

Khalaf edits the text sensibly, with sufficient commentary and a helpful glossary. It is most useful to have this edition, only the fourth in almost 170 years (Stevenson in 1849, Skeat in 1878, and Magoun in 1929). Taken overall, it is a very worthy volume in this series, where clear editorial and high scholarly standards continue to be upheld under the watchful eyes of the general editors, Margaret Connolly, William Marx, and Hans Sauer. Yet it is a great pity that they, and the publisher, continue to hide their lights under bushels and that there is no attempt to list previous volumes at the end of each new edition, something that is common practice in many other series and that would serve as a useful reminder to readers of what else is available in the excellent Middle English Texts series.

Veronica O'Mara, University of Hull

S. J. OGILVIE-THOMSON, ED.

The Index of Middle English Prose: Handlist XXIII: The Rawlinson Collection, Bodleian Library, Oxford.
Cambridge: D. S. Brewer, 2017.
xl + 367 pp.

This is the third of Sarah Ogilvie-Thomson's *IMEP* indexes of Oxford collections, the previous ones being Handlists VIII (Oxford College Libraries, 1991) and XVI (Laudian Collection, 2000). While the gap between publications is longer in this case than that between her first and second publications, the volume itself is much thicker, and in terms of the output of *IMEP* volumes, she has kept in time with the rate of publications (*IMEP* VIII, XVI, XXIII).

As with all *IMEP* volumes, as well as the necessary, and very useful, preliminaries and end-material, there is an introduction in which Ogilvie-Thomson introduces the reader to Richard Rawlinson, his unsatisfactory family, the need to sell his brother Thomas's fine library, and his heroic recovery of much of it, together with other manuscripts, to the number of over 5,000. On his death in 1755, the Bodleian was faced with the task of housing his extraordinarily eclectic collection. Ogilvie-Thomson also explains her editorial practice, particularly the inclusion of seventeenth- and eighteenth-century transcribed and translated material from medieval texts, and recipes (always a problem in *IMEP* listings) even in sixteenth-century hands.

This is a fascinating volume and would probably repay reading from end to end (which this reviewer confesses to not having done). Instead (as reviewers tend to do), I have looked at those manuscripts in the Rawlinson collection, which I know well. This practice (while convenient to the reviewer) tests the indexer to the full, since the reviewer has spent more time with the manuscript than the indexer. MS Rawlinson A 381 is the best manuscript of the Group B recension of the *Festial*, and Ogilvie-Thomson properly lists all the *Festial* sermons it contains ([7] to [69]). (This is a return to *IMEP*'s original practice, which was unfortunately proscribed for some years under different editorship from the present.) She suggests that the sermons have been "treated cursorily" (xxi), but that is all that is needed, as she says, when a collection has been edited. Her note on "Other texts" is exemplary in its completeness and provides a brief historiography of *Festial* sermons in relation to editions, articles, *IPMEP*, and *IMEP* itself.

The entries for John Gaytryge's sermon (*The Lay Folks' Catechism*) in MSS Rawlinson C 285 [12], an extract, and 288 [2] refer the reader to Anne Hudson's important articles "A New Look at the Lay-Folks' Catechism" and "The Lay Folks' Catechism: a Postscript" (*Viator* 16, 1985; 19, 1988) but not to my later "The Transmission and Circulation of The Lay Folks' Catechism,"[1] which benefited much from Hudson's two articles and was followed, and its hypothesis confirmed, by Robert Swanson's "The Origins of 'The Lay Folks' Catechism'" (*Medium Aevum* 60, 1991). This is not, of course, a criticism (for the reasons outlined above), but an attempt to indicate later scholarship on the subject that should be read after Hudson's seminal articles. Ogilvie-Thomson quite properly notes omissions and inconsistencies in other *IMEP* volumes in relation to this text: for example, that Gaytryge is not indexed in the Trinity College Cambridge volume "as its editor judged it to be verse" (it is included, she notes, in *NIMEV* and *DIMEV*). The question of whether it is verse or prose has been much discussed (see David Lawton's argument summarised in Powell, "The Transmission and Circulation," 72–73) and is perhaps unresolvable, but the fact of its omission in *IMEP* Handlist XI is important and should be added to any future amalgamated index of *IMEP* volumes.

As for material unknown to the present reviewer, two important pieces of information were revealed to me by this volume: one has already been incorporated into current research, and the other will become the subject of a future *JEBS* "Nota Bene." First, the volume alerted me to MS Rawlinson liturg. f. 36 and its version [5] of Caxton's *Fifteen Oes* (currently being edited by myself and Alexandra Barratt for the Middle English Texts series); secondly, it led me to another Prologue and Life of St Jerome, a very important discovery of a manuscript (MS Rawlinson D 112) that "has not been previously noted" (213). This is exactly what *IMEP* volumes should be doing, and one is grateful to them for such discoveries (easy to find with the summary list of contents, which precedes the index proper).

A slight cavil—entirely undeserved by Ogilvie-Thomson, since it is expressly not the aim of *IMEP*: Latin is not indexed in any way, apart from in the macaronic indexes at the end of *IMEP* volumes. For example, in the case of MS Rawlinson C 506, one might assume that Latin material (more likely than English verse, the other entirely justifiable exclusion) filled the gaps between entries [11] and [12], or between [12] and [13], or between [13] and [14].[2] In the case of [13], Ogilvie-Thomson notes that this is an "English passage in a Latin conjuration to raise spirits," but for the others one must consult the manuscript.[3] The macaronic index properly notes a list of Latin and English herbal names in Works in Latin and English [A 15]. As medievalist scholars have become increasingly interested in the total make-up of manuscripts, and as the blind spot with relation to Latin texts has only increased among English-speaking medievalists, it would be highly desirable now for there to be at least an indication of Latin (and verse, and even blank or missing folios) in the afternote to an entry, e.g., "followed by ten Latin medical recipes," "followed by an item in verse," "the following 5 folios are missing." However, that is a personal cavil, and one that, if implemented, would further delay the production of volumes.

While one must commiserate with Ogilvie-Thomson that the delights of working in Duke Humfrey's library when she began this volume gave way to the (temporary) horror of the Radcliffe Science Library, with her we must be grateful for the comfort of the new Weston Library (especially of its chairs in comparison with those of Duke Humfrey's), while agreeing that "it will never be the same, and I look back on the past with deep nostalgia, regret and gratitude"(vii).

Susan Powell, University of Salford (emerita), University of Leeds

NOTES

1. In *Late-Medieval Religious Texts and their Transmission*, ed. A. J. Minnis (Cambridge: Brewer, 1993), 67–84.
2. [11] ends f. 26v, [12] begins f. 29r; [12] ends f. 29r, [13] begins f. 40r; [13] ends f. 40v, [14] begins f. 53r.
3. In practice, the online Quarto Catalogue reveals that f. 27r introduces English verse on bloodletting, that ff. 29v-31v contain a table and English verse, followed by two missing and five blank folios, that the conjuration begins on f. 39r and is followed by a Latin text, and that the whole of ff. 42-53 is missing.

SUSAN POWELL
The Birgittines of Syon Abbey: Preaching and Print.
Texts and Translations 11.
Turnhout, Belgium: Brepols, 2017.
xxii + 345 pp.

A central element in Susan Powell's productive career has been her work on Syon abbey, England's only Birgittine house, and in this new book she provides a collection of her essays on this topic. The format she has invented is notably successful. Each essay is preceded by a headword that explains how and when it was first published and is followed by an afterword that summarizes research by others that appeared after the essay's original publication. The headnote for Chapter 2, for instance ("Preaching at Syon Abbey"), explains the piece's intellectual genesis as well as the circumstances of its composition—both valuable in appreciating the essay's thrust. The afterword then provides three pages that summarize recent publications on Syon sermons. Still more helpful is the author's perspective on her earlier work: what remains to be done now and what might have been done differently. Thorough, detailed, judicious, this arrangement of information is so useful to the reader that it might be recommended for all collections of previously published work.

In the volume's first half, devoted to preaching, Chapter 3 provides an investigation of a little-known, privately owned manuscript, Cox MS 39. It is a collection of sermons bound at Syon and owned by a Syon brother, John Lawsby. One of its sermons addressed to a fellow religious might have been delivered on a Syon profession day, as Powell suggests, but she points out that the whole collection deserves further study as "the only extant sermon collection by a Syon brother" (101). Chapter 4 was also originally impelled by the desire to identify (more) Syon preaching. Might the sermons printed by William Caxton at the end of his 1491 edition of Mirk's *Festial* be Birgittine? This chapter gives a condensed version of the introduction to Powell's edition of *Three Sermons for Nova Festa Together with the Hamus Caritatis* (Heidelberg, 2007), and it presents several intriguing answers to this question. Most likely to be Birgittine texts are the sermon for the feast of the Transfiguration, since it was one of Syon's important pardon days, and the curiously named *Hamus Caritatis* (fishhook of love). which Powell thinks likely to have been the work of Thomas Betson, Syon's librarian, because of resemblances to his later writing.

The book's second half is devoted to Syon's printing, which, because of its multiplicity and its anonymity, continues to offer the opportunity for further research. In this account of Syon's publishing, 1519 has been chosen as a significant date. In that year the *Orcharde of Syon* appeared, its epilogue giving the story of its Syon publication, and in a 1519 Book of Hours the beautiful and well-known Syon woodcut of St. Birgitta made its first appearance, accompanying the *Fifteen Oes*. In Chapter 5, Powell gives a series of suggestions that might enlarge the list of pre-1519 publications (e.g., more work on Syon-associated saints such as Barbara, Dorothy, and Jerome) and then treats in more detail the better-known post-1519 books. Together the *Orcharde* and the Birgittine woodcut image mark a significant moment in Syon's publishing—and it is true that in the period before 1519 we have very little certain information and a great deal afterward. Yet as Powell several times implies, the earlier period is underexplored—something she tries to remedy in the book's new introductory chapter, "The Birgittines of Syon Abbey," in a section titled "Books for Sisters," which attempts a chronological overview. Given Syon's connections with Caxton and hence with the beginning of printing in England, the abbey's involvement with the press lasted for about sixty years. The question might be asked: How best to describe the changing character of Syon's mission, and hence of its publishing, over these six decades of institutional life?

Chapter 6, "Lady Margaret Beaufort: Books, Printers, and Syon Abbey," draws on Powell's earlier published work on Lady Margaret's books and on her relation with Syon. The emphasis here is on the latter topic, and the addition of much new material drawn from Lady Margaret's household accounts, which Powell is editing, has been invaluable in presenting the king's mother's "prominent role in the commissioning and disseminating of printed books" (152). Both here and in the book's final chapter, "Syon Abbey in the Reign of Henry VIII and Beyond," material from these accounts adds completely new information. For instance Margaret Windsor, a nun whose name is found in four Syon books, is identified as Lady Margaret's goddaughter, for whom in May 1506 Lady Margaret paid ten pounds to Syon on her profession day (she would later become Syon's prioress). This chapter gives an account of Syon's final days, and it ends with new work in which Powell attempts to do for Syon's nuns' printed books what Christopher de Hamel did for the Syon brothers' manuscripts—that is, to trace the books' movements after the dissolution. Suggestively, eight brief case studies show that Syon books were often later held in recusant families.

The intention to make study of Syon as accessible as possible is everywhere evident in the book's content and its arrangement. The book's front matter, for instance, provides "A Note on the Bibliography of the Abbey and the Birgittine Order," a five-page bibliographical essay that gives admirably complete guidance on how to do research on Syon. The two appendices, one "A Bibliography of Syon Texts before and after 1519" and the other "A List of Printed Woodcuts of St. Birgitta," are also the product of careful thought about accessibility. (The latter includes a previously unnoticed 1537 image of the saint facing a full-length Image of Pity, not in Edward Hodnett or Isak Collijn.) Such imaginative assistance for the reader, together with the generous and inclusive analysis of current research by others that is offered in the afterwords, make this book an indispensable guide not only to Syon but more generally to the study of late-medieval devotion.

Mary Erler, Fordham University

R. M. THOMSON

The Fox and the Bees: The Early Library of Corpus Christi College Oxford: The Lowe Lectures 2017.

Cambridge, UK: D. S. Brewer for Corpus Christi College, 2018.

viii + 95 pp. 23 color plates.

Corpus Christi celebrated its half-millennium last year. For this occasion, the college commissioned a series of books celebrating its distinguished library: many hyperillustrated "coffee-table" volumes directed at old members rather than a scholarly audience (such as Pormann, reviewed in *JEBS* 19 [2016]). But scholarship did not always lag behind: the lecture series that memorializes Corpus's most distinguished paleographical member, E. A. Lowe, was dedicated to an accurate history of the college's distinctive early library.

Here Corpus was particularly fortunate in its presenter. Rod Thomson's credentials and his intimate knowledge of the college library are impeccable. In 2011, he produced a descriptive catalogue of the extensive manuscript holdings (mainly, as he points out here, donations of the seventeenth century). Thomson followed this up four years later by bringing to conclusion volume 16 of the long-running Corpus of British Medieval Library Catalogues (reviewed in *JEBS* 20 [2017]). This covers all the libraries of Oxford's secular colleges and includes extensive documentation of Corpus's library, including its acquisition of printed books, down to an initial catalogue of 1589. The Lowe Lectures (and the present volume) relied upon this bibliographical background; here, Thomson offers a richly nuanced narrative that contextualizes and fruitfully extends these somewhat inert earlier published materials.

Thomson's account reproduces the three public lectures that formed the 2017 Lowe series. The first outlines the vision of the founder, Bishop Richard Fox, and his distinctly "revolutionary" vision for a college. This was to be devoted to "The New Learning," an emphasis upon the classical languages and literary study; this focus necessarily prioritized modern printed editions rather than manuscripts. This first lecture outlines the founder's book donations and the way in which they actuated his vision; Thomson makes a good case here for this "revolution."

The second lecture is devoted to the activities of Fox's protégé, the college's first president, John Claymond (1468–1537). Here Thomson demonstrates the continuation of Fox's program, most especially in Claymond's extensive commentary on Pliny, and the addition of Hebrew, the third "great language," to college collections. In the third lecture, Thomson takes the narrative past mid-sixteenth century (when Corpus Christi, belatedly, one might think, began acquiring specifically Reformation printed materials). The volume is richly illustrated (particularly with images of original bindings, many produced by prominent members of the trade) and capped off with an extensive series of bibliographic appendixes: a listing of all surviving college books, print and manuscript, from the 1589 catalogue, arranged by donor; all entries in the college accounts pertaining to the library; and two letters associated with John Claymond (one heretofore unpublished). This is a very rich trove indeed.

To this account, I would add only a couple of grace notes, both concerning Claymond. Thomson laments the total loss of Claymond's "lighter writing" (22). While scarcely "light," at least one piece of this, surprisingly in the vernacular (and certainly predating his presidency), does survive. (In Thomson's defense, I would say it escaped even the indefatigable A. B. Emden, although not the authors of the Bodleian *Summary Catalogue*.) MS Wood F.34, folios 1–8, has an early-sixteenth-century copy of "Mr Claymondis treatise of repentance," with incipit "Conuertimini ad me in toto corde. . . . Hytt ys ye propurte and condycion off euery wyse man." Although Anthony Wood continues, "written with his owne hand," this is in fact a scribal copy (although it still retains vestiges of Claymond's native Lincolnshire dialect).

As his conclusion, Thomson offers an anecdotal account of the continuing usefulness of this sixteenth-century collection (52). In editing William of Malmesbury, he and Michael Winterbottom had to rely for their references on Corpus's 1524 printed Latin Josephus, unavailable in any modern edition. Here bibliographical *nous* may have slipped a bit; although the volume lacks any indication of the fact, this may represent a publisher's "comp copy," not a purchase, since the editor of the work was one of Claymond's sometime correspondents, one D. Erasmus.

But grace notes only: this is a richly rewarding account, with Thomson, as one of Fox's busy bees, carrying his activities into a new half-millennium.

Ralph Hanna, Keble College, Oxford

DANIEL WAKELIN

Designing English: Early Literature on the Page.
Oxford: Bodleian Library, 2018.
215 pp. 89+ color plates (some subdivided).

This entrancing and informative book was written to coincide with the excellent exhibition of the same name (Designing English) in the Weston Library of the Bodleian from December 1, 2017 to April 22, 2018. With its emphasis on graphic design, the exhibition (and the book) illustrate (literally) the perhaps surprising continuity between an interest in designing texts during the Middle Ages and today. *Ordinatio* has become an academic focus of medievalists in the past twenty-five years, as manuscript studies have become broader and to some extent have left behind "literature" (a word used, interestingly, in the subtitle of the book) in favor of codicology. This book fully demonstrates the link between text and design, a link that Bodley's Librarian, Richard Ovenden, suggests in the foreword was essential to make the underrated vernacular communicate to its new readership.

For this book Daniel Wakelin must have looked at every single one of the nearly nine hundred and fifty Bodleian manuscripts that Ovenden notes contain some English material. The majority of the Bodleian's thousands of manuscripts are in Latin, but even minor uses of English are relevant to this exhibition, although the major English works such as *The Peterborough Chronicle* and manuscripts of *The Canterbury Tales* and *Piers Plowman* are included, too. Not all the manuscripts illustrated and discussed are from the original Bodleian collections, but only eight other libraries are listed in the "Index of Manuscripts": in Cambridge, the libraries of Corpus Christi and Trinity, together with Cambridge University Library; Chicago University Library; Lambeth Palace Library; the National Archives; and elsewhere in Oxford, the libraries of Jesus College and University College.

Wakelin writes with fluency, elegance, and intelligence. Although entirely suitable for academic reading, his text is also accessible to the knowledgeable reader or visitor of the exhibition: in the introduction he explains why we might have "prejudices about the so-called 'Middle Ages'" (6) that would lead us to question an early interest in design, and he foregrounds the craft, handicraft, and craftsmanship of the period. His descriptions of scribes and illuminators is transparent and calculated to diminish the distance between the perhaps unfamiliar terms and the reality of those who did these activities: "a *scribe* is merely somebody doing the task of copying and an *illuminator* the task of painting (*illuminating* or *limning*)" (11). One of the four illustrations to the introduction is not even of a manuscript but of a copper jug from Ghana (property of the British Museum).

Each of the six sections of the book is elegantly illustrated and textually informative: "Making Space for English," "Making Pages," "Pages for Reading," "Decorating Pages," "Pages for Voicing," "English in Space." Each of these has a subtitle from a text discussed and illustrated to start the chapter. Chapter 1 is "In fruma wæs word" (In the beginning was the Word), illustrated by a manuscript where the English words (very small) gloss the same Latin verse decorated in the manner of a Bauhaus design (but at the turn of the eighth century). Having started with marginalized English (sometimes literally marginalized), Chapter 2, "In wat syde of heven that thy be," takes its subtitle from a line in the *Prick of Conscience*, the very page illustrated alongside the text. Materials are dealt with in this chapter: the process of making parchment (including "small, holey scraps of parchment," [53]), of reusing manuscripts as palimpsests, of folding (or rolling) manuscripts to various sizes and shapes, of squeezing words into margins, and all sorts of other ways of manipulating material to its textual and social purpose, until "perhaps by the late fifteenth century the bound book was too strong a model for storing or reading not to be followed" (71).

Chapter 3, perversely but perhaps deliberately, begins, "Here begins Book IV." It introduces the first four letters of Bede's Book IV as intertwining orange and green birds and beasts. Here the reader is introduced to medieval paratexts (Wakelin supplies a list, 73–74), such as different scripts, paraphs, changes of font (as we would say today), running heads, contents pages, glosses, and marginal annotations, all copiously illustrated. Chapter 4, "xii signes that reigneth," opens with a zodiac man and asks (and answers), "What is this picture for?" "So what do pictures and diagrams in English manuscripts achieve?" (99). The chapter deals with images: their construction and purpose, the importance of convention in religious pictures ("not because the culture was narrow or restrictive, but because it was through shared patterns of images that people found a way to show their personal piety" [106]), and the role of images in presenting magnificence, in entertaining, and in educating. Among the manuscripts are some a medievalist may never have seen before: drawings of antlers to instruct the reader in the different ages and designations of deer; a page illustrating four of *The Twenty Jordans,* with a real jordan (urine flask) alongside (from the Museum of London); a unique diagram illustrating problems in chess, with an ivory chess piece (from the Ashmolean) *en face.*

Chapter 5 is "tæc us hu we magon us gebiddan" (teach us how we can pray), the words of the apostles to Christ that led to the exposition of the Lord's Prayer. It opens with a folio from one of Ælfric's sermons, including these words and the Pater Noster itself, and the chapter deals with devices to enable reading aloud in numerous situations: preaching, chanting the liturgy, group reading, reading verse, singing, performing and reading plays.

Finally, Chapter 6 begins with an invocation to the Virgin and to Christ: "Lady, Jhesu, mercy!," taken from a brass memorial to Thomas Peyton and his two wives, with a picture of one of them with this inscription folded into her elaborate headdress. The theme of the chapter is "Books and other objects are more alike than they seem" (157). There are five manuscript pages illustrated, but the majority of illustrations are of other types of inscribed artifact: the brass from Cambridgeshire; an Anglo-Saxon knife from Kent; a silver brooch from Sutton Hoo; a gold ring from Godstow Priory; a piece of a sandstone cross from Dewsbury; another brass from Norfolk; and various much better known inscriptions: John Baret's cadaver tomb from Bury St. Edmunds, together with the decorated ceiling with his motto, "grace me gouerne"; the *Prick of Conscience* glass from All Saints, North Street, York; John Lydgate's verses on the walls of the Clopton chapel in Long Melford. Even the manuscript pages are unexpected: verses jotted down from the walls of a Cornish priory; Lydgate's Long Melford verses as they appear in manuscript; an illustrated poem on the instruments of Christ's Passion; the tau-cross as a charm for childbirth; and a charm for toothache to be written on a loaf or on butter or an apple for the sufferer to eat.

The research for this volume (and exhibition) must have been phenomenal—relatively few are thanked in the acknowledgments, which suggests prodigious hard work on their part, but among them are the endowers of Wakelin's Oxford Chair (which is in memory of the gifted codicologist Jeremy Griffiths, who died too young), "brilliant students in the Faculty of English in Oxford," and "my dad, Roger Wakelin, for travelling round East Anglia with me to make brass rubbings and take photographs of inscriptions." Copious thanks are due to Wakelin himself for a book that should be prescribed reading and teaching in any manuscript-oriented course from now on for a very long time.

Susan Powell, University of Salford (emerita), University of Leeds

JOCELYN WOGAN-BROWNE, THELMA FENSTER, AND DELBERT RUSSELL, EDS. AND TRANS.

Vernacular Literary Theory from the French of Medieval England: Texts and Translations, c. 1120–c.1450.
Cambridge, UK: D. S. Brewer, 2017.
xix + 590 pp. 10 B&W figs. and 2 maps.

The indefatigable and indefatigably scholarly Jocelyn Wogan-Browne has, we know, been responsible, along in each case with a team of other eminent scholars, for two previous large-scale and comprehensive anthology volumes on topics loosely related to those of this new volume: with Nicholas Watson, Andrew Taylor, and Ruth Dean on *The Idea of the Vernacular* (Exeter, UK: University of Exeter Press, 1999), and with Carolyn Collette, Maryanne Kowaleski, Linne Mooney, Ad Putter, and David Trotter on *Language and Culture in Medieval Britain* (Cambridge, UK: York Medieval Press, 2009). The present, monumental volume is another comprehensive source-book and critical tool designed in the first instance for the scholar and the student of Anglo-Norman but which will be extremely useful also for scholars of Middle English literature, for scholars of Continental French, and for scholars of medieval literatures more widely. *The Idea of the Vernacular* was a compilation of excerpts from Middle English literary texts, drawn principally from prologues, that demonstrate the sheer vigor of their literary landscape. *Language and Culture in Medieval Britain* was a collection of essays by many of the most eminent of today's Anglo-Normanists that aimed to "change the narrative" of studies of the languages of medieval Britain by showing its "great linguistic mix": how far French and English (and indeed Latin) were imbricated one with another.

This new collection focuses, says the preface (xiii), on the French-language writings of England "in their most self-reflexive moments," when their authors reflect on their own literary-linguistic strategies and their relation with their audiences. The major part of the book (9–400) consists of editions and translations of a series of forty-four texts from across the twelfth, thirteenth, fourteenth, and fifteenth centuries; this is supplemented by ten Middle English versions of the French originals used in the main part of the anthology; by two essays, on "England and French" and "Poetry and Prose in the French of England" (401–429); by lists, surprisingly revelatory, of the contents according to criteria different from those employed in the anthology proper (so arranged by date of text, by patron, by author, compiler, or translator, by place, by genre, by form, or by manuscript); by a timeline for French in England; by a comprehensive glossary and a general index.

The main body of this book is, of course, the forty-four texts, which are divided into five principal sections whose scope defines the range and ambition of the book overall. The first, "*Faus franceis* and *dreit engleis*: On Language," discusses the "situatedness" of French in a linguistically and ideologically complex environment: it runs from the late-twelfth-century *De Bretaine* to John Gower's *Mirour de l'omme*. The second, "*Si sa dame ne li aidast*: Authorship and the Patron," explores vernacular ideas of authorship in relation to audience and patron: it runs from Benedeit's *Voyage de saint Brendan* (ca. 2011) to Thomas Grey's *Scalacronica* (1355–1364). The third, "*Primes dirrum ka dreyte fei*: The Conduct of Reading, Hearing and Seeing," discusses "the conduct both of texts and their audiences": questions of reception and performance; it runs from Guillaume le Clerc's *Bestiaire divin* to William Waddington's *Manuel des pechiez*. Part IV, "*Ki vault oïr*: Forming Audiences and Creating Textual Communities," discusses the nature of audiences: the production community, the inscribed community, the historical audience. And last, Part V, "*Si come en latyn trovay escrit*: The Lineage of the Text," deals with issues to do with translation, provenance, and inheritance; the texts date from the later twelfth century to the first half of the thirteenth, from Everart's *Distichs of Cato* (late twelfth–early thirteenth century) to a poem on the Old Testament. Each part is preceded by a short introduction setting out its critical, cultural, and linguistic parameters.

Each text is newly edited from a single, specified manuscript source, translated into English, and introduced with notes specifying its date of composition and provenance, its author and/or sources, its literary nature, its audience and circulation, its manuscript source and its bibliography; each text is also followed by comprehensive and valuable notes exploring or explaining textual, linguistic, or translational problems and questions of prosody and pointing to its relevance to the overall theme of the particular part in which it appears. This richness of information will be particularly helpful to graduate students and indeed undergraduates, not just in Anglo-Norman but also in English and Continental French: text 21, for instance, *Sermons on Joshua*, provides excellent material on the dangers of eloquence; text 25b would be equally valuable in discussions of learned as against lay writers and audiences; text 20d, accompanied by three illustrations clearly legible, though only with a magnifying glass, would be an ideal demonstration of the importance of lineage and descent.

It is captious and greedy to ask for more when we have been given so much, but I wonder if it might not have been useful to extend the general index to include a subject index for the texts provided. I can imagine circumstances, for instance, in which I might want to know that text 27 addresses (273) issues of truth versus fiction/lies and hence the social responsibility of the writer; that text 32b is interesting on the question of what it is proper to couch in rhyme (312–313); that naming and the evolution of names is discussed, fascinatingly, in text 41 (380–381). But this is only a most minor cavil. The book is, very visibly, a labor of love: it has required from the three editors a quite monumental work of coordination. The clever choice of texts, often previously unedited, and sometimes unexpected, the thoroughness of the critical apparatus, the liveliness and focus of the accompanying essays speak to an energy and enthusiasm that, it is to be hoped, will help to form a new generation of Anglo-Normanists and to ensure that students and scholars of Middle English take full account of the French-speaking writers whose work threads exhilaratingly through the literary landscape of their period.

Jane H. M. Taylor, Durham University

About the Authors

Keith Busby is Douglas Kelly Professor of Medieval French Emeritus at the University of Wisconsin-Madison. His most recent book is *French in Medieval Ireland, Ireland in Medieval French: The Paradox of Two Worlds* (2017).

Amy Conwell is a Ph.D. candidate in Medieval Studies at the University of Toronto. Her Ph.D. analyzes the impact of the medical tradition on illness narratives in late medieval England.

Helen Cooper is Emeritus Professor of Medieval and Renaissance English at the University of Cambridge. She holds Emeritus and Honorary Fellowships at University College, Oxford, and a Life Fellowship at Magdalene College, Cambridge. She has particular interests in the cultural continuations across the medieval and early modern periods, including early printed editions of Middle English texts. Her books include *Pastoral: Mediaeval into Renaissance* (Ipswich, 1978); *Oxford Guides to Chaucer: The Canterbury Tales* (Oxford,1989); *The English Romance in Time* (Oxford, 2004); *Shakespeare and the Medieval World* (London, 2010); and a modern-spelling edition of Malory's *Morte Darthur* for Oxford World's Classics (Oxford, 1998).

Martha W. Driver is Distinguished Professor of English and Women's and Gender Studies at Pace University in New York City. A co-founder of the Early Book Society for the study of manuscripts and printing history, she writes about illustration from manuscript to print, manuscript and book production, and the early history of printing. In addition to publishing some 60 articles in these areas, she has edited twenty-two journals over twenty years, including *Film & History: Medieval Period in Film* and the *Journal of the Early Book Society*. Her books include *The Image in Print: Book Illustration in Late Medieval England* (British Library Publications and University of Toronto) and *An Index of Images in English MSS*, fascicle four, with Michael Orr (Brepols). She contributed to and edited *Preaching the Word in Manuscript and Print in Late Medieval England: Essays in Honour of Susan Powell* with Veronica O'Mara (Brepols, 2013). She recently published "Revisiting *Nychodemus Gospell*" in *Middle English Texts: Editing and Interpretation: Essays in Honour of William Marx*, edited by Margaret Connolly and Raluca Radelescu (Brepols, 2018). She also oversees the Texts & Transitions book series published by Brepols.

A. S. G. Edwards, FSA, FEA, is Honorary Visiting Professor at the University of Kent and at University College, London and Deputy Editor of *The Book Collector*. He is currently general editor, with Professor Julia Boffey, of the Cambridge Edition of the Works of Geoffrey Chaucer.

Mary Erler is Distinguished Professor in the Department of English at Fordham University, New York. She is the author of *Women, Reading and Piety in Late Medieval England* (Cambridge, 2002) and *Reading and Writing During the Dissolution: Monks, Friars and Nuns 1530–1558* (Cambridge, 2013).

Alexandra Gillespie is Professor of Medieval Studies and English at the University of Toronto, where she is also Director of University of Toronto's Digital Humanities Network, Department Chair and Special Advisor to the Vice Principal Research at the Mississauga campus. She has recently finished a monograph, *Chaucer's Books,* and is now working on a collaborative Mellon-funded project, "The Book and the Silk Roads."

Ralph Hanna is Professor of Palaeography emeritus and emeritus fellow of Keble College, Oxford. His most recent major publication is *The Penn Commentary on Piers Plowman*, Volume 2: *C Passus 5-9; B Passus 5-7; A Passus 5-8* (Philadelphia, 2017). Other publications include editions for the Early English Text Society, *Richard Rolle: Uncollected Verse and Prose, with Related Northern Texts* (o.s. 329, 2007), *Speculum Vitae: A Reading, Editions I and II* (o.s. 331-2, 2008), and *Editing Medieval Texts* (Liverpool, 2015). *Richard Rolle: Unprinted Latin Writings* (Liverpool University Press); "The Taill of Rauff Coil3ear" (Scottish Text Society, Boydell); and with the late A. I. Doyle, *Hope Allen's* Writings Ascribed to Richard Rolle: A Corrected List of Copies (*Publications of the Journal of Medieval Latin*) will appear in 2019.

Cynthia Johnston is a Lecturer in the History of the Book and Communication at the Institute of English Studies, School of Advanced Study, University of London where she convenes the MA in the History of the Book.

Caroline Koncz is a Ph.D. candidate in the History of Art department at the Ohio State University. Her current research examines how certain paintings and works on paper regulated social norms, specifically concerning those of gender and sexuality, in early modern Venice. Other recent research projects of hers include exploring Venice's relations with the Mamluks during the Renaissance as well as investigating the roles that desire and the body played in sacred images from the Cinquecento.

Veronica O'Mara is Professor of Medieval English Literature in the School of Arts/English at the University of Hull. Her main research areas are Middle English religious literature, female literacy, preaching, and the relationship between manuscript and print. She edited (with Martha W. Driver) *Preaching the Word in Manuscript and Print in Late Medieval England: Essays in Honour of Susan Powell*, (Turnhout: Brepols, 2013), and (with Virginia Blanton and Patricia Stoop) *Nuns' Literacies in Medieval Europe: The Hull Dialogue*, Medieval Women: Texts and Contexts, 26 (Turnhout: Brepols, 2013), and *Nuns' Literacies in Medieval Europe: The Kansas City Dialogue*, Medieval Women: Texts and Contexts, 27 (Turnhout: Brepols, 2015).

Patrick Outhwaite is a Ph.D. candidate in English literature at McGill University, and has undertaken work placements at the Wellcome and Osler libraries. He has published on medieval medical manuscripts, palaeography, and theology. His Ph.D. addresses the intersection of medical and religious controversy in England and Central Europe.

Oliver Pickering is Honorary Fellow in the School of English, University of Leeds, and a Fellow of the English Association. He has published widely in the field of medieval English texts and manuscripts (often on aspects of the *South English Legendary* collection), and he has been co-editor of the Middle English Texts series and editor of *The Library*.

Nancy P. Pope is a former Associate Dean of the Graduate School at Washington University in St. Louis. She has retired from a career of academic administration and teaching in order to have a research career. She plans to focus on National Library of Wales MS Brogyntyn ii.1, formerly Porkington 10.

Susan (Sue) Powell is Emeritus Professor of Medieval Texts and Culture (University of Salford) and a Visiting Research Fellow in the School of History at the University of Leeds. She is an editor of manuscripts and early printed books, and her research focusses on religious and devotional texts and institutions. Her latest books are *Saints and Cults in Medieval England* (Donington: Shaun Tyas, 2017) and *The Birgittines of Syon Abbey: Preaching and Print* (Turnhout: Brepols, 2017).

Pamela Robinson is Senior Research Fellow at the Institute of English Studies, University of London. She is currently compiling a Catalogue of Medieval Manuscripts containing Latin commentaries on Aristotle in London Libraries, as part of a British Academy project to compile inventories of such manuscripts in British libraries

Martha Rust is an Associate Professor of English at New York University, specializing in late-medieval English literature and manuscript culture. Her first book, *Imaginary Worlds in Medieval Books: Exploring the Manuscript Matrix* (Palgrave, 2007), envisioned the confines of a medieval manuscript as the potential territory of a virtual world; her current book project, *Item: Lists and the Poetics of Reckoning in Late-Medieval England* theorizes the list as a device that enables thinking in a variety of modes.

John Scahill teaches at Insearch, University of Technology, Sydney. He is responsible for the volume *Middle English Saints' Legends* in the D. S. Brewer series Annotated Bibliographies of Old and Middle English Literature, and as a member of the Tokyo Medieval Manuscript Reading Group, collaborated in a series of editions of the *Ancrene Wisse* Group. He is currently co-editing an edition of the Temporale and Old Testament from Caxton's *Golden Legend.*

Misty Schieberle is Associate Professor of English at the University of Kansas. She is the author of *Feminized Counsel and the Literature of Advice in England, 1380–1500* (Brepols, 2014). Her research focuses on women, manuscript studies, and French literature in England. She is currently preparing a dual edition, *Christine de Pizan's Advice to Princes in Middle English: Stephen Scrope's The Epistle of Othea and the Anonymous Lytle Bibell of Knyghthod* (Medieval Institute Press).

Valerie Schutte earned her Ph.D. in history from the University of Akron. She is author of *Mary I and the Art of Book Dedications: Royal Women, Power, and Persuasion* (2015) and has edited four collections on queens, royal Tudor women, and Shakespeare. She is currently working on a monograph on books related to Princess Elizabeth Tudor.

Joe Stadolnik is a Junior Research Fellow at Institute of Advanced Studies, University College, London. His current book project, *Subtle Arts*, considers the language practices of medieval science as a repertoire of styles and genres available to writers across Middle English literary culture (ca. 1350–1500). His other research studies the movement of Middle English texts, books, and readers in the fifteenth-century Atlantic, and medievalism in the Americas.

Jane H. M. Taylor is Professor Emerita of medieval French at Durham University. Her publications in this latter field include *The Poetry of François Villon: Text and Context* (Cambridge University Press, 2001) and *The Making of Poetry: Late-Medieval French Poetic Anthologies* (Brepols, 2007). In other fields, she has recently published *Rewriting Arthurian Romance in*

Renaissance France: From Manuscript to Print (D. S. Brewer, 2014); with Roberta L. Krueger, a translation of Antoine de La Sale's "Petit Jehan de Saintré" (University of Pennsylvania Press, 2014); and with Craig Taylor, a translation of *The Chivalric Biography of Boucicaut, Jean II le Meingre* (D. S. Brewer, 2016).

Mari-Liisa Varila is a Lecturer at the Department of English, University of Turku, Finland. She received her Ph.D. in English from the University of Turku in 2016. In her dissertation, she examined a group of three sixteenth-century English manuscripts with scientific contents. She is currently working on a book project focused on the scribal transmission of scientific texts. Her other research interests include the interaction between manuscript and print and paratextual communication in early English books. She has also recently co-edited a volume combining book studies with linguistics, *Verbal and Visual Communication in Early English Texts* (Brepols, 2017).

Sarah Wilma Watson received her Ph.D. in English Literature from the University of Pennsylvania in May 2018 and is currently a visting Assistant Professor of English at Haverford College. She has published essays on Anglo-French literary culture and on gender and reading. Her current book project, *Reading Across the Channel: Christine de Pizan in England, France, and Burgundy*, examines a transational community of late-medieval Francophone readers.

Mary Beth Winn is Professor Emerita of French Studies at the University at Albany, SUNY. Her research has focused on early French printing and on associated issues of patronage, transitions between manuscript and print, and correlations of text, image, and music. Text editor for the chansons of composers Thomas Crecquillon and Jean Mouton, she is currently establishing, with Louis-Gabriel Bonicoli, a database on the work of Anthoine Vérard while completing critical editions of two Vérard publications: *Le Roman de Tristan* (1489) and *Les Loups ravissans* (ca. 1505).

The twenty-first volume of the *Journal of the Early Book Society*
was published in Fall 2018
by Pace University Press

Cover and Interior Layouts by Jessica Estrella
The journal was typeset in Arno Pro
and printed by Lightning Source in La Vergne, Tennessee

Pace University Press

Director: Manuela Soares
Associate Director: Stephanie Hsu
Graduate Assistants: Jessica Estrella and Alicia Hughes
Student Aide: Erica Magrin

www.ingramcontent.com/pod-product-compliance
Lightning Source LLC
Chambersburg PA
CBHW060232100726
47907CB00003B/602

* 9 7 8 1 9 3 5 6 2 5 2 9 2 *